Successful Direct Marketing Methods

Sixth Edition

Bob Stone

Chairman Emeritus, Stone & Adler, Inc.

NTC Business Books
NTC/Contemporary Publishing Group

Library of Congress Cataloging-in-Publication Data

Stone, Bob.
   Successful direct marketing methods / Bob Stone. — 6th ed.
     p.   cm.
   Includes index.
   ISBN 0-8442-3003-0
   1. Direct Marketing.   I. Title.
  HF5415.126.S757   1996
  658.8′4—dc20

                                          96-9100
                                          CIP

Published by NTC Business Books
A division of NTC/Contemporary Publishing Group, Inc.
4255 West Touhy Avenue, Lincolnwood (Chicago), Illinois 60646-1975 U.S.A.
Copyright © 1997 by NTC/Contemporary Publishing Group, Inc.
Printed in the United States of America
International Standard Book Number: 0-8442-3003-0
18   17   16   15   14   13   12   11   10   9   8   7   6   5   4   3

Contents

S E C T I O N   I

Direct Marketing and Databases

SECTION II

The Media of Direct Marketing

SECTION IV

Managing the Creative Process

About the Author

Bob Stone

Position
Chairman Emeritus of Stone & Adler, Inc.

Articles
Author of more than 200 articles on direct marketing, which have appeared in *Advertising Age* magazine since 1967.

Awards
Six-time winner of the Direct Marketing Association's Best of Industry Award. The firm he cofounded, Stone & Adler, has received the Direct Marketing Association's highest honors, including the Silver and Gold Echo Awards as well as the International Direct Marketing & Mail Order Symposium's Bronze Carrier Pigeon Award. Member of the Direct Marketing Hall of Fame. Recipient of the Edward N. Mayer, Jr., Award for contributions to direct marketing education, the Charles S. Downes Award for direct marketing contributions, and the John Caples Award for copy excellence.

Affiliations
Former director of the Direct Marketing Association
Former president of the Chicago Association of Direct Marketing
Former membership chairman of the Direct Marketing Association
Former president of the Associated Third Class Mail Users
Board member of the Direct Marketing Educational Foundation
Adjunct Professor at the University of Missouri
Adjunct Professor at Northwestern University

Foreword

Bob Stone has observed, experienced, recorded, and taught direct marketing for more than five decades. During all of that time, he has practiced what he preaches, being actively engaged as a direct marketing entrepreneur as well as having been cofounder of the first advertising agency to devote itself exclusively to direct response promotion. His on-the-firing-line accumulation of experience and expertise is legendary. No one is more qualified on the subject of direct marketing—nor is anyone more authoritative—than is Bob Stone.

For more than 20 years, Bob Stone's *Successful Direct Marketing Methods* has recorded the evolution (more recently, the *revolution*) of the direct marketing process: the discipline, the strategies, the goals, the techniques. Through five editions and multiple printings—and with continuous reign as a best seller—the "direct marketing bible," as many refer to it, has nearly doubled in number of pages.

This sixth edition, however, so as to be relevant, readable, and most valuable, now concentrates on the contemporary state of the art of direct marketing. Although many reference books become cumbersome as they evolve through subsequent editions, Bob Stone's newest work confines itself to what the successful direct marketer needs to know, here and now. The result is a remarkably easy-to-grasp book, one written for reading clear through rather than being a thick tome to be stored on a shelf for reference only as needed. It presents what direct marketing is all about, today!

Significantly, in two new chapters, major attention is paid to the subject of database, a concept now generally recognized as being at the core of the direct marketing process. Databases make possible the creation and cultivation of customer relationships, and so it is terribly important to know how to design, maintain, and use these as well as to profit from the information they should contain.

The emerging technology and direct response promotion opportunities of the new interactive electronic media, notably the Internet, warrant much attention in this new edition too. These run the gamut from the various on-line information services accessed by personal computers . . . to the hook-up of the television medium (for presenting offers) with the telephone medium (for response and action). Bob Stone deals with these along with the state of the art of traditional direct mail, print, and broadcast media.

In addition to the media, the message aspects of direct marketing continue to be dealt with in this sixth edition. Few would dispute Bob Stone's well-documented expertise in developing offers and creating direct mail packages and catalogs as well as print and broadcast advertising. The management of the direct marketing process—strategy, mathematics, research, testing—continue to receive major attention, too. So do applications for lead generation and traffic building, as well as that use from which direct marketing emerged: mail order selling.

Throughout his multifaceted career, Bob Stone has been a teacher, sharing not only what he has experienced himself but also what he has learned from others. He continues presenting the skills he has developed and the knowledge he has acquired as an Adjunct Professor of Direct Marketing at the University of Missouri–Kansas City. And he brings it all to you in this current edition of his notable book, *Successful Direct Marketing Methods*.

Now I urge you to read it . . . cover-to-cover . . . and *learn*!

Martin Baier
Director
Center for Direct Marketing Education and Research
University of Missouri–Kansas City

Preface

Fax on demand. Electronic kiosks. Interactive TV. CD-ROM/diskette, on-line services marketing, World Wide Web/Internet marketing. Buzz terms all.

One might say these are the new faces of direct marketing. Most certainly none of today's electronic wizardry existed when the first edition of *Successful Direct Marketing Methods* was published in 1975.

This, the sixth edition of *Successful Direct Marketing Methods,* includes all the new and exciting evolutions. But a caveat should be noted: *new media does not replace old media.* Instead, new media increases our options and expands our arsenals. Yes—direct marketers are the happy recipients of windfalls, new combinations of ways to build databases, new ways to serve and communicate with customers.

Our new opportunities fit well with the trend towards integrated communications. Evolution has brought maturity. Most direct marketers of the '70s and '80s took a stance of "us against them," i.e., direct marketing vs. general advertising. Then cooler heads started thinking—"Suppose we were to integrate direct marketing with general advertising, sales promotion and public relations." It worked; it made sense.

Has direct marketing reached its pinnacle? Of course not. History says the evolution will continue. New sophistication is certain to come from bright young people inspired by the Direct Marketing Educational Foundation and taught by leading colleges and universities across our nation.

In signing off on the sixth edition of *Successful Direct Marketing Methods*, I want to acknowledge, as I did with all previous editions, that this book is not the work of one person. Instead, it is the combined contributions of the author and some of the most outstanding practitioners in our profession.

The best of success to you!

Bob Stone

Acknowledgments

As with all editions of *Successful Direct Marketing Methods*, the materials in this sixth edition in no way reflect the sole thinking of the author. Instead, this book is a reflection of all that is happening in direct marketing, with generous contributions from a host of people and organizations.

Thanks to the Direct Marketing Association for the statistics it has provided. To Pete Hoke, publisher of *Direct Marketing*, for his contributions. To Stan Rapp and Tom Collins, cofounders of Rapp & Collins, for their contributions on magazines and the techniques of creating print advertising.

And my thanks go likewise to Jack Schmid, president of J. Schmid & Associates, Inc., for his input on catalogs. To Vic Hunter, president of Hunter Business Direct, for his contributions on business-to-business direct marketing. To Martin Baier, director of the University of Missouri Center for Direct Marketing, for his contributions on data bases. To Bob Kestnbaum, president of Kestnbaum & Company and Pamela Ames, VP, for their input on the mathematics of direct marketing. And to Ron Jacobs, president of Jacobs & Clevenger, Inc. for his input on new media.

Numerous present and former staff members of Stone & Adler contributed to this book. Special thanks go to Jerry Wood for his contributions on strategic planning. To Don Kanter for his input on creating mail packages. And to Vince Copp for his contributions on direct marketing research.

Thanks also go to Frank Daniels for his input on idea development. And finally—a special thank you to Aaron Adler, cofounder of Stone & Adler, for lending his wisdom to the chapter on selecting and selling merchandise.

Direct Marketing and Databases

CHAPTER ONE

The Uniqueness of Direct Marketing

The scope of direct marketing has continued to expand for decades, and new applications have been numerous. Long trumpeted as a stand-alone discipline, direct marketing has matured and is rapidly taking its place as a key component in the total marketing mix.

Economic Impact of Direct Marketing

The size and economic impact of direct marketing in the United States had been debatable for decades until the Direct Marketing Association (DMA) commissioned a study in 1992 to analyze the extent of direct marketing in the United States and to develop an economic model for forecasting purposes.

The WEFA Group—a collaboration of Chase Econometrics and Wharton Economic Forecasting—was selected to conduct the study. Three solid years of research were devoted to this landmark comprehensive study. And so it was that the DMA was able to announce in October 1995 that U.S. sales revenue attributed to direct marketing for that year was estimated to be $1.1 trillion.

The $1.1 trillion economic impact figure, coming from an organization known worldwide for its forecasting accuracy, was a bombshell. Many had thought the economic impact to be in the $350 billion range.

It is significant that growth in direct marketing sales is outpacing growth in total U.S. sales, especially in business-to-business marketing.

- Business-to-business marketing sales were forecasted to be $498.1 billion in 1995. Sales grew by 8.1 percent per year between 1990 and 1995 and are forecast to grow by 10.2 percent per year between 1995 and 2000—to $810.4 billion. Total U.S. business-to-business sales grew by 4.3 percent per year between 1990 and 1995 and are expected to increase by 6.53 percent per year between 1995 and 2000.

- Consumer direct marketing sales were forecasted to reach $594.4 billion in 1995. They increased by 6.1 percent per year from 1990 to 1995 and are expected to grow by 6.5 percent per year from 1995 to 2000—to $841.2 billion. This compares with overall U.S. consumer sales growth of 5.3 percent per year and 5.5 percent per year for those five-year intervals, respectively.

Direct Marketing Defined

The definition of direct marketing has evolved over time (see Exhibit 1–1). The current definition given by the Direct Marketing Association follows:

Direct marketing is an interactive system of marketing that uses one or more advertising media to effect a measurable response and/or transaction at any location, with this activity stored on database.

Some people argue that, with continuing growth and development in the field, a standard definition is no longer valid. There are those who would drop the term *direct marketing* in favor of such terms as *directed marketing*, or *relationship marketing*, or *action advertising*, or *integrated marketing*. Where the debate will end, no one knows.

Nevertheless, it is important to have a thorough understanding of the current official definition:

- **Interactive:** One-on-one communication between marketer and prospect/customer.

Notes to Exhibit 1–1
ME = Media Expenditures ($ billions)

[a] Arnold Fishman (Marketing Logistics), U.S. Census, Robert J. Coen (McCann-Erickson).
[b] Direct response expenditures are calculated as a percentage of total expenditures in each media: direct mail (100%), telephone (50%), broadcast (45%), newspaper (45%), magazine (45%), misc. (100%).
[c] The mail order sales figure excludes roughly $50,490 billion of charitable mail order contributions, which are not included in the $14,088 trillion of U.S. aggregate sales.
[d] Personal visit to seller includes $1.655 billion of consumer product sales at retail plus 90 percent of consumer services sales. Ten percent of consumer services sales are conducted by salespeople visiting the buyer.

Total advertising for 1993 was $232.080 billion. It is estimated that $149.970 billion, or 65 percent, was direct advertising. The flow chart reports direct components of overall media advertising expenditures. A growing percentage of broadcast, newspaper, and magazine advertising dollars can be categorized as direct advertising. The percentage is growing rapidly as marketers learn the efficiency of measuring advertising performance.

Source: Martin Baier, Henry R. Hoke, Jr., and Robert Stone, "Direct Marketing . . . An Aspect of Total Marketing," *Direct Marketing* magazine, 224 Seventh Street, Garden City, NY 11530–5771.

Exhibit 1-1.   Direct Marketing Flow Chart

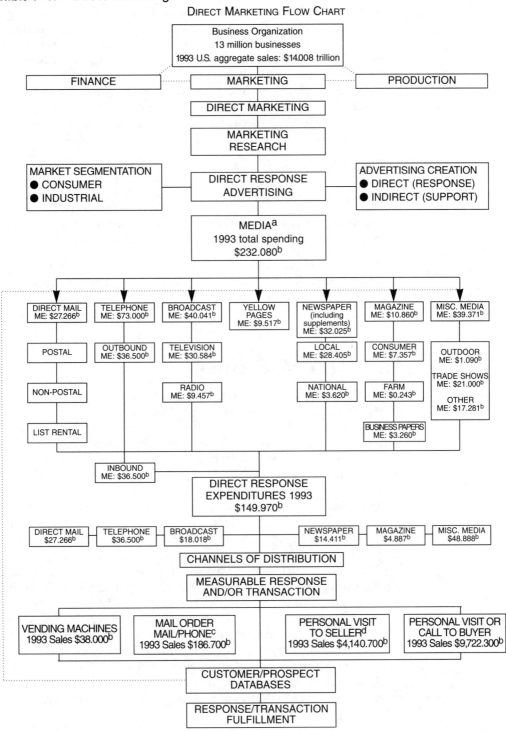

DIRECT MARKETING FLOW CHART

Business Organization
13 million businesses
1993 U.S. aggregate sales: $14.008 trillion

FINANCE   MARKETING   PRODUCTION

DIRECT MARKETING

MARKETING
RESEARCH

MARKET SEGMENTATION
● CONSUMER
● INDUSTRIAL

DIRECT RESPONSE
ADVERTISING

ADVERTISING CREATION
● DIRECT (RESPONSE)
● INDIRECT (SUPPORT)

MEDIA[a]
1993 total spending
$232.080[b]

| DIRECT MAIL ME: $27.266[b] | TELEPHONE ME: $73.000[b] | BROADCAST ME: $40.041[b] | YELLOW PAGES ME: $9.517[b] | NEWSPAPER (including supplements) ME: $32.025[b] | MAGAZINE ME: $10.860[b] | MISC. MEDIA ME: $39.371[b] |

POSTAL   OUTBOUND ME: $36.500[b]   TELEVISION ME: $30.584[b]   LOCAL ME: $28.405[b]   CONSUMER ME: $7.357[b]   OUTDOOR ME: $1.090[b]

NON-POSTAL   RADIO ME: $9.457[b]   NATIONAL ME: $3.620[b]   FARM ME: $0.243[b]   TRADE SHOWS ME: $21.000[b]   OTHER ME: $17.281[b]

LIST RENTAL   BUSINESS PAPERS ME: $3.260[b]

INBOUND ME: $36.500[b]

DIRECT RESPONSE
EXPENDITURES 1993
$149.970[b]

| DIRECT MAIL $27.266[b] | TELEPHONE $36.500[b] | BROADCAST $18.018[b] | NEWSPAPER $14.411[b] | MAGAZINE $4.887[b] | MISC. MEDIA $48.888[b] |

CHANNELS OF DISTRIBUTION

MEASURABLE RESPONSE
AND/OR TRANSACTION

| VENDING MACHINES 1993 Sales $38.000[b] | MAIL ORDER MAIL/PHONE[c] 1993 Sales $186.700[b] | PERSONAL VISIT TO SELLER[d] 1993 Sales $4,140.700[b] | PERSONAL VISIT OR CALL TO BUYER 1993 Sales $9,722.300[b] |

CUSTOMER/PROSPECT
DATABASES

RESPONSE/TRANSACTION
FULFILLMENT

- **One or more advertising media:** Direct marketing is not restricted to any one medium. Indeed, direct marketers have discovered there is synergism among the media. A combination of media often is far more productive than any single medium. The variety of media available to direct marketers is ever-expanding. On-line information services such as CompuServe, America On Line, and Prodigy are rapidly gaining prominence in the total media arsenal. And direct marketers can be expected to establish a presence on the Internet via the World Wide Web. What makes "new media" so exciting to direct marketers is that their inherent uniqueness—measurability—applies to new media just as it always has for print, direct mail, and broadcast.

- **Measurable response:** Measurability is a hallmark of direct marketing. Everything in the field, with rare exceptions, is measurable. Direct marketers know what they spend, and they know what they get back.

- **Transaction at any location:** The world is direct marketing's oyster. Transactions can take place by telephone, at a kiosk, by mail, at home, at a store.

- **Database:** A compilation of known data about a prospect or customer, including such data as history of purchases, source of inquiry, credit rating, and so on.

The Basics of Direct Marketing

The basic purpose of any direct marketing program is to get a measurable response that will produce an immediate or ultimate profit. To create a measurable response there must be an offer—a call to action. An offer to sell a product or service direct to the consumer or a business is but one way to create a measurable response. Offers that create leads for salespeople, get people to send for information, lead to visits to retail stores, impel people to give to causes are all measurable.

Traditionally, direct marketers have identified three key components to producing response, regardless of media used. The three components and ranking of importance has been as follows: list (40 percent), offer (40 percent), creative execution (20 percent).

Today, lists that contain only names of individuals, or names of business firms, are being supplanted by enhanced databases that help to profile prospects and customers, thus making it possible to target specific market segments.

The offer, sometimes referred to as the proposition, remains key to success. It has been said, with wisdom, that even brilliant creative execution cannot overcome an offer without strong appeal to the market approached. If the offer doesn't convey perceived value, response will suffer.

While creative execution is not ranked as high as list and offer, it is a mistake to assume that different degrees of creative make little or no difference. To the contrary, given the right lists and the right offers, superlative creative often increases response by 50 percent or more.

The ultimate objective of a successful direct marketing program is to build the lifetime value of a customer. This objective applies whether direct marketing methods are applied solely to a mail order business or to other channels of distribution. Either way, the customer database is available to cultivate customers.

As later chapters will reveal, direct marketers often avail themselves of rather sophisticated calculations. However, four terms—lifetime value (LTV) and recency, frequency, monetary (RFM)—summarize the financial dimensions of direct marketing. Brief definitions will be sufficient at this point.

- **Lifetime value:** The total of financial transactions with a customer over the life of a relationship

- **Recency:** The amount of time since a person or firm last purchased

- **Frequency:** The number of times a customer buys within a season, or a year

- **Monetary:** The amount of money a customer spends within a season, or a year

Knowing the lifetime value of a customer reveals how much you can afford to invest in a customer and still realize a satisfactory profit. Keeping tabs on customers by recency of last purchase, by frequency of purchase within a given period, and by amount spent enables the marketer to identify segments of the customer base that offer the greatest profit potential.

The 30 Timeless Direct Marketing Principles

Direct marketing is in the forefront of new technology, but the knowledge base that is the heritage of direct marketers has not diminished in value. Following are 30 principles that have stood the test of time:

1. All customers are not created equal. Give or take a few percentage points, 80 percent of repeat business for goods and services will come from 20 percent of your customer base.

2. The most important order you ever get from a customer is the second order. Why? Because a two-time buyer is at least twice as likely to buy again as a one-time buyer.

3. Maximizing direct mail success depends first on the lists you use, second on the offers you make, and third the on the copy and graphics you create.

4. If, on a given list, ''hotline'' names don't work, the other list categories offer little opportunity for success.

5. Merge/purge names—those that appear on two or more lists—will outpull any single list from which these names have been extracted.

6. Direct response lists will almost always outpull compiled lists.

7. Overlays on lists (enhancements), such as lifestyle characteristics, income, education, age, marital status, and propensity to respond by mail or phone, will always improve response.

8. A follow-up to the same list within 30 days will pull 40–50 percent of the first mailing.

9. ''Yes/No'' offers consistently produce more orders than offers that don't request ''No'' responses.

10. The ''take rate'' for negative option offers will always outpull positive option offers at least two to one.

11. Credit card privileges will outperform cash with order at least two to one.

12. Credit card privileges will increase the size of the average catalog order by 20 percent or more.

13. Time limit offers, particularly those that give a specific date, outpull offers with no time limit practically every time.

14. Free-gift offers, particularly where the gift appeals to self-interest, outpull discount offers consistently.

15. Sweepstakes, particularly in conjunction with impulse purchases, will increase the order volume 35 percent or more.

16. You will collect far more money in a fund-raising effort if you ask for a specific amount from a contributor. Likewise, you will collect more money if the appeal is tied to a specific project.

17. People buy benefits, not features.

18. The longer you can keep someone reading your copy, the better your chances of success.

19. The timing and frequency of renewal letters is vital. But I can report nothing but failure over a period of 40 years in attempts to hype renewals with ''improved copy.'' I've concluded that the product—the magazine, for example—is the factor in making a renewal decision.

20. Self-mailers are cheaper to produce, but they practically never outpull envelope-enclosed letter mailings.

21. A preprint of a forthcoming ad, accompanied by a letter and response form, will outpull a postprint mailing package by 50 percent or more.

22. It is easier to increase the average dollar amount of an order than it is to increase percentage of response.

23. You will get far more new catalog customers if you put your proven winners in the front pages of your catalog.

24. Assuming items of similar appeal, you will always get a higher response rate from a 32-page catalog than from a 24-page catalog.

25. A new catalog to a catalog customer base will outpull cold lists by 400 percent to 800 percent.

26. A print ad with a bind-in card will outpull the same ad without a bind-in up to 600 percent.

27. A direct response, direct sale TV commercial of 120 seconds will outpull a 60-second direct response commercial better than two to one.

28. A TV support commercial will increase response from a newspaper insert up to 50 percent.

29. The closure rate from qualified leads can be from two to four times as effective as cold calls.

30. Telephone-generated leads are likely to close four to six times greater than mail-generated leads.

Integrated Communications

As direct marketing continues to expand in scope and to mature as a discipline, a trend seems to be developing to include direct marketing in a total loop along with general advertising, sales promotion, and public relations. Hence the term *integrated communications*.

The concept makes a lot of sense. But if integrated communications is to be the bright future for direct marketing, as many predict, then both advertising agencies and direct marketers must begin to look at direct marketing in a different way.

The boom years of direct marketing—from the late 1950s to the 1980s—saw direct marketing enjoy fantastic growth as a stand-alone discipline and as a separate profit center. Integrated communications dictates integrated budgets, a concept contrary to the way direct marketing units are set up in most general advertising agencies. There is a problem with most national advertisers, too: Direct marketing units, for the most part, are separate and apart from general advertising, sales promotion, and public relations budgets. This situation leads to turf battles, direct marketing being the Orphan Annie in the fight for budget dollars in many cases.

There are two notable exceptions to these turf battles: Leo Burnett USA, which does not operate direct marketing as a separate profit center, and IBM, which has integrated all forms of communication and has assigned a ''police-man'' to allocate budget dollars according to the marketing needs for the imple-mentation of each given program (see Exhibit 1–2).

Recognizing the trend toward integrated communications, the American Association of Advertising Agencies has settled on the following definition:

> *Integrated communications:* A concept of marketing communications plan-ning that recognizes the added value in a program that integrates a variety of strategic disciplines, e.g., general advertising, direct response, sales pro-motion and public relations—and combines these disciplines to provide clarity, consistency and maximum communications impact.

Jerry Reitman, former executive vice president of Leo Burnett, paraphrases the definition by stating: ''Campaigns should have the same tonality, the same creative direction . . . and, more importantly, the same strategic direction.''

The case for integrated communications is thoroughly explored in a 1993 book, *Integrated Marketing Communicaions*. In describing the content of the book, the publisher states:

> *Integrated Marketing Communications* challenges business to confront a fundamental dilemma in today's marketing—the fact that mass media adver-tising *no longer works*. This landmark book reveals that strategies long used to deliver selling messages to a mass culture through a single medium are obsolete—and shows marketers how to get back on track.
>
> The answer lies in database-driven marketing, a key planning tool that can—in today's diverse, fragmented marketplace—create a complete picture of the lifestyles, attitudes, and motivations of distinct buyer groups.[1]

The authors identify the database as the linchpin necessary for the effective functioning of an integrated marketing communications program. Exhibit 1–3 illustrates the ideal planning model for such a program. Commenting on the planning model, the authors state:

> As can be seen, we start with a database of information on both customers and prospects. While the database should be as complete as possible, we recognize that many companies, particularly those that market through retail channels, often have only limited information about their actual customers. This is especially true of large, high-penetration, fast-moving consumer prod-ucts. Yet this type of information is critical to the future success of an integrated marketing communications program.
>
> The planning model that we illustrate is idealized, that is, it represents the best of all worlds. Few organizations have reached this point as yet in database development. There are some, however, who have been gathering data about their users for several years.

---

[1]Don E. Schultz, Stanley I. Tannenbaum, and Robert F. Lauterborn, *Integrated Marketing Commu-nications* (Lincolnwood, Ill.: NTC Business Books, 1993).

Exhibit 1–2.   IBM Integrated Marketing Communications Model

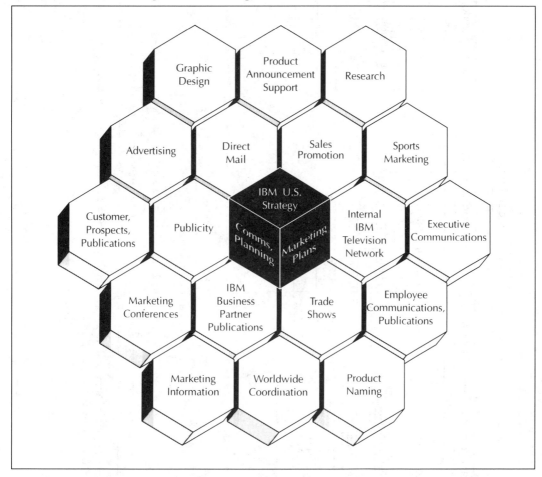

IBM's U.S. marketing communications disciplines are integrated into a single group, Marketing Services and Communications (MS&C), pictured here as a honeycomb of interlinked cells. Each represents a specialty with a defined role to play in achieving the larger marketing communications objectives of IBM United States.

Source: Association of National Advertisers, *The Advertiser* (Fall 1991).

Tobacco companies, for example, have very complete databases on their users. Automobile companies are also building detailed databases on ownership and histories of purchase patterns. Direct marketers such as American Express, Visa, MasterCard, and financial organizations also have detailed information on their customers and prospects. In our experience, service organizations and business-to-business marketers are generally far ahead of

Exhibit 1–3.   Ideal Planning Model

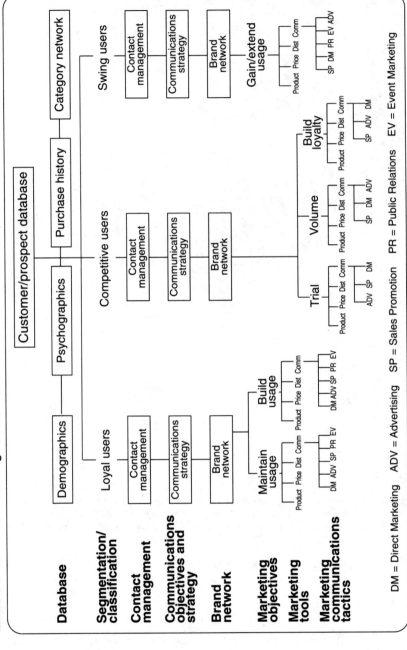

Source: Don E. Schultz, Stanley I. Tannenbaum, and Robert F. Lauterborn, *Integrated Marketing Communications* (Lincolnwood, Ill.: NTC Business Books, 1993).

consumer product companies in developing usable databases for integrated marketing communications.

As shown, the database should contain at a minimum such hard data as demographics, psychographics, and purchase history. In addition, attitudinal information such as the customer's category network and how consumers associate the products they use is vital for a solid integrated marketing communications approach. (Note: The planning form we have illustrated was developed for a consumer product. The database for a service organization would likely be quite different as would that for a business-to-business organization.)

The integrated marketing communications process begins with a business problem, does not assume an advertising solution, takes the time necessary to research and develop an integrated strategy, puts all elements in place before pulling the trigger, measures everything, and accepts accountability.

There are the new criteria of business success—if not survival—as the millennium dawns.[2]

For an understanding of how the concept of integrated marketing communications is implemented, let us look at a campaign developed by Allstate Insurance Company.

Case Study: Allstate Insurance Company Life Campaign

Introduction

In support of the Allstate agency force, an integrated life insurance campaign was developed in 1991. This promotion included:

- An overall theme: "I want to be your agent for Life" (a double entendre)

- National and local advertising support utilizing the Life theme

- An agent-paid and company-subsidized targeted lead-generation mailing

Background

The 1991 annual sales promotion was geared to increasing the number of Life sales in the Allstate agent's current book of business/customer base. Research has shown that Allstate's current customer base was virtually an untapped market in terms of cross-selling life insurance. Research also indicated that there was an increase in property and casualty insurance retention if there was Allstate life insurance present in a household.

[2]*Ibid.*

Program Objectives

- Promote Allstate's financial strength and rating in the life insurance business.
- Create awareness of Allstate's Life products and promote agents as the prospect/customer's primary source of contact for more information.
- Increase Life sales within agent's own customer base.
- Meet or exceed the Life Company's 1991 premium plan.
- Increase retention through cross-selling life insurance.

Program Strategies

- Develop a comprehensive communication plan integrating all marketing efforts.
- Increase life insurance cross-line sales through lead-generation mailings and co-op advertising.
- Provide national advertising support for the Life Campaign.
- Create employee awareness of the Life Campaign.

Target Audience

- Current customers with and without life insurance.

Program Components

- National advertising campaign: television, radio, print
- Local advertising (agent and company participation in cost)
- Lead-generation mailing program (agent and company participation in cost)
- Sales support material
- Billing messages
- Employee awareness
- Agent communication

Results and Advertising Support

Life Company year-end premium plan was exceeded (102 percent) and promotion results were 40 percent over the prior year's. Putting together an integrated campaign calls for a sophisticated planning process. Here is how advertising support was orchestrated.

The advertising message was twofold: (1) Allstate agents can take care of their customers' life insurance needs and (2) a long-term relationship with an Allstate agent is important.

National Advertising
Television.
- Messages used the ongoing, distinctive campaign currently airing that included the highly successful combination of live action with animation and capitalized on one of Allstate's best-recognized assets, the "Good Hands."

- Advertising messages ran throughout the promotion period on programs that supported Allstate's objectives of product awareness and agent support.

- Two 15-second executions were utilized that emphasized the "I want to be your agent for Life" message. These executions highlighted the lead lines (auto/home) as a transition into the life insurance sale.

Radio.
- National radio advertising via Paul Harvey supported the product message during the promotion period.

- Radio scripts were developed that focused on the life insurance product message and were aired where appropriate.

- National radio schedules were integrated with television air dates.

Print.
- Print ads featured the same look and message as the television messages.

- Print ads lent topspin to the promotion effort and provided merchandising consideration to agents.

- Print ads were featured in national magazine publications.

- National print schedules were integrated with television and radio schedules.

Local Advertising.
A portfolio of new Life Co-op advertising materials was developed for Allstate agents' individual use. It focused on the same theme as the national advertising message: "I want to be your agent for Life."

Television. Two 30-second Life Co-op television commercials were developed based on the national messages; they included a 15-second tag for agent personalization.

Radio.   A 30-second live-read radio script was developed that could be personalized for each agent's use.

Print.   Two versions of a Life print ad were developed that focused on the "I want to be your agent for Life" message and incorporated a new concept that allowed agents to personalize the ad with their signature.

Telephone (office support).   Life product scripts for agent offices' use with customer-on-hold phone systems were developed.

With advertising support in place, the next step was to create lead-generation support for those Allstate agents involved in the total campaign.

Mailing/Lead-Generation Support

Mailing Package.   The letter emphasizes the agent-customer relationship and makes an effort to review the customer's current insurance portfolio to make certain existing coverage is keeping pace with current lifestyle.

Features.
- Professionally written and designed mailing package

- Business card with the agent's name, address, and phone number

- "I want to be your agent for Life" theme printed on business card

- Multiline reply device offering various life products

- Business reply envelope

List Selections.   Agents had the choice of mailing to several targeted lists:

- Auto customers with homeowners

- Auto customers with property

- Property customers

- Auto customers

- Life customers

- Customers without Life

- Other line customers

Special Offer.   To encourage agents to order the lead-generation mailings, the company subsidized 50 percent of the mailing cost for letters sent to the agent's customers.

Follow-up.   As with any lead-generation effort, follow-up is critical for success. Agents received an extensive follow-up list for each of their mailings that included the following:

- Customer name

- Customer address

- Customer phone number

- Description of mailing package

- Date that the mailing package was sent

Sales Support Materials

Agents were provided with an array of product support materials.

- Brochures

- Counter cards

- Buttons, banners

- Letters, mailing kits, postcards

- The words "Your Allstate agent wants to be your agent for Life" were even printed on the policy-billing envelope.

Internal Support

- A comprehensive *Administrative Guide*, which gave a clear picture of what the Life Campaign was all about, was produced and distributed to field managers so they could review the program details with their agents.

- The internal theme "Jazz up your Life" contained various award levels that were appropriately named for famous jazz musicians. To win one of the awards, an agent needed to sell a specified amount of life insurance.

- Agent support was also provided through internal communications—desktoppers and letters touting the theme "I want to be your agent for Life."

- "Jump Start Your Market"—a starter kit consisting of actual samples and ordering information on all of the marketing materials available—was provided for all agents.

The Life Campaign was a remarkable program from the standpoint of planning and execution. Exhibit 1–4 presents representative executions. Exhibit 1–5 is one of two Life Co-op television commercials that included a 15-second tag for agent personalization.

Exhibit 1–4.   Ad Campaign Mailings

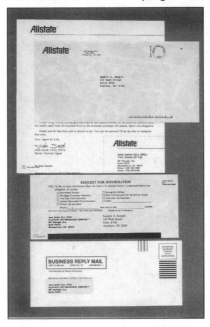

Lead-Generation Mailing

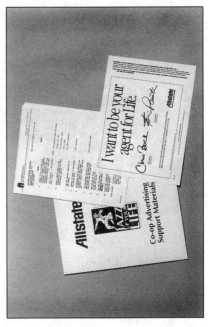

Co-op Mailing

Agent-Support Materials

Employee Awareness

Exhibit 1–5.   Life Co-op Television Commercial

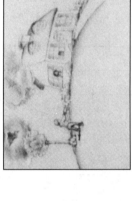

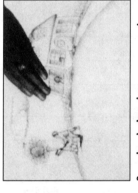

(MUSIC: UNDER THROUGHOUT)
1. (AVO): The Allstate agent...

2. who helps insure your home...

3. (SFX: THUNDER)
(AVO): can give you a hand with a plan for life insurance.

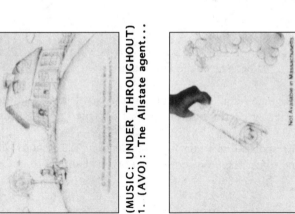

4. ...

5. Life insurance, your Allstate agent wants to be your agent for life.

6. You're In Good Hands With Allstate.

SELF-QUIZ

1. In order of effectiveness, maximizing direct mail success depends on:

   a. _____

   b. _____

   c. _____

2. Credit card privileges will outperform cash with order at least _____ to _____.

3. People buy _____, not _____.

4. Telephone-generated leads are likely to close _____ to _____ times more often than mail-generated leads.

5. Define *direct marketing*: _____

   _____

   _____

6. Define *integrated communications*: _____

   _____

   _____

7. Direct response lists will almost always outpull compiled lists.

   ☐ True   ☐ False

8. A follow-up to the same list within 30 days will pull _____ percent to _____ percent of the first mailing.

9. The "take rate" for negative option offers will always outpull positive option offers at least two to one.   ☐ True   ☐ False

10. A direct response direct sale TV commercial of 120 seconds will outpull a 60-second direct response commercial better than two to one.

    ☐ Yes   ☐ No

PILOT PROJECT

You are the catalog manager of a women's apparel catalog. You discover that 80 percent of your business is coming from 20 percent of your customer base.

Your assignment is to come up with a program to maintain the loyalty of that important 20 percent of the customer base. Develop an outline of incentives you would employ to retain the loyalty of your best customers.

CHAPTER TWO

Databases in the Marketing Process

The terms *direct marketing* and *database marketing* may be considered to be synonymous. Certainly, success in direct marketing is impossible without knowing how to target customers by applying the techniques of database marketing. This is why databases are introduced in the first section of this book. Chapter 10 provides more detailed discussion of the design, use, and maintenance of databases.

Databases enable direct marketing efforts to be targeted. The process begins with knowing about customers. It continues with knowing about their transactions. It is enhanced by information merged from other databases. It is further enhanced through affinity, relationship. And environmental data defines market potential even more.

Customers are anywhere. Customers are everywhere. But how do you target your customers? Databases allow you to create new customers and cultivate current customers. It is not surprising that "Target Marketing Expert" was one of the "Hot Tracks in 20 Professions" listed by *U.S. News & World Report*.

Any enterprise, whether selling to consumers or industries, can benefit from database-directed marketing. Databases describe customers in terms of their individual as well as their response characteristics. They relate past actions by customers to their future preferences in order to fit promotions to needs and add value to customer relationships. They enable profiling of prospects.

Databases can also describe environments, such as ZIP codes or Standard Industrial Classification (SIC) codes, in which a high propensity to respond (or not to respond) to an offer is likely.

Adapted with permission from Martin Baier, *How to Find and Cultivate Customers through Direct Marketing* (Lincolnwood, Ill.: NTC Business Books, 1996). Baier is director of the Center for Direct Marketing Education and Research at the University of Missouri–Kansas City and a member of the Direct Marketing Hall of Fame.

They can be enhanced with data from other sources so that they become even more descriptive and ever more predictive. They can provide the basis of scientific analysis and evaluation, which are key characteristics of direct marketing.

The most important database is that of your own customers. A customer database will enable you to cultivate your customers through continuity selling and cross-selling. It will also enable you to develop statistical profiles, even by product preference, and thus create more customers like those you already have. And a customer database will enable you to put lifetime value on your customers to guide your future decision making. The first sale to a newly acquired customer is but a forerunner of additional sales to that customer in the future, so a customer database should be viewed as an asset, like buildings, equipment, inventory, and accounts receivable.

Unlike such tangible assets, however, customers are a source of future revenues and future profits, which can go well beyond recovering the initial costs of acquiring these customers through selling, advertising, and other sales promotion. The value of a customer database is much more than that shown on a line, sometimes found on balance sheets, called "goodwill."

Database Marketing and Customer Relationships

Customers are not a homogeneous lot. Their one common characteristic is the relationship or affinity they form with companies they favor with their custom—and often their continued loyalty. When customers perpetuate such relationships, they expect in return to receive quality, value, and service. Organizations, in turn, seek customer loyalty in the hope of creating an affinity that will cement the relationship and keep customers coming back.

Relationships or affinities with customers can be developed to such a degree that loyal customers trust and buy the company's brands above all competitive offerings. Affinity and good customer relationships extend their value, too, well beyond the first sale . . . to cross-selling of unrelated products/services, even from unrelated organizations. The power of the marketing database makes all of this and more possible.

Customer Relationships and Lifetime Value (LTV)

The creation of customers is only a first step in building a successful business. The next—and more important—step is to keep and cultivate these customers. In the past, the nurturing of customer relationships has been difficult, in fact almost impossible, to evaluate. Though businesses might have known that the number of customers increased or decreased, that advertising attracted some new customers or that competitors took away others, there were few ways of knowing which customers came or went or why.

But database technology has changed that. An organization can at last identify its loyal customers, its repeat purchasers and its one-time-only "triers," especially within well-defined market segments. Moreover, marketers can now trace each customer's actions and transactions. This ability makes customers a significant—and measurable—asset.

Mail-order firms, faced with high front-end printing and circulation costs, long ago adopted the concept of lifetime value of a customer (LTV) to guide marketing decision making.

A 1993 Supreme Court decision could hasten a more universal adoption of the LTV concept. The case involved a New Jersey newspaper that claimed depreciation deduction for its acquisition of a paid-subscriber customer list as part of a sale transaction. In its ruling, the court rejected the categorical argument presented by the IRS that customer lists are a form of goodwill and therefore never depreciable.

Direct marketers truly appreciate LTV when they engage in both continuity selling and cross-selling . . . when they develop a database of customers. The LTV approach, too, is ideally suited to determining the market value of an enterprise in cases where an acquisition or a sale is contemplated. Since such an asset valuation of a database reflects anticipated future performance, it can be a better gauge of value than are commonly used multiples of sales or profits. The arithmetic involved in determining LTV is calculated in Chapter 19, "Mathematics of Direct Marketing."

Customer "Lists" versus Customer "Databases"

A list is commonly thought of as a list of customer names. Sometimes this list includes inactive customers, those who have inquired or been referred by a customer, or selected prospects.

Often, a company with a customer list seeks new customers by obtaining lists of prospects from external sources. Basically, there are two types of external lists available: lists of those who have responded to other offers (called *response lists*) and lists of those obtained from public sources of information (called *compiled lists*) such as automobile and driver's license registrations, membership rosters, or manufacturers' warranties.

An organization's own customer list, especially when enhanced as a database, is most productive and responsive. This is because of the special relationship— or goodwill—that any organization enjoys with its own customers. It is not uncommon for a house list to be four or even ten times as responsive as an external list with which there is no customer relationship.

Of course, active customers—those who have recently bought from the organization—are the most valuable segment of the house list. Of lesser potential, but still more responsive than lists from outside sources, are buyers who have become inactive, those who have inquired but have not purchased, and those who have been referred or recommended by present customers.

The value of any list—house, response, or compiled—can be substantially increased by turning it into a true database of usable customer or prospect information. To do so, you need to collect much more than your customer's name and address. A database becomes more useful as it includes more details about the customer's demographic and buying habits. Besides allowing you to sell more goods and services to current customers, such a database lets you identify prospects who resemble your customers.

Your database can also guide your continuity selling, cross-selling, and prospecting efforts efficiently and effectively. Properly used, a database can help avoid misdirected and cost-ineffective marketing efforts. A database is a planning tool. It also provides the means for analysis and evaluation. It enables the direct marketer to dig beyond traditional accounting reports into the intricacies of marketing success.

Although great strides have been made in making databases sophisticated planning tools, thus maximizing profits from house lists, the ever-present need for acquiring new customers remains. The more clearly the database defines the customer profile, the more likely it is that the marketer will be able to build the customer base in a cost-efficient manner. Working with competent list brokers is imperative.

Why You Need a Database

The following checklist will help support the decision to develop a customer database. A database can:

- Match products/services to customer wants and needs.

- Help you select new lists or use new media that fit the profile of existing customers.

- Maximize personalization of all offers or customer contacts to individual customers.

- Provide for ongoing interaction with customers and prospects.

- Pinpoint ideal timing and frequency for promotions.

- Measure response and be accountable for results.

- Help you create the offers most likely to elicit response from your customers.

- Help you achieve a unique selling proposition (USP) targeted to appeal to your customers.

- Integrate direct response communication with other forms of advertising.

- Demonstrate that customers are valuable assets.

What Information Should Your Database Contain?

The core of a customer database is a name and address record that is complete, accurate, and current. Beyond that, there is no cut-and-dried checklist stipulating how much information your database should contain or how detailed that information should be. Different organizations have varying needs. Consumer buyers differ from industrial buyers. But this list of essentials can get your database off to a good start:

- A unique identifier such as an ID or match code

- Name and title of individual and/or organization

- Mailing address, including ZIP code

- Telephone number

- Source of order, inquiry, or referral

- Data and purchase details of first transaction

- Recency/frequency/monetary transaction history by date, and by amounts of purchase, by product (lines) purchased

- Credit history and rating (scoring)

- Relevant demographic data for consumer buyers, such as age, gender, marital status, family data, education, income, occupation, length of residence at address given, geodemographic cluster information, and other data of value

- Relevant data for industrial buyers such as standard industrial classification, size, revenues, number of employees, length of time in business, socioeconomic information about the organization's location, and even data about the personality of individual buyers

What data you include depends entirely on its future value in use. "Nice to know" or "we may need that somewhere down the line" are not valid reasons for accumulating data, even though today's technology encourages it. Information costs money and that cost must return a value.

Information is also a perishable commodity. Not only does the degree of customer activity (or inactivity) fluctuate, but the people and organizations comprising your database are far from static. Their demographics change as they get older or raise families. They change jobs, within as well as between organizations. Their attitudes and preferences change. They die. They move. In 12 months, 20 percent of an average customer list could change address.

Such volatility demonstrates the importance of adequate mailing list maintenance. It demonstrates, too, that customer lists that are mailed to and maintained religiously have greater deliverability value to the direct marketer than do lists compiled without data qualification, from directories or rosters.

Data about customers and their transactions must be kept up to date. No advertiser, but especially not the scientific direct response advertiser, wants to distribute communications indiscriminately. It is important to make sure that the message is not only deliverable, but also that it is properly targeted. Cost without benefit is to be avoided. To achieve this end, you need to be concerned with mailing list maintenance as well as with ongoing updating of the transaction and other data contained within each customer record.

What Kind of Database Do You Need?

A database can be an added strength to a company's marketing efforts, or it can—as with direct marketing organizations—drive the entire operation. Following are five categories of database development and utilization, with a brief description of each. Decide which of these you currently have or need—then consider how you might develop and utilize your own database further.

The Customer Database

The simplest, yet most important, database may be little more than a collection of customer information. It can be used to identify the company's most valuable customers and communicate with them in ways that are likely to elicit response, based on their past preferences. Purchase history can be combined with demographic and psychographic data to predict future purchases. This database can further categorize customers as follows:

- **Active customers:** What action have customers taken in the past? How recently have they purchased? How frequently have they purchased? How much did they spend? What are their product or service preferences? From what promotion source were they acquired? Identifying your most active customers can help you concentrate resources on the most profitable segment of your customer list.

- **Inactive customers:** How long have prior customers been inactive? How long had they been active? What was their buying pattern while active? How were they initially acquired? What offers have they received since? This information can help you design promotions that reactivate your inactive customers.

- **Inquiries:** From what media source did inquirers come? What was the nature of the inquiry? Do you have any demographic or psychographic information on inquirers?

- **Referrals:** Who recommended these as prospects? For what purpose? Can the name of the referrer be used?

The Prospect Database

The databases of existing customers can enable you to identify new prospects most likely to become customers, and thus begin a prospect database.

- Profile customers in your existing database first, then seek prospects like them.

- View such profiles in terms of lists—of readers, viewers, listeners—in order to effectively utilize all advertising media and not just direct mail.

- Think in terms of market segmentation and product differentiation. Then position differentiated products (such as recordings of rock music) to market segments (high school students, for example).

- Employ a rifle rather than a shotgun approach to prospecting. Aim for those with similar characteristics to existing customers, not the mass market.

- Experiment with prospect lists . . . *test them*.

The Enhancement Database

Highly sophisticated computer matching technology now permits overlaying one or multiple databases on your own in order to transfer relevant information. Database enhancement can substantially increase the amount and quality of information you hold on each customer or prospect.

In its simplest form, an enhancement might be the addition of age (from a driver's license record) or telephone number (from a directory record). Other possibilities include past transactions; demographic and psychographic data; credit experience, if pertinent; people on the move, evidenced by an address change; significant characteristics of a business; and a multitude of customer behavior and transaction data.

By overlaying multiple databases, you can eliminate duplications between and among the lists and identify ''hotline names'' (those who responded most recently) and ''multibuyers'' (those who appear on more than one list). Negative screening, such as a credit check, can be used to remove a record from a solicitation database.

The Cluster Database

Consider expanding your database using publicly available information on people, groups, and businesses. Certainly a major database for direct marketers is that of the decennial Census of Population and Housing. The census is particularly useful in explaining the characteristics of a small geographic cluster (such as a ZIP code area) and from this evaluating a buying environment in order to predict response. Look also at the following:

- Affinity groups such as associations or neighborhoods where people with like interests tend to cluster. (Behavior within such clusters, including buying habits and attitudes, tends to be influenced by common interests.)

- Geographic reference groups small enough to facilitate prediction through environmental demographic databases such as census tracts, block groups, and ZIP code areas

- Lifestyle (psychographic) reference groups, having common activities, interests, and opinions

- Industrial data for business purchasers, including information such as size, sales revenue, capital, number of employees, and standard industrial classification (SIC)

The Analytical Database

Use your database not just to collect information and segment your lists, but also to aid decision making—both in marketing and in overall business strategy. Using your database as an analytical tool incorporates the statistical techniques and findings of research as well as the results of testing. It also includes models and simulations used to support your decisions. Use your database for any of the following:

- To measure response and keep records for accountability purposes

- To analyze, interpret, and evaluate the effect of every marketing decision you make

- To predict future response

How to Use a Database to Find Your Most Profitable Customers

An essential tool for identifying your best customers is the recency/frequency/monetary (RFM) formula. By carrying within each customer's record the date, volume, and nature of purchases, it is possible to determine the performance record of each customer. This enables you to estimate the future potential of that customer and relate the cost of future promotion to the potential benefit to be derived from each customer in the database.

The RFM formula is not new. It has been a standard for general merchandise catalogers for half a century. Originally developed by George Cullinan for his company, Alden's, the formula has been followed by many others. To a mail-order customer who complained when he or she didn't receive a seasonal or sale catalog, the pat answer was that the customer's RFM score didn't warrant the expense of sending it!

The exact RFM formulation for each direct marketer will vary according to the relative importance given to each of the three variables:

- Recency of purchase

- Frequencey of purchase

- Monetary value of the purchase

Under certain conditions, there might be a need for further weighting of the calculations of particular promotions as, for example, those to customers who had purchased most recently.

Exhibit 2–1 illustrates the use of the RFM formula in evaluating customers in an organization's database according to the combined RFM values of their transactions over a period of time. In this hypothetical example, three customers (identified as A, B, and C) have a purchase history calculated over a 24-month period. Points are assigned to each transaction, according to a historically derived RFM formula exclusive to this organization. Further weighting is given to recency of purchase (times 5), frequency of purchase (times 3), and monetary value of purchase (times 2). Thus, on a scale of 10, recency is weighted at 50 percent, frequency at 30 percent, and monetary at 10 percent.

The resultant cumulative scores—202 for A, 709 for B, and 280 for C—indicate a potential preference for customer C. Based on C's RFM history, a greater number of promotion dollars (such as mailing a seasonal catalog) could be justified. Sending a catalog could also be warranted for customer A. Customer B might be an unlikely risk and sending a catalog could be a misdirected marketing effort.

While recency of purchase has been given the greatest weight in this hypothetical example, each organization must determine through its own analysis the factors that influence purchases. As a rule of thumb, however, the buyer who has purchased most recently is the one most likely to buy again.

Market Tests

Every database for a product starts with an initial test—a market test—to determine *if* there is a market for the product and, if so, what the potential size or

Exhibit 2-1.   Evaluation of Customer Database Records by Recency, Frequency, and Monetary Values of Transactions (RFM)

Recency of transaction:
20 points if within past 3 months
10 points if within past 6 months
5 points if within past 9 months
3 points if within past 12 months
1 point if within past 24 months

Frequency of transaction: Number of purchases within 24 months × 4 points each (Maximum = 20 points)

Monetary value of transaction: Dollar volume of purchases within 24 months × 10% (Maximum = 20 points)

Weighting assumption:
Recency = 5
Frequency = 3
Monetary = 2

Customer	Purchase	Recency (months)	Assigned Points	(×5) Weight Points	Frequency	Assigned Points	(×3) Weight Points	Monetary	Assigned Points	(×2) Weight Points	Total Weight Points	Cumulative Points
A	1	3	20	100	1	4	12	$ 30	3	6	118	118
A	2	9	5	25	1	4	12	100	10	20	57	175
A	3	24	1	5	1	4	12	50	5	10	27	202
B	1	12	3	15	2	8	24	500	20	40	79	79
C	1	3	20	100	1	4	12	100	10	20	132	132
C	2	6	10	50	1	4	12	60	6	12	74	206
C	3	12	3	15	2	8	24	70	7	14	53	259
C	4	24	1	5	1	4	12	20	2	4	21	280

universe of that market is. Whether your company is well established and simply introducing a new product to an existing line or is a new company introducing its very first product, it is essential to use the direct mail test to determine the potential universe for the product. Initial preconceptions about ultimate sales penetration and about target markets are usually restrictive and rarely accurate.

In addition, the initial test mailing is sometimes too small to be projectable to a large continuation mailing. For example, an initial test of 50,000, which usually includes offer and package tests, is not projectable to a continuation mailing of 500,000 or more. Yet in many instances this is the stated objective. It is therefore recommended that no less than a 100,000 quantity, and preferably 150,000, be used, particularly if tests other than the market test are being conducted.

To identify the market, a test known as a *spectrum test* is recommended. Working with 20–30 lists, you construct a ladder of three tests—a sort of X, Y, Z arrangement. Your middle group, the Y of the spectrum, is drawn from lists that appear to be right on target. Your X group is drawn from those that, because of certain affinity factors, could be considered good prospects. The Z group, while it reflects a very different profile, inferentially could have reasons for being interested. This type of spectrum testing yields clues about how deeply you can mail because it is a two-dimensional sample. You are sampling the universe of lists as well as the people on the particular lists chosen.

Then there is always the question of what to do on a test mailing of, say, 150,000. Are you better off testing 30 lists of 5,000 each or 15 lists of 10,000? The answer depends on the growth pattern established in the original forecast plan.

Let's run through, as an example, a magazine called the *Glory of Art*. The first step was an "Overview of List Markets." The intention of this overview is to provide a feel for the potential universe and to decide on the specific lists to be selected from each category. (See Exhibit 2–2.) On the *Glory of Art*, it was

Exhibit 2–2.   *Glory of Art:* Overview of List Markets

Category	No. of Lists	Potential Universe
Art/antiques/collectibles	31	2,995,900
Upscale gifts and decorating items	24	2,088,600
Luxury foods and gifts	16	3,316,200
Photography	5	968,900
Women's high fashions	8	843,500
Cultural books and magazines	31	5,232,200
Regional publications	20	2,732,100
Cultural arts	7	485,400
Miscellaneous (credit card)	5	1,732,000
Total	147	20,394,800[a]

[a] Can be reduced by approximately 25 percent due to the duplication factor.
Source: © Rose Harper, The Kleid Company Inc.

decided to go with 30 lists, because the market testing was crucial in determining whether this was a viable publication in the marketplace. (See Exhibit 2–3.)

Note that, although the schedule is concentrated in the more targeted categories, other categories, such as women's fashions, were explored with an eye toward market evaluation and expansion.

In analyzing by category in the initial stages, it is better to look at the number of lists tested in each category and at the success ratio, rather than

Exhibit 2–3. *Glory of Art:* List Test Schedule (150,000)

Category	Universe	Test Quantity	No. of Lists
Art/antiques/collectibles	1,215,600	45,000	9
Upscale gifts and decorating items	383,000	20,000	4
Luxury foods and gifts	1,871,900	25,000	5
Photography	150,000	5,000	1
Women's high fashions	185,000	5,000	1
Cultural books and magazines	876,900	25,000	5
Regional publications	267,000	10,000	2
Cultural arts	245,000	10,000	2
Miscellaneous (credit card)	125,000	5,000	1
Total	5,319,400	150,000	30

Source: © Rose Harper, The Kleid Company Inc.

Exhibit 2–4. *Glory of Art:* Analysis Success Factor by Category

	No. of Tests	No. of Continuations	Percentage of Success
Y:			
Art/antiques/collectibles	9	7	77.8%
Cultural books and magazines	5	5	100.0
Cultural arts	2	1	50.0
Subtotal	16	13	81.3%
X:			
Upscale gifts and decorating items	4	1	25.0%
Photography	1	1	100.0
Regional publications	2	2	100.0
Subtotal	7	4	57.1%
Z:			
Luxury foods and gifts	5	2	40.0%
Women's high fashions	1	1	100.0
Miscellaneous (credit card)	1	—	—
Subtotal	7	3	42.9%
Total	30	20	66.6%

Source: © Rose Harper, The Kleid Company Inc.

averaging response in each category. Averages can be misleading: One list in a particular category that responds dramatically higher or lower than the other lists can influence the overall average.

This type of analysis should be considered directional and not an absolute. In some instances the ratios are reliable, and in some instances they're not. For example, where only one list was tested in a category and proved responsive, that category must be approached more cautiously than the category where five lists were tested and were all responsive. (See Exhibit 2–4.)

The most important element to consider, however, is that the dynamics of each testing situation are dissimilar, particularly the objectives, the time frame, and the financials. These variables must be studied and given consideration in structuring the initial test.

SELF-QUIZ

1. The most important database is _____ _____

   _____.

2. What is the difference between a customer *list* and a customer *database*?

   _____

   _____

3. What information should a database contain?

   • A unique identifier such as an ID or match code

   • Name and title of individual and/or organization

   • Telephone number

   • Data and purchase details of first transaction

   • _____

   _____

   _____

4. Once vital data are entered into a database, you are set for three years.

   ☐ True   ☐ False

5. There are five categories of databases:

   a. The Customer Database

    b. The Project Database

    c. The Enhancement Database

    d. The Cluster Database

    e. The _____ _____

6. What does RFM stand for?

    R _____

    F _____

    M _____

7. Using the RFM formula on a scale of 10, weight the three criteria:

    R—__ percent

    F—__ percent

    M—__ percent

PILOT PROJECT

The chairman of the board of your company thinks that a database is simply a fancy term for a mailing list. You have asked for a $50,000 budget to build a state-of-the-art database. Develop a list of ten reasons why the investment is justified.

The Media of Direct Marketing

CHAPTER THREE

New Media for Direct Marketers

No area of marketing is receiving more attention from consumers, business, and the press than that of new media. There are many options available. For the purpose of this chapter, we limit the discussion to a group of electronic media that offer two-way interactive communication between prospects/customers and marketers. These include fax on demand, interactive television, CD-ROM/diskette, electronic kiosks, on-line services, and Internet/World Wide Web. This chapter will define the scope of the new media marketplace and show how and why it should be included in the mix of direct marketing media.

The strength of the new media marketplace is in its ability to give instant access to incredible amounts of information in a cost-efficient manner. This information is stored and distributed in digital form. Unlike print or direct mail media, new media is not constrained by page sizes, printing cut-offs, or weight. This information is available on demand, when a consumer needs it, not necessarily when a marketer wants them to receive it. Once created, it requires little human intervention on the part of the marketer, except for periodic updates.

These new media allow true dialogue building. They allow consumers access to unprecedented amounts of product information. They offer marketers the opportunity to capture vast amounts of information on their prospects and customers. Because they are interactive, they offer the opportunity to customize messages to each consumer. Many pioneering direct marketers have already had success with these media. This chapter will show you how to benefit from what they've learned.

Ron Jacobs, the author of Chapter 3, deals with new media for his clients at Jacobs & Clevenger and teaches in the Medill School Integrated Marketing Communications Program at Northwestern University.

The New Media Marketplace

New media offer a paperless, digital environment where marketers can efficiently deliver their messages to target groups as small as one. However, unlike traditional media, new media are mainly invitational, where consumers actively seek the relationship. Marketers must work hard to let their target markets know where to find them. To support these efforts, they usually rely on traditional media, such as direct mail, print, and television. They often develop enticing incentives for consumers to locate them and return again and again. The technologies of new media enable marketers to achieve the promise of individual marketing. Unless the content of their offering is informative, engaging, and relevant, no dialogue will ensue.

The nature of that content takes on many forms. It may be in the form of an electronic shopping mall, retail store, catalog, product demonstration, advertisement, or directory. It may be content that allows a prospect to request or access additional product information (e.g., features, benefits, prices, dealer locations, availability) or allows them to complete the purchase directly. No matter what the form or content, new media are one of the hottest growth areas for direct marketing activity today.

According to Simba Information Inc., a unit of Cowles, publishers of industry publications *Direct* and *Catalog Age*, new media expenditures were $476.8 million in 1994, with on-line and interactive television services garnering the greatest share of spending. They estimate that this will grow to $2.4 billion in 1998 and $4.7 billion by 2000.

The greatest spending is coming from consumer goods marketers, who see new media as another channel of information distribution. Advertisers testing new media come from nearly every category. They include automobile manufacturers Ford, Chrysler, and Toyota; liquor brands such as ZIMA malt beverage, Stolichnaya vodka, and Jim Beam; and restaurants McDonald's, Pizza Hut, and

Exhibit 3–1. Percent of On-Line Shopping Revenues in the Year 2000

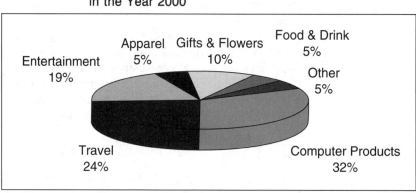

Source: Forrester Research

TGI Fridays. It is likely that the bulk of these dollars is coming from budgets otherwise earmarked for awareness-building media (television, newspapers, magazines, etc.). However, the need for consumer goods marketers to build relationships and retain customers in increasingly fragmented markets means that some of this spending would have gone to direct mail or other direct marketing executions.

Traditional and nontraditional direct marketers are a growing segment of electronic media. With increased postage costs, paper shortages, and decreased prospecting response rates from direct mail, many familiar direct marketers such as Spiegel, L.L. Bean, Sharper Image, and Williams-Sonoma are testing new media. In the past, there were barriers to new media direct marketing:

- The Internet's anti-commerce sentiment

- Primarily male demographics

- Poor graphic quality

- Insecure payment methods

Many of these barriers are coming down, and with them greater expectations for future growth.

According to Forrester Research, revenue generated from electronic transactions will grow from $518 million in 1995 to $6.6 billion by the year 2000. Ten to fifteen companies are estimated to be earning revenues in the $15 to $20 million range by the year 2000. Top growth categories for on-line commerce include computer products, travel, entertainment, gifts and flowers, apparel and food/drink (see Exhibit 3-1). Some companies having more than $1 million in online sales in 1996 include CD Now, JC Penney, Internet Shopping Network, 1-800 FLOWERS, L.L. Bean, NECX Direct, Netscape's Company Store and Spiegel.

New Media Is about Information

The main commerce of new media is information. This parallels what's going on in much of the world around us. In the words of Nicholas Negroponte, director of the MIT Media Lab, ''Information about information is more valuable than the information it is about.'' Negroponte points out that all of us are willing to pay handsomely for information that we are interested in. He cites the fact that *TV Guide* is more profitable than the four TV networks combined!

It should be no surprise that new media have proven to be powerful information-gathering devices. With one call to IBM, consumers can get up-to-date product information sent to their fax machine. They can look up features from one of more than 50,000 products stored on the CD-ROM catalog of an industrial supply company. They can scan vast digital libraries, finding articles on specific diseases from the National Cancer Foundation, locate population growth figures from the U.S. Census, look up data on any of 10 million U.S. businesses supplied by American Business Information, or request product specs from a company in Copenhagen.

Using simple agent or filtering programs, users can program their own personal interests. The filtering programs scan huge databases, on-line articles, press releases, etc. They capture only the information that users have determined is relevant to them. These articles can be sent to the users as collected or batched on an hourly, daily, or weekly basis, depending on the users' needs. Users get just the information they've asked for, without having to weed through information that they have not requested.

Marketers can gather information about consumers as well. It might be the ease of use, or ease of responding, but marketers seem to be able to gather more information electronically than from traditional printed means. They can do this passively, recording browsing activity, time on-line, and purchase behavior on a product-by-product basis. They can capture e-mail addresses and store information on each user in a database.

Marketers can also capture data using active means. They can encourage users to fill out questionnaires, capturing vast amounts of demographic, psychographic, and leisure information about buyers and browsers. Donnelley Marketing Inc. has successfully tested an on-line version of its Share Force™ questionnaire using the Prodigy on-line service and the Microsoft Network. Such information gathering is one of the most effective uses of new media. While it raises privacy concerns among some, an opt-out selection helps to ensure that information is used in a manner consistent with consumers' wishes.

Key Elements of Successful New Media

A variety of product categories have been early adopters in the new media marketplace. These groups have crossed over from both the consumer and business-to-business marketplace. Categories such as computers, office supplies, apparel, sporting goods, home furnishings, flowers and other gift items, airline tickets, and even fireworks are being sold direct via one or more new media.

Simba information has identified six key elements for new media success. Marketing will profit from new media if it:

- Uses an existing customer base

- Makes an existing marketplace more effective

- Brings together buyers and sellers that are physically separated

- Is easily accessible (has wide distribution)

- Offers decision support information (value-added services)

- Has the ability to close the sale direct

The parallels between the elements of successful new media campaigns and direct marketing are clear. It's no wonder that direct marketers have had some of the earliest successes with new media. It's also not surprising that marketers unschooled in direct marketing have had some of the costliest and most complete failures. Acceptance of new media technologies is growing rapidly, but it is still a narrow target market. Good, solid direct marketing skills are necessary to break through and impact these markets.

The Technology of New Media

New media is defined by technology. Each of these electronic technologies brings together buyers and sellers in a unique way. All require the use of an intermediary electronic device such as a computer, CD-ROM reader, fax machine, or telephone. The future of these media are tied to both the willingness of consumers to learn and use these new technologies and the proliferation of these tools in homes and offices.

Some marketers might find that they can make use of many of these media. Others will not be so lucky. One thing is for certain—if consumers find using these digital media for commerce more difficult than their analog competitors, only a handful of technophiles will use them.

Fax on Demand

One medium that nearly any direct marketer can take advantage of is fax on demand (FOD). In a typical system, promotional copy and marketing information is stored on a fax server. The server, often a dedicated personal computer, runs specialized software that can store pages of information such as catalog sheets, product descriptions, and price lists. Consumers calling an FOD line are given prompts that lead them to the information they are looking for. They are then prompted to enter their own fax number. Within moments of completing the call, the server dials the caller's fax number and delivers the requested information.

Growth of FOD has been spurred by the increase in fax machines in homes and offices. According to BIS Strategic Decisions, the fax market will go from $887 million in 1993 to $3 billion by 1998. This rapid growth is due in part to the increasing use of computer fax modems, which will swell to 17 million units during that same period.

The use of FOD is particularly appropriate for companies that offer large numbers of products, have lengthy technical specs, or want to offer 24-hour access to information with no staffing requirements. Companies in high-tech industries have found FOD particularly effective.

The IBM personal computer division has been a leader in the use of FOD. It includes the FOD phone number in print ads, brochures, and even in its catalogs. Users can access specifications on the latest computer models, price lists, warranty information, and even specials on discontinued and factory-serviced models.

Electronic Kiosks

Over the last few years, electronic kiosks have made a tremendous comeback in the marketplace. These freestanding electronic displays were once large unwieldy boxes, crammed full of electronic switches, tubes, video players, line printers, etc. Reductions in the size of computers, liquid crystal displays, and CD-ROM technology have changed all this. Today these units can be handsome stainless steel affairs, unobtrusively placed in well-trafficked areas.

According to Simba, kiosks represent less than 1 percent or $5 million in media transactions. This market is expected to grow from 70,000 units in 1994 to 600,000 by 1998. Most of this growth will come from using the kiosk for information delivery: helping consumers learn more about products and services, informing them of special promotions, and delivering coupons. Retailers have found kiosks particularly helpful for sampling music or locating records by title, artist, or category. Blockbuster and Best Buy are two retailers that have had great success using kiosks in such a supporting role.

Most tests of kiosks have attempted to sell general merchandise from a variety of catalogers in malls, hotels, and offices. Consumers seem uncomfortable using such devices in highly public places. The need to display a purse, wallet, or credit card while focused on such a device gives some consumers a feeling of vulnerability. Kiosks offering products and services to niche markets located in targeted locations, such as health clubs or grocery stores, have improved results with less traffic. Testing in various traffic flows is now commonplace. Moving a kiosk just 50 feet to a more private location can increase results by two to three times.

Today's kiosks are powerful, reliable, and portable. They can be quickly deployed with compelling applications that make the most of interactive media. At a cost of $10,000–25,000 each, they are not cheap. But they can be successfully used as part of an overall new media strategy.

Interactive Television

Tests of interactive television (ITV) have been going on for more than a decade. Companies such as Time Warner, Knight-Ridder, Bell Atlantic, Cox Communications, US West, Bell South, TCI, and Microsoft have invested heavily in trials of various technologies and service options. They have been constrained by the requirements of evolving digital technologies and the high costs associated with these changes. ITV systems require enormous amounts of data flow for two-way, interactive communications. This additional bandwidth makes possible increased channel options, high-quality video, and acceptable response time. Going digital is the most popular answer to improving these systems to meet such expectations. Most of the current interactive trials require that test neighborhoods first be upgraded with fiber optic cables. This costs millions of dollars per system.

Another technology hurdle for ITV is set-top decoder boxes necessary to convert digital signals for use on home TVs. The set-top boxes, which can include microprocessors, printers, and computer hookups, can cost $1,000–5,000 each. As providers move into national roll-outs, they expect the price of set-top boxes to be a more reasonable $300–450. To gain consumer acceptance, ITV providers will have to give away or subsidize the cost of hardware, even during roll-outs.

The expectations for ITV are great. It offers consumers the ability to do a variety of different things from their living rooms, and it gives them the ability to shift these activities to their own personal "prime time." Some of the options tested include on-demand programming of movies, news, sports, and broadcast network TV programs. Interactive banking, investing, and bill paying are also popular options. On-line travel planning and reservations also find favor, as consumers search for the best deals or find their plans changing overnight. Interactive government, where you can attend and participate in local city council and school board meetings and even vote on-line, promises to bring government to the people. Even interactive gaming and gambling have spurred a lot of interest and controversy.

The list of proposed and tested ITV options go on to include interactive video personals, Internet access, local phone service, utility management, and home security management. For marketers, the promise of ITV includes on-demand coupons, sweepstakes promotions, on-demand catalogs, and interactive shopping. Is this what consumers want?

A 1994 Dataquest survey of consumers in the top seven U.S. ITV trial markets asked what ITV services the consumers would pay for. This survey found that home shopping finished dead last. Other surveys have found that most consumers are happy with their current TV options and don't have high interest levels in ITV. A study by Simba Information Inc. concluded that ITV might not provide enough personal interaction for large numbers of consumers to use it for on-line shopping. Ordering merchandise with a remote control device does seem to lack the comfort of calling an 800 number and speaking with a telephone sales rep.

However, ITV tests of home shopping continue. Interaxx is working with seven cable operators to implement ITV tests using a "smart analog" set-top box, which requires a lower investment than other systems. Interaxx has signed up 300 merchants for a 2,000-home trial in Coral Gables, Florida. According to Kenneth Angel, senior vice president and marketing director, "Even if consumers tell you (interactive home shopping) is fifth or sixth in importance, this is what they are going to use." He continued, "Convenience is a major factor."

With billions of dollars already invested in ITV, it's clear that testing will continue but that roll-outs are still 5–10 years away. However, what form this will ultimately take is not clear. At a recent cable TV trade show, the items gaining the most attention were cable TV modems. These allow cable subscribers to hook up their computers to the already laid mid-band coaxial cable in their homes.

The benefit to the consumer of cable modems is on-line access at a low cost and at speeds up to a thousand times that of twisted-pair phone lines. This speed allows real multimedia and interactive capabilities unachievable with phone lines. It gives cable system operators the ability to deliver interactive and multimedia services using much of their existing infrastructure, at a fraction of the cost of most ITV tests. This is a notable step toward the much-heralded convergence of television and computers. If it gains acceptance, it will change the nature of ITV and delay roll-outs further into the next century. (See Exhibit 3–2.)

CD-ROM/Diskette

An area that has shown great promise for direct marketers is the use of interactive CD-ROM and computer diskettes as marketing tools. They can combine text, graphics, still or full-motion photography, and animation with sound and music to create compelling response to applications. They can show demonstrations of products in use, show diagrams of the inner working of machines, and even accommodate pricing based on consumer-selected options. They often include games or contests to increase interest and make them more interactive.

Exhibit 3–2.   Interactive TV Trials

Name	Company	Location	Size
InTV	ACTV	Ventura County, CA	250 homes[a]
Stargazer	Bell Atlantic	Fairfax, VA	1,000 homes[b]
Interactive Systems Inc.	ISI	Beaverton, OR	1,500 homes[c]
NYNEX	NYNEX	Manhattan, NY	50 VOD homes/ 2,500 VDT homes[d]
Interactive Channel	Source Media Inc./ Sammons	Denton, TX	175 homes[e]
PersonalVision	Southern New England Telephone	West Hartford, CT	350 homes[f]
Time Warner	Time Warner	Orlando, FL	90 terminals[g]
Tele-Choice	US West	Omaha, NE	45,000 homes passed[h]

[a] Free during test/$10.00 thereafter.
[b] No monthly fee during test; will pay $0.49–4.49.
[c] Tests started 4th quarter 1995.
[d] Test ran September 1994–January 1996; concluded until digital technology available.
[e] Users pay $2.00 per month.
[f] No initial charge; will charge when system goes digital.
[g] Includes interactive couponing from CUC.
[h] Awaiting tariff approval from FCC to begin test.
Source: Interactive TV Strategies, © 1995.

Marketers as diverse as software companies and automakers have used diskette promotions to demonstrate their products and generate leads. Distributed on 3.5'' diskettes, they can be mailed to homes as part of a direct mail prospecting program. In the case of a test for Toyota, diskettes were distributed in private airline clubs to reach frequent business travelers who are target markets for the model promoted.

Prospective auto buyers can learn about the latest models and available options and even calculate the manufacturer's suggested list price. By filling out and returning an enclosed survey, users signal their buying interest, budget, timetable, etc. Information from the reply cards is added to the automaker's prospect database. Respondents might receive a number of mail efforts over time. And, depending on their survey scores, names can be distributed to local dealers for follow-up.

Although diskettes offer many advantages, they have limited space for the rich digital content marketers find most effective in new media. One CD-ROM can hold the equivalent of 250,000 pages of information, or 450 times the information on a 3.5'' diskette! The medium has quickly gained favor as increasing numbers of home and business computer users purchase computers with CD-ROM readers. In 1994 there were estimated to be four million computers with CD-ROM readers in use. Two out of three computers sold that year were equipped with them.

This medium offers a highly interactive way for consumers to learn about product benefits. They can see apparel products on a model. By pointing and clicking, they can change colors or styles interactively, look at the product from a variety of angles, and even see short movies with product use demonstrations or celebrity endorsements.

However, consumers are still not as comfortable with this method of purchasing as they are with television home shopping or ordering by phone. Simba estimates that purchases from CD-ROMs account for no more than 3 percent or $10 million in new media purchases. It estimates that software sales via CD-ROM were just $5 million, despite the efforts of more than 20 companies marketing such discs and the natural affinity for software one might expect from CD-ROM users. Of greater concern are that only half of marketers testing cooperative CD-ROMs have returned to them during roll-outs. These pioneers might have found that the critical mass of potential users has yet to develop.

CD-ROM catalogs can be expensive to produce. Cost is based on the amount of content. This can range from $10,000 for an electronic catalog with 25–30 products, up to $100,000 for a full CD-ROM. Add in duplication costs of $1.00–$2.00, plus additional promotional materials, and it's easy to see why marketers have been quick to test cooperative CD-ROM catalogs such as Shopping2000 or 2Market. Although marketers must still bear high production costs, they greatly reduce their distribution costs.

The holiday 1995 edition of 2Market includes 20 marketers, including the Chef's Catalog, FAO Schwartz, 1-800 Flowers, Hammacher Schlemmer, The Nature Company, and The Sharper Image. Users can browse through the catalog at their leisure. To view the latest updates or request help from a 2Market "gift expert" via e-mail, users can access 2Market's area on America On Line. Orders are placed through 2Market, and they take a small commission on each order.

2Market's hybrid approach helps to overcome the objection by marketers that CD-ROMs are a static medium—meaning that once they are pressed, prices, products, etc., can't change. However, the chances for success of this medium improve with the continued growth of CD-ROMs in the installed base of personal computers.

On-line Services Marketing

On-line services are proprietary networks that allow dial-in access using personal computers with modems, personal digital assistance (PDAs), or cable television set-top boxes equipped with modems. They include consumer on-line services such as CompuServe, America On Line, Prodigy, Delphi, eWorld, and the Microsoft Network and specialized business on-line services including ARI Network Service, Data Transmission Network, IndustryNet, LEXIS/NEXIS, and Dialog.

Growth of the consumer on-line services has been fueled by the increase in home multimedia-compatible personal computers. There is greater consumer spending on personal computers for home use than on televisions. It is estimated that there were more than 50 million multimedia PCs in use at the end of 1995. By September 1995, the six top consumer on-line services had a combined 9.9 million subscribers, adding 3.5 million in the first nine months of 1995 alone. Even the most conservative estimates expect this total to be 18 million subscribers by 1998. (See Exhibit 3–3.)

According to Simba Information Inc., consumer and business-to-business on-line services accounted for $324.9 million in new media transactions in 1994.

Exhibit 3–3. On-Line Service Growth Slowing, Role Evolving

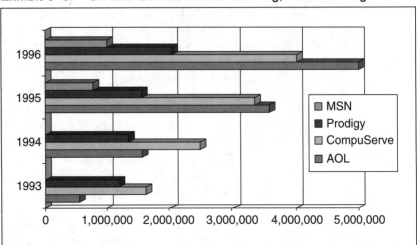

Consumer services accounted for $108.3 million of this, and business on-line services accounted for $216.6 million. The largest transaction-generating on-line services were Prodigy with $40 million and CompuServe with $50 million.

The on-line services are often described as gated villages. Subscribers feel a high degree of safety when in the controlled environments of these networks. A sense of community has developed among users. They find areas of specific interest to them, which they visit regularly.

On-line transactions have not taken hold within these environments as many marketers would hope. The feeling of security within the networks indicates that the sharing of financial data such as credit cards is not the greatest issue. It would seem that the right content and the ability to locate it are greater factors, as is the invitational nature of the on-line environment. Members spend a lot of time on-line using chart areas and e-mail. Indeed, these are the top services in use within the on-line communities. Nonetheless, as the on-line services mature, they offer great opportunities to marketers who can identify users' needs and crack the code with appropriate content.

All of these services share features that make them ideal for direct marketing activities. But first marketers must understand the network environments. Rob Jackson, executive vice-president, general manager of CMS (Customer Management Services, a database marketing services company in Chapel Hill, N.C.) and an authority on electronic media, points out three characteristics shared by all on-line services:

- They are highly effective information media.

- They are significant distribution channels for a wide range of products and services.

- They are sophisticated marketing databases.

Jackson notes that most marketers have yet to adequately transfer their successful response strategies to on-line content development. He points out that early on-line attempts have been more like mass media executions than direct marketing executions. He concedes that there must be more entertainment value in on-line content than in traditional direct marketing media. But not treating the on-line environment as a database marketing opportunity means that marketers are truly missing some of the strengths of this medium.

For example, on-line marketers have all of the tools necessary to complete transactions, but they seldom do. Marketers have the ability to capture significant amounts of information from prospects and customers, but they have yet to actively seek this kind of information. By adding a database component to an on-line area, consumers can complete orders on-line, instantly check inventory, and check the status of an order. Marketers can fulfill orders quicker; reduce staffing, telephone, and paperwork costs; and more efficiently operate their businesses. This is the reality for a tiny few marketers.

Within the on-line environment, marketers have two main choices before establishing a presence: they can go solo or they can be part of an on-line shopping mall. Translating a 64-page catalog to a stand-alone on-line environment will cost $35,000–50,000. Adding additional content can range from $300 to $500 per page. By having your own area, you may share in royalties of 2–4 percent of what the on-line service charges users for the time they spend in your area. This may change, however, as on-line services rethink their billing structures to remain competitive with each other and a host of Internet providers.

On-line malls typically have top retail anchors, such as Nordstrom or J.C. Penney, which helps attract users to the area and benefits smaller, lesser-known marketers. Costs to design a storefront area within a mall range from $10,000–25,000. In addition, the mall manager will take a commission on all sales. On CompuServe, for example, commissions range from 2 percent to 5 percent.

Hammacher Schlemmer has been one of the earliest adopters of new media. The Chicago-based cataloger and retailer of electronic gadgets and unique products has been testing on-line services since 1988, when they started testing on CompuServe.

CompuServe was chosen because of its close demographic match with Hammacher Schlemmer's customers. CompuServe's subscribers are typically male, 42 years of age, with a household income of $92,000. Hammacher Schlemmer's customers are 50 percent male/50 percent female, 36–49 years of age, with a household income of $75,000.

Hammacher Schlemmer uses an off-line system for orders. Users browse through its area then go to an order form and fill it out. The system handles orders as e-mail messages. They are downloaded nightly by HS staff, who handle them as they would a phone order. The low quality of on-line service graphics and the inability of users to check inventory on-line are the greatest weaknesses of the HS system.

Hammacher Schlemmer is pleased with its efforts. It reports that 2–3 percent of on-line service users enter their electronic storefront each month. Eighty percent of these buyers are ordering for the first time. The implication is that HS is reaching a market segment that would have remained unknown to them if not for their on-line presence. The average order size in the electronic environment of $112 is less than the $120 average order from print catalogs. With response rates 30 percent higher than in direct mail, and more than $2 million annually in on-line sales, Hammacher Schlemmer plans to continue and expand these efforts.

The future of the on-line services is in doubt. Consumer demand has caused all to offer Internet access. In addition, Prodigy, CompuServe and AOL have all started Internet service provider subsidiaries. These companies offer Internet only access at far lower rates than full on-line services customers pay. Microsoft Network has announced plans to convert to an all Internet service.

For unsophisticated users, and those with security and privacy concerns, the on-line services fill an important niche. Competition among these services, and their falling fees are good news for consumers hoping to save money. They are also helping to spur growth of this new medium. With growing consumer acceptance of the Internet, and its wealth of content, the on-line services may not be able to compete on cost. That would be a tragedy, as their role has been so important during the early stages of on-line market development.

World Wide Web/Internet Marketing

No form of new media has gripped the imagination of consumers and marketers more than the Internet (the Net). It is the modern descendant of a government and academic computer network started two decades ago. The Net is a vast, global network of 45,000 interconnected computer networks, which are able to seamlessly connect an estimated 30 million users worldwide. No one owns the Net, and no organization or government controls it. The fiercely independent, yet cooperative nature of the Internet is one of its most prominent features.

The Net includes a series of different applications. E-mail is the most common of these applications. It allows people to instantly communicate across networks and vast reaches of the Internet. Usenet is a series of more than 6,000 discussion groups where users with similar interests share ideas. E-mail groups (known as listservs) are similar to Usenet, but they use e-mail for communication, rather than special Usenet readers.

For a direct marketer, the existence of such lists might seem like a great opportunity. They are not the same as mailing lists in the traditional sense. Commercial applications in e-mail listservs and Usenet have been resisted. "Net-iquette," an unwritten code of Net conduct, prohibits the sending of unrequested advertising or promotion messages, except in areas designated for such activity. Violators ("spammers") are subjected to "flaming," a form of public e-mail humiliation that can include sending thousands of unpleasant messages to an offender's mailbox.

Growth of new Net users have been estimated at 60–85 percent annually. Low-cost access, minimal regulatory constraints, and the wealth of information available have all contributed to this growth. Another recent growth spurt has come as the consumer on-line services have given their subscribers Net access. This has forever changed the perception of the Net as a strictly academic and research tool.

A 1995 study by Yankelovich Partners Inc., "The Cybercitizen Report," found that 83 percent of Internet users also subscribed to at least one on-line service. They observed that 14 percent of the U.S. adult population are on-line service users, although only half of these have used the Internet proper. A 1995 study by O'Reilly & Associates pegged Internet demographics as 63 percent male, 33 percent female; median household income between $50,000 and $75,000; age 35–44.

Commercial activity has been slowly coming to the Internet. According to Simba Information Management, in 1994 the Internet accounted for just 6 percent of new media transaction activities, a total of $20 million. This is changing rapidly. The influx of new users, advent of relatively secure credit card transactions, and sheer number of commercial Web sites on-line has created a virtual gold rush of commercial Web sites on-line. Consumer demand still lags behind. A recent Gallup/Interactive Age survey showed that 24 percent of those polled intended to make a purchase of the Internet. (See Exhibit 3–4.)

Nonetheless, thousands of companies are on-line, with more setting up on-line every day. Most are setting up in an area of the Internet known as the World Wide Web. Unlike other areas of the Net, which are mainly text-based, the Web uses a graphic interface that offers interactive capabilities including animation, sound, and full-motion video. Documents created for the Web include words or pointers (known as *hypertext links*) that connect users with documents and files at other Web sites. These links are an important part of the communal information sharing that is the heart of Internet and Web culture.

Users access these documents, known as home pages, using one of a number of browsers created specifically to take advantage of the latest Web technology. Web browsers are often downloaded without cost to the user from home pages created by developers such as Microsoft, Mosaic, or Netscape. These companies' profits come from selling the software servers that run complex World Wide Web applications. Software and hardware can cost from $5,000 for a simple information server to $50,000 for a server that includes a complete on-line catalog, ordering, fulfillment, and a full-time, open connection to back-end databases.

Exhibit 3–4.   Intention to Use the Internet for Product Purchases

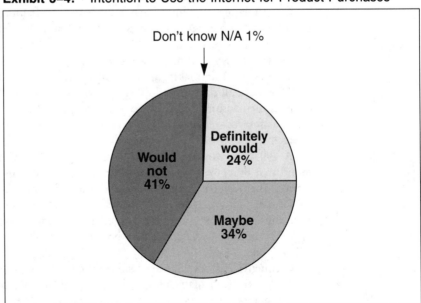

Source: Gallup/*Interactive Age,* 1995.

Costs for creative development of a home page have escalated sharply as the level of multimedia sophistication and programming has increased. Creative costs for a typical Web site range from $10,000 to $50,000, with updates and maintenance adding thousands of dollars annually. A recent study of Fortune 1,000 companies by Forrester Research showed average costs of $304,000 for promotional sites (on-line brochures), $1.3 million for content sites (sites that offer information or entertainment content) to $3.4 million for fully transactional sites (secure commerce sites with on-line ordering, on-line database, and multimedia graphics). Many marketers are choosing to develop and maintain Web pages in-house to help control and manage these costs.

Designing a successful Web presence requires graphic arts skills, experience with Web design tools, and constant updating. For example, Java, software that offers expanded multimedia capabilities to the Web, was included in the servers and browsers of Web developers within weeks of introduction. Many Web sites were updated with applications taking advantage of these new capabilities within a few months.

In order to have a successful Web presence, it's important to follow a few basic guidelines. Here are ten key elements to a successful Web site:

- Provide information that is perceived as valuable.

- Use good copy and compelling graphics that download quickly.

- Make it easy to use and include a frequently asked questions (FAQ) document.

- Update it frequently, so that users will return often.

- Offer an incentive (e.g., free software or screen saver downloads).

- Include a chat area.

- Survey and capture visitor information.

- Voluntarily capture e-mail addresses of users.

- Count and record the number of hits (i.e., visits) to the site.

- Become an information resource by linking to complementary home pages.

The World Wide Web is both a communication and a collaboration medium. It is profoundly changing the definition of an advertising medium. Its growth has been explosive, although not for transactions. The Federal Express home page allows visitors to check on the status of their shipments. CNN offers the latest news in a multimedia format. MCI has created Grammercy Press, a fictitious company, to help illustrate the benefits of MCI Business Internet services. Even the White House and Congress are on the Web, offering speeches, news, and information on important legislation. Many organizations are also developing *intranet* sites. These closed loop sites are designed to allow communication between an organization and its employees, customers, or other stakeholders.

Access to an *intranet* site is limited to designated users, but the objectives of creating bonds or offering various kinds of information are the same as with other Web sites.

Getting prospects to a Web site is not easy in this self-directed medium. Most users start an information quest by searching one of hundreds of Web directories (e.g., Yahoo!, Excite, Magellan, and so on). In order to get users to their sites, it's imperative that marketers develop a thorough directory listing strategy. This includes designing page headers that encourage more hits from the directories, listing in secondary as-well-as primary directories, and linking with as many complementary sites as possible.

Banner advertising is another strategy used to get users to an organization's Web site. Many popular Web sites, including the major directories, offer paid advertising that hot links back to the advertisers' own home page. It is estimated that companies will spend $10 million in on-line advertising in 1996 and $2.2 billion by the year 2000. Cost of such ads vary. *HotWired* charges up to $15M a month for an ad that rotates with dozens of others. When evaluating potential ad sponsorship opportunities (or deciding if your site could offer such sponsorship), look for site volume of more than 10,000 hits per day.

With rising Web costs, measurement of results has taken on even greater importance. The most common measurement is "hits," or any user click onto a page. This method is flawed. If a page is accessed three times in a session, this counts as three hits. Independent log audits offer better results. They track a user's hits across the entire Web site, not just a single hit. Two leading independent audit services are I/Pro (owned by A.C. Nielsen) and I/Audit (this service is used by Netscape and Yahoo).

The most foolproof tracking method is to ask users to "subscribe" to the site before allowing them across. Users must first fill out a brief survey which includes their name, e-mail address and any other demographic information the site owner deems valuable. Upon submitting this information, subscribers lock in a unique user name and password, which allows their activity to be tracked each time they enter the site. This does reduce overall traffic to a site, but it allows for much better qualification and tracking.

The Web has proven itself a valuable source of information as well as an excellent method for building relationships and generating leads. As the culture of the Net evolves, it is starting to prove itself as a successful means of selling products direct as more secure ordering systems become available. Many experts predict that the Web will be supporting billions of dollars in commerce by the year 2000.

Phantom Fireworks Home Page

Phantom Fireworks is a mail order and retail marketer of fireworks. It mails four catalogs a year to residents in states where fireworks are legal. It also has 17 retail stores in the Midwest, Northeast, and Southeast United States. Its Web site was created with the objectives of building traffic for the retail stores, generating prospect names for the catalog, and selling products direct. The legal restrictions on fireworks sales meant that Phantom needed to find a method of identifying the home state of prospective buyers.

The first step was to request an easy-to-identify domain name. The domain name is a key part of the Web site's Internet address. Having a readily identifiable domain name makes it easier for Web users to find your site. Phantom's domain is fireworks.com.

The site was then created with the objectives in mind. Copy and photos for 40 products were included in an on-line catalog. The catalog had an order form for on-line ordering; however, credit card information was not taken on-line. Those ordering were given a confirmation number and instructed to call a 24-hour, toll-free phone number. Upon giving the operator their confirmation number, customers' orders were confirmed and payment information taken.

Maps and directions for each of the retail stores were included in another part of the site. (See Exhibit 3-5.) A down-loadable coupon was included as

Exhibit 3-5.   Phantom Fireworks
World Wide Web Home Page

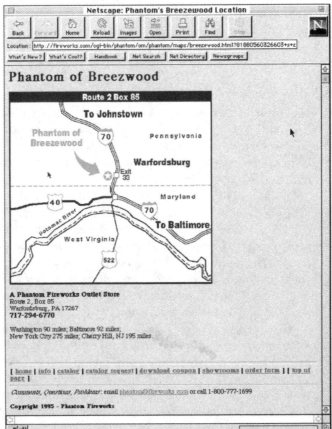

a value-added incentive. Special offers were changed regularly to coincide with promotions in other media. A chat area was created so that online users with a fireworks interest could share stories and information. A catalog request form included a survey to capture demographic and lifestyle information of prospects.

To maintain legal compliance, users reaching the home page were asked to input their ZIP code before entering the site. If they were from a ZIP code where it is legal to ship fireworks, they were allowed full catalog ordering privileges. If they weren't in a legal ZIP code, users were blocked from ordering, but were told that they could browse the catalog and instructed on how to find the maps and directions of their nearest retail store.

The Phantom home page cost approximately $25,000, including design and software. It runs on a leased server in another state, with no direct connection to Phantom's in-house computer system. Order are received as e-mails from the server as they are input. This affords significant "firewall protection," in the event the site is broken into by hackers.

Although no results or sales figures were disclosed, the site has met its initial objectives. In fact, it continues to receive catalog requests and orders throughout the year, unlike Phantom's other sales channels. It is a good example of how a company in a niche market can take advantage of the World Wide Web's capabilities and be successful on a modest budget.

Some Final Comments

The future of new media is bright. The promise of $500 Internet terminals, fast cable TV computer modems, and a plethora of interactive new media applications over the next few years will increase interest across all levels of the market. With computing costs coming down and postage and production costs going up, many direct marketers need to test new media as an alternative.

Traditional direct marketers such as mail order marketers and catalogers are in a great position to maximize the interactive nature of new media. The growth of the business-to-business uses of new media for generating leads, filling information requests, or giving automatic quotes for complex sales requests seems certain. Nontraditional direct marketers, such as commercial and investment banks, and those offering other kinds of niche market services might find even greater success than those companies selling general merchandise and tangible goods. But all marketers testing the electronic marketplace must be patient.

New media's greatest benefit today is that it is another way of providing information that consumers need to make purchase decisions. Many direct marketers are uncomfortable in the role of information brokers for consumers. After all, most of us expect results, such as sales. New media are much more soft sell. Its best uses are to help create, build, and maintain long-term relationships. But because it's invitational, it gives the consumer the option of having the kind of relationship they choose. That's not likely to change.

Nonetheless, the benefits of new media and the relatively low cost of entry make it worth testing. While the window of opportunity won't close, early adopters have the advantage of learning what works and what doesn't. This, and early recognition in today's less cluttered new media environment, makes it a good bet that you should be testing some form of new media today.

SELF-QUIZ

1. What is particularly unique about new media?

    a. They involve two-way dialogue.   ☐ True   ☐ False

    b. They can customize messages to each consumer.

    ☐ True   ☐ False

    c. They offer a paperless, digital environment.

    ☐ True   ☐ False

2. A key element for new media success is the use of an existing _____ base.

3. Name three options available to the consumer through interactive television.

    a. _____

    b. _____

    c. _____

4. Diskettes offer many advantages to marketers, but what is the one major disadvantage?

    _____

5. What is the major advantage of testing a cooperative CD-ROM catalog?

    _____

6. Name three of the major consumer on-line services.

    a. _____

    b. _____

    c. _____

7. Describe the World Wide Web.

_____

_____

8. The Net is mainly text-based. ☐ True ☐ False

   The Web uses a graphic interface. ☐ True ☐ False

9. What is a home page?

_____

_____

10. "New media" tends to be more "soft sell" than "traditional media."

    ☐ True ☐ False

PILOT PROJECT

You are the marketing director of an office supply firm that distributes a 120-page catalog to likely business firm prospects each year.

The company president has been reading a lot about the "new media" and has asked you to recommend a test program. Using a test budget figure of $100,000, please outline your plan.

CHAPTER FOUR

Magazines

Where Do You Go First?

The advertising pages of magazines are to the direct response advertiser what the retail outlet is to the manufacturer selling through the more traditional channels. A magazine that performs consistently well for a variety of direct response advertisers is like a store in a low-rent, high-traffic location. It's far more profitable than a store selling the same merchandise on the wrong side of town.

Such a magazine just seems to have an atmosphere that is more conducive to the mail response customer. The mail order shopping reader traffic is high in relation to the publication's cost per thousand. Magazines in this category (and this is by no means a complete list) are *National Enquirer, Parade*, and the mighty *TV Guide*. Women's publications also doing well for mail-order advertisers are *Family Circle, Better Homes & Gardens, Good Housekeeping, Cosmopolitan, Woman's Day, Seventeen*, and *Redbook*. Men's publications include *Home Mechanix, Moose, Playboy*, and *Penthouse*. SRDS (Standard Rate and Data Service) identifies magazines that provide a structured mail order atmosphere in its magazine edition.

But just as retail locations come into and go out of favor with each passing decade, so do publications in the mail order marketplace. I can remember in the 1950s looking to *Living for Young Homemakers, Harper's, Atlantic*, and *Saturday Review*—and the *Saturday Evening Post* could be counted on for good results. Times change.

Regional Editions: When Is the Part Bigger than the Whole?

For the buyer of space in magazines today, most publications with circulations of over 1.5 million offer the opportunity to buy a regional portion of the national circulation. But it was not always so.

Although it has been said that the *New Yorker* was the first to publish sectional or regional editions in 1929, it wasn't until the late 1950s that major magazines began selling regional space to all advertisers, not just to those that had distribution limited to a particular section of the circulation area.

The availability of regional editions for everyone opened important opportunities to the mail order advertiser. Here are a few of the things you can do with regional buys:

1. You don't have to invest in the full national cost of a publication to get some indication of its effectiveness for your proposition. In some cases, such as *Time* or *TV Guide*, by running in a single edition you can determine relative response with an investment at least 20 percent less than what it costs to make a national buy.

2. Some regions traditionally pull better than others for the mail order advertiser. For many mail order products or services, nothing does better than the West Coast or worse than the New England region. You can select the best response area for your particular proposition.

   Remember that in most publications you will be paying a premium for the privilege of buying partial circulation. If you are testing a publication, putting your advertising message in the better-pulling region can offset much of this premium charge.

3. Availability of regional editions makes possible multiple copy testing in a single issue of a publication. Some magazines offer A/B split-run copy testing in each of the regional editions published. For example, in *TV Guide* you can test one piece of copy against your control in one edition, another against your control in a second edition, another against your control in a third, and so on. As a result, you can learn as much about different pieces of copy in a single issue of one publication as you could discover in several national A/B copy splits in the same publication over a span of two years or more.

4. When testing regionally, don't make the mistake of testing too small a circulation quantity. It is essential that you test a large enough circulation segment to provide readable results that can be projected accurately for still larger circulations.

   Warning: Buying regional space is not all fun and games. You will have to pay for the privilege in a number of ways. As mentioned, regional space costs more.

Another factor to keep in mind is the relatively poor position regional ads receive. The regional sections usually appear far back in the magazine or in a ''well'' or signature of several consecutive pages of advertising with no editorial matter to catch the reader. As you will see later in our discussion of position placement, the poor location of an ad in a magazine can depress results as much as 50 percent below what the same advertisement would pull if it were in the first few pages of the same publication. If you are using regional space for testing, be certain to factor this into your evaluation.

Exhibit 4–1 shows how various factors must be weighed in utilizing regional circulation for test purposes. Because full-page, four-color inserts have been extremely profitable for some of the large mail-order advertisers, this size unit was tested for the XYZ Yarn & Craft Company to see whether such inserts could bring in a lower lead cost than could be obtained from a black-and-white page and card.

Because women's publications are the most successful media for this advertiser, the company went to two that offered the mechanical capabilities for regional testing of such an insert. Although May and June are not prime mail order months, it is necessary to test then in order to allow turnaround time for the next season's scheduling. Therefore, the following factors would have to be taken into consideration in projecting test results to learn whether this unit would be successful in prime mail order months with full circulation: (1) regional premium, (2) month of insertion, (3) position in book, and (4) relative value of specific media.

Pilot Publications: The Beacons of Direct Response Media Scheduling

When planning your direct marketing media schedule, think about the media universe the way you think about the view of the sky in the evening. If you have no familiarity with the stars, the sky appears to be a jumble of blinking lights with no apparent relationship. But as you begin to study the heavens,

Exhibit 4–1.   Regional Test Schedule for XYZ Yarn & Craft Company

Redbook	
Space:	Full-page, four-color insert
Position:	Back of main editorial (regional forms)
Issue:	June
Space cost:	$14,235 (printing cost not included)
Editions used:	New England, Mid-Atlantic, South Atlantic
Total test circulation:	1,121,000 (35 percent of total circulation)
Regional premium:	None
Family Circle	
Space:	Full-page, four-color insert
Position:	Back of main editorial (regional forms)
Issue:	June
Space cost:	$3,800 (printing cost not included)
Editions used:	Los Angeles (383,000), San Francisco (209,000)
Total test circulation:	592,000 (15.3 percent of total circulation)
Regional premium:	None

you are soon able to pick out clusters of stars that have a relationship to one another in constellations.

The magazine universe is no different. There are nearly 400 consumer magazines published with circulations of 100,000 or more. The first step in approaching this vast list is to sort out the universe of magazines into categories. Although this process is somewhat arbitrary, it is useful to have a mental map of major magazine groupings. Once you begin to think of magazines as forming logical groupings within the total magazine universe, you can begin to determine the groupings offering the most likely marketplace for your product or proposition. Exhibit 4–2 is a basic magazine category chart and lists some of the publications currently available for the direct response advertiser.

Exhibit 4–2. Basic Consumer Magazine Categories

Demographic	Category	Sample Publications
Dual audience	General editorial/ entertainment	Grit, National Enquirer, National Geographic, New York Times Magazine, Parade, People, Reader's Digest, TV Guide
	News	Time, Newsweek, Sports Illustrated, U.S. News & World Report
	Special interest	Architectural Digest, Business Week, Elks, Foreign Affairs, High Fidelity, Modern Photography, Natural History, Ski, Travel & Leisure, Wall Street Journal, Yankee
Women	General/service/ shelter (home service)	Better Homes & Gardens, Cosmopolitan, Ebony, Family Circle, Good Housekeeping, House Beautiful, House & Garden, Ladies' Home Journal, McCall's, Redbook, Sunset, Woman's Day
	Fashion	Glamour, Harper's Bazaar, Mademoiselle, Vogue
	Special interest	Brides, MacFadden Women's Group, McCalls Needlework & Crafts, Parents, Working Woman
Men	General/ entertainment/ fashion	Esquire, Gentlemen's Quarterly, Penthouse, Playboy
	Special interest	Field & Stream, Home Mechanics, Outdoor Life, Popular Mechanics, Popular Science, Road & Track, Sports Afield
Youth	Male	Boy's Life
	Female	Teen, YM
	Dual audience	Scholastic Magazines

Within each category there are usually one or more publications that perform particularly well for the direct response advertiser at a lower cost than other publications in the group. We call those magazines the *pilot publications* for the group. If you use the pilot publications and they produce an acceptable cost per response, you can then proceed to explore the possibility of adding other magazines in the category to your media schedule.

In selecting the pilot publications in a category, keep in mind that you are not dealing with a static situation. As indicated earlier, a publication's mail order advertising viability changes from year to year, and what is a bellwether publication this season may not be the one to use next year. What is important is that you check your own experience and the experience of others in determining the best places to advertise first in each category, and the next best, and the next best, and so on.

Think of your media-buying program as an ever-widening circle, as illustrated in Exhibit 4–3. At the center is a nucleus of pilot publications. Each successively larger ring would include reruns in all profitable pilot publications plus new test books. In the same way, you can expand from campaign to campaign to cover wider levels of the various media categories until you have reached the widest possible universe.

Exhibit 4–3. Circle Approach to Media Selection

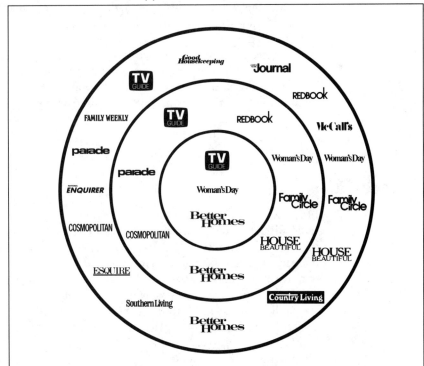

Bind-In Insert Cards

The reason for the success of the insert card is self-evident. Pick up a magazine, thumb through its pages, and see for yourself how effectively the bound-in cards flag down the reader. Each time someone picks up the publication, there is the insert card pointing to your message. Another reason is the ease with which the reader can respond. The business reply card eliminates the trouble of addressing an envelope, providing a stamp, and so on.

Before the development of the insert card, the third and fourth covers of a magazine were the prime mail order positions and were sold at a premium. The bind-in insert card has created a world in which three, four, five, or more direct response advertisers can all have the position impact once reserved for the cover advertisers alone.

When you go to purchase space for a page and an accompanying insert card, you must face the fact that the best things in life are not free. Insert card advertising costs more. You must pay a space charge for the page and the card and sometimes a separate binding charge, and you must then add in the cost of printing the cards. How much you pay, of course, depends on the individual publication, the size of the card, and a number of other factors. There is no rule of thumb to follow in estimating the additional cost for an insert card. Space charges alone for a standard business reply card can be as little as 40 percent of the black-and-white page plus additional binding charges.

When the cost of the insert unit adds up to as much as four times the cost of a black-and-white page, you will have to receive four times the response to justify the added expense.

For most direct response advertisers, the response is likely to be six to eight times as great when pulling for an order and as much as six to eight times as great in pulling for inquiries. As a result, you can expect to cut your cost per response by 50 percent or more with an insert card as opposed to an ordinary on-page coupon ad.

Bingo Cards

Insert cards have a dramatic effect on response, and so do bingo cards. Bingo cards, often referred to as *information cards* were developed by magazine publishers, both consumer and business, to make it easy for the reader to request more information. *Bingo card* is really a generic term for any form—a reply card or printed form on a magazine page—on which the publisher prints designated numbers for specified literature. The reader simply circles the number designated for the literature desired. (See Exhibit 4-4.)

Typically, an advertiser placing a specified unit of space in a magazine is entitled to a bingo card in the back of the publication. Ads reference these bingo cards with statements such as ''For further information, circle Item No. 146.'' The cards are sent directly to the publisher, which sends compiled lists

Exhibit 4-4. Bingo Card for *Better Homes & Gardens*

Information

WORTH WRITING FOR

**Better Homes and Gardens®
REMODELING IDEAS,
Summer 1987 Dept. SURI7
P.O. BOX 2611
CLINTON, IA 52732**

Issue 66

TO ENSURE PROMPT HANDLING OF YOUR ORDER FOLLOW THESE INSTRUCTIONS:

- Circle your choice
- Enclose cash, check, money order for cost of booklets plus $1.00 service charge (no stamps/foreign)
- Send coupon and remittance to address above
- ALLOW 4-6 WEEKS FOR DELIVERY
- Coupon expires July 19

FREE LITERATURE Circle numbers below corresponding to items in this issue.
Please include $1.00 for handling charge

5.	214.	323.	400.	406.	1321.	1810.
9.	300.	324.	401.	602.	1602.	4056.
55.	301.	330.	402.	613.	1664.	
59.	303.	344.	403.	919.	1666.	
71.	322.	376.	405.	1205.	1668.	

PRICED LITERATURE Numbers below refer to items on which there is a charge.
Please include proper remittance.

25 ...... 35¢	73 .... 50¢	332 .... 50¢	762 .... $2.00	1256 .. $10.00	1305 .... $2.95	1679 .... $2.00
27 ...... 25¢	74 .... $3.00	407 .... $1.25	802 .. $14.50	1271 .... $3.95	1306 .... $2.95	1808 .... $1.00
35 .... $3.00	75 .... $1.00	410 .... 25¢	821 .... $3.00	1272 .... $4.95	1307 .... $2.95	1816 .... 50¢
57 .... $2.00	94 .... $1.99	415 .... 15¢	827 .... $1.00	1273 .... $5.95	1335 .... $1.00	1824 .... $2.00
60 .... $1.00	95 .... $1.99	420 .... 75¢	828 .... $1.00	1274 .... $4.95	1359 .... $1.00	4011 .... $1.00
61 .... $1.00	150 .... 35¢	426 .... 50¢	844 .... 25¢	1275 .... $3.95	1361 .... $12.00	4012 .... $1.00
62 .... $1.00	205 .... 25¢	430 .... 25¢	855 .... $1.99	1290 .... $9.75	1362 .. $12.00	4013 .... $1.00
63 ...... 50¢	217 .... $1.00	437 .... $2.00	902 .. $14.50	1291 .... $8.75	1363 .. $12.00	4014 .... 25¢
67 ...... 50¢	310 .... 25¢	438 .... $1.00	911 .... 25¢	1293 .... $8.75	1364 .. $12.00	
68 .... $1.00	316 .... 35¢	612 .... $1.00	1001 .... 40¢	1294 .... $3.75	1365 .. $12.00	
69 ...... 25¢	321 .... $1.00	614 .... $1.00	1005 .... 40¢	1296 .. $28.00	1604 .... $2.00	
70 .... $1.00	327 .... $1.00	616 .... $1.00	1217 .... $5.00	1303 .... $2.95	1672 .... $2.00	
72 .... $1.00	329 .... 50¢	744 .... $1.00	1244 .... $5.00	1304 .... $2.95	1673 .... 25¢	

Name (please print) _____

Address _____

City _____

State _____ Zip Code _____

I AM ENCLOSING:

$_____ for priced items

$___1.00___ for handling

$_____ total remittance

---

of inquiries to participating advertisers. The respective advertisers then send fulfillment literature to all who have requested it.

A neat system, to be sure, but a caveat is in order. ''We get tons of requests for literature from bingo cards, but they're not worth anything'' is a frequent advertiser complaint.

On the other hand, ''Bingo cards can be very productive,'' states Adolph Auerbacher, who has been publisher of 22 special-interest publications for *Better Homes & Gardens* (BH&G). Auerbacher points to two prime reasons for poor sales conversions: (1) failure of advertisers to respond to inquiries quickly and (2) failure of advertisers to qualify prospects properly. Pointing to a survey by BH&G of 203 companies to which they responded, Auerbacher reports the following response times. During the first week 13 percent sent literature. At the end of the first month they had heard from 62 percent. Thirty-eight percent of the companies had not responded a month after the first response was received.

And 10 percent were never heard from. (For maximum effectiveness, all advertisers should have responded within two weeks.)

In regard to qualifying prospects properly for a better likelihood of sales conversion, Auerbacher gives some interesting theories and facts. Responding to the age-old question, "Should the advertiser charge for literature or send it free?" he makes this key point:

> If an air conditioner advertiser, for example, has a literature cost of $1, he has a natural tendency to want to get his dollar back. But he may lose sight of the fact that his real objective is to sell a $500 air conditioner.
>
> Even taking into account that those who pay $1 for the literature might be more qualified, the ratio of free requests to dollar payments may be so overwhelming that more air conditioners in total might be sold to consumers who requested free literature.

But often it is best to charge for literature as a qualifier. The question is, "How much?" Here Auerbacher provides some hard facts. Exhibit 4-5 refers

Exhibit 4–5.   Tabulation of Literature Requests: *Better Homes & Gardens* Publications

Price	Median Response	Percentage of Free	High[a]	Low[b]	Ratio H/L[c]
		Remodeling Ideas			
Free	672		1,171	192	6:1
$0.10	148	22%	373	113	3:1
0.25	213	32	408	51	8:1
0.50	130	19	540	51	10:1
1.00	82	12	240	3	80:1
2.00	19	3	129	2	65:1
		Building Ideas			
Free	781		1,501	252	6:1
$0.10	108	14%	199	60	3:1
0.25	298	38	430	109	4:1
0.50	297	38	722	97	7:1
1.00	95	12	431	3	143:1
2.00	31	4	164	3	55:1
		Decorating Ideas			
Free	491		1,420	21	67:1
$0.10	62	13%	72	49	1.5:1
0.25	193	39	400	68	6:1
0.50	138	28	646	35	18:1
1.00	102	21	282	17	16:1
2.00	79	16	123	19	6:1

[a] The highest number of requests for the literature of a given advertiser in a particular issue.
[b] The lowest number of requests.
[c] The ratio of response of the best puller contrasted to the worst puller.

to three titles among the BH&G stable of special-interest books with the details of response by amount charged for literature. Free-literature request had the greatest response in every case, as one would expect. But note the differences in response between varying amounts requested. For *Remodeling Ideas*, for example, a 10-cent request pulled 22 percent as many requests as free. But 25 cents pulled more requests than 10 cents. And in the case of *Building Ideas*, a 50-cent request pulled as well as a 25-cent request. With the exception of *Decorating Ideas*, both a $1 and a $2 request got a very poor response, perhaps suggesting upper limits of resistance.

So, as Auerbacher points out, success in the use of bingo cards depends, to a major degree, on rapid fulfillment of literature requests and qualifying prospects in the most cost-efficient way. Two additional factors must be taken into account: (1) The closer the literature offered ties to the special interest of the book, the better the response is likely to be; and (2) advertiser awareness is an important response factor.

Magazine Advertising Response Pattern: What Do These Early Results Mean?

There is a remarkable similarity from one insertion to another in the rate of response over time for most magazines. Monthly publications generally have a similar pattern for the rate of response from week to week. However, the pattern of response for publications in different categories can vary. For example, a mass circulation weekly magazine (*TV Guide* or *Parade*) will pull a higher percentage of the total response in the first few weeks than a shelter book (such as *House & Garden* or *Better Homes & Gardens*). A shelter book has a slower response curve but keeps pulling for a long time because it is kept much longer then a mass circulation magazine.

Also, subscription circulation will pull faster than newsstand circulation. Subscribers usually receive their copies within a few days, whereas newsstand sales are spread out over an entire month. Consequently, the response pattern is spread out as well.

If you are running an ad calling for direct response from a monthly magazine, here is a general guide to the likely response flow:

After the first week	3–7%
After the second week	20–25
After the third week	40–45
After 1 month	50–55
After 2 months	75–85
After 3 months	85–92
After 4 months	92–95

From a weekly publication such as *Time* or *TV Guide*, the curve is entirely different; 50 percent of your response usually comes in the first two weeks.

These expectations, of course, represent the average of many hundreds of response curves for different propositions. You will see variations up or down from the classic curve for any single insertion.

As a general rule for monthlies, you can expect to project the final results within 10 percent accuracy after the third week of counting responses. If you are new to the business, give yourself the experience of entering daily result counts by hand for dozens of ads. Before long you will develop an instinct for projecting how an ad for your particular proposition is doing within the first ten days of measured response.

Timing and Frequency: When Should You Run? How Often Should You Go Back?

Once you determine where you want to run, timing and frequency are the two crucial factors in putting together an effective print schedule. Some propositions will do best at one specific time of the year. For example, novelty items are likely to be purchased in October and November or even as early as late September for Christmas gifts. But for nonseasonal items, you can look forward to two major print advertising seasons for direct response.

The first and by far the most productive time for most propositions is the winter season, which begins with the January issue and runs through the February and March issues. The second season begins with the August issue and runs through the November issue. The best winter months for most people are January and February. The best fall months are October and November. For schools and book continuity propositions, September frequently does as well or better.

If you have a nonseasonal item and you want to do your initial test at the best possible time, use a February issue with a January sale date or a January issue with a late December or early January sale date of whatever publication makes the most sense for your proposition.

How much of a factor is the particular month in which an ad appears? it could make a difference of 40 percent or even more. Here is an example of what the direct response advertiser can expect to experience during the year if the cost per response (CPR) in February were $2: January, $2.05; February, $2; March, $2.20; April, $2.50; May, $2.60; June, $2.80; July, $2.60; August, $2.40; September, $2.60; October, $2.20; November, $2.20; December, $2.40.

These hypothetical relative costs are based on the assumption that the insertion is run one time in any one of the 12 issues of a monthly publication. But, of course, if you are successful, you will want to run your copy more than once. So now you are faced with the other crucial question: What will various rates of frequency do to your response? Should you run once a year? Twice? Three times? Or every other month?

The frequency factor is more difficult to formulate than the timing factor. Optimum frequency cannot be generalized for print media advertising. Some propositions can be run month after month in a publication and show very little difference in cost per response. At one time, Doubleday & Company had worked out optimum frequency curves for some of its book club ads that required a 24-month hiatus between insertions.

How, then, do you go about determining ideal frequency of insertions? Try this procedure: The first time your copy appears in a publication, run it at the most favorable time of the year for your special appeal. If you have a nonseasonal proposition, use January or February issues.

If the cost per response is in an acceptable range or up to 20 percent better than expected, wait six months and follow with a second insertion. If that insertion produces results within an acceptable range, you probably are a twice-a-year advertiser. If the first insertion pulls well over 20 percent better than the planned order margin, turn around and repeat within a three- or four-month period. If the response to the test insertion in January or February was marginal, it usually makes sense to wait a full year before returning for another try in that publication.

The best gauge of how quickly you can run the next insertion aimed at the same magazine audience is the strength of the response from the last insertion. What you are reading in the results is a measurement of the saturation factor as it relates to that portion of the circulation that is interested in your selling message.

Of course, like all the other factors that affect response, frequency does not operate in a vacuum. The offer of a particularly advantageous position in a particular month or a breakthrough to better results with improved copy can lead you to set aside whatever carefully worked out frequency you had adopted earlier.

Determining Proper Ad Size: How Much Is Too Much?

A crucial factor in obtaining an acceptable cost per response is the size of the advertising unit you select. Ordinarily, the bigger the ad, the better job the creative people can do in presenting the selling message. But there is one catch: Advertising space costs money. And the more you spend, the greater the response you need to get your money back.

What you want to find is the most efficient size for your particular proposition and for the copy approach you have chosen. Just as with frequency, there is no simple rule of thumb here.

Generally speaking, advertising for leads or prospects or to gain inquiries requires less advertising space than copy that is pulling for orders. Many companies seeking inquiries or running a lead item to get names for catalog follow-up make use of advertising units of less than one column. Only a handful of companies looking for prospects can make effective use of full-page space. Going one step further and using a page and insert card to pull for leads runs the risk of being too effective. This unit can bring in inquiries at very low cost, at the expense, possibly, of good quality. Find out at your peril.

For example, if you use a black-and-white page with a tear-off coupon that generates leads at $5 each and that converts at a 10 percent rate, then your advertising cost per sale is $50. Take the same insertion and place it as a page and insert card, and the cost per response could be as low as $3. If the conversion rate held up at 10 percent, the advertising cost per sale would be only $30. But it is more likely that the advertiser would experience a sharp conversion rate drop to perhaps 5 percent, with a resultant $60 cost per sale plus the cost of processing the additional leads.

When a direct sale or a future commitment to buy is sought, the dynamics usually are different from those when inquiries are sought. As a general rule, the higher the unit of sale or dollar volume commitment, the larger the unit of space that can be afforded, right up to the double-page spread with insert card. However, there are a number of additional factors to be considered:

1. The nature of the product presentation might require a particular space unit. For example, in tape club and book club advertising, experience has shown that a maximum number of books and tapes should be displayed for best results. As a consequence, many of these clubs run a two-page spread as their standard advertising unit. And in a small-size publication such as *TV Guide*, they might take six or even eight pages to display the proper number of books and tapes.

2. Some propositions, such as Time-Life Books in the continuity bookselling field, require four-color advertising in order to present the beautiful color illustrations that are an important feature of the product being sold.

3. Usually, full-page ads appear at the front of a publication and small-space ads at the back. So going to a full-page unit is often related to the benefits you can expect from a premium, front-of-publication position.

4. If you are successful with a single-page ad with coupon, test using an insert card before you try to add a second page. If the page and insert card work for you, give the spread and card a try.

5. Most mail-order advertising falls into one of three size categories: (a) the spectacular unit—anything from the page and standard card insert to the four-page preprinted insert, (b) the single full-page unit, or (c) the small-space unit less than one column in size.

The awkward sizes in pulling for an order appear to be the one-column and two-column units. These inserts seldom work better than their big-brother pages or little-sister 56-line, 42-line, and 21-line units, although a "square third" (2 columns by 70 lines) can be a very efficient space unit.

Always remember that space costs money. The objective is to take the minimum amount of space you need to express your proposition effectively and to return a profit. Start by having the creative director at your advertising agency express the proposition in the amount of space needed to convey a powerful selling message. Once you have established the cost per response for this basic unit, you can experiment with other size units.

If you have two publications on your schedule that perform about equally well for the basic unit, try testing the same ad approach expressed in a smaller or larger space size in one of those two publications while running the basic control unit in the same month in the other publication.

Four-Color, Two-Color, Black-and-White: How Colorful Should Your Advertising Be?

All magazines charge extra for adding color to your advertising. And there will be additional production expense if you go this route. Usually the cost of adding a second color to a black-and-white page does not return the added costs charged by the publication for the space and the expense of producing the ad. If the copy is right, the words will do their job without getting an appreciable lift from having headlines set in red or blue or green. An exception might be the use of a second-color tint as background to provide special impact to your page.

It is with the use of four-color advertising that the direct response advertiser has an opportunity to profit on an investment in color. A number of publications (*Esquire, Time, Woman's Day, Ladies' Home Journal*) allow you to run a split of four-color versus black-and-white, in an alternating copy A/B perfect split-run. Test results indicate an increase of anywhere from 30 percent to almost 60 percent where there is appropriate and dramatic utilization of the four-color process.

Given a striking piece of artwork related to the proposition or an inherently colorful product feature to present, you can expect an increase in response when you use four-color advertising. You will need more than a 20 percent increase in most publications to make the use of color profitable, so it is wise to pretest the value of this factor before scheduling it across the board. Some products, such as insurance, simply do not benefit from color.

If you plan to use four-color advertising, the increase in publication space cost is only one of the cost factors to be weighed. The cost of the original four-color engravings for a 7" x 10" page runs from $3,000 to $5,000 depending on the copy and artwork being used. This compares with a black-and-white engraving cost that could be from $200 to $300. In addition, any dye transfers or other four-color preparatory work will probably increase mechanical preparation costs by 50 percent or more over a comparable black-and-white insertion.

The Position Factor

Position in life might not be everything, but in direct response it often means the difference between paying out or sudden death. By *position*, we mean where your advertisement appears in the publication. There are two rules governing position. First, the closer to the front of the publication an ad is placed, the better the response will be. Second, the more visible the position, the better the response will be.

The first rule defies rational analysis. Yet it is as certain as the sun's rising in the morning. Many magazine publishers have offered elaborate research studies demonstrating to the general advertiser that an ad in the editorial matter far back in a publication gets better readership than an ad placed within the first few pages of the publication. This could well be true for the general or institutional advertiser, but it is not true for the direct response advertiser.

Whatever the explanation is, the fact remains that decades of measured direct response advertising tell the same story over and over again. A position in the first seven pages of the magazine produces a dramatically better response (all other factors being the same) than if the same insert appears farther back in the same issue.

How much better? There are as many answers to this question as there are old pros in the business. However, here is about what you might experience the relative response to be from various page positions as measured against the first right-hand page arbitrarily rated at a pull of 100:

First right-hand page	100	Back of the publication	
Second right-hand page	95	(following main body of	
Third right-hand page	90	editorial matter)	50
Fourth right-hand page	85	Back cover	100
Back of front of the publication		Inside third cover	90
(preceding editorial matter)	70	Page facing third cover	85

The second rule is more easily explained. An ad must be seen before it can be read or acted on. Right-hand pages pull better than left-hand pages, frequently by as much as 15 percent. Insert cards open the magazine to the advertiser's message and thereby create their own "cover" position. Of course, the insert card introduces the additional factor of providing a postage-free response vehicle as well. But the response from insert cards is also subject to the influence of how far back in the magazine the insert appears. Here is what you can expect in most publications (assigning a 100 rating to the first card):

First insert card position	100
Second insert card position	95
Third insert card position	85
Fourth insert card position	75[a]
Fifth insert card position	70[a]

[a] If position follows main editorial matter.

The pull of position is as inexorable as the pull of gravity. Well, almost. There are a few exceptions. In the fashion and the mechanics magazines, card positioning seems to make little or no difference. Another exception involves placing an ad opposite a related column or feature article in a publication (e.g., a *Home Handyman's Encyclopedia* ad opposite the Home Handyman column). Another exception involves placing an ad in a high-readership shopping section at the back of a magazine.

How to Buy Space

Because mail-order advertising is always subject to bottom-line analysis, the price you pay for space can mean the difference between profit and loss. Florence Peloquin, head of Florence Peloquin Associates, New York City, provides the following basic questions the advertiser should ask the publisher or the publisher's agency before placing space:

1. Is there a special mail-order rate? Mail-order rates are usually 10–30 percent lower than general rates.

2. Is there a special mail order section, a shopping section where special mail order ads are grouped? (This section is usually found in the back of the book.)

3. Does the magazine have remnant space available at substantial discounts? Many publishers offer discounts of up to 50 percent off the regular rate.

4. Is there an insertion frequency discount or a dollar volume discount? Is frequency construed as the number of insertions in a time period or consecutive issues? Many publishers credit more than one insertion in an issue toward frequency.

5. Do corporate discounts apply to mail-order? Sometimes the corporate discount is better than the mail-order discount.

6. Are there seasonal discounts? Some publishers have low-volume advertising months during which they offer substantial discounts.

7. Are there spread discounts when running two pages or more in one issue? The discount can run up to 60 percent on the second page.

8. Is there a publisher's rate? Is this in addition to or in lieu of the mail order rate? It can be additive.

9. Are per-inquiry (PI) deals accepted? In PI deals, the advertiser pays the publisher an amount for each inquiry or order, or a minimum flat amount for the space, plus so much per inquiry or order.

10. Are "umbrella contracts" accepted? Some media-buying services and agencies own banks or reserves of space with given publications and can offer discounts even for one-time ads.

11. Is bartering for space allowed? Barter usually involves a combination of cash and merchandise.

When bought properly, tested properly, and used properly, magazine advertising represents a vast universe of sales and profit potential for the direct response advertiser.

SELF-QUIZ

1. Name five magazines that provide a conducive atmosphere for direct response advertisers.

   a. _____

   b. _____

   c. _____

   d. _____

   e. _____

2. Name the four major advantages of using regional editions of magazines.

   a. _____

   b. _____

   c. _____

   d. _____

3. What are the two negative factors involved in buying regional space?

   a. _____

   b. _____

4. Name five basic consumer magazine categories.

   a. _____

   b. _____

   c. _____

d. _____

e. _____

5. Define *pilot publication*.

_____

_____

_____

6. What is the theory of an expanded media-buying program based on an ever-widening circle?

_____

_____

_____

_____

7. What is the principal advantage of an insert card in a magazine?

_____

_____

_____

8. When direct response advertisers use insert cards, the response is likely to be _____ to _____ times as great when pulling for an order and as much as _____ to _____ times as great in pulling for inquiries.

9. What are the two prime reasons for poor sales conversions to bingo cards?

a. _____

b. _____

10. As a general rule, when direct response advertisers use a monthly magazine, they can usually expect to have about 50 percent of their total response after _____ weeks.

11. For weekly publications, 50 percent of total response can be expected after _____ weeks.

12. From a timing standpoint, which is the most productive season for most direct response propositions?

_____

13. Which is the second most productive season?

_____

14. When is the best possible time to test a nonseasonal item?

_____

_____

15. The cost per response (CPR) is likely to vary _____ percent between the best-pulling month and the poorest-pulling month.

16. Provide guidelines for frequency factors in magazine advertising.

   a. If the cost per response is in an acceptable range or up to 20 percent better than expected, wait _____ months and follow up with a second insertion in the second half of the year.

   b. If the first insertion pulls well over 20 percent better than allowed order margin, turn around and repeat within _____ or _____ months.

   c. If response to the test insertion in January or February was marginal, it usually makes sense to wait _____ before returning for another try in that publication.

17. Generally speaking, which requires more space for effective direct response advertising?
   ☐ Pulling inquiries   ☐ Pulling orders

18. What is the prime advantage of a full-page ad versus a small ad in a magazine?

_____

_____

19. If a single-page ad with coupon is successful, what is the next logical test?

_____

_____

20. What are the three size categories for most mail order advertising?

   a. _____

   b. _____

   c. _____

21. When four-color is tested against black-and-white, results indicate an increase of anywhere from _____ percent to almost _____ percent where there is appropriate and dramatic utilization of the four-color process.

22. What are the two rules governing the position factor for the direct response advertiser?

    a. _____

    b. _____

23. Right-hand pages pull better than left-hand pages by as much as _____ percent.

24. If a 100 rating is assigned to a first insert card position in a publication having five insert card positions, the fifth insert card rating would be _____.

25. Mail-order rates are usually _____ percent to _____ percent lower than general rates.

PILOT PROJECT

You are the advertising manager for a publisher of children's books. It is your assignment to test-market a new continuity series of 10 books written for age levels 6 to 10. Each book in the series will sell for $4.95. Outline a plan for test marketing in magazines.

1. What pilot publications would you schedule for testing?

2. Will you use any regional editions? Why or why not?

3. Do a circle approach to media selection indicating what additional publications you will expand to if the pilot publications prove successful.

4. Prepare a timing schedule, indicating when your pilot ads will break and when your expanded media-buying program will take place.

5. What ad size will you use? Will the ad be black and white, two colors, or four colors?

CHAPTER FIVE

Newspapers

For sheer circulation in print, there is nothing to compare with the daily and Sunday newspapers. There are over 1,500 daily newspapers in the United States with an average daily circulation of about 60 million. Thus the circulation available through newspapers offers an exciting opportunity for direct response advertisers. It is significant that many direct response advertisers spend all or a major portion of their budgets in newspapers.

Newspapers are unique in that they can serve as a vehicle for carrying direct response advertising formats foreign to their regular news pages. Remarkable results have been achieved by using these special formats.

Newspaper Preprints

Use of newspaper preprints by direct response advertisers is a phenomenon of this decade. Preprints became a viable method for direct marketers in 1965. In the first five months of that year there was only one preprint mail order advertiser (Time-Life Books) in million-circulation newspapers.

Columbia Record & Tape Club followed Time-Life Books in 1965. Wunderman Worldwide, the club's agency, first tested preprints in newspapers in six markets (*Akron Beacon, Dallas Times Herald, Des Moines Register, Minneapolis Tribune, Peoria Journal Star,* and *Seattle Times*). Hundreds of millions of preprints have since been run in newspapers by Columbia. There are two obvious advantages to preprints such as those used by Columbia. First, they provide abundant space for the detailed listing of items available. Second, a perforated postpaid return card can be imprinted, which, because of the weight of the stock used, closely resembles an ordinary postcard and can be mailed easily by the respondent. (See Exhibit 5–1.)

The dramatic impact of preprints in a newspaper must be measured against the greatly increased cost. Comparing a four-page preprint with a fourth cover

Exhibit 5–1.   First Page of a Six-Page Newspaper Insert for Columbia House

in a syndicated Sunday supplement, one finds the preprint costs almost four times as much. The tremendous volume of preprints found in the Sunday newspaper is good evidence that the increased cost often is more than warranted. Printing costs of the inserts must be added to the space cost for them. Careful note should be taken of the fact that the cost per thousand (CPM) tends to be lower for large metro papers. Thus, if a direct marketer has a proposition that appeals only to small towns, the chances for successful use of preprints are greatly diminished.

Size depends on the newspaper's policy and equipment, but, generally speaking, minimum size is 5½" x 8⅛". Maximum size is 10¾" x 14½". These minimum and maximum sizes are folded sizes—unfolded size could be larger. For example, a standard format size of 21½" x 14½" printed on heavy stock could fold in half to 10¾" x 14½".

Syndicated Newspaper Supplements

Imagine placing three space insertion orders and buying newspaper circulation of 65 million plus! This is indeed possible if you place insertion orders in the three major syndicated newspaper supplements: Sunday Magazine Network (Mag/Net), *Parade*, and *USA Weekend*.

Distribution of the three syndicated supplements breaks down about this way. Sunday Mag/Net is distributed by about 24 member newspapers. Those carrying Sunday Mag/Net supplements offer a choice of 26 top metro areas for advertising. *USA Weekend* is generally carried by the newspapers with smaller circulations. *Parade* is included in some of the Sunday Mag/Net newspapers, but generally it is more evenly distributed among the top 100 metro areas.

Obvious advantages of syndicated supplements are their relatively low CPM and the possibility of reaching top metro areas as well as smaller cities, depending on the supplement used. One thing going for the syndicated supplements is their mail-order atmosphere. *Parade*, for instance, points out that 60 percent of its advertising carries some kind of coupon that enables the advertiser to measure results.

Among the syndicated supplements, *Parade* and *USA Weekend* offer a mail order booklet inserted on a regular basis. This booklet, commonly called a Dutch door, usually runs 12 pages. Its page size is one-half that of the supplement. Some issues are taken over entirely by one advertiser. Other issues contain a variety of small mail order ads.

Obviously, a direct marketer that has not previously placed space in one of the syndicated supplements would not go full run without testing. *Parade*, for example, offers remnant space to mail-order advertisers at a 20 percent discount. Remnant space is advertising space left over when package-goods advertisers buy only in those markets where they have distribution. Second to testing in remnant space is testing in regions.

With about 722 Sunday and weekend magazines, both syndicated and locally edited, a direct response advertiser has an incredible amount of distribution available at low cost.

Comics as a Direct Marketing Medium

Perhaps the biggest sleeper as a medium for direct marketers is the comics section of weekend newspapers. Comics are not glamorous, nor are they prestigious. But their total circulation, readership, and demographics constitute an exciting universe for the direct response advertiser. Here are some of the fascinating facts and figures about comics as an advertising medium.

Each week, usually on Sunday, millions of color comics are distributed through nearly 400 different newspapers. These comics literally saturate the major and secondary markets, providing the better coverage in strategic metro markets of the country. The major comics network is Metro-Puck Comics, distributed in 250 newspapers with a total circulation of more than 46 million.

The demographic characteristics of comics readers are quite a surprise to most advertisers, who seem to have ill-conceived ideas about this type of reader. The median age of the adult comics reader is 39 years, slightly younger than the overall median age of 40.2 years in the United States. One misconception about comics readership is that the higher one's education, the less likely one is to read the comics. Statistics dispute this. Finally, there is the misconception that the higher one's income, the less likely one is to read comics. Again, statistics refute this.

The availability of the ad-and-envelope technique in conjunction with comics-page advertising serves a genuine need of photo finishers, because they are able to provide an envelope in which the prospect can return completed film rolls. The standard charge for a freestanding envelope or for affixing a card or envelope to the ad averages about $40 per thousand, plus the cost of printing the response vehicle. With ad-and-envelope, the direct response advertiser provides the same impetus to response with a reply card or reply envelope. (See Exhibit 5-2.)

Opportunities obviously exist for a host of direct response advertisers seeking mass circulation at low cost. Comics-page advertising traditionally limits advertising to one advertiser per page. Thus full-page advertising is not essential to gain a dominant position. Comics, like syndicated supplements, should be tested before going full run.

Run-of-Paper Advertising

We have been exploring formats carried by newspapers: preprints, syndicated supplements, and comics. Not to be overlooked, of course, is run-of-paper

Exhibit 5–2.   Comics-Page Advertising

This ad calls attention to an envelope inserted loose in a newspaper comics section.

(ROP) advertising. Generally, direct response advertisers have failed to get the results with ROP advertising that they have obtained from newspaper preprints and syndicated newspaper supplements. One obvious reason is that four-color advertising is not generally available for ROP. Another is that ROP ads don't drop out for individual attention. But many successes can be cited for small space ROP ads that have run frequently year after year in hundreds of newspapers. When small-space ads are run over a long period with high frequency, the number of reader impressions multiplies rapidly in proportion to the cost.

Effect of Local News on Results

A major difference between newspaper advertising and all other print media is that the newspaper reader is more likely to be influenced by local news events. All newspaper advertising appears within the atmosphere of the local news for a given day. A major scandal in local politics or a catastrophe such as a tornado in a local area can have a devastating effect on the advertising appearing in a given issue. Magazines, on the other hand, do not tie in closely with local events. Magazines are normally put aside to read during hours not taken up by involvement in local events. Because local events have a strong effect on response, positively or negatively, markets with similar demographics don't always respond in the same manner. All newspaper advertising tends to be local, even if a schedule is national.

Developing a Newspaper Test Program

When direct response advertisers first consider testing newspapers as a medium, they have a myriad of decisions to make. Should they go ROP, the newspaper preprint route, local Sunday supplements, syndicated supplements, TV program supplements, comics? What papers should they test? Putting ad size and position aside for the moment, there are two initial considerations: the importance of advertising in a mail-order climate and the demographics of markets selected as they relate to the product or service being offered.

If you had one simple product, a stamp dispenser for instance, and a tiny budget, you might place one small ad in one publication. You could run the ad in the mail order section of the *New York Times Sunday Magazine*. Generally, if you don't make it there, you won't make it anywhere. Running such an ad would give a "feel." If it works, it would be logical to test similar mail order sections in major cities such as Chicago, Detroit, and Los Angeles. (See Exhibit 5-3.)

Simple items, which are suited to small-space advertising in mail order sections, greatly simplify the testing procedure. But, more often than not, multi-city testing in larger space is required. Prime direct response test markets in the

Exhibit 5–3.   Mail Order Shopping Guide from the *Chicago Tribune Sunday Magazine*

United States include Atlanta, Buffalo, Cleveland, Dallas–Fort Worth, Denver, Des Moines, Indianapolis, Omaha, and Peoria. In the selection of test markets, you should analyze the newspaper to make certain it has advertising reach and coverage and offers demographics that are suitable to your product. If there are two newspapers in a market, it is worthwhile to evaluate both of them. Let us say that because of budget limitations advertising can be placed in only a limited number of markets. Such criteria as circulation, household penetration, male or female readers, and advertising lineage relating to the product to be advertised should be measured.

A number of sources will provide the data necessary for evaluation. You would begin with SRDS's *Newspaper Rates and Data* for general cost and circulation information. *SRDS Circulation Analysis* would provide information about metro household penetration. *Simmons Total Audience Study* could then be used to isolate male or female readers of a particular age group. Other criteria to be measured are retail lineage in various classifications and spendable income by metro area.

Demographics are a major consideration whether you are using ROP, preprints, local supplements, syndicated supplements, or TV progam supplements. Once an advertiser develops a test program that closely reflects the demographics for the product or service, expansion to like markets makes possible the rapid acceleration of a full-blown program. But selecting newspapers is tedious, because there are hundreds from which to choose as compared with a relative handful of magazines whose demographics can be more closely related to the proposition. As an example, a test newspaper schedule could be placed in the following markets: Atlanta, preprint; Cleveland, Metro comics; Dallas–Fort Worth, ROP; Denver, preprint; Des Moines, ROP; Indianapolis, preprint; Omaha, Metro comics; and Peoria, *Parade* remnant. If there is more than one newspaper in a test market, the paper with the most promising demographics should be selected.

A test schedule like this would be ambitious in terms of total dollars, but it would have the advantage of simultaneously testing markets and formats. Once a reading has been obtained from the markets and formats, the advertiser can rapidly expand to other markets and will have the advantage of using the most productive formats.

Advertising Seasons

As in direct mail and magazine direct response advertising, there are two major newspaper direct response advertising seasons. The fall mail order season begins roughly with August and runs through November. (A notable exception is a July insertion, which is often useful especially when using a pretested piece.) The winter season begins with January and runs through March.

Exceptions to the two major direct response seasons occur in the sale of seasonal merchandise. Christmas items are usually promoted from September through the first week of December. A nursery, on the other hand, will start promoting in late December and early January, then again in the early fall. Many nurseries follow the practice of promoting by geographic regions, starting earlier in the South and working up to later promotion in the North.

Timing of Newspaper Insertions

Beyond the seasonal factor of direct response advertising in newspapers, timing is important as it relates to days of the week. According to the *E&P Yearbook, Bureau of Advertising Circulation Analysis*, the number of copies of a newspaper sold per day is remarkably constant month after month—despite such events as summer vacation and Christmas holidays. And people buy the newspaper to read not only the editorial matter but also the ads. According to an *Audits & Surveys Study*, the percentage of people opening an average ad page any weekday, Monday through Friday, varies less than 3 percent, with Tuesday ranking the highest at 88 percent.

There is no question that the local newspaper is an integral part of practically everyone's daily life. Magazines are often set aside for reading at a convenient time, but newspapers are read the day they are delivered or purchased or are not read at all. Monday through Thursday are favorite choices of many direct response advertisers for their ROP advertising. Many direct response advertisers judiciously avoid the weekday issue containing grocery advertising.

As we have seen, more and more newspapers are accepting preprints for weekday insertions. This can be a major advantage, considering the larger number of preprints appearing in most metro Sunday newspapers.

Newspaper Response Patterns

Newspapers have the shortest time lapse from closing date to appearance date of all print media. In most cases, ads can appear in the newspaper within 72 hours after placement. Depending on the format used, up to 90 percent or more of responses will be reached for a typical direct response newspaper ad within these time frames: ROP, after the second week; preprints, after the third week; syndicated newspaper supplements, after the third week; and comics, after the second week.

Naturally, response patterns vary according to the proposition. Thus it is important for advertisers to develop their own response pattern. But the nature of newspaper advertising permits a quick turnaround. *Dow Theory Forecasts*, for instance, has run ads in hundreds of newspapers. Dow is able to project results, giving the advertiser the option of deciding whether to repeat an ad, within a week after the first orders are received.

Determining Proper Ad Size

In direct response newspaper advertising, as in retail or national newspaper ads, few people dispute the claim that a larger ad generally will get more attention than a smaller one. But whether the full-page ad gets twice the attention of the half-page ad or four times the attention of the quarter-page ad is debatable. It is cost per response that counts. Just as in magazine advertising, less space is usually indicated for inquiry advertising and more space for a direct order ad.

According to one study conducted by the Bureau of Advertising relating to mail-back newspaper coupons, the size of the space seems to be a factor in reader response only to the extent that it is a factor in initial reader attention. In this study, 85 percent of newspaper inserts ran ads of 1,000 lines or more. Only half used fewer than 1,000 lines, with a minimum of 500 lines per ad.

A low-budget advertiser often must choose between a single full-page ad and several small ads over an extended time. The proper guide to follow in determining the initial size of ads is to base the size on the space required to tell the *complete story*.

Trying to sell membership in a video and tape club in a small space would be ludicrous. Experience shows that a wide selection of videos must be offered in the ad to get memberships. The same is true for a book club. On the other hand, if you are selling a single item at a low price—say, a cigarette lighter for $4.95—the complete story can be told in a small space. Where small-space advertising can tell the whole story, consistency and repetition often prove to be keys to success.

Aside from the obvious requirement of using a full page or more for a proposition, constant testing of ad sizes will establish the proper size to produce the most efficient cost per inquiry or per order.

The Position Factor

Newspapers and magazines have many similarities in respect to the importance of position in direct response advertising. Research has demonstrated high readership of newspaper ads, whatever the position. However, direct response advertisers still prefer right-hand pages. Generally, such advertisers find that ads are more effective if they appear in the front of the newspaper rather than in the back. Placement of coupon ads in the gutter of any newspaper page is almost always avoided.

All newspapers are printed in sections. Special consideration should be given to the reading habits of men and women as they relate to specific sections of a newspaper. Readership habits of men and women are similar, with the exception of four sections: food and cooking, home furnishings, gardening, and sports.

Color versus Black and White

The possibilities of using color in newspaper advertising may be regarded as similar to those for magazine advertising, with one major exception. If you plan to use one or more colors other than black in an ROP ad, you simply can't get the quality that you can in a color magazine ad. This does not mean that ROP color shouldn't be tested. A majority of newspapers that offer color will allow A/B splits of color versus black and white.

Studies have used split runs and the recognition method to test the attention-getting power of both two-color and full-color ROP ads. These studies show increases of 58 percent for two-color ads and 78 percent for full-color ads above the level of results for black-and-white versions of the same ads. Comparable cost differences are 21 percent and 25 percent, respectively.

When Starch "noting score" norms are used to estimate the same attention-getting differential, a different conclusion is reached. The differences are about 10 percent and 30 percent, respectively (when size and product category are held constant). Using norms means comparing a black-and-white ad for one product in another city at another time. These variables inevitably blur the significance of comparisons.

For the direct response advertiser, these studies are interesting. However, you should remember that genuine controlled testing is the only way to get true figures.

SELF-QUIZ

1. Name the two obvious advantages of preprints.

    a. _____

    b. _____

2. Which is the most popular format for a preprint?
    ☐ Card   ☐ Multipage

3. Name the three major syndicated newspaper supplements.

    a. _____

    b. _____

    c. _____

4. Define *Dutch door*.

    _____

    _____

    _____

    _____

5. What is remnant space?

    _____

    _____

    _____

    _____

6. The higher one's education, the less likely one is to read the comics pages.
    ☐   True   ☐   False

7. The higher one's income, the less likely one is to read the comics pages.
    ☐   True   ☐   False

8. What is the advantage of the ad-and-card and ad-and-envelope for comics-page advertisers?

    _____

    _____

    _____

9. How many advertisers per page are allowed in comics-page advertising?

    _____

10. What major advantage over ROP advertising is offered to direct response advertisers by preprints and supplements?

    _____

    _____

11. In regard to potential results, what is the major difference between newspaper advertising and all other print advertising?

_____

_____

_____

12. What are the two initial considerations in the development of a newspaper test program?

a. _____

b. _____

13. If you have a single item that is suitable for advertising in a small space and a limited budget for testing, which publication would you test first?

_____

14. What are the two main seasons for newspaper direct response advertising?

a. _____

b. _____

15. Depending on the format used, up to 90 percent or more of responses will be reached for a typical response newspaper ad within these time frames:

ROP: after _____ week(s)

Preprints: after _____ week(s)

Supplements: after _____ week(s)

Comics: after _____ week(s)

16. When running ROP, direct response advertisers should specify:
    ☐ Left-hand page   ☐ Right-hand page

17. What is the major disadvantage of running color ROP?

_____

_____

_____

_____

PILOT PROJECT

You are the advertising manager of a mail order operation selling collectibles. You have been successful in magazines offering a series of historic plates. You have never used newspapers, but now you have a $75,000 budget to test the medium.

Outline a newspaper test plan. (*Note:* If you use preprints, your total space budget should cover printing costs.)

1. Select your test cities.

2. Will your test run in the Sunday edition or the weekday edition, or both?

3. What formats will you test: preprints, supplements, comics, local TV guides, ROP?

4. What size preprints or ads will you test?

5. At what time of the year will you run your tests?

CHAPTER SIX

TV/Radio

Electronic Media Applications

Broadcast TV

The range of TV direct response offers has greatly expanded in recent years. Although direct selling of magazines, tapes and CDs, and innovative products certainly still exists, many different types of direct response offers have surfaced.

Lead-generation commercials for high-ticket products and services such as home mortgages, insurance, and exercise equipment are now common. In addition, many *Fortune* 500 companies have started incorporating TV direct response into the marketing mix. The diversity of TV direct response offers is evidenced by broadcast direct response agency A. Eicoff & Company's client roster: American Express, Time-Life, Beltone Electronics, Rodale Press, and St. Jude Children's Hospital, among others.

A truly unique application of broadcast TV involves White Castle. Hundreds of thousands of Midwesterners were practically raised on White Castle hamburgers. Each year many of those same Midwesterners move to other regions of the country. Even without a White Castle nearby, the taste lingered on.

White Castle solved the availability problem by initiating a unique TV campaign with the theme, "White Castle has the taste some people won't live without." Outside of the White Castle trading area, commercials ended with this tag line: "Hamburgers to Fly. Call 1–800–W CASTLE." Over 10,000 hamburgers were being sold a week, with a minimum order of 50 hamburgers for $57! (See Exhibit 6–1.)

Cable TV

Broadcast TV, both local and network, has long been a major medium for consumer direct response advertisers, producing inquiries, supporting other me-

Exhibit 6–1.   White Castle Campaign

DAUGHTER: I miss you, momma. I miss the city, too.

MOMMA: What if we sent you a little bit of your home town.

DAUGHTER: Now, how are you gonna do that?

White Castle hamburgers from back home! You can't get them out here.

My folks sent them!

ROOMMATE: Hey! Johnson's got White Castles!

GANG: White Castles!

DAUGHTER: You know, on my first date we stopped at a White Castle.

SINGERS: WHITE CASTLE HAS THE TASTE SOME PEOPLE WON'T LIVE WITHOUT.

dia, and selling goods and services to the consumer. But in the last five years, in particular, cable has come on strong.

Cable TV looks like broadcast TV, but it is different in many ways. First, the cable TV audience is highly defined. Cable operators know who is tied into the system—they send them a bill every month. This demographic information and some psychographic information is available to the advertiser. With many more channels available than are available for broadcast TV, cable, not unlike the audience selectivity traits of radio and special-interest magazines, provides more special-interest programming. Thus, the direct response advertiser can tie offers to predefined audiences with a proclivity toward special interests such as sports, news, or entertainment.

One of the most firmly established special-interest channels is Home Box Office (HBO). Its appeal is to those who have a particular interest in movies, sports, and special events. To be successful, not only must HBO offer superior programming, but also it must sell subscriptions for the programs.

Home Shopping Shows

A phenomenon of our times is the home shopping TV show. The telephone is integral to its explosive growth. The pioneer was HSN (Home Shopping Network). A later entrant, QVC Network, has experienced dramatic growth. The QVC shopping channel is broadcast live 24 hours a day, 7 days a week. QVC built its huge volume by featuring prescheduled programs, offering products from specific product categories such as jewelry, electronics, and apparel. Under a new policy, customers may order any item presented on QVC at any time that's convenient to them, providing the item is still in stock. Throughout all TV broadcasts, the QVC toll-free number is flashed constantly. Phone response is almost instantaneous. To promote viewership, QVC mails extensively to cable subscribers, providing them with free memberships in the QVC Shoppers Club and notifying them about free prizes awarded each day. (See Exhibits 6–2 and 6–3.)

Radio

Radio has two things going for it over broadcast TV: (1) program formats to which advertisers can better target and (2) much lower costs for similar time periods. Targeting to the right program formats is the key. For example, if an advertiser is soliciting phone-in orders for a rock album or tape, there's no problem running a radio commercial on scores of stations that feature rock music; these listeners are the very audience the advertiser is seeking. Or if a financial advertiser is soliciting inquiries from potential investors, there are program formats that help the advertiser reach a target audience: "Wall Street Report," for example, or FM stations with a high percentage of upper-income listeners. This 60-second radio commercial by Merrill Lynch was run in conjunction with program formats with a high percentage of listeners who match its customer profile:

(Music up and under)
ANNOUNCER: A word on money management from Merrill Lynch. Today, many banks are trying to copy our revolutionary Cash Management Account

Exhibit 6–2.   Cover Panel of Folder Announcing Free Prizes to Cable Viewers

financial service. Here's why they can't. Bank money market accounts are simply that: bank accounts. A Merrill Lynch CMA gives you access to the entire *range* of our investment opportunities. Instead of just an account, you get an Account Executive, backed by the top-ranked research team on Wall Street. Idle cash is automatically invested in your choice of *three* CMA money market funds. You enjoy check writing, a special Visa card, automatic variable-rate loans up to the full margin loan value of your securities—at *rates* banks aren't likely to match. So give your money sound management, and *more* to grow on. The all-in-one CMA financial service. (*Music*) From Merrill Lynch. A breed apart.

LOCAL ANNOUNCER: For more complete information and a free prospectus, including sales charges and expenses, call 000–0000. Read it carefully before you invest or send money. That's 000–0000.

Exhibit 6–3.   First Page of Two-Page Letter to Cable Subscribers
with Free Membership Card for QVC Shoppers Club

```
MultiVision
QVC Network
Channel 23
```

1·800·345·1515	**1·800·345·1515**
QVC MEMBERSHIP NO.	QVC MEMBERSHIP NO.
1449–3828	1449–3828
1·800·345·1515	**1·800·345·1515**
QVC MEMBERSHIP NO.	QVC MEMBERSHIP NO.
1449–3828	1449–3828

> ## QVC SHOPPERS CLUB
>
> ★ **MEMBERSHIP CARD** ★
>
> MEMBERSHIP
> NUMBER   1449–3828
>
> Mr. Don Corley
> P.O. Box 641
> Cambria, IL 62915
>
> QVC – Cable Channel 23

```
       CAR-RT SORT    **B009
```
*↖ Place these stickers on your phones so you'll
always have your membership number and
QVC phone number handy!*

```
Mr. Don Corley
P.O. Box 641
Cambria, IL 62915
```

Dear Cable Subscriber:

   Because you're a MultiVision cable subscriber,
we're pleased to award you a FREE membership in
the QVC Shoppers Club!

   Your exclusive membership number is valuable.
It's your key to winning great prizes on QVC. And
you'll have lots of opportunities to win, because
QVC GIVES AWAY HUNDREDS OF PRIZES EVERY DAY!

   <u>Hourly</u> $25 prizes. <u>Daily</u> $1000 shopping sprees.
And <u>weekly</u> grand prizes such as new cars and dream
vacations -- all to help introduce cable viewers to
QVC, the <u>new</u> way of shopping, on Cable Channel 23.

   QVC stands for Quality, Value and Convenience.
Tune in to channel 23 <u>anytime,</u> day or night,
for a wide variety of high-quality products to
help you look your best, beautify your home and
make your life easier. You can order any item
by phone, with <u>a 30-day money-back guarantee.</u>

   However, you don't have to buy <u>anything</u> to win
prizes on QVC. Here's just <u>one</u> way you could win:

   Tune in for QVC's hourly Lucky Number drawings.
Every time the number drawn matches <u>either</u> the
first 4 digits <u>or</u> the last 4 digits of your QVC
membership number, YOU'RE A WINNER! Just phone
QVC before the next Lucky Number is drawn and
you'll <u>instantly</u> win $25 credited to your QVC
account. Plus, you'll automatically be entered
in QVC's DAILY $1000 GRAND PRIZE DRAWING!

   Your membership number is 1449-3828, which gives
you <u>two</u> opportunities to win during each drawing!
Every time 1449 <u>or</u> 3828 is drawn, YOU'RE A WINNER!

                              Over, please...

Videocassettes

Today more than half of all TV homes have one or more VCRs. This could be bad news for movie theaters: Close to $3 billion annually is spent on movie rentals. The onslaught of VCRs isn't good news for TV networks either: Millions use their TV sets to watch taped movies, sporting events, and special events without commercials. But for the direct marketer, VCRs offer an opportunity rather than a threat: Direct marketers have the opportunity to become sponsors of videocassette programming.

By incorporating commercial messages in the program, producers can defray the high cost of production and sell their tapes at a lower price. In addition, they might be able to open new distribution outlets. As an example, the hour-long "Mr. Boston Official Video Bartender's Guide," sponsored by Glenmore Distilleries, is available through liquor stores as well as the more usual outlets. Along with the cassette goes an eight-page catalog of each Glenmore product.

With such a catalog, or with specific sales and response information incorporated into a taped presentation, a sponsored videocassette might prove so productive for an advertiser that it could afford to sell the tape cheaply, use it as a self-liquidating premium, or even give the tape to videocassette outlets for low-rate rental. Videocassette catalogs also show potential for high-ticket items that benefit from demonstration.

Direct Response TV

Buying and scheduling TV and radio time is best left to the experts—direct marketing agencies and some select buying services. But for a direct marketer to recognize the opportunities and pitfalls of advertising in these media, it is imperative that the basics be understood. The following comments about buying and scheduling TV apply equally to radio.

Ratings

It is important to keep in mind that the cost of a commercial time period is based on its rating. This is a measure of its share of the total TV households viewing the show. The more highly rated the show, the higher the cost. One rating point equals 1 percent of the total households in the market. A show with a 20 rating is being watched by 20 percent of TV households.

When the total ratings of all the time periods in a schedule are combined, the result is called *gross rating points* (GRPs). Simply stated, if a television schedule has 100 GRPs per week, it is reaching the equivalent of 100 percent of TV households in the market in that week. Obviously, this is a statistical reach with varying degrees of duplication. It does not guarantee 100 percent of the individual homes will be reached.

Commercial Lengths

Although 30 seconds is the most common length for general or image advertising, direct marketers seldom find it adequate to tell their selling story in a persuasive way. Ninety to 120 seconds is usually required for a direct sale commercial, and 60 to 90 seconds is usually required for lead-generation commercials. On the other hand, support commercials with sufficient GRPs prove effective with a combination of 10-second and 30-second commercials. But key outlet marketing usually requires longer lengths.

Of course, with the popularity of 30-second announcements and the premium broadcasters can get for them, it is not always possible to clear longer-length commercials, particularly during periods of high demand.

Reach and Frequency

TV advertisers use two terms in measuring the effectiveness of their television schedules. *Reach* refers to the number of different homes exposed to the message within a given time segment. *Frequency* is a measure of how many times the average viewer will see the message over a given number of weeks. Frequency also can be measured against viewer quintiles (e.g., heaviest viewers, lightest viewers).

The combination of reach and frequency will tell you what percentage of the audience you are reaching and how often on average they will see your message. Television schedules often are purchased against reach and frequency goals and actual performance measured in postanalysis.

For most direct marketers, reach and frequency are not as important as actual response rates, which represent a true return on the media dollar. But a knowledge of what reach and frequency are is critical when television is used in a supporting role.

Buying Time

Buying specific time periods is the most expensive way to purchase television time. You pay a higher price to guarantee your message will run at a precise time within a predetermined program environment. Television time also can be bought less expensively. Stations will sell run-of-station (ROS) time—time available during periods the station has been unable to sell at regular rates. This is particularly true with independent (non-network) stations, which often have sizable inventories of unsold time. If the station, however, subsequently sells the time to a specific buyer, your commercial will be preempted.

Preemptible time can be an excellent buy for direct response advertisers because of the combination of lower cost and quite respectable response rates. When buying preemptible time, it also is possible to specify the dayparts (daytime, early fringe, late fringe, and so on) for slightly more than straight ROS rates. This can be important for direct marketers with a specific target audience for their product. Such spots still may be preempted at any time, however.

Television time also can be purchased on the basis of payment per inquiry (PI) and bonus-to-pay-out. PI allows the station to run as many commercials as it wishes, whenever it wishes. There is no charge for the time, but the station receives a predetermined sum for every inquiry or sale the advertisement generates for the advertiser. The advertiser is not committed to pay for a spot until it delivers an inquiry or sale and then only in relation to responses.

But there are disadvantages. It is almost impossible to plan methodically for fulfillment. Such programs cannot be coordinated reliably with other efforts or promotion timetables. And because the station will run the commercials that it thinks will perform best for it, your spot might never run and you will not know it until it has jeopardized your entire selling program.

Bonus-to-pay-out involves a special arrangement with the station to deliver a certain number of responses. A schedule is negotiated with the station to guarantee a certain minimum schedule. If at the end of the schedule the response goal has not been reached, the station must continue to run the commercial until it is reached. This method provides a better planning base for the direct marketer.

With television time in high demand, such opportunities are not as available as they once were. But if they can be located, they can be a superb vehicle for direct marketers.

TV Schedules

What kind of broadcast TV schedule is most productive and/or efficient for the direct marketer? It depends on the objective. For direct sale or lead-generation commercials, which require the viewer to get up and take some action within minutes, certain criteria apply. For example, the TV viewing day is divided into various dayparts. There are weekday daytime, early evening or fringe, prime time, late night or fringe, and weekend. Each daypart tends to reach one group or combination of viewers better than the others.

It is important to know your primary target group so you can select the most appropriate daypart. Prime time is so called because it reaches the largest audience with the most exciting shows. It is also the most expensive. The more attentive viewers are to the show, the less likely they are to respond immediately. Therefore, times of lower viewer involvement and attentiveness are better and less expensive for the advertiser who expects a direct response. Reruns, talk shows, old movies, and the like often are the best vehicles for direct response advertising. These tend to run predominantly in daytime, fringe, and late-night time slots.

Similarly, because independent stations tend to run a higher percentage of syndicated reruns and movies, their viewers tend to have a lower level of attentiveness to the programming. But even on independent stations, avoid news shows and other high-interest programming. Check the ratings. They are a good guide.

Seasonality is another factor in direct response TV. The first and third quarters are the best seasons for television response, just as they are for print and mail. Moreover, television time pricing is related to viewing levels, which are seasonal and vary month to month as well as by daypart.

Market Performance. Some geographic locations are good for certain products or offers. Others are simply not receptive. It pays to know ahead of time what a market's propensity is. Previous experience with mail or print can be a reasonably reliable guide.

In any event, it, is not necessary to jump in up to your neck. Start with a handful of markets—say, two to five—and test the waters. Try a one- or two-week schedule. As few as ten commercials per week can give you a reading. Monitor your telephone response daily. You'll know within two or three days if it's bust or boom. After a week or so you'll have an even more precise fix on how well your commercial is doing. If it holds up, stay with it until it starts to taper off. Then stop. Don't try to milk a stone.

Meanwhile, move on to other markets in the same methodical and measured way. You always can return to your most successful markets later in the marketing year after your commercial has had a rest. Or you can come back with a new offer.

Advantages and Disadvantages of Different Types of Stations. Media-buying decisions have become more complex because of the expansion and success of various cable and broadcast stations and programming packages. Let's examine the advantages and disadvantages of the five major options for most TV direct response offers.

Network. The four major networks are ABC (195 affiliated stations), CBS (189 affiliated stations), NBC (186 affiliated stations), and Fox (134 affiliated stations). The advantage of the network option is that network reaches 95 percent of the potential U.S. TV households with each spot. The disadvantages are as follows:

1. There are few, if any, 120-second spots available.

2. It is generally cost-prohibitive.

3. Telemarketing blockage problems would occur in most dayparts.

4. Talent payments could present a problem.

Though once considered prohibitively expensive, with astute planning the network option can be a viable direct response vehicle.

Spot TV. The use of spot TV is a localized way of making a buy, and it can be done through independent stations and/or affiliates. Whether you buy one or five stations in a spot market, you are reaching only one TV market. Rates vary greatly, depending on the station's ranking in and the size of the market. One advantage of spot TV is that it is cost-efficient. Because of competition within a market, reasonable buys generally can be made. Also, you can maximize efficiencies in the better-performing markets and on the better-performing stations. The disadvantage is that for a national campaign, it's more labor-intensive to buy each market individually. Spot TV is the common approach for most direct response television campaigns.

Network cable. The total cable penetration in the United States is 61 percent. There are 32 advertiser-supported cable networks and 16 regional cable networks. The advantages of network cable are as follows:

1. It is cost-efficient.

2. It enables targeting an offer to a cable network.

3. Back-end tends to be better on cable than on broadcast TV because cable has a more upscale audience.

The disadvantage is that there are limited availabilities, especially if you have a two-minute spot. Network cable is especially appropriate if you have a one-minute spot and an offer perfectly matched to a cable network's audience.

Local cable. Unlike cable network, local cable enables you to buy on a market basis or, in some instances, on a neighborhood basis. One advantage of local cable is that it allows a very targeted approach that works for products with narrow market segments. Also, it allows securing of additional cable time when networks are tight. The disadvantages include the following:

1. There are no two-minute breaks.

2. Rates aren't particularly cost-efficient.

3. You have to work with five or more cable operators to cover one market.

4. It offers a very fragmented audience.

Local cable is best used for offers that target a narrowly segmented market.

Syndication. Syndication is the sale of a TV program for airing on a market-by-market, station-by-station basis. Though generally associated with reruns and game shows, syndication can include first-run movies and original, first-run TV shows. Some direct marketing agencies have also been able to buy time within a syndicated program, ensuring that the spot will air every time the show runs.
    The advantages of syndication are as follows:

1. It is difficult to preempt a syndicated program.

2. It reaches 80–90 percent of the country (similar to network).

3. There are no telemarketing headaches, because each station airs a particular show at a different time of day or on a different day of the week.

4. It allows product-to-program matching—a useful targeting tool.

The disadvantages are that it usually accepts only 60-second spots and for cost efficiency, buyers often have to wait for "distressed" or unsold time within a syndicated program. Syndication is well-suited to one-minute offers that are matched to a specific program, and it is a good choice for direct marketers having problems with preemptions.

Creating for Direct Response TV and Radio

Creating for TV

In wrestling with concepts for television, remember that it is a visual medium and an action medium. And you are using it in a time of great video literacy. Your concept must be sharp and crisp. It must be designed to jar a lethargic and jaded audience to rapt attention. Your concepts, therefore, require the best and most knowledgeable of talent.

When you have arrived at your concept, it's time to write a script and do a storyboard. The script format is two adjacent columns, one for video descriptions and one for copy and audio directions. The two columns track together so that the appropriate words and sounds are shown opposite the pictures they will accompany. Video descriptions should make it possible to understand the general action in any given scene. It is not necessary at this point to spell out every detail.

Some people prefer to work only with storyboards, while others combine scripts and storyboards. The storyboard is a series of artist's drawings of the action and location of each scene. There should be enough individual pictures (called *frames*) to show the flow of the action and provide important visual information. Most concept storyboards run eight to sixteen frames, depending on the length of the commercial, the complexity of the action, and the need to show specific detail.

Novices make two important errors when preparing TV storyboards. One is failure to synchronize the words and the pictures. At no point should the copy be talking about something different from what the picture is showing, nor should the picture be something that is unrelated to the words.

The second mistake is failure to realize that most people who evaluate a storyboard equate frames with the passage of time. Each frame in an eight-frame storyboard will often be interpreted as one-eighth of commercial time. If some intricate action takes place over five seconds, it could take four or five frames to illustrate. Meanwhile, a simple scene that may run ten seconds can often be illustrated with one or two frames. Imagine the confusion the reviewer of the storyboard faces. Make sure your storyboards show elapsed time. Often an elapsed time indicator next to the picture will do the trick.

Of course, the criteria presented above are only guidelines. They are not rules. Even if they were, the essence of all great advertising, including direct response, is to break the rules to reach people in a way they haven't been reached before. But it is something quite different to violate principles that have been developed over years of observation. Do so only at your own peril.

There is a set of rules that relates to the law. Various industry self-regulatory bodies and instruments of the government watch over the airwaves. They require that advertising be truthful and not misleading. Don't say (or picture) anything in your commercial that you can't substantiate or replicate in person. And don't make promises your product or service can't deliver.

As you design your direct response commercial, there are some important techniques to keep in mind. If at all possible, integrate your offer with the rest of your commercial. It will make it easier for the viewer to comprehend and respond. And it will give your offer, and your product or service, the opportunity to reinforce each other in value and impression.

Also, if possible, integrate the 800 toll-free number into the commercial. You should plan to have the telephone number on the screen for at least 25 seconds or more, depending on the length of the commercial. Try to find ways to make it ''dance'' on the screen. Bring it on visually as it is announced on the sound track.

Once you have developed a television storyboard that you believe is a good representation of what you want to accomplish, it is possible to evaluate it using the following criteria:

1. **Immediacy.** Is there a sense of urgency to ''Call this number now''? Does it make viewers feel that an opportunity will be lost if they don't run to the phone?

2. **Clarity.** Is the offer clear? Do people understand exactly what they will receive, or is there room for doubt and ambiguity?

3. **Lack of retail availability.** If the advertised product is not available in any store, make sure that point is communicated to the viewer.

4. **Increased value.** Many tactics can heighten the offer's value, for example, making a ''special television offer'' and stating ''for a limited time only.''

5. **Limited options.** If the spot provides viewers with too many choices, they will be confused. Yes-or-no offers usually do better than multiple-choice ones.

6. **Early close.** Ask for the order early and often. If the commercial waits until the final seconds or makes only one request for the viewer to call, it is usually too late.

7. **Less is more.** If you're asking for installment payments, focus the viewers' attention on the installment amount. Do not emphasize the sum total of all the installments.

8. **Show and tell.** It the product does more than one thing, show it. This is the only way viewers will become familiar with the product. Demonstrations work. Make sure the commercial conveys exactly what viewers are getting when they buy the product.

A support television commercial differs from a straight response commercial in ways worthy of note. Because it seeks to reach the largest number of people, it usually runs in time periods when 30 seconds is the prevalent availability. It must have a greatly condensed message, placing a premium on simplicity. As it seeks no immediate response, but directs the viewer elsewhere, such as to a newspaper insert, memorability and a positive attitude about the advertiser become extremely important.

Creating for Radio

In its early days, television was perceived by many copywriters as nothing more than illustrated radio. With the evolution of the medium, we learned how limited that vision was. Now, in this age of video, there is a tendency to think of radio as television without the pictures. That perception is equally wrong.

Radio is the "writer's medium" in its purest sense. Words, sounds, music, and even silence are woven together by the writer to produce a moving tapestry of thought, image, and persuasion. Connection with the listener is direct, personal, emotional, primal.

In writing for radio, it is important to consider a station's format. The country-and-western station has a different listening audience from the all-news station. Different people listen to classical music than talk-back or rock programming. Tailor your message and its style to the format of the station it is running on. That doesn't necessarily mean make it sound exactly like the station's programming. Sometimes it makes sense to break the flow of programming to stand out as a special message, but only within the framework of the format that has attracted the station's listeners.

Remember also that radio is more personal than TV. Radios are carried with the listener—in a car, at the beach, at the office, in the bathroom—and even joggers with their earphones are tuned into the radio cosmos. Moreover, because the radio listener can supply important elements in the message mosaic, the conclusion drawn from it is likely to be more firmly held than that which the individual has not participated in. Do not fill in all the blanks for your listeners. Let them provide some of the pieces. At the same time, be sure the words you use are clear in their meaning and emotional content. Be sure the sounds are clearly understandable and recognizable. If not, find some way to augment them with narrative or conversation that establishes a setting that is easy to visualize.

Use music whenever you can justify its cost and consumption of commercial time. Music is the emotional common denominator. Its expression of joy, sorrow, excitement, romance, or action is as universally understood as any device available to you. When it comes time to consider music, contact a music production house. There usually are several in every major city. Los Angeles, New York, and Chicago have scores of them. Or consider library music that can be purchased outright at low cost.

Another aspect of radio is its casualness. Whereas television tends to command all of our attention and concentration, radio usually gets only a portion of it. It is important to keep radio commercials simple and intrusive. Devices such as special sounds (or silence) can arrest your listener's attention. To hold it, the idea content must be cohesive and uncomplicated. Better to drive one point home than to flail away at many. If many points must be covered, they all should feed to a strong central premise. This advice is appropriate for all advertising. But for radio it is critical.

The length a radio commercial runs is usually 60 seconds. This not only should be adequate for most commercial messages, but it also is the time length listeners have become accustomed to. Thirty-second commercials are available but are not a good buy for direct response purposes.

One other thing that everyone who listens to radio will appreciate is that radio lends itself to humor. For some reason we have become used to hearing humor on radio, and we respond positively to it. The following radio commercial employs humor effectively to address small-business owners while talking to the public at large.

Husband:	How did we get into this anyway?
Wife:	Who knows, we tried to make it work.
Husband:	Well, I guess it's over.
Wife:	We better get on with it.
Husband:	Okay, you get the car.
Wife:	Right.
Husband:	I get the sofa bed. You get the fridge.
Wife:	Right.
Husband:	I get the Bell System Yellow Pages Directory. You get the . . .
Wife:	Hold on—that doesn't mean the Gold Pages Coupon Section, does it?
Husband:	Why, sure it does.
Wife:	I get the Gold Pages Coupons.

Husband:	Well come on—you're getting the bedroom set too.
Wife:	You can have the bedroom set. I want the Gold Pages Coupons good for discounts at local merchants.
Husband:	I'll tell you what.
Wife:	What?
Husband:	I'll throw in the oil painting and the end tables.
Wife:	I want the Gold Pages.
Husband:	Look, you can have everything else. Just let me keep the Gold Pages Coupons.
Wife:	Get off your knees. You really want them that bad?
Husband:	I do absolutely.
Wife:	We could split them.
Husband:	You mean . . . tear them apart?
Wife:	You're right . . . it won't work.
Husband:	No. Neither will this.
Wife:	It won't work.
Husband:	You mean . . .
Wife:	We'll just have to stay together.
Husband:	Dolores—what a mistake we almost made.
Wife:	Lorraine.
Husband:	Lorraine—what a mistake we almost made.
Wife:	Who's Dolores?

TV in the Multimedia Mix

For decades marketers have regarded electronic media as stand-alone media. But the astute marketers of the 1990s have joined the trend toward integrated communications. A classic example of this trend was the multimedia campaign for Ryder used trucks, created by Ogilvy & Mather Direct.

Exhibit 6–4 gives a precise description of the campaign. Note that the campaign included direct mail, direct response, TV, print, and radio.

Exhibit 6–5 shows a print ad that appeared in ensuing vertical publications. A vertical publication is one that caters to a specific category of business, such as banking, or a specific interest such as jogging, boating, etc. The headline ''Buy a Ryder Road Ready Used Truck and You'll Find One Problem. The Mechanics Hate to See Them Go'' carries the campaign theme.

Exhibit 6–6 reveals the 120-second TV commercial. It was tagged as ''The Crying Commerical,'' because it paid off on the theme ''The mechanics hate to see them go.''

How successful was this multimedia campaign? The combination of direct mail, print, TV, and radio produced a total of 46,046 responses, beating the previous controls by 245 percent.

Exhibit 6–4.   Description of Ryder Campaign

Product or Service

Used vehicle sales, including vans, gas and diesel straight trucks, refrigerated trucks, tractors, and trailers. Range in price from $7,000 to $35,000.

Target Audience

- Owners/presidents of small service businesses, small wholesalers/retailers, small trucking companies and light manufacturing companies (cabinetry, auto parts, electronic parts, clothing/candy)
- Owner/operators
- Used truck purchasers in large companies with 10 + vehicle fleet size

Medium/Media Used

Direct mail: 300,000 pieces. Lists included previous customers, Dun & Bradstreet selects (targeted industries; less than 100 employees; transportation titles), *Fleet Equipment* subscribers, *Fleet Owner* subscribers, *Allied Truck Publication* subscribers.

DRTV: :60 and :120 local television in spot markets. 3–5 stations/market, 10–15 spots/week/station, for 2–4 week flights

Print: local trade publications (*Truck Trader*)

Radio: local spot stations

Marketing Strategy

To remain competitive in its primary business—truck rental and leasing, Ryder needs to keep its truck fleet current. Selling its used vehicles helps Ryder fund the purchase of new vehicles while providing an additional source of revenue.

Problem:
- Increasingly depressed market for used vehicle sales
- Aggressive sales objectives within a more competitive category environment
- Inconsistent awareness that Ryder also sells trucks

Solution:
- Leverage Ryders' reputation for quality in truck rental and leasing to sell its vehicles at a premium price.
- Establish "Road Ready" as a symbol of reliability, safety, and value through a lfietime of maintenance.
- Provide a continuous presence in the marketplace to generate awareness that Ryder sells trucks.
- Generate immediate, qualified leads through an offer of a free "How to Buy a Used Truck" booklet.

Exhibit 6–5.   Print Ad for Ryder Campaign

Exhibit 6–5 *(Continued)*.

Exhibit 6–6.   The Crying Commercial

Ogilvy & Mather Direct

CLIENT: RYDER
PRODUCT: USED TRUCK SALE
TITLE: "CRYING"
COMML No.: RTLR 0111 :120

(SFX-TRUCK HORN) (MUSIC UP-
SENTIMENTAL THEME)
MECHANIC #1: There goes my
baby.

STEVE: Here we go again. I knew
it, every time Ryder sells a used
truck this happens.
(SFX-SOBBING, BLOWING NOSE)

STEVE: Alright, there, there.

You didn't know Ryder sells
trucks? They do, they sell them.
Excuse me.
(SFX-SOBBING)

The same quality trucks they rent
and lease to businesses, they also
sell to businesses.

Makes these guys fall apart.

MECHANIC #2: We've been
caring for them since they were
new.

STEVE: See what I mean? They
look after these trucks like they
were their own.

MECHANIC #3: They've got their
whole lives ahead of them.

STEVE: You're going to be okay,
don't worry about it. Do you
believe these guys?

Ryder sells more kinds of used
trucks than anyone. Trucks, vans,
tractors, trailers.

Even specialized equipment.

Just call and they'll tell you where
to get 'em. They'll even--

MECHANIC #1: (VO) Steve, not
the book!
STEVE: Eh, I have to do this.

They'll even give you free advice
before you look. It's in here:
"How to Buy a Used Truck."

You gotta get this. It's the inside
story. What to look for, and
avoid. Whether you're buying
now or just kicking some tires.

Course, with a Ryder used truck
you know what you're getting
into.

See this tag, "Road Ready." It
means this truck has been
maintained at the highest
standards since it was new.

Ryder has the records to prove it.
And a limited warranty to back it.
Impressive stuff.

How ya doin'? (MUSIC UP-
SENTIMENTAL THEME)
MECHANIC #4: Great.

Exhibit 6–6 *(Continued).*

STEVE: These guys put their hearts into these trucks. They even fix things before they go wrong.

MECHANIC #4: Brakes. Steering. Engine.

STEVE: You'll love your Road Ready truck as much as they do.

MECHANIC #2: Oh please , I don't want to see you go.

STEVE: Only you'll get to keep yours. So call for the Ryder Road Ready Center near you. Ask about financing.

MECHANIC #1: (VO) Steve! STEVE: It's okay, relax.

MECHANIC #1: Don't give him the number, please.

Just call for the free book: "How to Buy a Used Truck."

Even if you're not buying now, you'll be an expert.

But you gotta call.

MECHANIC #4: Please take good care of them.

STEVE: Don't worry. They'll get more trucks. Sorry, I'm out of tissues.

It's a new jacket, get off me. I'm not kidding!

(SENTIMENTAL MUSIC UP AND OUT)

The Phenomenal Growth of Infomercials

The use of 60-second and 120-second TV commercials to sell tapes, CDs, and a wide assortment of merchandise has now been standard fare for a number of years. The "new kid on the block" within the last decade has been the infomercial. The kid, so to speak, is now a grown-up with impressive credentials. Larry Jaffee, reporting for *DM News* in September 1995, stated that approximately 2,200 people were at the National Infomercial Association conference in Las Vegas.

It is estimated that infomercials collectively generate more than $1 billion in sales and at least $500 million in media time expenditures on cable and broadcast television. NIMA stated that the number of *Fortune* 500 firms using infomercials as a direct marketing tool will nearly double over the next three years.

Bruce D. Goodman, writing in the September 18, 1995, issue of *DM News*, quotes Sam Catanese, president of Infomercial Monitoring Service, as stating, "There are infomercials running somewhere on broadcast television or on cable every hour of the day, 24 hours a day, seven days a week, nationally and internationally." Claire Kogler, president of the *Direct Response Television Monitoring Report*, believes there are 250–300 infomercials actively on the air at any one time.

With all the good things there are to report about infomercials, the other side of the coin is that selling or traffic building with infomercials as the medium is no sure thing: a gambling spirit with fairly deep pockets to match are required. The *DM News* articles on infomercials point out that creating and producing an infomercial today costs anywhere from $100,000 to $500,000. And testing costs to determine how well an infomercial will perform will run $30,000 to $40,000.

To test retail sales impact, the articles point out, your infomercial should run ten times a market per week for a minimum of four weeks so the before and after impact can be measured. Depending on the size of the market, the media cost can range from $5,000 to $50,000 per market per week. A typical retail sales test runs in two to four markets.

SELF-QUIZ

1. Which of these two TV audiences is highly defined?
   ☐ Broadcast TV   ☐ Cable TV

2. HBO is a premium subscription TV channel. It offers subscribers:

   a. Movies

b. _____

c. _____

3. Radio has two advantages over broadcast TV:

a. Program _____

b. Lower _____ for similar time periods

4. How might direct response advertisers benefit from videocassettes?

_____

_____

_____

_____

5. Define *gross rating points* (GRPs)

_____

_____

6. Define *reach* and *frequency*.

Reach: _____

_____

Frequency: _____

_____

7. Within what time frame can a direct response advertiser learn how well a commercial is doing?

☐   One week

☐   Two to three weeks

☐   A month

8. The dayparts of radio are:

a. Day

b. Early evening

c. Prime

d. _____

e. _____

9. If you use a toll-free number as part of your TV commercial, you should plan to have the telephone number on the screen for at least:

☐ 10 seconds   ☐ 25 seconds   ☐ 60 seconds

10. Name three types of radio program formats:

a. Country and western

b. _____

c. _____

PILOT PROJECT

Your assignment is to sell an album of rock music by a "hot" group for $19.95. The medium you are to use is radio. Prepare a 60-second commercial for a rock station.

CHAPTER SEVEN

Co-Ops

As advertising costs have continued to spiral over several decades, marketers have sought out ways to reduce their circulation costs. The co-op sharing advertising costs has proved to be one solution.

Package-goods firms, for the most part, disavow direct marketing as a part of their marketing mix. And yet a direct marketing vehicle—the cents-off coupon—is integral to most of their marketing programs. Cents-off coupons qualify as direct marketing because they meet the three requirements of a direct response proposition: (1) a definite offer (a discount on a specified product), (2) all the information necessary to make a decision, and (3) a response device (the coupon, when presented at the checkout counter). Promotions come and go, but cents-off coupons continue to grow. When consumers are asked why they redeem coupons, they give two major reasons:

1. Coupons inform consumers about old-line products and encourage them to try new products.

2. Coupons reduce the cost of the products consumers buy.

When asked for the reasons why package-goods firms use couponing, Donnelley Marketing, publishers of the Carol Wright co-op, gave these reasons:

• To generate short-term incremental volume

• To reward loyal users

• To counteract competitive-coupon pressure

• To support retail-merchandising events (synergy)

• To build the brand franchise base, attracting new users through the communication of added value

• To generate trial and optimize repeat for a new brand

• To build brand/corporate equity with the retailer/consumer

- To preempt competitive promotional, introductory activity by ''protecting'' current users.

Mass Market Penetration

The Carol Wright mail co-op is distributed to 30 million selected households ten times a year. Selections are made from a consumer database of 87 million identified households.

The program is so sophisticated that through targeting Donnelley can identify a competitive user and also one who buys more of a given product. Similarly, Donnelley can target by product categories such as, for example, household products, nonprescription remedies, beverages, personal care products, and pet products. Selectivity is further enhanced by demographic profiles. (See Exhibits 7–1 and 7–2.)

Redemption Rates

Exhibit 7–3 shows that redemption rates vary by category and by circulation vehicle. Mail distribution of cents-off coupons, although it is highly effective

Exhibit 7–1.   Carol Wright Co-op Demographic Profile (30 Million Households)

	Total U.S. Households	Total Co-op	Index	Younger Families	Index	Established Families	Index
Head of Household Education							
Not high school grad	24.1%	12.5%	52	10.5%	44	15.0%	62
High school grad	36.0	35.6	99	37.2	103	33.7	94
Some college/college grad	39.9	51.9	130	52.3	131	51.3	129
Marital Status							
Married	57.2	74.7	131	75.3	132	73.8	129
Children under Age 18							
None	62.6	40.7	65	32.0	51	52.1	83
1	15.0	21.0	140	20.6	137	21.5	143
2	14.2	25.0	176	30.2	213	18.2	128
3 or more	8.2	13.3	162	17.2	210	8.2	100
Average children	.7	1.2	171	1.4	200	.9	129
Presence of Children							
Children under 6	18.1	29.6	164	42.2	233	13.1	72
Children 6–11	18.3	31.7	173	39.2	214	21.9	120
Children 12–17	16.1	23.4	145	17.8	111	30.7	191

Source: Donnelley Marketing Inc.

Exhibit 7-2.   Carol Wright Co-op Demographic Profile (30 Million Households)

	Total U.S. Households	Total Co-op	Index	Younger Families	Index	Established Families	Index
Household Size							
1-2	56.4%	34.0%	60	29.6%	52	39.9%	71
3 or more	43.6	66.0	151	70.4	161	60.1	138
Average persons	2.6	3.2	123	3.4	131	3.0	115
Head of Household Age							
18-24	5.8	3.1	53	4.7	81	1.1	19
25-34	22.6	31.9	141	48.8	216	9.7	43
35-49	29.7	43.9	148	37.2	125	52.7	177
50-64	20.7	17.9	86	6.5	31	32.9	159
65 and over	21.2	3.2	15	2.8	13	3.6	17
Median age	44.1	38.0	86	33.4	76	45.6	103
Household Income							
$40,000 and over	31.2	48.1	154	44.4	142	52.9	170
$25,000-39,999	22.8	26.9	118	29.1	128	24.1	106
Under $25,000	46.0	25.0	54	26.5	58	23.0	50
Median income	$27,380	$38,919	142	$37,171	136	$41,858	153
Average income	$34,703	$45,643	132	$42,864	124	$49,278	142

Source: Donnelley Marketing Inc.

compared to freestanding inserts, magazines, and newspaper space, has by far the highest per-thousand circulation cost.

Traditional Co-ops

Most participants in Carol Wright co-ops are package-goods firms, but some direct marketers also include mail order offers in their co-ops. However, most

Exhibit 7-3.   Redemption Rates by Category and by Method Categories

Method	Refrigerated and Frozen	Dry Grocery and Beverage	Health and Beauty Aids	Household Products
Bounce-back	28.9%	23.6%	42.0%	36.8%
Direct mail	5.5	6.5	10.0	5.4
Freestanding insert	2.5	2.5	1.7	2.7
In-ad	0.8	4.0	0.7	1.1
In-pack	6.0	4.9	4.1	3.0
Instant redeemable	21.9	24.3	39.1	29.8
Magazine	0.9	0.6	0.3	1.1
Newspaper ROP	0.8	1.0	0.8	1.0
On-pack	5.5	6.4	4.9	6.8

direct marketers that use co-ops tend to use those that have a greater number of direct response offers. Types of direct response co-ops available break into the following categories:

1. **Mail order co-ops.** These are arranged by direct marketers that put their own co-ops together. They induce other direct marketers to join forces with them and make combined mailings to their buyer list. The income from other marketers naturally reduces mail circulation cost for the sponsor.

2. **In-house co-ops.** A variation of the commercial co-op is the in-house co-op. In this case the sponsor (marketer) co-ops only products or services that it sells. The advantage is that selling costs are spread over several offers, rather than applied to a single offer.

3. **Vertical co-ops.** Here we are talking about specific groups, such as business people, college students, new mothers, schoolteachers, accountants, lawyers, engineers, and so forth.

4. **Magazine co-ops.** Many magazines sponsor a co-op of their own, their circulation list serving as the channel of distribution. This service offers two major advantages to the sponsoring magazine: (1) a chance for additional revenue from regular magazine advertisers, and (2) an inducement to prospective advertisers to test the responsiveness of the magazine's market. (See Exhibit 7–4.)

Standard Rate & Data Service (SRDS) has an entire section devoted to co-op mailings in its periodic directory, *Direct Mail List Rates and Data*. The listings contain much valuable information.

Sales/Cost Ratios

Quoting averages is always dangerous, but as a rule of thumb response for individual pieces in a co-op is about one-fourth the response of a solo mailing. The cost, however, is similarly about one-fourth. Response rates do vary, of course. A 50 percent discount offer from *Time*—so well known that little explanation is necessary—is likely to pull much better than that for an unknown publication. Also, a new-product offer, because of restricted space in a co-op, is likely to pull far less than one-fourth of a solo mail effort.

Co-op Formats

Direct marketers have two basic formats available to them: postcard and ''loose'' inserts. (See Exhibit 7–5.) Most postcard publications carry three postcards to

Exhibit 7-4.   A Co-op Mailing

A store redemption coupon and a direct response offer among 43 inserts in a typical Carol Wright co-op.

the page, the reply card unit size measuring approximately 6" × 3⅝". An advertiser can purchase a single card or two or three adjacent cards. (See Exhibit 7-6.)

Sponsors determine the size and weight limitations for loose inserts. Typically, the weight limitation is one-quarter ounce, and the size limitation is 5" × 8". If the advertiser exceeds the weight limitation, it is usually subject to a surcharge.

Getting Co-ops Read

Participants in co-ops face fierce readership competition. You can greatly improve your chances for getting your piece read and acted on by knowing the behavior patterns of people who receive co-ops. Phil Dresden, an expert on co-oops, provides a valuable insight:

> I have witnessed a number of focus group research interview sessions through a one-way mirror. Different groups of housewives were brought in and handed co-op envelopes filled with coupons and offers. There was an amaz-

Exhibit 7–5.   Three Examples of Participants in *Advertising Age*'s Loose-Pack Postcard Deck

SUPER SALESMAN

Need a sales rep who's hard working, loyal, who never gets tired and always delivers your sales message just the way you intended it?

Panasonic's new CT-130V Monitor/VCR is all of these and more. It combines a compact VHS video recorder and big 13″ color monitor for **foolproof** delivery of your important sales presentations.

For details, send in this card or call Midwest Visual, Chicago's largest and most respected audio-visual dealer, at (312) 478-1250.

Authorized Dealer

Panasonic

Name _____   Title _____

Company _____   Phone _____

Address _____ City _____ State _____ Zip _____

WIN A VACATION FOR TWO IN SUNNY SOUTHERN CALIFORNIA!

Yes, I would like the opportunity to win a vacation for two, courtesy of Western Airlines and Disneyland Hotel. Please include my name in the June 14 drawing.

Name_____

Title_____

Company_____

Address_____

City_____ State_____ Zip_____

Daytime Telephone (_____)_____

Disneyland Hotel

OFFICIAL HOTEL OF THE MAGIC KINGDOM
A MOBIL ★★★★ AND AAA ★★★★ RESORT
ANAHEIM, CALIFORNIA 92802 • A WRATHER HOTEL

Western Airlines
Count on us

All entry forms must be received by June 10, 1985. Drawing will be held on June 14, 1985. Reservations for travel and lodging must be completed by December 31, 1985 and are subject to availability. Crain Communications employees, suppliers and their families ineligible to participate.

Steal this color copier.

Not a sale. Not a bargain. At 29% savings, it's a steal. For only $995 a brand new Savin 7010 gives you:

- One of the smallest personal copiers made.
- Two-sided copying.
- Book copying.
- Letter and legal size copies.
- Faithfully reproduces solids and halftones.
- Copies on label stock and transparencies.

- Fastest 1st copy speed in its class 10 seconds.
- 10 crisp copies per minute.
- Microprocessor controls.
- Fiber optics.
- 100 sheet paper tray.
- Short jamproof paper path.
- Reliability.
- Color copies.

Only $995

Was $1395 — you save $400.

FOR MORE INFORMATION CALL:
Jim Cook, Sales Manager   (312) 640-9595
Or return this card filled out.

savin

The Dependable Decision

NAME_____ TITLE_____

COMPANY _____

ADDRESS_____

CITY _____ STATE _____

ZIP _____ PHONE _____

*Price valid if purchased by phone or demonstrated at Savin sales offices.
Savin and Savin logotype are registered trademarks of Savin Corporation.
© Copyright 1983 Savin Corporation. Stamford, CT 06904

Exhibit 7–6.   Three Examples of Postcard Advertisers in
Physicians Market Place

ingly consistent behavior pattern. The participants, without exception, sorted each envelope's contents into two piles. Later when they were asked what was the basis for the two piles, they answered: "Interesting—not interesting; like—dislike; value—no value." Your offer must find its way to the right pile during that initial sorting.

The way to get into the first pile is to have a simple message clearly stated with effective graphics. The more alternatives you offer, the less your response will be. In a phrase, don't get sorted out; keep it simple. You only have a few seconds to make an impact. Inserts in direct mail co-ops are more like ads in a magazine than like regular direct mail. If the offer appears to be too much trouble, if it appears that the message is going to take some time and effort to get at, the housewife goes to the next offer.

Before you release your final mechanical to the printer, write two questions down on a piece of paper and see if you can answer them honestly: (1) Have you given the potential respondent an opportunity for dialog with you? (2) What precisely are you asking the potential respondent to believe and to do?

Generally, in co-op direct response advertising, the recipient sees little and remembers less. Any purchase is basically made on impulse, and response levels can be seriously impacted if the potential respondent does not act within a short time span. The products and services should fall into the pattern of something wanted or needed now.

Testing a Co-op

As Phil Dresden points out, testing co-ops is a tricky business. When you test an insert in a co-op, you are doing so with one group of partners; when you "roll out," you are likely to be participating with a different group of partners. So you must live with this variable. Here are a few simple rules for testing co-ops that are based on the Dresden experience:

1. Because testing is a trial for a subsequent major promotion, it is important to ensure that conditions for the major promotion will be as close to those of the original as possible.

2. Know what your break-even point is and test a sample large enough so your result can be acted on.

3. Test the co-op first and leave the segments for later unless your product clearly suggests a particular segment. For example, if your product is aimed entirely at a female market, test only the female portion of a co-op mailing.

4. Test a cross-section of the complete co-op list. If no "*n*th" sample is available, request distribution in several different markets—all widely dispersed.

5. Don't let too much time elapse between your test and your continuation, especially if the item you are testing is of a seasonal nature.

Package Inserts

The never-ending quest for reducing selling costs has led many major direct marketers to offer package insert programs to noncompeting advertisers. Jack Oldstein, president of Dependable Lists Inc., states:

> Package inserts offer immediacy, guaranteed mail-order buyers, with no waste circulation, the understood endorsement by the mailer of your product to his loyal customers, and the names used are fresher than the next update.

The late Virgil D. Angerman, formerly sales promotion manager of Boise Cascade Envelope Division, gave this sage advice about package insert programs:

> The planning of a package insert program is much like planning a direct mail campaign. The advertiser should evaluate the type of person who will receive the package insert. The advertiser should ask if he or she is the logical prospect for a particular merchandise or service. The questions should be raised, will the insert do a thorough selling job? Is the offer attractive? Have you made it easy to send an inquiry or order?

Just as with mailing lists, best results are realized when you match your offer to the market. If you are selling insurance to older people, using package inserts with vitamin shipments makes sense. If you are selling sports apparel, using package inserts with shipments going to fishermen and hunters makes sense, and so forth.

Professional mailing-list brokers will provide list cards of firms that accept package inserts just as they supply list cards of direct marketers that make their mailing list available for rental.

Co-op Enhancements

Although card packs dominate co-ops, the following case history details how co-ops can be enhanced. It introduces you to a variety of alternative media that can greatly expand your co-op program.

Hanover House

About ten years ago, WEB Specialties Inc., of Wheeling, Illinois, started working with Hanover House, of Hanover, Pennsylvania. Hanover had 21 catalogs at the time, each with a different name and each targeted to a different audience. It needed an alternative to the expensive, time-consuming, two-step catalog process.

The challenge was to develop a low-cost miniature, four-color catalog with a built-in envelope and coded order form that weighed less than one-third ounce. WEB met the challenge at the budgeted cost with a $3^3/_4'' \times 5^3/_4''$ catalog of 16 pages plus envelope and order form. The catalog was dubbed the "mini storybook." (See Exhibit 7–7.)

Featuring Hanover's best values and hottest-selling items at a variety of price points, the mini storybook was tested in 100 different package insert programs for a total cost of less than 10 cents each to create, print, insert, and deliver to a targeted audience of proven mail-order buyers.

The program was a big success. On average, across all programs, the profit from the sale of merchandise featured in all of the mini storybooks exceeded Hanover's total print and media costs. The company actually began to make a profit prospecting for new customers.

Hanover didn't stop with package inserts. Since it weighed only a half-ounce, the mini storybook could ride along with an order acknowledgment, an invoice, a statement, a dun notice, or other customer correspondence.

As for WEB Direct Marketing, with the success of Hanover under its belt, the firm decided, as the saying goes, "We're in business." It went on to develop a business plan that incorporated alternative media and product categories. The alternative media were the following:

—Card decks

—Cable billing statements

—Package inserts

—Co-op mailings

—Catalog bind-ins

—Magazine bind-ins

—Billing statements

—Self-mailers

—Take-ones

The prime product categories were as follows:

• Catalog firms

• Office suppliers

• Credit card companies

• Phone companies

Exhibit 7–7.   Mini Storybook Covers

Covers of two mini storybooks typical of those included in co-op programs.

- Encyclopedia companies

- Hotels and travel packages

- Hearing-aid firms

- Eye-care programs

- Book publishers

- Major service organizations

- Merchandise clubs

- Sales organizations seeking leads, both consumer and business-to-business

Card Deck Enhancement.   With its business plan in hand and a marketing plan to go with it, WEB's major target was card decks for, as partner Joe Kallick pointed out, circulation is huge. There are approximately 950 card decks with circulation in excess of 280 million.

The WEB strategy went beyond being included in a card deck. Instead, WEB told card deck publishers that it wanted to purchase the window position for its mini storybook clients. WEB was willing to pay a premium for this position. Kallick's position with the card deck publishers was that WEB's attractive four-color mini storybooks induce the recipient to open the deck and that other participants with one- and two-color cards benefit thereby. The publishers bought into that.

Cable Billing Statements.   In its Hanover House program, a second major target for WEB was cable companies. Cable companies combined mail over 50 million statements a month.

After analyzing the cable market and negotiating with cable system operators, WEB developed 574 market selections from a 19 million universe that they could target on a national, regional, or local basis. To further enhance response, WEB overlaid the markets with 29 demographic selections that included age, income, education, housing, and even a special affluence index.

Putting Together a Media Schedule.   How does a direct marketer match its profile against the total alternative media available? WEB recognized this problem at the outset and included profiling against media as part of its total service operation.

To illustrate the testing procedure for the mini storybooks, I asked WEB to prepare a test budget for a hypothetical credit card operation using four media alternatives: (1) cable billing statements, (2) card packs, (3) package inserts, and (4) catalog bind-ins. The test budget WEB provided is shown in Exhibit 7–8.

The recommendations are "turnkey in the mail" costs. They include media research, media recommendations, and placement, as well as complete print production, tracking codes, and shipping charges. There are no extras except for creative and film. A three-way perfect split for testing is available.

Exhibit 7–8.   Test Recommendations for Using a Mini Storybook in Alternative Media

Mini storybook in cable billing statements (Circulation 1,000,000 @ $115/M[a])	$115,000
Mini storybook in card packs (10 decks) (Circulation 1,000,000 @ $110/M)	110,000
Mini storybook in package inserts (20 programs) (Circulation 1,000,000 @ 120/M)	120,000
Catalog bind-ins (4 catalogs) (Circulation 1,000,000 @ $100/M)	100,000

[a] The per-thousand prices are based on a combined test circulation of 4 million.

Exhibit 7–9. Overview for Package Insert Media Recommendations: Small-Business Executives

Marketplace/Program Name	Annual Circulation (000)	Distributed
1. Drawing Board Business Enclosure Program	475	Monthly
2. Safeguard Business Systems PIP[a]	1,300	Monthly
3. Quill Office Supplies/Equipment PIP	2,600	Monthly
4. Reliable Office Supplies PIP	1,330	Monthly
5. Misco Computer Supplies PIP	130	Monthly
6. Newsweek Movers & Shakers PIP	300	Monthly
7. Tools for Business Success PIP	120	Monthly
8. Newbridge Communications Book Club PIP		
Executive program	215	Monthly
Small computer program	278	Monthly
9. Brooks Brothers PIP	273	Monthly
10. Joseph A. Bank Clothiers PIP	233	Monthly
11. Hanover & Bostonian Shoes PIP	167	Monthly
12. Professional Book Club PIP	600	Monthly
13. Rapidforms PIP	240	Monthly
14. Darby Group PIP	700	Monthly
15. 20th Century Plastics PIP	242	Monthly
16. Prentice-Hall Bus. Information & Prof. PIP	480	Monthly
17. Fordham Electronics Business Catalog PIP	122	Monthly
18. Histacount Corp. PIP	120	Monthly
Total Annual Circulation: 9,875,000		

[a] PIP (Package Insert Program)

To zero in on a specific category of the hypothetical credit card company—small-business package insert programs—I asked for insert recommendations. Exhibit 7–9 lists 18 recommendations.

Co-ops are a major tool for direct response advertisers when used correctly. They are not suitable for selling a $400 camera, but they are excellent for getting inquiries about a $400 camera. Co-ops are highly preferred for in-store coupon redemptions and for scores of direct response offers requiring a minimum of information for a targeted audience.

SELF-QUIZ

1. Why do cents-off coupons qualify as direct marketing?

2. Heavy users of cents-off coupons skew toward families with:

☐ Annual income under $10,000

☐ Annual income over $25,000

3. Which is the largest distribution channel for cents-off coupons?

☐ Newspapers   ☐ Magazines   ☐ Direct mail

4. Which medium shows the highest average redemption rate?

☐ Newspapers   ☐ Magazines   ☐ Direct mail

5. Name four types of traditional co-ops.

a. _____

b. _____

c. _____

d. _____

6. A co-op is likely to pull about one-fourth the response of a solo mailing at about _____ the cost.

7. What is the difference between ''loose'' insert co-ops and postcard co-ops?

_____

_____

_____

8. Describe how homemakers tend to sort out the contents of co-op envelopes.

_____

_____

_____

_____

9. What is the one variable you must live with in scheduling the continuation of a co-op you tested previously?

_____

_____

10. Name five advantages of package inserts.

a. _____

b. _____

c. _____

d. _____

e. _____

11. Name two advantages of mini storybooks.

   a. _____

   b. _____

PILOT PROJECT

You have beome promotion director of the *Advertising Age* postcard program, which is distributed several times a year to its 70,000+ subscribers.

As a prelude to developing your promotion program, it is your assignment to develop a list of prospects whose propositions you believe will appeal to advertising agency personnel, marketing executives, advertising managers, advertising research executives, and graphic arts personnel.

Break your prospect categories into two segments: primary and secondary. Expand the list for each to twelve, using the first three as starting points.

Primary

1. Advertising and marketing books
2. Premiums
3. TV production
4. _____
5. _____
6. _____
7. _____
8. _____
9. _____
10. _____
11. _____
12. _____

Secondary

1. Investment opportunities
2. Office forms
3. Office equipment
4. _____
5. _____
6. _____
7. _____
8. _____
9. _____
10. _____
11. _____
12. _____

CHAPTER EIGHT

Telemarketing

Telemarketing is as much an advertising medium for direct response advertisers as print, broadcast, or direct mail. Telemarketing is particularly powerful when it is integral to other media. The toll-free number in a direct response commercial, a direct response ad, or a direct mail package becomes a major force in overcoming human inertia.

The power of telemarketing begets a responsibility to use the medium with discretion. Intrusive, high-pressure telephone calls at times inconvenient for the consumer are most often counterproductive. Telemarketing is most effective when helpful dialogs are maintained with existing customers and qualified prospects.

Although favorable impact on sales is a given for both consumer marketers and business-to-business marketers, little is known about the major criteria that influence consumers favorably toward proactive telemarketing.

A Landmark Study: The Wyman Survey

The first formal research on the attributes that influence consumers' acceptance of telemarketing when marketers take the initiative (proactive telemarketing) was conducted in 1989 by John Wyman, a former vice-president of AT&T.

Methodology

A structured telephone interview was used to obtain information from a statistically valid, nationwide, random sample of 1,000 consumers who have phones. The sample was obtained from the M/A/R/C Inc. Telno telephone database.

Much of the material in this chapter was previously published in Bob Stone's *Successful Telemarketing*, 2d ed. (Lincolnwood, Ill.: NTC Business Books, 1992).

The database is designed to ensure that virtually all operating phones, listed and unlisted, have an opportunity to be in the sample. The design of the size of this sample enabled inferences to be drawn with a high degree of confidence.

Results

In the survey the consumers were first asked about their expectations with using the phone for information or for purchasing products and services. They were then asked about toll-free 800 service (reactive telemarketing), and finally about receiving proactive telemarketing sales calls.

Telephone Experience.   The consumer reported positive experiences in utilizing the phone. Fifty-four percent believed the phone is good for obtaining information or purchasing a product or service. Sixty percent indicated they had made purchases using the phone, and, of those, 74 percent were satisfied with phone shopping.

Reactive Telemarketing.   The consumers also had had very positive experiences with using a toll-free 800 number. Eighty-three percent of the consumers had used an 800 number. Eighty-nine percent of the consumers who had used an 800 number reported they were satisfied with the experience.

Proactive Telemarketing.   Consumers were then asked three questions about their reaction to receiving a proactive telemarketing sales call. An acceptance index (dependent variable) was developed by combining the consumers' answers to the following three questions:

1. How would you rate your acceptance of telephone sales calls made by telephone salespeople who give you information or offer you a wide range of products or services?

2. How likely is it that the information you receive from a telephone sales call will be useful?

3. How likely is it that you would purchase the product or service being offered by a telephone sales call?

While the consumers were clearly not as receptive to receiving proactive telemarketing calls as they were to making reactive telemarketing calls, an initial acceptance rate of 13 percent was noted.

Calling Attributes.   The consumers were then asked to rate the importance of six calling attributes and the likelihood that the six calling attributes existed on telemarketing sales calls that they had received. (See Exhibit 8–1.) The six calling attributes were originally identified by a focus group of telemarketing experts and further defined through a pilot research study. The consumers found all six calling attributes to be important, and there was a reasonable likelihood that the six calling attributes had existed on telemarketing sales calls that they had received.

On a scale of one to six, with six being very important, the consumers rated the mean of all six attributes at 4.9. On the same scale, with six being very likely to occur, the mean score was 3.6.

The consumers were told to assume that all six calling attributes were present on the telephone sales call they received. They were then asked the same three questions that comprised the original acceptance index. With these six calling attributes present, 34 percent of the consumers shifted from nonacceptance to acceptance. This resulted in a total acceptance of 47 percent.

It is interesting to note that the most important calling attribute is that the salesperson is professional and courteous. It is also rated as the most likely to occur. A person calling, rather than a computer, is second in importance; even with the perception of the increase in electronic calling, the consumers felt a person calling would be highly likely to occur. It was somewhat surprising to see that the consumers' previous positive experience with the company was least important, and having an interest in the product or service was next to last in importance.

Differences between Acceptors and Nonacceptors of Proactive Telemarketing. The consumers were then divided into two groups: acceptors and nonacceptors (acceptors include both initial acceptors and those who shifted

Exhibit 8–1.　Telephone Sales Call Attributes

Calling Attributes	Importance		Likelihood	
	Mean	Standard Deviation	Mean	Standard Deviation
The salesperson is professional and courteous.	5.254	1.409	4.680	1.308
The person calls at a convenient time.	4.892	1.644	3.260	1.677
The company calling has a good reputation.	5.011	1.569	3.680	1.585
You have an interest in the product.	4.679	1.760	2.794	1.595
You have had a good previous experience with the company.	4.537	1.801	2.833	1.719
A person calls rather than a computer.	5.133	1.598	4.307	1.617
All six attributes.	4.918		3.592	

to acceptance with the presence of the six calling attributes). The study then determined the differences between the two groups based on the consumers' response to questions in the three categories of previous telemarketing experience, calling attributes, and demographics.

The consumers were asked questions related to 24 independent variables. Nine of these were in reference to telemarketing experience, 6 to calling attributes, and 10 to demographics.

Telemarketing Experience.   The consumers were asked if they had ever used the phone to make a purchase. Sixty-five percent of the acceptors had used the phone to make a purchase, compared to 56 percent of the nonacceptors. Those who had made purchases were asked about their satisfaction level when purchasing by phone. The satisfaction level was not significantly different between the acceptors and the nonacceptors.

Consumers were then asked about their experience with using an 800 number. Having previously used an 800 number did not make a difference between the acceptors and the nonacceptors. Since 83 percent of all the consumers had used an 800 number, it would be difficult for this variable to discriminate between the two groups.

Consumers were then asked about their satisfaction with using an 800 number. While 89 percent of the consumers who had used an 800 number reported they were satisfied with the experience, satisfaction with using 800 numbers was not significant in determining acceptance of proactive telemarketing. The mean score on satisfaction was 5.22 for the acceptors and 5.17 for the nonacceptors, compared to a maximum score of 6. Both groups were very satisfied with using an 800 number.

They were next asked about the number of 800 calls they had made in the preceding three months. The mean number of calls for the preceding three months was 3.62 for the acceptors and 2.91 for the nonacceptors. The means of the two groups are not significantly different. (See Exhibit 8–2.) It is concluded that there is no significant difference between acceptance groups based on positive experiences with the use of an 800 number.

The consumers were next asked about their experiences with proactive telemarketing sales calls. The acceptance of proactive telemarketing was significantly lower for consumers who had recently received a large number of telephone

Exhibit 8–2.   Phone Calls Made by Respondents to Toll-Free Numbers in the Preceding Three Months

Number of Calls	Acceptors	Nonacceptors
0	29.3%	35.9%
1–3	40.1	42.6
4 or more	30.6	21.5

sales calls. The mean number of calls received by acceptors during the preceding three months was 4.89, while the nonacceptors had a mean of 8.14. (See Exhibit 8–3.) The difference between the two means is statistically significant. Sixty percent of the acceptors reported receiving three or fewer calls in the preceding three months, compared to 48 percent of the nonacceptors.

It should be noted that the number of calls reported as received by the consumers could involve both an estimation on their part and a perception. There may be a possible correlation between the consumers' attitude about acceptance and their perception of the number of calls received.

The consumers were also asked to state the number of purchases made from proactive telemarketing calls received within the preceding three months. Fifteen percent of all respondents said they had made a purchase from a call received. The acceptor group reported 23 percent had made purchases in the preceding three months, compared to 8 percent for the nonacceptors. This difference is statistically significant; however, even the percentage of sales to nonacceptors is a relatively successful rate.

Telemarketing Calling Attributes.   There was a significant difference between the acceptors and the nonacceptors in terms of their view of the importance of the calling attributes and the likelihood that the attributes would exist in the telephone sales calls they received. The acceptors found attributes to be very important, with a mean score of 5.3 compared to the nonacceptors' mean score of 4.6. The acceptors also viewed the likelihood of these attributes existing on calls they received to be relatively high, with a mean of 4.0; the nonacceptors had a mean of 3.2.

Demographics.   Age plays an important role in understanding the difference between acceptors and nonacceptors of proactive telemarketing. A regression analysis found this variable to be the most significant. In the acceptance group, 21 percent of the respondents were between the ages of 18 and 24, as compared to 10 percent in the nonacceptance group. There is relatively no difference between ages 25 and 44. At age 45 and beyond, 42 percent are nonacceptors, while the acceptors' category is only 30 percent. At age 55 and beyond, 26 percent are nonacceptors, compared to 16 percent for acceptors. There is clearly

Exhibit 8–3.   Proactive Telemarketing Phone Calls Received by Respondents in the Preceding Three Months

Number of Calls	Acceptors	Nonacceptors
Fewer than 3	59.8%	47.7%
4–9	23.0	25.2
10 or more	17.2	27.1

a greater acceptance of proactive telemarketing by consumers who are younger. (See Exhibit 8–4.)

Education is also an important factor in determining acceptance of proactive telemarketing. Forty-six percent of the acceptors had a high school education or less, while only 29 percent of the nonacceptors were in this category. At the higher end of the education spectrum, 37 percent of the nonacceptors had a college degree or above, while only 21 percent of the acceptors were at that education level. The acceptors of proactive telemarketing are definitely less educated than the nonacceptors. (See Exhibit 8–5.)

Total family income is another significant factor in the acceptance of proactive telemarketing. Twenty-six percent of the acceptors have an income of $15,000 or less, while only 15 percent of the nonacceptors are in that income range. The higher-income range of $35,000 a year or above accounts for 44 percent of the nonacceptors and only 26 percent of the acceptors. Acceptors of proactive telemarketing have significantly lower incomes. (See Exhibit 8–6.)

There are important differences between acceptors and nonacceptors based on their demographics—in particular, age, education, and family income.

Listening to the Sales Message.   In another effort to determine how strongly consumers felt about receiving a proactive telemarketing call, they were asked "How likely is it that you would hang up or terminate the telephone sales call before the caller was finished?" An extremely high number of consumers, 60 percent initially and 65 percent after the calling attributes were introduced,

Exhibit 8–4.   Ages of Consumers

Age (in Years)	Acceptors	Nonacceptors
18–24	20.70%	9.52%
25–34	27.89	26.79
35–44	21.57	22.82
45–54	13.94	15.08
55–64	8.06	13.49
65 and over	7.84	12.30

Exhibit 8–5.   Education of Consumers

Education	Acceptors	Nonacceptors
High school or less	46.09%	29.05%
Some college (business or technical)	32.61	33.99
College graduate	15.00	23.12
Postgraduate	6.30	13.83

Exhibit 8–6.   Family Income of Consumers

Income	Acceptors	Nonacceptors
Under $10,000	11.86%	7.43%
$10,000–14,999	14.53	7.43
$15,000–24,999	25.92	19.31
$25,000–34,999	21.79	21.77
$35,000–49,999	12.83	22.03
$50,000–74,999	8.23	15.84
$75,000 or more	4.84	6.19

reported they would not hang up or terminate a sales call before the caller was finished. One may assume that a large number of people considered hanging up or terminating a call to be impolite. It also demonstrates that a high percentage of people, for whatever reason, are willing to listen to the telemarketing sales message.

Calling at a Convenient Time of Day.   It had been shown previously that making a telephone sales call to a consumer at a convenient time was an important attribute. The consumers also provided the day of week and time of day that each considered to be the most convenient for them, as displayed in Exhibit 8–7.

It is interesting to note the wide distribution of the consumers' preference for receiving a telephone sales call. In particular, only 23 percent of the consumers preferred to receive their call on weekday evenings, while it is estimated that approximately 80 percent of all proactive telemarketing calls to consumers occur on weekday evenings. Because the consumers also stated that calling at a convenient time was an important attribute, there is considerable opportunity to better adapt calling programs to a time preferred by consumers.

Ten demographic variables were analyzed for consumers in each of the nine time-of-day and day-of-week cells to provide insight about the people in each cell. Some general conclusions can be drawn from the results of this analysis. The consumer groups that prefer receiving phone calls on weekday mornings and afternoons are older, include more females, tend not to be employed outside of the home, include retired and unemployed people, and have a slightly lower

Exhibit 8–7.   Most Convenient Time of Day and Day of Week to Receive a Telephone Sales Call

	Weekdays	Saturday	Sunday
Morning	22.2%	10.4%	2.9%
Afternoon	19.5	9.8	3.5
Evening	23.2	3.5	5.0

level of education and total family income. The people who prefer to receive their phone calls on weekday evenings or on Saturdays and Sundays have a higher total family income, are employed outside of the home, and have a somewhat higher level of education.

The other demographic variables had relatively the same mean scores across each cell. This information should be useful in developing telemarketing programs that try to contact consumers at a time they find more convenient.

The findings of the Wyman study can be invaluable in catering to consumer preferences, but it should be noted that a similar study for the business-to-business field would undoubtedly produce findings that would be significantly different.

The Spectrum of Telemarketing Applications

One way to explore telemarketing opportunities is to look at a telemarketing sales continuum as a means of identifying applications. (See Exhibit 8–8.)

Order taking usually begins with a catalog or other promotion mailed to potential customers. The prospect is encouraged to use the convenience of calling an 800 number to place an order. It is estimated that mature catalog operations like Spiegel receive more than 75 percent of their orders via an 800 number. Additionally, an order-taking operation offers the possibility of upgrading by

Exhibit 8–8.   Telemarketing Sales Continuum

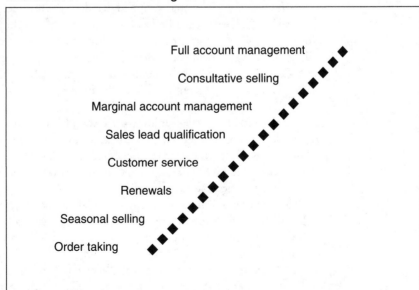

including limited cross-selling, new-product couponing, and even simple marketing research.

Seasonal selling is another telemarketing application. The Swim Shop—a company in Nashville, Tennessee, that supplies gear to summer swim teams—offers an example of how to extend a limited sales season. The peak swimming season lasts about 12 weeks—too brief for the shop to rely on traditional methods to fill orders. Therefore, the Swim Shop made available an 800 number so orders could be received and filled promptly late in the season. Avoiding the mail stretched out the firm's sales season.

Renewals are another widely used aspect of telemarketing. These applications are now an integral part of a magazine's circulation subscription program. One phone call can produce what it might take several subscription renewal letters to accomplish. The technique has been used successfully also for selling other products: fruit, cheese, and even plants.

As a major user of telemarketing for policy renewals, one insurance company's "conservation program" saves about $20,000 per month by using telemarketing to conserve policies about to lapse.

Customer service, another area for improved effectiveness and cost control, is the next step up the telemarketing continuum. Using a unique system, the 3M Company offers an 800 number to assist its telecommunication equipment customers. The 3M National Service Center, located in St. Paul, Minnesota, is staffed 365 days a year, 24 hours a day, with skilled technicians and coordinators. Through systematic questioning and a variety of facsimile, ASCII communication terminals, store-and-forward electronic message distribution terminals, the latest electronic monitoring and testing equipment, and a sophisticated on-line computer system, the staff can pinpoint the failure as an equipment problem or operator error.

Sales lead qualification is designed to reduce the number of wasted in-person sales visits. The better qualified a prospect is, the greater the sales call's potential for success. When a prospect is prequalified by phone, telemarketing helps to direct outside salespeople to where the highest sales potential exists.

Marginal account management allows a marketer to capitalize on the revenue potential of smaller accounts without the high cost burden of face-to-face sales visits. Banding together marginal accounts spread over a wide geographic area permits profitable coverage at low cost. To handle such targeted accounts profitably, Hallmark Cards Inc., the social-expression company, uses telemarketing. Hallmark uses a combination of direct mail and telemarketing to give its remote outlets the same highly personal, current card selection as any large urban card shop or department store.

Consultative selling is a highly personal, involved sales technique. With telemarketing, a customer's needs are probed by a specially trained sales representative. Personalized solutions are designed during the telephone contact, when possible.

Full account management is at the very zenith of the marketing spectrum. It involves order taking, answering questions about order status, inventory availability, shipment scheduling and billing, credit checking, and product consultation. This full-service operation includes both selling and customer service.

Telemarketing in the Advertising Mix

Direct Mail

Telemarketers learned early on that if you give direct mail recipients the choice of either making a toll-free call or returning a reply card, total response is usually increased. AT&T has found, as have many others, that those who inquire by phone are more likely to order. Exhibit 8–9 is a good example of how long-distance services emphasize their toll-free number in both their letter and reply card. The bottom line is that those who respond by phone prequalify themselves as better prospects. Closure rates are often four to six times greater than mail response.

Of all the advertising applications of the 800 number, none has proved more successful than toll-free phone order privileges for catalog buyers. Catalog director after catalog director reports the average phone order to be 20 percent greater than the average mail order. Thus, if a catalog firm gets an average of $70 by mail, it can expect an average phone order of $84.

The reason for the larger order is easy to explain. A woman ordering a dress by phone, for example, puts the telephone communicator into a natural consultative selling situation. Consider this dialogue:

> Fine, Mrs. Smith. You want Size 18 in the royal blue. Have you considered the scarf on page 32, item number 1628? This would really look beautiful with the royal blue. . . . Good, I'll include it with your order. Shipment will go out via UPS tonight. Thank you.

Print Advertising

It is common today to see in newspapers and magazines ads that feature either a local number or an 800 number to get information or to place an order. Indeed, the 800 number has changed the way many marketers do business. To illustrate the power of integrating the 800 number into print advertising, let us look at two unique examples.

It's not unusual for consumers to order merchandise by phone in the $10–100 range. But it's most unusual for consumers to order gold or silver by phone in units of $1,500, $2,500, $5,000, $10,000, and more. And yet they do—in the aggregate of millions of dollars. By phone! Exhibit 8–10 is typical of the sort of advertisement that Monex International has run consistently in the *Wall Street Journal* and other publications appealing to the serious investor. What is so unique about Monex's use of print and phone is that major purchases of precious metals are consummated entirely by phone.

Exhibit 8–9. A Letter from AT&T with a Reply Card

AT&T

2301 Main Street • P.O. Box 549 • Kansas City, Missouri 64141 • 1 800 821-2121, ext. 626

Dear Executive,

We are pleased to be able to present our special AT&T long distance services in one comprehensive "Business Services Guide."

This gives you the opportunity to review just what the new AT&T is offering. From AT&T Long Distance Service to AT&T Data Services, we bring you the best telecommunications network anywhere.

Our services are designed to help your business grow, and grow with your business, no matter how small or large your company is.

And along with the thorough outline of our services in your enclosed Business Services Guide, we're also offering a free consultation with a professional Consultant, to help you choose the AT&T long distance services that are right for you.

> Simply call us toll-free at 1 800 821-2121, ext. 626 to speak
> to an AT&T Network Consultant.

Our Consultants have worked with businesses of all sizes across the country, so we can help you decide which services make sense for your company. And your Consultant will offer personalized service and advice to help your business use them to cut costs, increase your sales, and help your business grow faster. He or she can even coordinate implementation of the services for you.

So take some time to read through your Business Services Guide. And be sure to contact your Network Consultant at our toll-free number, or mail the enclosed postpaid card, to put these services to work for your business.

Sincerely,

Judy DeVooght

Judy DeVooght
Manager, Network Consultants

FIND OUT HOW YOUR BUSINESS CAN CUT COSTS AND IMPROVE PROFITABILITY WITH AT&T LONG DISTANCE SERVICES

CALL TOLL-FREE

1 800 821-2121, ext. 626
OR MAIL THIS POSTPAID CARD

YES! Please tell me more about
AT&T long distance services.

Please fill in Phone Number _____
(Area Code)

If address is incorrect, fill out information below

Name Title _____
Company _____
Address _____
City _____ State _____ Zip _____

33U-073

Exhibit 8–10.   Monex International Advertisement

The second example of a unique application of print and phone involves what is commonly referred to as "dealer-locator advertising." Consider the problem a major marketer with hundreds or thousands of dealers faces when a very special service is offered only through a select number of its dealers. Telemarketing turns out to be the ideal solution. The Chevron ad in Exhibit 8–11 is a classic example of the solution. Note how Chevron makes it easy for

Exhibit 8–11.   Chevron Dealer-Locator Ad

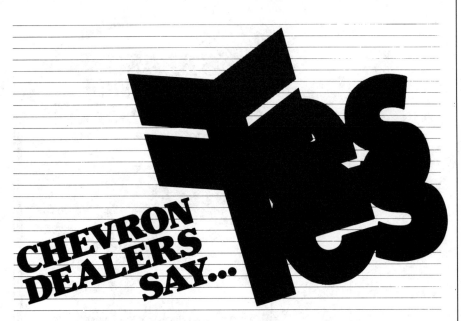

6-Point Car Service Warranty Protection

While many gas stations are saying no to choices and services, Chevron Dealers say Yes. Yes to a *6-point warranty protection plan* on many car care services at Chevron Hallmark Award Stations.

1. **90 DAYS or 4,000 MILES GUARANTEED**
Whichever comes first. Warranty covers all parts and labor.

2. **PROBLEM SOLVED OR MONEY REFUNDED**
If a problem occurs, either the work will be done over at no cost to you, or the entire cost will be refunded, at the dealer's option.

3. **ADVANCE WRITTEN ESTIMATES**
You'll know the cost before work begins. If additional repairs are needed, your approval will be obtained first.

4. **RETURN OF REPLACED PARTS**
At your request, all replaced parts will be returned for your inspection.

5. **HONORED AT HALLMARK AWARD STATIONS WITH REPAIR FACILITIES**
If a problem occurs, take your car back to the station where the service was performed. If you're more than 50 miles from that station, your warranty will be honored by any Hallmark Award Dealer who performs that type of service.

6. **ON-THE-ROAD HOTLINE**
There are over 1000 Hallmark Award Dealers with service facilities in the U.S. You can call toll-free **(800) 227-1677** for the nearest station which will honor your warranty.
You'll find that all Chevron Hallmark Award Dealers—including those who do not offer car care service—maintain the highest standards of customer service. For the nearest Chevron Hallmark Award Station call:

(800) 227-1677

Complete Details of Warranty available at your Chevron Hallmark Award Station

the consumer to learn the name and address of the nearest dealer offering "6-Point Car Service Warranty Protection." More and more national advertisers are offering a dealer-locator service by providing a toll-free number in their print advertising. It's faster and more cost-efficient.

TV Advertising

There are few direct response TV commercials these days that do not include an 800 number. The 800 number makes instant response a reality. We have already discussed the impact of the telephone on TV's home-shopping shows. Millions of dollars in merchandise are being sold via TV with the phone as the catalyst.

The Mathematics of Telemarketing

The power of telemarketing is beyond question. Its place in the totality of direct marketing is firmly established. But the mathematics of telemarketing is not clearly understood by many. For starters, we face up to the fact that the telephone is the most expensive advertising medium on a per-thousand basis after face-to-face selling. So telemarketing has to be very cost-effective to be successful. And for thousands of marketers, it is. To obtain the numbers, we went to Rudy Oetting, senior partner of Oetting & Company, an international marketing consulting firm located in New York City.

Inbound/Outbound Costs

Two sets of numbers are key to estimating telemarketing costs: (1) cost per call for handling *inbound* calls from business firms and consumers, and (2) cost per decision-maker contact in making *outbound* calls to business firms and consumers. Exhibit 8–12 provides the range of costs for each.

The difference in cost range between inbound and outbound calls should be explained. In the case of inbound calls, the initiator is always a prospect or customer: the caller phones at a time of his or her convenience with a view of

Exhibit 8–12. Per-Call Costs for Inbound and Outbound Calls

Category	Range of Cost
Inbound	
Business	$2.50–7.00
Consumer	1.50–3.00
Outbound	**Range of Cost**
Business	$6.00–16.00
Consumer	1.15–4.00

getting further information or negotiating an order. In the case of outbound calls, the initiator is always the marketer. The call might be made at an inconvenient time for the prospect, and the caller might have to generate awareness about a new product or service. Consequently, outbound calls are usually of longer duration and often require more experienced, higher-paid personnel.

The range of costs, whether for inbound or outbound, depends a great deal on the telemarketing application and the complexity involved for each application. Exhibit 8–13 indicates where ranges of costs are most likely to fall, on average, by application.

Developing Worksheets

Knowing the average range of costs for inbound and outbound calls is key, but it is just a start. The operation of an in-house telemarketing center requires a full range of personnel. Also, it is subject to taxes, fringe benefit costs, incentive costs, equipment costs, and collateral materials costs. To get a true picture of all monthly costs, worksheets are advised.

Oetting has provided us with two representative worksheets (Exhibits 8–14 and 8–15), one for inbound and one for outbound. It is important to note that the term *phone hour* means workstation time, *not* connect time.

It is easy to see how worksheets lead to capturing all the numbers. The key numbers to explore are (1) cost per phone hour, (2) cost per call, and (3) cost per order (or response). A review of the computations for Exhibit 8–14 (inbound) shows a significant difference in cost, for example, when phone representatives are able to handle 15 incoming calls per phone hour as contrasted to 12 calls per phone hour. And the cost per order drops dramatically if the representative is able to close six orders per phone hour, for example, as contrasted to one order per phone hour.

Exhibit 8–13.   Range of Costs by Application[a]

Application	Low Range	Mid Range	High Range
Order processing	X		
Order increase		X	
Customer service		X	
Sales support		X	
Account management			X
Sales			X
Sales promotion	X		

[a] More and more companies are beginning to realize that through the strategy of "customer education and awareness" (helping customers buy), carefully trained and coached inbound representatives using the proper tools and materials can convert sales inquiries to orders and increase the average revenue of an order. There have been recorded differences of as much as $900 per hour between high-end and low-end representatives in the same group, at the same basic cost.

Exhibit 8-14.   Monthly Expense Statement—Inbound: 9 a.m. to 5 p.m.

Direct Expenses	Cost	Cost/Phone Hour
Labor		
Manager (⅓ time)[a]	$ 1,250	$ 1.01
Supervisor (full time)[b]	2,750	2.23
Representatives[c] (10 @ 123.5 hours/month)[d]	16,000	12.96
Administrator (full time)[e]	1,213	0.98
Incentives (reps only)	2,000	1.62
Tax and benefits[f]	7,730	6.25
Subtotal	$30,943	$25.05
Phone		
Equipment and service[g]	$ 1,146	$ 0.93
WATS line[h]	7,770	6.29
MTS (Message Toll Service) line	—	—
Subtotal	$ 8,916	$ 7.22
Automation		
Depreciation[i]	$ 2,500	$ 2.02
Maintenance[j]	750	0.61
Subtotal	$ 3,250	$ 2.63
Other		
Lists	—	—
Mail/catalogs (F/S & result of requests)	$ 2,470	$ 2.00
Postage	1,235	1.00
Miscellaneous	1,000	.81
Subtotal	$ 4,705	$ 3.81
Total direct expenses	$47,814	$38.72
G&A (15%)	7,172	5.81
Total	$54,986	$44.53

[a] $45,000/year × ⅓ allocation = $1,250/month
[b] $33,000/year × full allocation = $2,750/month
[c] $9.23/hour × 40 hours/week × 52 weeks ÷ 12 months = $1,600/month
[d] 6.5 phone hours/day × 19 days/month = 123.5 phone hours/month
[e] ($7.00/hour × 40 hours/week × 52 weeks) ÷ 12 months = $1,213/month
[f] 33.3% of wages (including contest incentives)
[g] $50,000 depreciated over 5 years + $3,750 annual maintenance
[h] Average 40 min. (60%) per labor hour. WATS connect time: 40 min. ×
  $0.15/min. avg. cost + access charges for 10 lines
[i] $6,000 per workstation for 15 stations (additional for growth)
  depreciated over 3 years
[j] 10% of total purchase cost

Note: The average number of calls handled per rep phone hour is 12 @ 3.1 min.
each (as high as 15 per phone hour during peaks).

- 12 calls/hour = $3.71/call
- 15 calls/hour = $2.97/call
- 1 order/rep phone hour = $44.52/order
- 6 orders/rep phone hour = $7.42/order

Exhibit 8–15.   Monthly Expense Statement—Outbound: 9 a.m. to 5 p.m.

Direct Expense	Cost	Cost/Phone Hour
Labor		
Manager (⅓ time)[a]	$ 1,500	$ 1.21
Supervisor (full time)[b]	3,000	2.43
Representatives[c] (10 @ 123.5 hours/month)[d]	18,000	14.57
Administrators (2 full time)[e]	2,426	1.96
Commissions[f]	12,529	10.14
Tax and benefits[g]	12,473	10.10
Subtotal	$49,928	$40.41
Phone		
Equipment and service	$ 350	$ .28
WATS line[h]	4,991	4.04
MTS (Message Toll Service) line[i]	1,112	.90
Subtotal	$ 6,103	$ 4.94
Automation		
Depreciation[j]	$ 3,542	$ 2.87
Maintenance[k]	1,063	.86
Subtotal	$ 4,605	$ 3.73
Other		
Lists	$ 3,088	2.50
Mail/catalogs	617	$ .50
Postage	358	.29
Miscellaneous	1,235	1.00
Subtotal	$ 5,298	$ 4.29
Total expenses	$65,934	$53.39
G&A (15%)	9,890	8.00
Total	$75,824	$61.39

[a] $54,000/year × ⅓ allocation = $1,500/month
[b] $36,000/year × full allocation = $3,000/month
[c] ($10.38/hour × 40 hours/week × 52 weeks) ÷ 12 months = $1,799/month
[d] 6.5 phone hours/day × 19 days/month = 123.5 phone hours/month
[e] ($7.00/hour × 40 hours/week × 52 weeks) ÷ 12 months = $1,213/month
[f] Reps, 40% of total remuneration; supervisor, 15% of total remuneration
[g] 33.3% of wages
[h] 25 min. per labor hour. WATS connect time: 25 min. × $9.15/min. + access charges for 10 lines
[i] 5 min. per labor hour. Connect time: 5 min. × $0.18/min.
[j] $8,500 per workstation for 15 stations (additional for growth) depreciated over 3 years
[k] 10% of total purchase cost

- 12 (TDs)/hour = $5.12/dial
- 15 (TDs)/hour = $4.09/dial
- 5 (DMCs)/hour = $12.28/DMC
- 6 (DMCs)/hour = $10.23/DMC
- 1 order/rep phone hour = $61.39/order
- 2 orders/rep phone hour = $30.67/order

In Exhibit 8–15 (outbound), similar significant differences are to be noted in costs at different levels relating to total dialings per phone hour, total decision-maker contacts per phone hour, and total orders per phone hour. Such computations provide a realistic approach to determining break-even point.

These two worksheets relate to the sale of products or services, but the same type of arithmetic can help predict likely costs for literature requests, product information, customer service calls, sales support, full account management, or sales promotion. The calls handled or made per phone hour might vary by application, but the principles are the same.

Call Ratios Favor Telemarketing

When comparing outbound sales calls to field sales calls, the pure ratios favor telemarketing. On the average, a field salesperson can make five to six calls a day (25–30 a week). On the average, a telemarketing salesperson can make 25–30 decision-maker contacts a day (125–150 a week). Therefore, to achieve the same contact level, on average five field salespersons would have to be added for every telemarketing salesperson.

The Training Process for Telemarketing

For those who opt for an in-house marketing operation, it must be emphasized that there is far more involved than putting a successful salesperson on the phone. As a matter of fact, more often than not, the worst thing one can do is put a successful staff salesperson into a telemarketing center. A field salesperson thrives on face-to-face interaction and resists being desk-bound.

To establish the traits of a successful telemarketing person and to learn what is involved in the ongoing training process, we went to the AT&T training center in Cincinnati, Ohio. We are indebted to Nancy Lamberton, staff manager, for sharing her experience with us.

Traits of a Telemarketing Person

Our first question to Lamberton was: "When recruiting, what traits do you look for?" She listed five traits:

1. Good communication skills, articulate, with a voice quality that is clear and pleasant

2. Persistence and ability to bounce back from rejection

3. Good organization skills

4. Ability to project phone personality—enthusiasm, friendliness

5. Flexibility, ability to adapt to different types of clients and new situations

AT&T uses a 90-minute assessment process for potential applicants for telemarketing sales positions. Applicants are put in several sales situations to determine whether they have the dimensions the firm is looking for.

Training for New Hires

AT&T's training program for newly hired personnel covers a period of 18½ days, broken down as follows:

1. **Orientation (4 days):** Salesperson learns overall structure and goals of AT&T Communications as well as general business functions.

2. **Network services (2½ days):** Salesperson receives basic knowledge of AT&T Communications products and services. This is what the salesperson will be selling. This course is delivered via computer-based education.

3. **Selling skills (3½ days):** Salesperson learns sales skills through the interactive video disc, then goes through four hours of role-playing with an instructor.

4. **Telemarketing (2 days):** Salesperson learns how to identify client's needs and telemarketing applications. Through casework, the salesperson practices implementing an application for a client.

5. **Account management (3 days):** Each salesperson has 400 accounts, which means prioritizing accounts by revenue potential, cycling accounts, and time management are critical.

6. **Advanced account management (3½ days):** After 3–8 months of experience, the salesperson gets advanced training on how to manage the highest-potential accounts.

The Seven-Step Selling Process

Students are schooled thoroughly in a seven-step selling process, a process developed over time, which leads the salesperson in logical steps from precall planning to the close and wrap-up. The following outline details these steps.

1. Precall planning
   a. Reviewing client information
   b. Planning objective for the call
   c. Psyching—getting mentally ready for the call

2. Approach/Positioning
   a. Identifying who you are and where you're from
   b. Stating purpose of the call
   c. Making interest-creating statement
   d. Building rapport

   e. Getting the decision maker
   f. Getting through the receptionist/screener

3. Data gathering
   a. Gaining general understanding of the client's business
   b. Moving from general to specific types of questions
   c. Questioning techniques
   d. Identifying a client's business need

4. Solution generation
   a. Tailoring communication solution to specific client need
   b. Asking in-depth questions to test the feasibility of the solution
   c. Gathering data for cost/benefit analysis
   d. Preparing client for the recommendation

5. Solution presentation
   a. Getting client agreement to area of need
   b. Presenting recommendation in a clear and concise manner
   c. Explaining benefits of use

6. Close
   a. Timing—when to close
   b. Buying signals
   c. Handling objections
   d. Closing techniques

7. Wrap-up
   a. Implementation issues
   b. Thanking client for the business
   c. Confirming client commitment
   d. Leaving name and number
   e. Positioning next call

Applying the Selling Process.   Now let us see how this selling process might be applied outside the field of communications. For our example, we'll create a wholesaler specializing in veterinary drugs. The purpose of the call is to introduce a new drug to a regular customer.

1. Precall planning. The telemarketer reviews the account file of the Whiteside Veterinary Clinic. He notes that Dr. Sargent ordered her usual drug supplies last month, but that she hasn't tried a new drug that L.L.M. Pharmaceutical has recently introduced via direct mail. The telemarketer reviews his introduction briefly, takes a deep breath and says "Smile!"

2. Approach/positioning. "Hello. This is Mark Wiley with L.L.M. Pharmaceutical. Dr. Sargent is usually available about this time. May I speak with her?

"Good morning Dr. Sargent. This is Mark Wiley with L.L.M. How have things been going at your clinic since I last talked to you? (*Pause*) I'm certainly glad to hear that! Dr. Sargent, as a buyer of many of our quality products, I knew you'd be interested in hearing about one of our innovative new drugs. If you have a minute, I'd like to ask you a couple of questions. . . ."

3. Data gathering. "Doctor, your practice pretty much covers a suburban area, doesn't it?"

   "Right now, when a dog is suffering from hookworm, what drug are you prescribing?"

4. Solution generation. "Many vets also used to prescribe that particular drug. Have you had many dogs suffering from various side effects from that drug?"

   "Would you be interested in prescribing a new drug that has few, if any, side effects?"

5. Solution presentation. "L.L.M. has introduced Formula XYZ that not only has fewer side effects, but also extensive laboratory tests have shown that the medicine takes effect 24 hours sooner than similar drugs."

6. Close. "I'm sure that your customers would appreciate faster relief for their pets. Can I add a case of Formula XYZ to your regular order?"

7. Wrap-up. "I'm sure that you will be pleased with the results, Dr. Sargent. We've gotten excellent comments back from many vets around the country. I'll get that shipment to you by early next week. Thank you for your business. I'll be calling you again the first of next month. Have a good day!"

Role Playing: A Key Teaching Device

Lamberton continued to share her telemarketing-training experience at AT&T by pointing out that one effective way to teach proper telemarketing procedures is to get students involved in role playing. Role playing is an excellent way to acclimate the student to the job. By putting students in different selling situations, the learning curve is accelerated. Students make their first mistakes with the instructor rather than the prospect.

Examples.   AT&T's instructors put students through role-playing situations and then evaluate their performance. Following are examples of a phone dialog, followed by evaluations. (These are abbreviated versions for demonstration purposes.) First we consider a poor example, Heritage Village Furniture:

Sue: Hello. May I speak to Steve Rooney?

Steve: This is he.

Sue: Oh, this is Steve? Well, Steve, this is Sue Jones, your new account executive. I'd like to talk to you about your phone services. Do you have a minute?

Steve: I didn't catch what company you're with. . . .

Sue: Oh, gosh, I'm sorry . . . I'm with AT&T.

Steve: Well, I'm pretty busy today. . . .

Sue: That's okay, I won't take much of your time. Can I just ask a few questions about your business?

Steve: If it only takes a minute. . . .

Sue: So, are you a furniture retail store?

Steve: No, actually we manufacture furniture.

Sue: Do you then sell it to retail furniture stores?

Steve: Yes, we do.

Sue: What is your sales volume a year?

Steve: I don't see what business that is of yours. Anyhow, why are you asking me all these questions? What has it got to do with my phone service?

Sue: Well, it helps me better understand your company so I can show you how to use telemarketing.

Steve: I'm not interested in telemarketing. You can't sell furniture over the phone.

Sue: A lot of companies are doing it.

Steve: Well, not my company! Maybe you should call me back when you can tell me how to save on my phone bill. I'm really quite busy. . . .

Sue: Can I call you tomorrow, Mr. Rooney?

Steve: Why don't you just send something in the mail? That would be quicker.

Sue: Oh, okay. I'll do that today. Thanks for your time, Mr. Rooney.

The evaluation of this dialogue is given in Exhibit 8–16. Let's consider the same selling opportunity, but with a good example of how it might be handled:

Sue: Hello. This is Sue Jones with AT&T Communications. May I speak to Steve Rooney?

Steve: This is he.

Sue: Oh, good. How are you doing today, Mr. Rooney?

Exhibit 8–16.   Role-Playing Evaluation (Poor Example)

ACCOUNT EXECUTIVE
TELEMARKETING SELLING SKILLS
Evaluation Sheets

ROLE PLAY/SKILL PRACTICE

Trainee: _Sue Jones_   Date: _6/14_

Which call (1st, 2nd, etc.) _2nd_   Case–Company name: _Heritage Village_

Instructor/Evaluator: _M. Saunderson_

Skill	ST	SAT	NI	NO	COMMENTS
APPROACH POSITIONING					
Managed screener: polite, persistent, used as a resource				✓	Sue obviously didn't have a plan going into this call. She confused the client by not explaining who she represented and the purpose of the call. She also didn't get the client's attention.
Completed positioning statement: who, where from, why calling			✓		
Made interest-creating opening statement			✓		
Asked for appropriate contact (if no name given prior to call)		✓			The poor introduction set the tone of the entire call – Sue never recovered.
Explained consultative role			✓		
Used listening skills		✓			
DATA GATHERING					
Made appropriate transition from AP		✓			Sue assumed Heritage was a retail store, which brought a negative response from the client. (a series of close-ended questions then followed. Sue needs to ask more open-ended questions to get the client involved in the conversation.
Verified existing LD services				✓	
Asked about immediate concerns			✓		
Learned about business operations			✓		
Structured questioning strategy			✓		

Performance rating: ST – Strong; SAT – Satisfactory; NI – Needs improvement; NO – Not observed.

Exhibit 8–16 *(Continued).*

Skill / Performance rating	ST	SAT	NI	NO	COMMENTS
Used open/closed questions appropriately			✓		*Her strategy was poor. Before she got the client comfortable, Sue asked about sales volume. At this point, the client's frustration with the call came out.*
Questions appeared directed toward objective(s)			✓		
Attempted to build credibility				✓	
Maintained conversational tone		✓			
Maintained control of dialogue			✓		
Demonstrated listening skills: –Probed and clarified –Paid attention to client –Followed client leads –Used silence –Demonstrated empathy –Tied together ideas			✓		
SOLUTION GENERATION/DEVELOPMENT					
Identified relevant/appropriate applications					
Collected appropriate specific data					
Dropped interest-creating hints					
Tailored application(s) to business operations & expressed needs					
SOLUTION PRESENTATION					
Reviewed & got agreement on client's objectives & concerns					
Tailored solution to client					
Focused on relevant benefits					
Demonstrated cost-effectiveness					
Anticipated impact of solution on client's business					

Exhibit 8–16 *(Continued).*

Skill	Performance rating				COMMENTS
	ST	SAT	NI	NO	
Made an organized presentation				✓	Sue tried to overcome the objection by talking about telemarketing. Many clients have preconceived notions about telemarketing. Don't throw the term around—show the client how it can benefit him!
Created interest and continuity in pres'n				✓	
Handled resistance & objections			✓		
Responded to buying signals				✓	
THE CLOSE					
Timed the close right				✓	Sue let the client off the hook, which was probably a good choice considering how the call was going.
Used appropriate technique(s)				✓	
Handled objections successfully				✓	
Gave client time to respond to close				✓	
Got clear commitment/Got an order				✓	
Wrapped up call: -Summarized call -Reinforced close -Arranged for next call -Clarified what client would do -Clarified what AE would do		✓			
FOLLOW-UP (if appropriate)					
Inquired about progress of implementation				✓	
Responded to client concerns				✓	

Steve: Well, actually I'm pretty busy today. . . .

Sue: I understand that you're a busy person, Mr. Rooney, but if I can show you how to get the most out of your communication dollars, would you have a few minutes to discuss some ideas?

Steve: Well, I guess I do have a couple of minutes, but what can AT&T do for me?

Sue: As your account executive, I will be working with you to show you how AT&T long-distance services can be a valuable part of Heritage's profit picture. To see exactly how I can be of service to you, it would be helpful if I understood your business better. Tell me a little about Heritage Village Furniture, if you would. . . .

Steve: We're a manufacturer of traditional home furnishings.

Sue: Whom do you sell to, Mr. Rooney?

Steve: Various retail outlets such as local furniture stores. A lot of it is custom work, special orders.

Sue: Where are these outlets located?

Steve: Mostly in the eastern part of the country.

Sue: That's a large area. How do you reach all of your customers?

Steve: We have a sales force that visits the stores to keep our name in front of them. The salespeople show new samples of fabrics and promote sales we have going. The most important thing is that the furniture retailer remember our name when his customer walks in the door.

Sue: Is that because you have a lot of competition?

Steve: You bet. I mean there are all sorts of furniture manufacturers. A lot of them with their own stores. We have to rely on the independent furniture store to sell our line.

Sue: Let's go back to your sales process. How do you get your orders?

Steve: Well, since most of the work is custom and we can never predict when an order will come in, most of the orders are mailed to us by the retailer. We have a form in the back of our sample book.

Sue: How long does it take to get that order in from the time it's mailed?

Steve: Oh, probably four days.

Sue: And how long does it take you to get the piece of furniture delivered to the customer once you've gotten the order?

Steve: Anywhere from six to eight weeks . . . depends if we have all the materials in stock.

Sue: I remember when I ordered a chair recently, that sure seemed like a long time. Would you be interested in cutting down that delivery time?

Steve: Well, sure, but it takes that long to make the furniture—that can't be cut down.

Sue: Oh, I understand, Mr. Rooney. But perhaps we could cut down the time it takes you to get the order from the retailer. Would you be interested if I could show you a way to shorten those four days to just a few minutes to get that valuable order?

Steve: What do you have in mind?

Sue: Instead of using the mail for your orders, you could use a toll-free number for your retailers to call in their orders. Not only would you receive the order immediately, but you could also check on inventory while the retailer was on the line. If you were out of a fabric, say, the retailer could consult his customer to see what they wanted to do. This would save additional time and perhaps even the sale. Don't you think a toll-free number would give you a competitive edge?

Steve: Well, I don't know of anyone else doing that. But what kind of costs are we talking about?

Sue: I think you'll be surprised to see how inexpensive it is to provide this service to your customers. Our 800 toll-free number actually costs less than a regular long-distance phone call. So for a couple of dollars for the phone call, you'll be making a sale worth hundreds of dollars, plus improving your long-term relationship with the retailers. Can I place that order for you today?

Steve: How can I say no? Let's give it a try.

Sue: I'm sure you'll see immediate results. I'll give you a call in a few days to set the installation date. I really appreciate your business, Mr. Rooney, I look forward to working with you on this and perhaps other ideas.

Steve: Sounds good. Be talking to you soon.

Sue: Thanks again, Mr. Rooney. Goodbye.

Exhibit 8–17 presents a positive evaluation of this dialog.

Summary

When integrated into the total marketing process, telemarketing can increase sales efficiency and profits by (1) qualifying leads, (2) increasing response from catalogs, direct mail, print, and broadcast advertising, and (3) maintaining contact with direct marketers' most priceless asset—their customer base.

Exhibit 8–17. Role-Playing Evaluation (Good Example)

ROLE PLAY/SKILL PRACTICE

ACCOUNT EXECUTIVE
TELEMARKETING SELLING SKILLS
Evaluation Sheets

Trainee: _Sue Jones_

Which call (1st, 2nd, etc.) _2nd_

Date: _6/16/84_

Case—Company name: _Heritage Village_

Instructor/Evaluator: _D. Pemberton_

Skill	Performance rating				Comments
	ST	SAT	NI	NO	
APPROACH POSITIONING					Sue got the decision-maker to talk to her by showing some empathy and creating some interest. This was very effective without being too pushy.
Managed screener: polite, persistent, used as a resource				✓	
Completed positioning statement: who, where from, why calling		✓			
Made interest-creating opening statement	✓				
Asked for appropriate contact (if no name given prior to call)		✓			
Explained consultative role	✓				
Used listening skills	✓				
DATA GATHERING					Sue twice her questions off the client's remarks, although she still kept the focus on her objectives. Some more in-depth questions may have been helpful, but Sue identified a business need.
Made appropriate transition from AP		✓			
Verified existing LD services				✓	
Asked about immediate concerns		✓			
Learned about business operations	✓				
Structured questioning strategy	✓				

Performance rating ST – Strong; SAT – Satisfactory; NI – Needs Improvement; NO – Not observed.

Exhibit 8–17 *(Continued).*

Skill	Performance rating ST	SAT	NI	NO	COMMENTS
Made an organized presentation	✓				
Created interest and continuity in pres'n	✓				
Handled resistance & objections		✓			
Responded to buying signals		✓			
THE CLOSE					
Timed the close right	✓				
Used appropriate technique(s)	✓				
Handled objections successfully		✓			Good timing and aggressiveness. Client's tone indicated that he was interested, but was worried about cost. Sue overcame the cost issue, and went for the close. Very effective!
Gave client time to respond to close		✓			
Got clear commitment/Got an order	✓				
Wrapped up call:					
-Summarized call					
-Reinforced close					
-Arranged for next call		✓			
-Clarified what client would do					
-Clarified what AE would do					
FOLLOW-UP (if appropriate)					
Inquired about progress of implementation				✓	
Responded to client concerns				✓	

Exhibit 8–17 *(Continued).*

Skill	Performance rating ST	SAT	NI	NO	COMMENTS
Used open/closed questions appropriately		✓			
Questions appeared directed toward objective(s)	✓				
Attempted to build credibility		✓			
Maintained conversational tone	✓				
Maintained control of dialogue		✓			
Demonstrated listening skills: -Probed and clarified -Paid attention to client -Followed client leads -Used silence -Demonstrated empathy -Tied together ideas	✓				*Overall, Sue did a good job. A few specific facts I like the value of a sale — would have helped build even a stronger case.*
SOLUTION GENERATION/DEVELOPMENT					
Identified relevant/appropriate applications	✓				
Collected appropriate specific data		✓			
Dropped interest-creating hints		✓			
Tailored application(s) to business operations & expressed needs		✓			
SOLUTION PRESENTATION					
Reviewed & got agreement on client's objectives & concerns	✓				*Sue used specific benefits to sell the client on the solution. Although she didn't use specific cost figures, her point was well made to the client.*
Tailored solution to client		✓			
Focused on relevant benefits	✓				
Demonstrated cost-effectiveness		✓			
Anticipated impact of solution on client's business				✓	

SELF-QUIZ

1. In the Wyman study of consumer attitudes about telemarketing, consumers were asked to rate six calling attributes:
   a. The salesperson is professional and courteous.
   b. The person calls at a convenient time.
   c. The company calling has a good reputation.
   d. You have an interest in the product.
   e. You have had a good previous experience with the company.
   f. A person calls rather than a computer.

   Of these attributes, which did consumers rate highest?

   _____

2. The Wyman survey results disclosed that age is an important factor in being receptive to proactive telemarketing. Which of these groups was more receptive?   ☐ 18–24   ☐ 25–34

3. The time of day is a factor in response to proactive calls. Which period is better when making weekday calls?   ☐ Morning   ☐ Afternoon   ☐ Evening

4. There are eight major applications of telemarketing. Complete this list:

   a. Order taking   e. _____

   b. Seasonal selling   f. _____

   c. Renewals   g. _____

   d. Customer service   h. _____

5. People who inquire by phone are:
   ☐ More likely to order   ☐ Less likely to order

6. What is the function of dealer-locator advertising?

   _____

   _____

   _____

7. Why are outbound calls more expensive than inbound calls?

   _____

   _____

8. On the average, a field salesperson can make _____ to _____ sales calls a day; a telemarketing salesperson can make _____ to _____ calls a day.

9. Field salespeople are most likely to succeed at telemarketing.

    ☐ True   ☐ False

10. Name two desirable skills of a successful telephone communicator.

    a. _____

    _____

    b. _____

    _____

11. Complete this list of seven steps involved in the telemarketing selling process.

    a. Precall planning   e. _____

    b. Approach positioning   f. _____

    c. Data gathering   g. _____

    d. Solution generation

PILOT PROJECT

You are the marketing director of an envelope company. You have a customer base of 100,000 small-business firms, all secured by direct mail. You have decided to test the efficiency of telemarketing.

Your assignment is to develop a telemarketing test plan. In developing this plan, please answer the following questions:

1. What data, or measures, will you use to estimate when inventories might be depleted for each customer?

2. What information might you request from each customer in the process of making your calls?

3. What special offers might you make in an effort to get repeat business by phone?

Strategies and Objectives

CHAPTER NINE

Strategic Business Planning

With the new professionalism that has come to direct marketing, the need for strategic business planning has emerged. Major traditional marketers that have established direct marketing units as separate profit centers have insisted on strategic business planning for these centers just as they do for their traditional operations. But strategic business planning is quite foreign to those who have built businesses based solely on direct marketing methods. Yet the rewards that can come from strategic business planning can be as great proportionately for the entrepreneur as for the giant corporation.

When facing the reality that large- and medium-size companies have been the stimulus for recent growth, it behooves today's direct marketers to take heed of the signals and make sure that their approaches are as contemporary as their potential targets. Because accountability is one of the key elements in direct marketing programs, it is necessary for us to ensure that we remain on track with our own marketing plans, that we are up to date with the emerging technologies, and, finally, that we optimize our own organization's resources.

Strategic Business Planning Defined

First of all, let's define our terms. *Strategic business planning* is a formal method of considering alternatives related to the growth, development, or other options of an enterprise, organization, or business. It has application for large and small companies in direct marketing, ranging from fund raising to lead generation to product sales. When properly developed, a strategic business plan should provide the following elements:

- A comprehensive review of the current business

- A description of the problems and opportunities that must be dealt with in the short term

- Clear direction

- A practical action plan

A strategic business plan is *not* a marketing plan. It is much broader in scope, but it does address marketing issues related to a business or company. A well-designed plan will permit much greater control over one's business, enabling the individual to deal with critical situations in a proactive rather than a reactive manner.

Direct marketers have countered the strategic planning issue with a number of comments, such as:

- "It's expensive and time-consuming."

- "My plan is based on past experience and current expectations."

- "We don't have the availability of talent in our organization to make planning work."

These comments seem valid, especially for smaller firms. Many are hard pressed to look further ahead than three months at a time. However, when the following questions are asked, companies of all sizes are likely to agree on the impact:

- Has your company felt the impact of new or revised federal regulations over the past few years?

- Is the current economic environment having an impact on profitability?

- Are sales increasing at the rate you forecasted?

- Are you comfortable with your organization's ability to adapt to change?

These questions, and many more like them, apply to virtually every business endeavor. Managing these responses and affiliated actions are the key to success in direct marketing today.

How to Develop a Plan

After disposing of the questions about what strategic business planning entails and how it applies to direct marketers, the next step is to develop a plan and determine what should be included. Let's agree on one more fact.

There are countless methods used for developing strategic business plans. They range from the efforts of a single, specially trained planning executive to extensive committee approaches. The range of the information developed is equally broad. A plan in some industries might dictate a company's action for a ten-year period, whereas in other cases it could suggest specific actions for a twelve-month period. Depending on the purpose and expectations, any approach can benefit an organization.

There does not seem to be any evidence that better results are achieved through any one methodology. However, for direct marketers, a simple, practical approach will yield the most actionable information. Further, while it would be nice to be able to project, with infinite wisdom, what will happen to our industry and organization or company over the next five years, it is next to impossible. Just review recent growth, technological change, and new applications of direct marketing, and you will understand the difficulty of accurate long-term planning. Also, the array of information to be included in a strategic business plan should be subject to the criterion of what is absolutely necessary, rather than what you would like to include. The simpler the plan and the process for developing it, the higher the likelihood of success.

To provide a clearer understanding of a business plan, look at the planning model in Exhibit 9–1. It has proved successful with a number of direct marketing operations. Initial examination of the model suggests a planning time span of three years. However, the meat of the plan is in the annual action plan that covers a twelve-month time frame. As stated, a twelve-month planning horizon seems to provide more than enough opportunity to manage change. Let's examine each of the components of the model in detail.

Exhibit 9–1.   A Model for Strategic Business Planning

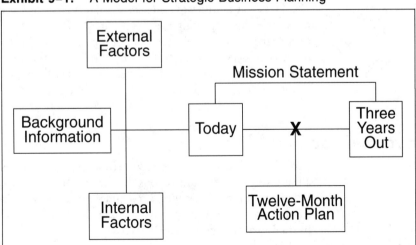

Background Information

In order to develop a strategic business plan, it is necessary to carefully and thoroughly investigate the company's performance. In effect, you are trying to take a "snapshot" of activities covering the current situation and extending back two or three years. As this is done, you can separate data into two categories: (1) financial and marketing/sales and (2) organizational data.

In the first case, you are looking for the following types of information:

- Growth

- Market share

- Expenditures in specific categories

- Seasonality of sales

- Profit levels

- Product/service line

- Financial resources

- Allocation of resources

- How you rate against your competition

In the second case, you must review how the organization and staff conduct the business. You must determine how the organization works rather than how it looks on the formal organization chart. You must get a "fix" on the company's personality.

For example, is the good work being accomplished on a daily basis spread evenly across the staff, or is it really accomplished by a core of dedicated people? Or, do the key employees understand what the business is trying to accomplish, rather than just reporting the "party line"? This case is every bit as important as knowing the financial operations of the business. However, it is the one most often overlooked in business planning. After collecting the raw data on business, marketing, and organizational issues, we are ready to proceed to the next step in the model.

External Factors

Simply stated, external factors, sometimes referred to as *exogenous factors*, are all of those activities and actions that have an impact on your business but are out of your immediate control. You might quickly say, "If we cannot exert any control over these factors, why include them at all?" The answer to this is twofold: positioning and contingency.

Examples of external factors are:

- Current economy

- Federal regulation

- Competition

- Availability of resources

- Postal rates

- Technology

If we examine one external factor—the current economy—you will get a clearer understanding of why it is important to determine what these factors are and how they impact your business. We certainly cannot control the current economy. However, consider for a moment some of the actions we might take to optimize our position:

- Better manage cash flow

- Reduce inventory

- Tighten receivables

By taking one or more of these actions, we can reduce some of the impact of this external factor on our business.

In the development of a list of external factors, two considerations are important. First, limit the list to the most important factors—ten or fewer for many companies. There is nothing more frustrating or less rewarding than considering all of the perils outside of your control and never getting to the major issues that affect your firm directly. Also, as you discuss and decide on each major external factor, be specific in defining what impact it has on your business. If this is impossible, discard the factor. After looking outside your company or business and sifting through the relevant information, it is time to move to the next phase of plan development.

Internal Factors

Internal factors are those you have control and influence over. Such factors are probably best described as the strengths and weaknesses of your company. These strengths and weaknesses are often referred to as the "building block" of a sound strategic business plan. Experience has indicated it is easier and more productive to start with the positive aspects—the strengths. Basically, strengths include those activities that you consistently complete extremely well—the things that give you an edge on your competition. They can include but are not limited to the following:

- Technology
- Product
- Marketing
- Process
- Service

- Systems
- People
- Organization
- Attitude

- Flexibility
- Management
- Communication
- Leadership

For example, in direct marketing, a company might refer to its preeminence in product development, production innovations, back-end service and performance, and so forth. All of these are significant attributes and must be defined. This will allow for leveraging real strengths against stated goals. One note of caution: Make sure your description of a strength is accurate. Often the definition of these considerations is completed cavalierly, and the strength turns out to be of less value than previously reported.

The next move in the development of internal factors is defining weaknesses. Actually, this is the toughest part in developing a strategic business plan. However, this part of the inspection will yield the greatest return. It is difficult to elaborate on the shortfalls of a business. In this case, we are often getting at subpar performance levels. How many executives really want to define what's wrong with the operation, the staff, or even their direction of them? Weaknesses can be described as what a company does poorly and can include the following:

- Technology
- Product
- Marketing
- Process
- Service

- Systems
- People
- Organization
- Attitude

- Flexibility
- Management
- Communication
- Leadership

A comprehensive review of internal factors will provide an accurate picture of the company as it is today. More often than not, when completed objectively, it is quite revealing. In content alone, it can include a number of documents and summary sheets. Gathering the data is only one step. The next is to condense those data into an accurate, readable document. And this brings us to the next component of the planning model.

Mission Statement

The mission statement is a condensation of what the company is today and what we want (expect) it to be tomorrow. Let's separate the mission statement into those parts and describe each individually.

Mission Statement—Today.   The purpose of this statement is to accurately define in business shorthand the position of the company as it now exists. It is derived from the microscopic review discussed earlier. It usually is restructured in length to one or two typed pages. If it is honest, it will probably sound somewhat pessimistic. But that's acceptable, for more often than not, where the company is today is not where it wants to be tomorrow.

Let's take a look at a mission statement. After considerable discussion, one direct marketing company, which for the sake of this discussion we'll call Leisure Time Activities, developed this statement of where it is today:

Leisure Time Activities Today

Today we are an established mail order company operating in the United States and Canada with a preeminent niche in the leisure activities market. In 1995, we had sales of $17 million and an embarrassing shortfall of $1.5 million in profits. Our recent growth has been sluggish and has not met our expectations. We have limited information on the market, but we do know we have a dominant share of the hobby segment. We have not extended this strength into the larger market of sporting goods.

The competition is intensifying, especially for sporting goods. Major companies have an edge, and they are expanding the market. This is all taking place in a market where there is little current product innovation. We feel technological change is coming, but we don't know when. As a company, we have moved from a leadership position to a company that follows.

Although we have good products and a good customer base, we have become complacent. We have not leveraged our small size and financial strength to the best advantage. Our marketing approach is lackluster. We have experienced a breakdown in leadership, management, and communications. This has confused our direction and has had a negative impact on company spirit and teamwork. As a result, we have had a breakdown in company performance in several areas.

Although we perceive our company and organization to be in a growth mode, we have not taken effective actions to make it happen. We have discussed an appetite for change and have developed a consensus on the major issues that must be resolved.

In summary, we are at a turning point. We must leverage our good name and products that have enabled us to become a major force in this industry, develop innovative marketing plans, and move in one direction, collectively.

Mission Statement—Tomorrow.   The purpose of this statement is to define reasonable goals to be achieved within a specific period. The length of time to cover for this type of statement varies. A three-year period for goal setting is often an agreeable compromise. Where does Leisure Time Activities see itself in three years?

Leisure Time Activities Three Years Out

By the end of 1999, we will be recognized as an aggressive, multiline direct marketing company. We will have demonstrated state-of-the-art marketing programs, a collective winning attitude, and financial results in line with written plans. We will have a sales volume of $20 million with a minimum of 25 percent ROI. And we will generate a profit on sales of 10 percent.

Our growth will be carefully planned. We will have expanded our capabilities and increased our share of the sporting goods market. Our product lines will include, but not be limited to, equipment and supplies, clothing, and related gift items, and will tend to have more proprietary products.

Our management has become a cohesive team which is directing a qualified, experienced, and motivated staff. This collective effort has provided a competitive edge and the flexibility to use our strengths in the best possible way.

Our financial performance has enabled the company to easily secure capital for further investment opportunities.

In summary, we have turned Leisure Time Activities around. This has been recognized by our stockholders, our employees, and the industry. We have replaced our former complacency with a demonstrated winning attitude.

If you manage to plan correctly, you will revisit these goals on an annual basis to make sure you remain on track and that changing conditions are updated. Remember, a plan is not a document that is put on the shelf and dusted off each December. In developing this section of the mission statement, you might wish to include the following:

- Sales/income
- Markets
- Technology

- Organization/size
- New products
- Position in market

The checklist in Exhibit 9–2 is provided to assist in structuring your mission statement.

You are now at a critical point in the planning model. The next step is to deal with the "gaps" in the mission statement, the differences between your strengths/weaknesses now and your expected position in three years.

Action Plans

The fundamental output from any good strategic business plan is the identification of those actions or activities that must be accomplished in order to reach

Exhibit 9–2. Mission Statement

General Information	Today	Three Years Out
Volume		
Profit		
Growth		
Market position		
External Factors		
Competition		
Industry factors		
Geography		
Internal Factors		
Strengths		
Weaknesses		
Product		
Summary		

your intended position. These actions or activities spring forth from your examination of internal and external factors and are summarized in the today section of the mission statement.

The question is, how do you prepare an action plan that guarantees progress toward your stated goals? There may be several ways to develop this kind of plan. However, there are a few fundamentals to success:

- Top management endorsement

- Clearly stated tasks

- Complete understanding by those who must implement the plan

- Realistic and attainable actions

If the above criteria can be met, the likelihood of success is greatly increased. Now, let's move on to the development of an action plan. An action plan defines the "must-do" tasks for completion, usually over a twelve-month period. These are the problems or opportunities that must be handled in order to achieve planning goals. They must be specific and precisely worded to ensure that those responsible for achievement have a clear understanding of the tasks to be accomplished. Participants must know *what* is to be accomplished, *how* it will be accomplished, *by whom*, and *within what time frame*. Anything short of these conditions will negatively impact performance against the plan.

There are some guidelines for developing objectives and strategies that detail the action plan. Let's start by clearly defining these terms:

- **Objective:** A statement that accurately describes what is to be accomplished over the next twelve months. In almost all cases, it is a must-do task.

- **Strategies:** A list of methods, events, and the like that describe how an objective will be achieved. Completed strategies always list who is responsible, for what, and when.

To simplify the discussion, let's divide it into two parts: how to develop good objectives, and how to develop effective strategies.

Developing Good Objectives

The first step in moving toward the development of action plan objectives is to review any notes taken during the strengths and weaknesses identification. Determine the problems (not the symptoms) and then review the problems and define them as clearly as possible. It is necessary at this stage to move from the general to the specific. It is easier to reduce a general concept by listing all situations or actions relating to the problem prior to specifically pinpointing it. Perhaps the following example will make this clear.

Example 1.   Let's take a look at the Leisure Time Activities company again. In the general area, one of the problems is the need to increase profits. If we dig deeper, we can expand this problem to include the following:

1. We need a 10 percent profit on all sales made in 1997–1998.

2. We must improve our marketing approach.

3. We must regain our leadership position.

4. We lack specific controls: financial, purchasing, inventory, marketing programs.

5. We need to develop systems to accurately project our financial future.

6. We need a minimum of 25 percent ROI.

All of the above statements are valid, but they do not relate directly to the same specific problem: No. 1 gets at the heart of the problem—how much and when. It further describes the scope of what is to be done. The others, 2–6, could either be strategies (how to do it) or be related to another problem. It is necessary to use this process for all problem areas so that accurate descriptions of the problems are developed.

The next step is to take the refined list for each problem and write an objective. As this is done, consider whether the problem or task is realistic and achievable. If you should feel that nothing can practically be done in a given situation, why continue working on it? This situation doesn't happen very often, but it should be acknowledged. Let's assume that the problem can be dealt with. You must now put it in a clear statement that describes what is to be accomplished. We have found that there are three integral parts in defining problems:

1. A clear, concise statement of the *task*

2. The *purpose* for completing the task

3. Reasonable *time* measurement(s)

Further, we have found that when these factors are included, the probability of successful completion is greatly increased.

The outline method seems to be the easiest approach in applying the factors. Here's an example:

Task	**Purpose**	**Time**
What do we want to do?	Why are we doing it?	When do we want it completed, or what interim time checks should we use?

Referring to an earlier situation, we can develop an objective that meets the criteria. (For sake of discussion, we have stated the real problem as the need to increase profits through planning.)

Task	**Purpose**	**Time**
• Achieve a sales volume of $20 million with a minimum 25 percent ROI.	• Increase profits. • Regain leadership position.	• Within next twelve months. • By December 1998. • Monitor progress quarterly.
• Develop short- and long-term plans.		

Using this information, we can develop an objective statement that clearly reflects our intention:

By December 1998,   *we must develop short- and long-term plans*
Time   **Task**

to achieve a sales volume of $20 million with a minimum 25 percent ROI
Purpose

and regain a leadership position in our market. Progress on this will be *formally monitored on a quarterly basis.*
Additional Measurements

At this point you might ask the question, Is all this really necessary? The best answer is simply this: If you do not take the time to clearly select and write the plan objectives, not much will happen. One other example might help to clarify this.

Example 2.   Managers at Leisure Time Activities found that after a comprehensive assessment there were a number of internal problems related to morale and communications. As they focused on the problem, it seemed that improved communications would really clear up the situation. After thrashing out problems, they then developed this objective: "We must improve company internal communications." From this point, they further identified five strategies that would be necessary to achieve the objective. After additional discussion, they agreed that even if all of the strategies were implemented, they would, at best, achieve only a partial solution to the problem. In reanalyzing the objective, they found these critical flaws:

1. Only part of the task was identified.

2. The purpose of the action was not specified.

3. There were no time measurements or checkpoints.

They went back to discuss the objectives. The following revision makes the point quite well:

Within six months, we will improve the interchange of information and ideas throughout the company about plans and activities affecting operations and policies, in order to encourage feedback and involvement of all employees.

You will notice, when we move into strategy development, that a clear objective reduces the difficulty of strategy selection.

Developing Effective Strategies

Now that you know what must be done, we will discuss approaches and methods to describe how it should be done. Strategies are events, methods, and the like that crisply define the kinds of actions that should be taken to solve a problem, that is, to complete an objective. If an objective has been clearly written, the strategies are easily developed.

One way to look at strategies is to think of an action plan. What kind of actions should you take to rectify this problem or improve that situation? At this point, you are not trying to get down to details. Rather, you are looking for a logical sequence of activity that will outline actions for the next twelve months or so (though some strategies will extend beyond a twelve-month period). To get a better fix, let's continue with the objective discussed in Example 2 above.

Within six months, we will improve throughout the company the interchange of information and ideas about plans and activities affecting operations and policies, in order to encourage feedback and involvement of all employees.

This objective is common for many companies, but the methods used to achieve it will vary considerably. A group must consider all of the problems, resources, and other considerations. Let's list some facts that seem apparent:

1. We know when we want to accomplish it.

2. We know the type of communication we want to disseminate (plans and activities).

3. We know what areas it will affect (operations and policies).

4. We know we need to encourage feedback and involvement.

What seems to emerge is that Leisure Time Activities management needs to improve interchange of information on a companywide basis. It now knows what it wants to do and needs to develop how it will do it. In discussing the matter further, management came up with the following action recommendations:

• Set up a departmental activities program.

• Set up an Operations Improvement Committee to answer questions and get employee feedback.

• Provide a forum for departmental information interchange.

• Meet informally with employees.

• Deliver a "State of the Company" message.

• Provide feedback on progress of plans and activities.

These action recommendations were refined and expanded as shown in Exhibit 9–3. As you can see, the group went from the general to the specific. When approaching it in this manner, you can see where the plan stands at all times. This company turned a normal problem into a reasonable and practical opportunity.

How to Manage the Plan

Once a strategic business plan is written, people forget about it and return to the daily grind. This happens in spite of the fact that the objectives that were developed during the process were must-do tasks. To ensure that must-do tasks

Exhibit 9–3.   Executing Strategies

Strategies	Responsibility	Due Date
1. Company orientation to department activities; set up program and schedule	Personnel and division managers	Monthly
2. Operations Improvement Committee set up to answer questions and obtain feedback from employees	A representative from each department	5/15
3. Management Committee to be the forum for interchange of departmental information and in turn inform their departments and get feedback	Management Committee	3/23
4. "State of the Company" message: where we are, how we are doing, etc.	President	4/1 and annual
5. Informal meeting of all employees	Executive Committee	6/1 and 12/1 and semiannual
6. Memo from Executive Committee to employees on how we are doing	Executive Committee	Monthly
7. Staff luncheons with informal meetings— opportunity for employees to ask questions	Management Committee	When necessary
8. New employee orientation	Personnel and department peer level	5/1
9. Social/athletic activities a. Set up program b. Schedule an "activity day"	Personnel Management Committee	4/15

are acted on and to make certain the plan functions as a road map, proceed as follows:

1. Set up a small planning coordination function (one to two persons). This function is responsible for managing the plan from the meeting to back on the job. The function should:
   a. Coordinate with each person responsible for an objective and make sure that the assigned objective is in final form with realistic due date, strategy

    assignments, and so forth. (During the planning meeting, appoint one or two persons to be responsible for each objective developed.)

  b. Consolidate all objectives and review background data (developed in the meeting).

  c. Submit it for management approval.

  d. Develop a short overview of the planning meeting that describes the highlights of the plan (no confidential information) for all employees. After management's approval, this should be discussed with all employees as appropriate.

  e. Stay on top of the plan. The coordination group should establish a practical method to evaluate progress against strategies. This should be put into a two-page report and presented to management on a quarterly basis.

2. A number of other practical approaches can be utilized. These range from getting lower-level organizational participation on strategies to individual departmental plans.

    In summary, strategic business planning is a management tool that enables an organization to focus on problems and opportunities, on current position and future direction, and, finally, on what to do next. Participating in the development of a strategic business plan is only one phase. Making it work is another.

SELF-QUIZ

1. Define *strategic business planning*.

_____

_____

_____

_____

2. What are the two types of data required for background information pertinent to developing a strategic business plan?

  a. _____

  b. _____

3. List six external factors that can have an impact on a direct marketing operation but cannot be directly controlled.

a. _____   d. _____

b. _____   e. _____

c. _____   f. _____

4. List six internal factors over which a direct marketing operation can exercise control.

a. _____   d. _____

b. _____   e. _____

c. _____   f. _____

5. Define *mission statement*.

_____

_____

_____

_____

6. What are the four fundamentals in making an action plan work?

a. _____

b. _____

c. _____

d. _____

7. Define *objective* as it relates to a business plan.

_____

_____

_____

_____

8. Define *strategy* as it relates to a business plan.

_____

_____

_____

_____

9. In moving toward the development of action plan objectives, one should determine the _____, not the _____.

10. What are the three integral parts involved in defining a problem?

a. _____

b. _____

c. _____

PILOT PROJECT

For three years your company has had a mail order catalog that offers women's apparel, home furnishings, and gift items. You are no match for competitors like Horchow and Neiman-Marcus. Your resources, both personnel and financial, are limited. As you are now positioned, it is obvious that you are fighting a losing battle.

Your objective is to change direction and establish a clearly defined niche in the marketplace, changing your merchandise mix to items not generally available from your competition.

Your assignment is to develop strategies and an action plan that will reposition your catalog in the marketplace over the next twelve months. (Among the strategies you might consider are: positioning your catalog as the source for apparel, home furnishings, and gifts for the career woman; or positioning your catalog as the source for apparel and gift items for those engaged in outdoor activities.)

CHAPTER TEN

The Design, Use, and Maintenance of Databases

A database is a perishable commodity. Unless it is kept up to date, information ages. When incorrect addresses or telephone numbers result in misdirected advertising promotions, the cost is twofold: (1) the cost of the wasted contact, and (2) the sacrifice of potential response.

As you design your database, strive to make it easy to maintain. Make sure that information is compiled and developed in a *uniform* manner. Only when such uniformity exists within a computerized list is it possible to use merge/purge or match codes with any assurance of reliability.

Designing the Database

There are two broad categories of database to consider when you are thinking in terms of reference and retrieval of relevant data: hierarchical and relational.

Hierarchical Databases

Hierarchical systems are built around the idea of a single, central record. For example, all information related to a customer is contained in a master record.

Adapted with permission from Martin Baier, *How to Find and Cultivate Customers through Direct Marketing* (Lincolnwood, Ill.: NTC Business Books, 1996). Baier is director of the Center for Direct Marketing Education and Research at the University of Missouri–Kansas City and a member of the Marketing Hall of Fame.

There is no need in such a system to cross-reference other sources. Airline and hotel reservation systems have been developed in this way. Single-record databases provide high-volume access and ease of use, but their analytical capabilities can be limited by the extent of the data available in restricted records. An example of a hierarchical data record, with typical information, is shown in Exhibit 10–1.

Relational Databases

Relational systems, which are a more recent approach to database development and utilization, provide the advantages of simplicity and flexibility, minimizing redundancy. Related information is drawn from different, independent database sources as needed. For example, a product database can be linked to a customer name/address database in order to direct promotion to those purchasing particular products. At the same time, the separate product file makes possible product line analysis regardless of customer. Links can be established, too, with billing and/or shipping and inventory records as relevant information is needed.

Sources of Information

Most of the information needed to begin a customer database is readily available within an organization. Accounting records, shipping and fulfillment records,

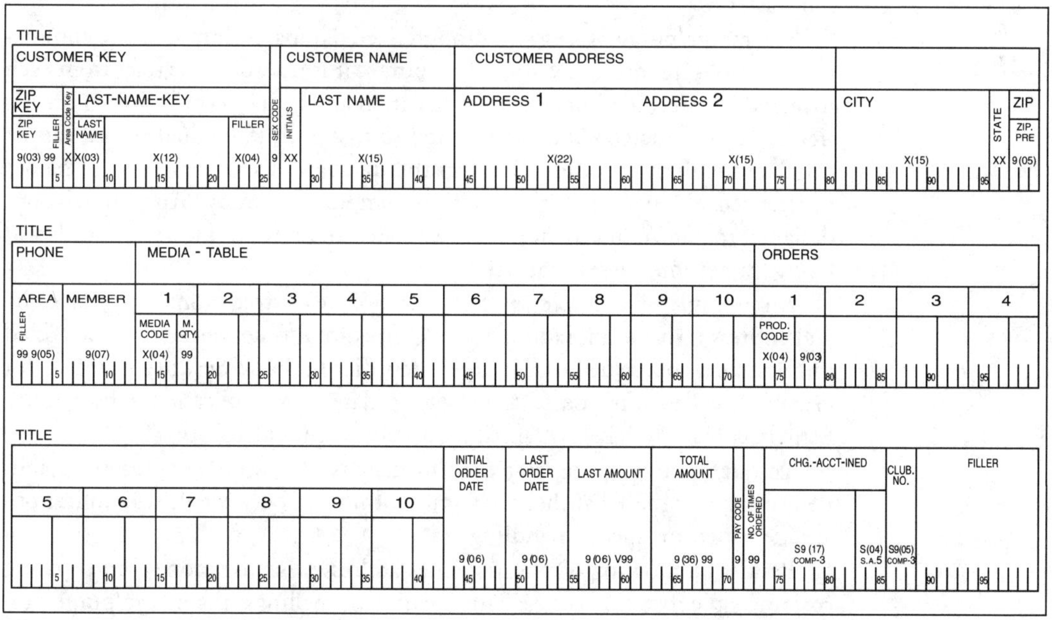

Exhibit 10–1.   Hierarchical Format of a Single-Source Record

service reports, inquiries, warranty cards, and survey research results can all yield valuable marketing information.

But just because the information is there does not automatically qualify it for entry into a marketing database. Some information is unnecessary; other information is too expensive to acquire. A guideline to follow is this: collect that data you think you'll need to know . . . and no more.

In order to identify prospects with the greatest potential to become customers, you might want to rely on an external database. Paying to use this kind of database as needed is probably wiser than bringing it in-house, where maintenance could be a problem. Compiled lists are a good example of an external source of information that can be rented without acquiring and maintaining infrequently used data.

Using Match Codes and Merge/Purge to Eliminate Duplication

For best results, a database must be designed so that it eliminates duplicated information and, therefore, wasted effort. The more that external lists are used to supplement a house list, the more complex this problem becomes. Customer lists from different sources might duplicate each other; response lists and compiled lists can contain a surprising number of duplicates, within and between lists; and many names could already be on your house list. The solution is to use match codes and merge/purge techniques to eliminate duplication on internal lists as well as on external lists being used for customer solicitation.

The merge/purge process on computerized databases simplifies the elimination of duplicate records. With merge/purge, it is possible to extract from each name/address record abbreviated information about that record. This abbreviation is called a match code, constructed so that each individual record can be compared with every other record in the database. Exact matching of name/address records requires a good deal of computer memory. An abbreviation, designed to reduce the chance that two match codes from different records will be the same, minimizes that need.

An example of a simple 18-digit match code derived from a typical name and address is shown in Exhibit 10–2. Quite often, other data might be added to the match code, such as a unique identifier (a Social Security number, for example), coded birth date, or expiration date of a publication subscription. Periodical mailing labels often contain match codes of this type.

Through a merge/purge system using match codes, millions of records potentially can be compared at the same time, within and between lists. Duplications are identified for special handling.

Besides eliminating duplicate names/addresses, saving money, and sparing customers the irritation of receiving redundant mailings, the merge/purge pro-

Exhibit 10-2.   Mailing List Match Code

EXAMPLE ADDRESS	DERIVED MATCH CODE
Melinda Barton	92173BRT5410SLI6M7
5410 Salisbury Drive	
Lexington, MA 02173	

Position	Item	Description
1	State	A unique code assigned to each state
2–5	ZIP code	Last 4 number of 5-digit ZIP code
6–8	Surname	1st, 3rd, and 4th alpha characters of surname or business name
9–12	Address	House or business street number
13–15	Address	1st, 3rd, and 4th alpha characters of street name
16	Surname	Count of characters in surname
17	Given name	Alpha initial of first name
18	Given name	Count of characters in first name

cess offers another, possibly even greater advantage. If the same name/address is found on two or more customer lists simultaneously, it is conceivable that individual, now identified as a multibuyer is an excellent prospect for future response. Experimentation has shown that the expectation of a higher rate of response from those names appearing on three lists is greater than the expectation from those names on two lists. The merge/purge process can identify these special multibuyers for special handling.

The merge/purge process can also effectively remove names of individuals who have expressed a desire not to receive particular solicitations as well as those who have been poor credit risks or are otherwise potentially undesirable customers.

Control and Maintenance Tasks

Your database will need constant control and maintenance. You will want to perform these three tasks on a regular basis:

1. Nixie removal

2. Change of address

3. Record status update

Nixie Removal

The term *nixie* refers to mail that has been returned because it is undeliverable as addressed and no forwarding address has been provided. This might result from a simple error in the street address or ZIP code. If such an error can be traced, the address can be corrected.

Other possible reasons for undelivered mail are that the person to whom mail is addressed is deceased or has moved and left no forwarding address. In such cases, the person should be removed from the mailing list portion of the database, leaving other records intact until a new address, if any, is known.

Often mail addressed to a deceased person will continue to be delivered to a surviving spouse. Or mail to an individual who has changed positions or left an organization will be received by the replacement in that position. Although the U.S. Postal Service will not send notifications in such instances, experienced direct marketers obtain list corrections through specially directed mailings. Or if a salesperson calls on the customer, corrected information can be obtained that way.

Other ways in which mailing lists can be updated to avoid nixies include references to news items and public records such as birth and death notices, marriage registrations, and divorce (annulment) proceedings.

Change of Address Update

Whenever possible, address corrections should be requested through the U.S. Postal Service. Mail prepaid with first-class postage is automatically returned if undeliverable or forwarded without charge if the new address is known. For a fee, the sender will be notified of the new address as well.

The U.S. Postal Service offers a variety of address correction procedures for third-class advertising mail. Most notable is the computerized National Change of Address (NCOA) file, which virtually all major mailers and a good number of minor ones, use regularly.

Direct marketers themselves often encourage those on their databases to inform them of any change of address or telephone number and provide the means for doing so.

Record Status Update

It is of vital importance to keep the record status of customers current. New transactions from customers should be entered into the database promptly, as they have major impact on the RFM formula described earlier. They also influence the success of future solicitations.

Above all, direct marketers do not want to distribute their direct response advertising indiscriminately. They want to make sure not only that their messages are delivered, but also that they are delivered to the right prospects at the right time.

Database Security

Like buildings, equipment, and inventories, computer databases are assets. Unlike more tangible assets, they are somewhat more portable. Millions of records can be packed on a single reel of computer tape or even on a pocket-sized cassette. Their loss or misuse through falling into the wrong hands can be highly detrimental to the organization. Unfortunately, because their value is intangible, they are not easily insurable, except for replacement and duplication costs.

For these reasons, special precautions must be taken to prevent destruction, loss, theft, or unauthorized use. Attention should be given to the following:

- Program administration, assigning responsibility for development, modification, and utilization

- Limiting exposures through secured location, proper storage, controlled access, cryptographic techniques, adequate erasure, and destruction

- Marking the list, to discourage unauthorized use

- Discouraging theft through visible security, awareness of misuse precautions, apprehension of violators

- Maintaining accountability for system and documents

The logical first step is to make sure the database is stored in a manner that protects it against natural hazards of fire and water damage, as well as theft or unauthorized use. To discourage theft, access to list files should be limited and controlled at all times.

How to Profit from an Enhanced Database

A customer list becomes a database when it is enhanced to include more than simply a name, an address, and a telephone number. It is enhanced when it records relevant information about each customer's transactions. It is further enhanced when demographic and/or psychographic information is appended for each consumer or industrial buyer. Enhancement of a database can also include environmental information such as data about ZIP codes for consumers or about Standard Industrial Classification (SIC) codes for businesses. In essence, enhancing your database lets you learn more about your customers and why they buy so you can nurture your relationship with them for many profitable years.

Any organization must first know about its own customers. This knowledge not only opens up the opportunities for continuity selling and cross-selling, but it also is the prelude to pinpointing prospects most likely to become customers in the future. A simple five-step sequence can help an organization profit from an enhanced database:

1. Identify your customers.

2. Enhance your database.

3. Overlay environmental data.

4. Utilize the tools of prediction.

5. Utilize your own analytical database.

These five steps can mean the difference between a profit and a loss in any enterprise. Building and enhancing a database is a means. It is not an end in and of itself. The true end is the success and stability of the enterprise.

Step One: Identify Your Customers

Many well-intended marketers spend considerable time and money on seeking new customers without first learning about the characteristics of their present customers. By answering some basic questions about your customers, you can more easily (and less expensively) find others like them.

- Who are your customers?

- Where are more like them to be found?

- How were these customers obtained?

- Which offer the most opportunity from continuity sales and cross-sales?

- How much can be spent to acquire them?

- What is their lifetime value?

These are the questions that your customer database, when enhanced, can answer.

Step Two: Enhance Your Database

First of all, make sure that you have a proper mechanism for the development and maintenance of your database. Then capture customer information that is relevant for pinpointing future revenues. This includes product(s) purchased, RFM, and other transaction data. It also might include significant demographic data derived from external databases.

Step Three: Overlay Environmental Data

Certain kinds of environmental data can help you predict future purchasing behavior. Perhaps the characteristics and variables within ZIP code areas influence response. Or industry characteristics of a business firm could impact response. Environmental data can be geographic, demographic, or psychographic in that it can be a predictor of lifestyle and buying behavior.

Step Four: Utilize the Tools of Prediction

Develop high regard for and a comfort level with numbers and statistics. Not every technique is complicated. At the low end, a simple response percentage can highlight the most productive segment of a response list. At the high end, a complex, multivariate regression analysis can correlate response variances with behavioral variables found within a cluster of ZIP code areas.

Step Five: Utilize Your Own Analytical Databases

Most response-oriented direct marketers experiment a lot. From these tests, they collect a great deal of data. Properly analyzed, such data can provide much guidance. Databases should contain more than "nice to know" information. They should tell you who your best customers are, where they are, and how to cultivate them. Such analytical databases, too, should track the lifetime value of a customer, because what better way is there to set promotion budgets for new customer acquisition?

A Guide to an Endless Array of Enhancements

Your database might already contain proprietary information such as actions taken, product preference and creditworthiness. But you might want to add information such as age (from a public record compilation of driver's licenses), a mobility indicator such as length of residence (from a telephone directory compilation), or a credit rating (from a credit rating bureau).

Your database can also be used as a negative screen to suppress promotion to those desiring not to be solicited (from the Direct Marketing Association's mail and telephone preference compilations) or an address where a prospect no longer resides (from the U.S. Postal Service's NCOA file).

All of this information is available from compiled lists, response lists, and credit reporting databases. But before you turn to external data sources, take a second look at your own files. One insurance company surveyed its policyholders to determine their ages, even though it already had this information in its underwriting database!

Compiled Lists

Carefully developed and maintained name/address compilations can be a key source of data. This information can be transferred to customer or other response lists to segment and qualify them.

Telephone Directory Compilations.   Drawn from white pages (individuals) or Yellow Pages (organizations), these enormous databases can yield a treasure trove of information. For households, you can estimate household mobility, identify multi-unit buildings or associate the address itself with a ZIP code or other small geographic area for which census data is obtainable. Phone numbers can be added where worthwhile.

For businesses and other organizations, you can discover SIC codes by cross-referencing Yellow Pages categories. You can determine the year the organization first appeared, or identify a franchise such as McDonald's, a brand affiliation such as General Electric, or membership in a professional society. As with households, telephone or fax numbers can be appended. The extent of Yellow Page advertising can be identified, too, if relevant to response.

Telephone directory compilations can themselves be enhanced from other databases and usually are. Gender can be approximated from first-name tables; ethnicity can be approximated from surname tables. Telephone surveys of directory listings of organizations provide names and titles of decision makers, number of employees, and sales volume. First-time listings of households on the move or of business start-ups can be isolated as well.

City (and/or Criss-Cross) Directories.   Where available, these household compilations can augment telephone directories, which omit both those who lack telephone service and those who, through their own choice, prefer not to be listed. City directories are typically compiled through mail survey or house-to-house canvassing. They often list all persons in the household, along with age, marital status and family relationships. Children are included as are senior citizens living with their children. City directories are readily obtainable for manual perusal, and they are often incorporated into the enormous databases offered by major list compilers.

Voter Registration Files.   Like city directories, these are locally compiled, typically by county election boards or commissions. Like city directories, they include many individuals who do not appear in telephone directories. But they are far from comprehensive. Not all U.S. residents are citizens and, of those who are, not all are registered as voters.

Voter lists might show party affiliation, an important qualifier for political parties and candidates, although party affiliation might not always be current. Addresses might also be out of date if the voter has not voted recently. For these reasons, voter lists are probably most effectively used when they are joined with other databases by a professional compiler.

Real Estate Records.   Information derived from public real estate records can provide considerable enhancement to a customer database, especially when offers relate to home furnishings, maintenance, gardening, and landscaping. Available data for either customer enhancement or prospect qualification includes type of dwelling unit (single or multi-family, condominium), month or year purchased, market value, and residence of owner.

Rosters.   The membership rosters of the local PTA, service clubs, neighborhood and trade associations, professional societies, and special-interest groups can be a useful source of customer and prospect information. The key qualification is the nature of the group with which an individual or organization is affiliated.

Because rosters are typically in hard copy, working with them can be cumbersome. Duplication can result when an automated means for merge/purge is unavailable. Roster information might not always be up-to-date, and many groups frown on their use as mailing lists.

Still, the information in rosters, especially evidence of affinity with a particular group and its interests, can be a worthwhile enhancement to a customer database. Sizable collections of rosters, drawing together local groups, are available in computer format.

Automobile and Driver's License Registrations.   Obtained from the various state motor vehicle departments, registration records can provide year, make and model for each automobile in a household. They can also identify new vehicle purchasers. Because certain vehicles can be associated with certain lifestyles, this can offer clues about a customer's lifestyle. The number of vehicles owned in a household, as well as their combined market value, can also be discriminate variables.

Because automobile registrations are recompiled annually, they can be used to update mailing addresses. Not so driver's license registrations, which are issued for as many as five years. However, driver's license registrations are a good source of age and gender information as well as height and weight statistics that can be important predictors of interest in products such as large or tall clothing sizes. A driver's license record can also indicate some degree of physical mobility and acuteness, important qualifiers for products such as insurance.

Lifestyle Compilations. Generally derived from warranty registrations returned to product manufacturers or from survey responses, this information comes from consumers themselves and often provides a variety of demographic data about individuals and households. Psychographic data volunteered by respondents also provide indicators of activities, interests and opinions. Coupled with environmental data obtainable for ZIP code areas, such databases become valid measurements of lifestyles.

Tens of millions of records, compiled month-to-month and regularly maintained through address correction procedures, comprise these lifestyle databases. Dozens of activities and interests from antique collecting to wildlife/environmental issues can be identified. Included are such diverse indicators as bible/devotional reading, casino gambling, snow skiing, gardening, motorcycling, and watching TV sports.

Demographic selections from such databases often include gender, title, age band, home ownership, marital status, income, occupation, credit card usage, children at home, education, religion, and ethnicity.

Direct marketers who effectively use lifestyle compilations as mailing lists will often initially transfer relevant variable information from these databases to their own customer records. Thus, they can model their customer penetration correlated with these variables so as to predict the likelihood of response to their offer from segments of the multi-million compilation. These segments become key sources of new customer acquisition.

Credit Reporting Databases. Major national credit-reporting organizations offer a broad array of enhancement and qualification screens, negative as well as positive. Their databases let you suppress promotion efforts to those with poor credit records and properly direct promotion efforts to those qualified for and likely to be interested in a particular offer. They are also excellent sources of up-to-date, deliverable addresses, because they are updated every month as consumers and businesses pay their bills.

A great deal of the demographic data offered as mailing lists by credit-reporting organizations is derived from sources external to them. For consumer records, this includes a variety of information about those in the household as well as the housing itself. For business records, primary and secondary industry classifications are shown, as are other non-confidential data derived from survey or observation.

The use of information from credit-reporting databases is, in the eyes of consumers and consumer advocates, controversial—especially when it is used for offers that do not grant a credit privilege. That is why highly personal and confidential information obtained in the process of credit checking and reporting is available to credit grantors only.

On the other hand, credit organizations have modeled the likelihood of bankruptcy without individually identifying bankrupt consumers. Without breaching individual confidentiality, this kind of modeling with predictive averages is a valid enhancement for a customer database as well as an important qualifier for an offer to be directed to a prospect mailing list.

Respondents to Direct Offers.   Experienced direct marketers know that the single most important qualification of a mailing list is history of response. Response or action taken can be predictive. It can help a direct marketer predict whether a prospect might make similar or related purchases in the future. A purchaser of a travel cruise to Alaska, for example, might be a more likely prospect for a world cruise than one who had bought a weekend Caribbean cruise. By enhancing your database with information from other response lists, you can learn a great deal about customers without invading their privacy.

Conducting a merge/purge of several response lists against each other and your own customer list can offer further predictive likelihood by identifying multibuyers. Large database compilers have facilitated this by marking mail order buyers from many, many individual response lists and identifying them by purchase dollar range and purchase method. In doing so, they have coupled the typically larger numbers of records available in compiled lists with qualifications of mail responsiveness, recency of purchase (hotline buyers) and frequency of purchase (multibuyers). The result is the best of both worlds: high volume and great qualification.

Predictive Modeling: Compiling a Customer Profile

The primary reason for enhancing your database is to develop an accurate profile of your customers—a profile you can use to identify prospects that are like the most profitable of the customers you already have. Organizations used to develop cursory profiles of their customers through primary research, surveying a sampling of them in order to determine their key characteristics. Today's database and analysis technology, however, provides opportunities for statistical modeling that can embrace not just a sampling but the entire customer file. Further, it can categorize these customers by products purchased, RFM analysis, credit experience, and a host of transactions variables. Then it can relate its findings to an infinite array of enhancements: geographic, demographic, and psychographic.

Because today's organizations—their product and promotion strategies, their databases, their markets—are dynamic, customer profiling through statistical modeling needs to be a never-ending process. As already emphasized, the collection and analysis of information costs money and should be undertaken only if benefits derived from better decision making exceed these costs.

A starting point for developing such profiles is through the calculation of market penetration. This, in its simplest form, is a percentage relationship of customers to some benchmark universe. It tells what percentage of the total universe of potential buyers are your customers. To be even more predictive, such arithmetic should be performed on customer segments: RFM categories, product lines, specific demographics.

The benchmark universe can be as broad as a total population or a count of all households or of all families. It could be as narrow as a count of mailings of a particular promotional effort to a particular list. Industrial organizations might view their prospect universe as all firms within an SIC, within a size category, or within a geographic area. The universe could be even further refined by age band, marital status, occupation, educational level, or numerous other restrictions.

When determining percentage penetration of customers in a potential market, it is well to keep in mind the "equal effort over time dilemma." You might have a higher concentration of customers in a particular segment—high-income households, for example—simply because your prior marketing efforts, for a good many years, have been directed to that segment. Without objective guidance, you might have unintentionally bypassed even more productive, lesser-income segments. A solution to this dilemma is to measure a controlled universe such as a direct mail effort across all household income segments with response key-coded by income category.

Suppose that you mail an offer to 19,600 households, each identified as falling into one of four low-to-high income ranges: A, B, C, and D. You receive 350 responses to your offer, an average of 1.79 percent response. When the response is tabulated by household income range, market penetration is shown to increase as household income increases:

Household Income Segment	Total Mailed	Total Responses	Percentage Response to Mailed
A	5,793	60	1.04%
B	2,735	33	1.21
C	6.731	138	2.05
D	4,341	119	2.74

From this table, it is readily apparent that the response rate from the direct mail offer is positively correlated with household income. That is, the response rate increases along with household income. Because the market potential has been defined with a direct mail effort sent to all available households irrespective of income, our market penetration, viewed as a series of response rates, is controlled. Thus, we are not faced with the "equal effort over time dilemma."

Now, let's assume that we have a list of 350 customers, who were acquired over a period of time from a market potential universe consisting of 19,600 households. Let's change only the column headings on the preceding table so it looks like this:

ZIP Code Cluster	Total Households	Total Customers	Percentage of Customers/ Households
A	5,793	60	1.04%
B	2,735	33	1.21
C	6,731	138	2.05
D	4,341	119	2.74

What we are showing here is a clustering of 350 customers according to their ZIP code locations and calculating the percentage of customers we have among all households in those ZIP code clusters. Once again, we see that market penetration increases from A to B to C to D. What we don't know, in this instance, however, is why!

If we had the means to correlate our customer penetration of the market potential of the four ZIP code clusters, we should be able to seek prospects and more readily convert these to customers in cluster D than in cluster A. The trick is to know what distinguishes D from A: demographically, psychographically, and geographically.

Try eyeballing the ZIP code clusters in which you have the greatest market penetration. What is different about each ZIP area? Are they rural or metropolitan? Are the housing structures multi-family? Are the neighborhoods "new" or "old"? Are the household heads young or old, college postgraduates or high school drop-outs? You might even look at a census of population and housing. From all of this data, it might be possible to discover what distinguishes the high penetration areas from those with low penetration. A customer profile— real or estimated—is the starting point in seeking out new prospects or prospect lists.

Case Study: Benefiting from Predictive Modeling with Databases

A travel company that offers package tours through mail order to older persons desires to increase its marketing effectiveness. It seeks to do this through segmentation of its marketplace within the state of Florida using demographic independent variables in addition to age. The firm has developed, from census and proprietary data sources, a total of 103 demographic variables describing each of 35,000 geographic ZIP code areas. These variables are expressed as either averages or frequency distributions.

Several of these variables have been normalized. That is, they have been indexed to some larger area such as a Sectional Center (the first three digits of a five-digit code) or a state (such as Mississippi versus New York) in order to achieve environmental, as opposed to absolute, measurement. This means that the relative income level in a rural Mississippi ZIP code area is compared with the relative income level of an urban area in New York City rather than in absolute dollars. A "high" dollar income level in the rural Mississippi area could be relatively "low" in New York City.

Variables have also been subjected to factor analysis in order to discover the typical lifestyle factors and the associated independent variables. The dependent variable is market penetration, defined in this instance as the response rate (total responses divided by the total number of pieces mailed) to the travel company's direct mail offer of tours to the older residents of Florida.

To maximize the number of observations and assure statistical validity of both measurement and prediction, the response rate is calculated within clusters of ZIP code areas with common characteristics produced using cluster analysis. Ultimately, these clusters will be described as market segments in which penetration levels can be correlated with their characteristics. At this stage, both environmental (indexed) measurement and interaction among the variables defining clusters are important considerations.

Calculation of penetration is simple. Within each cluster of ZIP code areas, the response rate is calculated as shown here:

ZIP Code Area Clusters	Total No. of Pieces Mailed	Total No. of Responses	Percentage of Responses
A	5,793	60	1.04%
B	2,735	33	1.21
C	6,731	136	2.02
D	4,341	118	2.74

From this table, it is readily apparent that there is an increasing rate of response from A to B, from B to C, and from C to D. These differences can be explained by evaluating the independent variables entering in and deemed significant through regression analysis shown in Exhibit 10–3, which enables the transfer of these findings from a sample to the total population without first having mailed that total population. The linear regression equation (of the form: $Y = a + bX$) becomes a formula for predicting estimated response rates from ZIP /code area clusters not yet solicited but having similar characteristics to those sampled.

Correlation analysis by the travel company identifies the strength of the relationship between cluster response rates (the dependent variable) and each of the 103 selected demographics (independent variables). Exhibit 10–3 reproduces a condensed printout of the stepwise multivariate regression analysis that

Exhibit 10–3.   Stepwise Multivariate Regression Analysis

```
VARIABLE ENTERING           X- 5
R = 0.583959      R SQ.  =   0.341008
  F LEVEL  =     23.8036
  STANDARD ERROR OF Y  =      0.06341
  CONSTANT TERM  =      0.27470726
```

VARIABLE NO.	COEFFICIENT	STD ERR OF COEFF
X- 5	-0.28683022E-01	0.00594

```
STEP # 2
  VARIABLE ENTERING           X- 2
R = 0.717396      R SQ.  =   0.514658
  F LEVEL  =     l6.1004
  STANDARD ERROR OF Y  =      0.05504
  CONSTANT TERM  =      0.25037676
```

VARIABLE NO.	COEFFICIENT	STD ERR OF COEFF
X- 2	0.11710477	0.02951
X- 5	-0.25006641E-01	0.00524

```
STEP # 3
  VARIABLE ENTERING           X- 16
R = 0.814453      R SQ.  =   0.663334
  F LEVEL  =     19. 4310
  STANDARD ERROR OF Y =      0.04637
  CONSTANT TERM  =      0.17120540
```

VARIABLE NO.	COEFFICIENT	STD ERR OF COEFF
X- 2	0.12946498	0.02503
X- 5	-0.21160301E-01	0.00450
X- 16	0.10500204E-01	0.00241

```
STEP # 4
  VARIABLE ENTERING           X- 14
R = 0.831825      R SQ.  =   0.691934
  F LEVEL  =     3.9919
  STANDARD ERROR OF Y  =      0.04488
  CONSTANT TERM  =      0.11676645
```

VARIABLE NO.	COEFFICIENT	STD ERR OF COEFF
X- 2	0.12659431	0.02427
X- 5	-0.18140811E-01	0.00462
X- 14	0.27103789E-01	0.01373
X- 16	0.99606328E-02	0.00235

```
STEP # 10
  VARIABLE ENTERING           X- 22
R = 0.896520      R SQ.  =   0.803748
  F LEVEL  =     2.8542
  STANDARD ERR OF Y  =      0.03766
  CONSTANT TERM  =      0.39812356
```

VARIABLE NO.	COEFFICIENT	STD ERR OF COEFF
X-2	0.13928533	0.02095
X-9	-0.20301903E-02	0.00064
X-10	-0.87198131E-02	0.00257
X-14	0.69082797E-01	0.01875
X-15	0.13623666E-01	0.00421
X-16	0.22368859E-01	0.00380
X-22	-0.15226589E-02	0.00091
X-23	-0.21373443E-02	0.00081

follows the correlation analysis. From 27 available independent variables, each a surrogate of a demographic characteristic of ZIP code areas, ten steps are taken. Eight variables remain at the conclusion of step 10. The reference numbers of these eight variables, together with their simple correlation coefficients, are shown at the bottom of Exhibit 10–3.

The resulting R^2 value of 0.803748 (the multiple coefficient of determination) indicates that 80 percent of the variance in response is explained by presence or absence of these eight variables. The derived regression equation enables a rank ordering of predicted response rates attributable to each five-digit ZIP code area within each cluster.

Exhibit 10–4 shows the highest to the lowest, as well as the cumulative, predicted penetration percentages (response rates). It also shows both individual and cumulative base mailing list counts for each ZIP code area within each cluster. Note the variance of the actual response rate, shown for each ZIP code area in the third column, attributable to the small number mailed in each area. Exhibit 10–4 reveals that, from a total mailing quantity of 1,277,262 pieces, the overall average response rate is predicted to be 1.95 percent. The response rate from the top cluster (#39) is predicted at 4.49 percent; that from the bottom cluster (#30) is predicted at 0.76 percent. The ratio, top versus bottom, is very nearly 1:6. Note, too, that the response rate from the top cluster is 2.3 times the overall average of 1.95 percent; that from the bottom is 39 percent.

To attain an average response of 2.55 percent (31 percent better than average), the company should stop after cluster #10, with marginal response of 2.06 percent, mailing 511,276 pieces. Limiting mailing quantity to 242,935 pieces, about 20 percent of the list availability, average response would be 2.87 percent, an improvement of 47 percent over the 1.95 percent overall average.

From this analysis, the company decides how big a market segment is needed, then predicts what overall response rate will be. It sets its minimum response rate requirement (average or marginal), then determines how many pieces it can mail. At this point, of primary importance to the travel company is a description of the profiles that exist in Florida. Just what influence might each of these exert on the response rate to a travel tour offer directed to older persons? Factor analysis produces these three explanatory lifestyle profiles, which are present in clusters with high response rates:

- **Rural residers.** Variables positively associated with this factor include rural farm and rural non-farm types of areas; farm manager and farm laborer occupations; housing in mobile homes and trailers; housing equipped with food freezers, lacking formal kitchens; East European ancestry. Negatively associated variables are access to public water and sewers; finance industry; multi-family dwelling units.

- **Social class.** "Lower half" variables positively associated with this factor include occupation as laborers, operatives, service workers, unemployed; poverty levels; divorced, separated, and widowed marital status; older housing; longer tenure of residence. "Upper half" variables, negatively associated, are high

Exhibit 10–4.   Rank Ordering of ZIP Code Area Clusters According to Response Rate Predicted by Regression Analysis

Cluster #	Zip #	Penetration Actual	Percentages**		****Base Counts****	
			Pred	Cum Pred	Zip Only	Cumulative
39	32009	.00	.0449	.0449	89	89
	32265	.00	.0449	.0449	4	93
	32560	.1070	.0449	.0449	93	186
	32563	.00	.0449	.0449	6	192
	32710	.00	.0449	.0449	37	229
	32732	.00	.0449	.0449	200	429
	32740	.00	.0449	.0449	42	471
	32766	.1500	.0449	.0449	200	671
	33070	.0460	.0449	.0449	651	1322
	33470	.00	.0449	.0449	132	1454
	33527	.00	.0449	.0449	716	2170
	33534	.0590	.0449	.0449	505	2675
	33550	.00	.0449	.0449	194	2869
	33556	.0750	.0449	.0449	528	3397
	33569	.0480	.0449	.0449	1637	5034
	33584	.0390	.0449	.0449	1001	6035
	33586	.00	.0449	.0449	62	6097
	33592	.0770	.0449	.0449	518	6615
	33600	.0750	.0449	.0449	398	7013
	33943	.00	.0449	.0449	139	7152
3	32600	.0420	.0342	.0363	28855	36007
11	32301	.0560	.0327	.0360	3533	39540
	32304	.0230	.0327	.0358	2532	42072
	32500	.0360	.0327	.0355	4873	46945
	32570	.0120	.0327	.0354	2312	49257
	32601	.0330	.0327	.0350	7826	57083
	33030	.0120	.0327	.0348	5564	62647
13	32211	.0240	.0246	.0291	6134	222185
	32303	.0160	.0246	.0290	4243	226428
	32561	.0330	.0246	.0289	1203	227631
	32701	.0140	.0246	.0289	2038	229669
	32751	.0140	.0246	.0288	3379	233048
	32786	.00	.0246	.0288	229	233277
	32789	.0170	.0246	.0287	7543	240820
	33511	.0370	.0246	.0287	2115	242935
10	33900	.0210	.0206	.0255	53503	511276
37	33062	.0170	.0111	.0198	6834	1234153
	33140	.00	.0111	.0198	56	1234209
	33154	.0060	.0111	.0198	3120	1237329
	33160	.0130	.0111	.0197	16354	1253683
	33306	.0100	.0111	.0197	986	1254669
30	33064	.0210	.0076	.0196	8210	1262870
	33516	.00	.0076	.1095	11202	1274072
	33570	.0090	.0076	.0195	3190	1277262

housing value; housing equipped with amenities such as air conditioning and dishwashers; 2 or more autos; high income; high education levels; occupations in management, sales, professional, technical; finance industry.

- **Ancestry/heritage.** Variables with positive association are native-born with English as a mother tongue; foreign-born with countries of origin including the United Kingdom, Canada, Ireland, Austria, and Germany; housing in owner-occupied single-family units. Negatively associated variables include foreign-born; immigrated from Cuba; Spanish is mother tongue; multiple family rental housing.

Because the overall response to this offer is double the break-even requirement for the acquisition of new customers, the travel company decides to validate its research. Six months after the first offer, the entire list is remailed, rank-ordered in quintiles of response as predicted from regression analysis. As expected, the overall response drops to about half that of the first effort. What is important, however, is that the relationship (response rate indices) of the quintiles are virtually the same for both efforts, as detailed in Exhibit 10–5.

Exhibit 10–5. Response Rate Indices for Each Quintile

Rank Ordered Quintile	No. of Pieces Mailed	First Effort Response (%)	First Effort Index	Second Effort Response (%)	Second Effort Index
1	242,935	2.87%	147	1.36%	143
2	268,341	2.26	116	1.08	111
3	230,592	1.94	99	0.96	99
4	290,001	1.54	79	0.81	84
5	245,393	1.19	61	0.67	67

Self-Quiz

1. A database is a perishable commodity. On a regular basis you will want to perform these three tasks:

   a. Nixie removal

   b. Change of address

   c. _____

2. What is the definition of *nixie removal?*

_____

_____

_____

3. Add three other enhancements to these three enhancements.

    a. Actions taken   d. _____

    b. Product preferences   e. _____

    c. Creditworthiness   f. _____

4. If it is important for you to know the ages of your prospects, what source would you use to learn exact ages? _____

_____

_____

5. Based on the following lifestyle characteristics, please indicate whether each characteristic would indicate a middle-class or upscale consumer.

    a. Owns a Porsche   ☐ Middle-class   ☐ Upscale

    b. Lives in a ZIP code with $30,000 median income
       ☐ Middle-class   ☐ Upscale

    c. Owns a house valued at $100,000
       ☐ Middle-class   ☐ Upscale

6. If you do a merge/purge on a number of lists and identify multi-buyers—those who appear on more than one list—you should consider these names to be poorer prospects than those that appear on only one list.
    ☐ True   ☐ False

7. Define *SIC.* _____

_____

8. Define *clustering*. _____

_____

_____

9. Define *predictive modeling*. _____

_____

PILOT PROJECT

You are a regional marketing director of an air conditioning firm that specializes in installing central air conditioning in homes. The market you are targeting is Milwaukee, Wisconsin. Based on research of your customer base, the profile of your customer base is as follows:

1. Lives in a house ten years old or more

2. Has a household income of $35,000 a year or more

3. Has lived in the same house for five years or more

Identify the sources you might use to build a list meeting the three criteria.

CHAPTER ELEVEN

The Offer

The propositions you make to customers—more often referred to as *offers*—can mean the difference between success and failure. Depending on the offer, differences in response of 25, 50, or 100 percent and more are commonplace. Not only is the offer you make the key to success or failure, but also the manner in which the offer is presented can have a dramatic effect. For example, here are three ways to state the same offer:

1. Half price!

2. Buy one—get one *free!*

3. 50 percent off!

Each statement conveys the same offer, but No. 2 pulled 40 percent better than No. 1 or No. 3. Consumers perceived No. 2 to be the most attractive offer.

Offers with Multiple Appeals

Exhibit 11–1 illustrates what appears to be an innocuous order card. But the multiple appeals used are certain to have a strong effect on front-end response. And the "conditions" for accepting are certain to have an immediate and long-term effect on how well the publisher does, both front-end and back-end.

Let's examine the appeals and conditions. "Please send me, free, the Premier issue of GEO." That's strong—you can't beat the appeal of something free. But note the slight condition ". . . and reserve a money-saving Charter Subscription in my name." The first appeal is followed by another appeal and a condition: "At the end of thirty days, if I have not instructed you to cancel my reservation, you may enter my subscription at the Charter Rate of $36 for one

Exhibit 11–1. Offers with Multiple Appeals and Conditions

FREE PREMIER ISSUE/CHARTER SUBSCRIPTION RESERVATION

Please send me, free, the Premier Issue of GEO, and reserve a money-saving Charter Subscription in my name. At the end of thirty days, if I have not instructed you to cancel my reservation, you may enter my subscription at the Charter Rate of $36 for one year (12 more monthly issues)—a savings of $12 off the annual cover price of $4 per issue.

As a Charter Subscriber, I am entitled to renew annually at savings of 25% off the newsstand price. Please bill me automatically each year. If at any time, for any reason, I elect to cancel my subscription, I will receive a full refund on all un-mailed issues. The Premier Issue is mine to keep in any case.

In addition, when I pay for my Charter Subscription, as a special gift I will receive a limited-edition copy of the GEO Premier Issue Cover Poster.

Please make any necessary corrections in your name or address. Return this reservation form in the postage-paid reply envelope enclosed.

H-PF-R   P.O. BOX 2552, BOULDER, COLORADO 80322

year (12 more monthly issues)—a savings of $12 off the annual cover price of $4 per issue.''

So the basic offer breaks out like this: First issue free (appeal); right to cancel at the end of 30 days (appeal); enter 12-month subscription at $36 unless instructed otherwise (condition); save $12 off the annual cover price (appeal).

But the offer doesn't end there. ''As a Charter Subscriber, I am entitled to renew annually at savings of 25% off the newsstand price'' (appeal). ''Please bill me automatically each year'' (condition). ''If at any time, for any reason, I elect to cancel my subscription, I will receive a full refund on all un-mailed issues. The Premier Issue is mine to keep in any case'' (appeal).

Finally, ''In addition, when I pay for my Charter Subscription, as a special gift I will receive a limited-edition copy of the GEO Premier Issue Cover Poster'' (both a condition and an appeal). In total, a brilliantly conceived and well-thought-through offer.

The Effects

This offer, one of many tested by *Geo* in the process of introducing the international magazine, can have a tremendous effect on immediate and long-term results. *Geo* and its agency know that offering the premier issue free will almost certainly bring a greater response than "tighter" offers that don't allow for cancellation after the first issue. But it also knows that, historically, its "loose" offer can result in cancellations of as high as 65 percent. So, to be determined is whether the superb quality of the magazine will overcome the historically poor conversion rate of this type of offer.

Guaranteeing in perpetuity a renewal rate of 25 percent off the newsstand price is a "safe" offer; this is a standard discount for the publishing industry. But "Please bill me automatically each year" could be a problem, or it could be a bonanza. This condition allows *Geo* to bill automatically without employing a renewal series, often six to eight efforts. The question is whether (1) the cancellation rate will be the same, better, or worse than when a renewal series is used and (2) whether the pay-ups will be the same, better, or worse than when a renewal series is used.

The sign-off offer—"In addition, when I pay for my Charter Subscription, as a special gift I will receive a limited-edition copy of the Premier Issue Cover Poster"—is smartly conceived. It is clear recognition on the part of *Geo* and its agency that not only do "loose" offers like this one historically result in a low conversion rate, but that pay-ups for those who don't cancel tend to be lower than for "tighter" offers. The question here is whether the lure of the free cover poster upon payment will increase the conversion rate and the payment rate.

Like any direct response offer, this one carries many immediate and long-term implications. That's why direct response professionals carefully consider ten basic factors for any offer before beginning the creative process.

Factors to Consider

Basically, when a direct sale is the objective, there are ten factors to consider when creating an offer:

1. *Price.* Nothing is more crucial than setting an appropriate price. Does the price allow for a sufficient markup? Is the price competitive? Is the price perceived by the consumer to be the right price for the value received? If you want to sell your item for $7.95 each, how about two for $15.90 (same price, but you get twice the average sale)? How about selling the first for $11.95 and the second for $3.95 (same total dollars if you sell two units— and if you don't sell two units, you get a higher price for a single unit)? Testing to determine the best price is vital to maximizing long-term payoff.

2. *Shipping and Handling.* Where applicable (usually not for a publication or service), shipping and handling charges can be an important factor in pricing. It's important to know how much you can add to a base without adversely affecting sales. Many merchandisers follow a rule of thumb that shipping and handling charges should not exceed 10 percent of the basic selling price. But again, testing is advisable.

3. *Unit of Sale.* Will your product or service be offered ''each''? ''Two for''? ''Set of *X*?'' Obviously, the more units you can move per sale, the better off you are likely to be. But if your prime objective is to build a large customer list fast, would you be better off to offer single units if you got twice the response over a ''two for'' offer? In the case of *Geo*, suppose it had offered six months for $18? Would it be better off in the long term?

4. *Optional Features.* Optional features include such things as special colors, odd sizes, special binding for books, personalization, and the like. Optional features often increase the dollar amount of the average order. For example, when the publisher of a dictionary offered thumb indexing at $2 extra, 25 percent of total purchases opted for this added feature.

5. *Future Obligation.* Subscribers to *Geo*, returning the illustrated order card, have agreed to automatic billing, if they don't elect to cancel. More common are book and tape offers that commit the purchaser to future obligation. (''Take ten tapes for $1 and agree to buy six more in the coming 12 months.'') A continuity program offer might state: ''Get Volume 1 free—others will be sent at regular intervals.'' Future obligation offers, when successful, enable the marketer to ''pay'' a substantial price for the first order, knowing there will be a long-term payout.

6. *Credit Options.* Many marketers believe that a major factor in the direct marketing explosion during the past decade was the proliferation of credit cards. It's rare today to receive a catalog that does not contain one or more of these options: ''Charge to American Express, Diners Club, Carte Blanche, Visa, Master Card, Discover.'' It pays: The average order is usually at least 15 percent larger than a cash order.

   Some major direct marketers offer credit for 30 days. (*Geo* did this), and others offer installment credit with interest added (oil companies are a good example). Whether it be commercial credit cards or house credit, history says credit options increase revenue.

7. *Incentives.* Incentives include free gifts, discounts, and sweepstakes. (*Geo* offered two incentives: the premier issue free with a conditional subscription and a free poster upon payment.) Toll-free ordering privilege is likewise an incentive—ease of ordering. Not unlike credit options, toll-free ordering privileges tend to increase the average order 15 percent and more. But incentives must be tested front-end and back-end. Are people ''buying'' the free gift or sweeps? Will they be as good repeat customers as those who bought in the first instance without incentive?

8. *Time Limits.* Time limits add urgency to an offer (*Geo*, for example, could have applied a time limit to its charter offer—with good logic.) One word of caution: If you establish a time limit, stick to it!

9. *Quantity Limits.* One of the major proponents of quantity limits is the collectibles field. (''Only 5,000 will be minted. Then the molds will be

destroyed.'') There is something in the human psyche that says, ''If it's in short supply, I want it!'' Even ''Limit—two to a customer'' often out-performs no limit. But if you set a limit, stick to it.

10. *Guarantees.* Of the ten factors to be considered in structuring an offer with the objective of making a sale, there is one that should never be passed up—the guarantee. *Geo* has two guarantees: Cancel the subscription if not pleased with the free premier issue and ''if at any time, for any reason, I elect to cancel my subscription, I will receive a full refund on all un-mailed issues.'' Hundreds of millions of people have ordered by phone or mail over the decades with the assurance their satisfaction is guaranteed. Don't make an offer without a guarantee. Nothing should happen in the creative process until you have structured an offer, or offers, that will make the creative process work. But remember this—what you offer is what you live with.

Checklist of Basic Offers

Following are 30 basic offers that may be used singly or in various combinations, depending on the marketer's objectives. Variations on some of these basic offers are illustrated in Exhibits 11–2 through 11–4.

1. *Free Information.* This is often the most effective offer, particularly when getting leads for salespeople is the prime objective or when non-prospects must be screened out at low cost before expensive literature is sent to prime prospects.

Exhibit 11–2.   Involvement Device

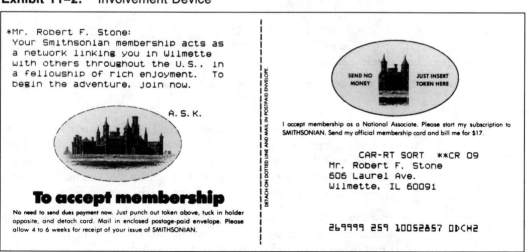

This order form, with a personal message from Smithsonian, *includes an involvement device.*

Exhibit 11–3. Postcard Mailing with Multiple Devices

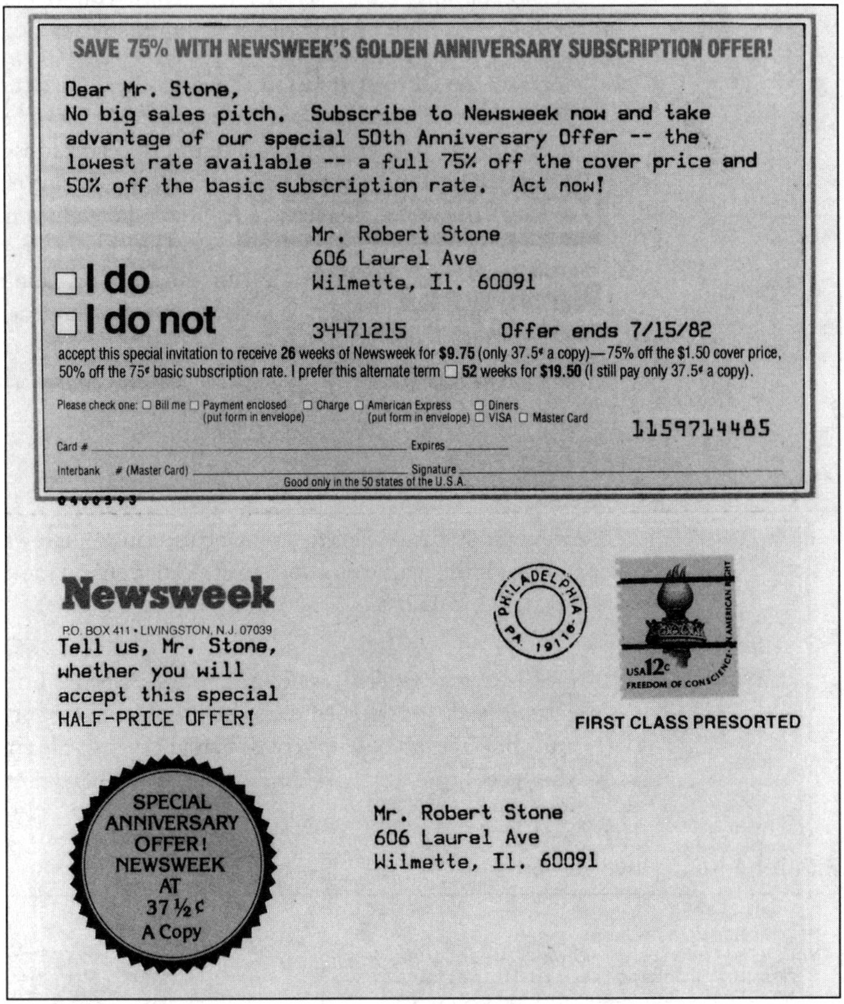

This simple postcard mailing from Newsweek *includes a sales message, yes-no offer, discount offer, and subscription card.*

2. *Samples.* A sample of a product or service is often a very effective sales tool. If a sample can be enclosed in a mailing package, results often more than warrant the extra cost. Consideration should be given to charging a nominal price for a sample. The recipient's investment in a sample promotes trying it, and this usually results in a substantial increase in sales.

3. *Free Trial.* This is the bellwether of mail order. Free trial melts away human inertia. Consider fitting the length of the trial period to the nature of the product or service, rather than the standard 15 days.

Exhibit 11–4.   Three-Tier Offer

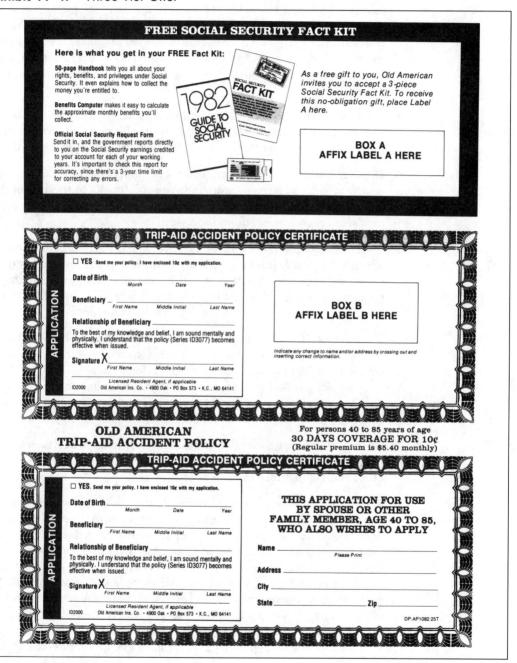

This three-tier offer from Old American Insurance Company offers: (1) a free Social Security Fact Kit, (2) an opportunity for the mail recipient to accept a 10-cent introductory offer for a Trip-Aid Accident Policy, and (3) the same opportunity for a spouse or other family member.

4. *Conditional Sale.* This prearranges the possibility of long-term acceptance based on a sample. Example: "Please send me, free, the premier issue of *Geo*, and reserve a money-saving Charter Subscription in my name. At the end of the thirty days, if I have not instructed you to cancel my reservation, you may enter my subscription at the Charter Rate of $36 for one year (twelve more monthly issues)—a savings of $12 off the annual cover price of $4 per issue."

5. *Till Forbid.* This prearranges continuing shipments on a specified basis. The customer has the option to forbid future shipments at any specified time. Works well for business-service offers and continuity book programs.

6. *Yes-No.* This is an involvement offer. The prospect is asked to respond usually through a token or stamp, indicating acceptance or rejection of the offer. Historically, more favorable responses are received with this offer than when no rejection option is provided.

7. *Time Limit.* Setting a time limit on a given offer *forces* action, either positive or negative. Usually it is more effective to name a specific date rather than a time period. It is important to test for the most effective time limit, because a short period might not allow sufficient time for deliberation. Too long a period, on the other hand, can promote inertia.

8. *Get-a-Friend.* This concept is based on the axiom that the best source for new customers is one's present list of satisfied customers. Many get-a-friend offers get new customers in a large volume at low acquisition cost. The best response, for a get-a-friend offer usually results from limiting the number of friends' names requested and offering a reward for providing names or securing new customers. (See Exhibit 11–5.)

9. *Contests.* These create attention and excitement. Stringent FTC rules apply. Contests are highly effective in conjunction with magazine subscription offers and popular merchandise offers.

10. *Discounts.* A discount is a never-ending lure to consumers as well as businesspeople. Discounts are particularly effective where the value of a product or service is well established. Discounts are widely offered for cash, for an introductory order, and for volume purchase. Discounts for volume purchases are often tied to levels of purchase. For example, "5 percent discount on orders up to $25; 10 percent discount on orders from $25 to $50; 15 percent discount on orders of $50 and over." Another play on basic discount offers is what is commonly referred to as *multiple time-dated discount offers*. The objective here is to get the customer into the habit of using your product or service. (Exhibit 11–6 is a good example of this technique.)

11. *Negative Option.* This offer, in popular use by book and record clubs, prearranges for shipment if the customer doesn't abort the shipment by

Exhibit 11–5.   Get-a-Friend Offer

The Literary Guild

231-3

New Applicant: Choose 4 books for $1 with membership!

Please accept my application for membership in The Literary Guild. Send me the 4 books indicated and bill me just $1, plus shipping and handling. I agree to the membership plan described in the enclosed circular and understand that I need buy only 4 more books at the regular low club prices whenever I want them. After buying 4 more books I may resign or remain a member for as long as I wish without further obligation to purchase books.

SATISFACTION GUARANTEED: If not completely satisfied with your Introductory package, return all four books within ten days. Your membership will be canceled and you'll owe nothing.

Write in code numbers of your 4 books here

Mr.
Mrs.
Miss
Ms.

(please print)

Address   Apt.

City   State   Zip

Present Member: Take 2 books FREE for each friend who becomes a member!

Write in code numbers of your 2 books here:

SPECIAL BONUS: Take one of these gifts free for each friend you introduce to The Literary Guild. Check one box for each friend:

☐ 88278 "Foot Notes" Memo Board
☐ 81075 The Literary Guild Book Jacket
☐ 85597 The Literary Guild Mini-Bag

81075

88278

85597

PRESENT MEMBER: In addition to your 2 FREE books, take one of these gifts free for each member recruited.

IMPORTANT: To avoid delay, please enter your current book club account number.

Name

(please print)

Address   Apt.

City   State   Zip

53   Order cannot be processed unless this card is filled in by both Present Member and New Applicant   FG033

In this get-a-friend offer from the Literary Guild, the member encourages a friend to fill out an application. The member fills in the balance of the card, indicating the bonus desired as a reward for acquiring a new member.

mailing the rejection form prior to deadline date. FTC guidelines must be followed carefully.

12. *Positive Option.* Every shipment is based on a direct action by the club member, rather than a nonaction, as exemplified by the negative option feature of most book and record clubs. Front-end response to a positive option is likely to be lower, but long-pull sales are likely to be greater.

Exhibit 11–6.   Time-Dated Discount Offer

U.S. News and World Report offers the first two issues free, with the right to cancel the conditional subscription for 24 additional issues. A token dramatizes the free offer.

13. *Lifetime Membership*. Under this plan, the member pays one fee, $5 for instance, at the time of becoming a member. In return, the member is guaranteed substantial reduction from established retail prices. There is no requirement that the respondent make a specified number of purchases. But the safeguard to the marketer is that members are more likely to make purchases because of their front-end investment.

14. *Load-Ups*. This proposition is a favorite of publishers of continuity series. Example: The publisher offers a set of 12 books, one to be released each month. After the purchaser has received and paid for the first three books, the publisher invites him to receive the remaining nine, all in one shipment, with the understanding that payments can continue to be made monthly. This load-up offer invariably results in more complete sets of books being sold.

15. *Free Gift*. Most direct response advertisers have increased response through free-gift offers. For best results, you should test several gifts to determine the most appealing. There's no set criterion for the cost of a gift as related to selling cost. The most important criteria are appropriateness of the gift, its effect on repeat business, and net profit per thousand circulation or distribution including cost of the gift.

16. *Secret Gift*. Lester Wunderman, chairman of Wunderman Worldwide, invented the secret-gift offer, commonly known as the "Gold Box offer." Conceived to measure the impact of TV on the pull of a newspaper or magazine insert, the viewer was told that there was a secret gold box on

the insert order form and that by filling in the box, the prospect would receive an extra free gift over and above the regular free-gift offer.

17. *Cash-up Free Gift.* Used primarily by publishers, cash-up offers stimulate cash with order. Incentives for advance cash payment usually involve one or two extra issues of a publication or a special report not available to charge subscribers.

18. *Add-on Offers.* One of the most innovative offers ever developed for increasing the unit of sale was first used, I believe, by the Horchow Collection. The offer was directed to catalog buyers about to place a toll-free phone order. The direction was, "When you place your phone order, ask about our Special of the Month." The special was always a discount on a catalog item. One catalog marketer adapted this idea and consistently sold the "special" to 10–15 percent of phone-order inquirers.

19. *Deluxe Alternative.* Related to the famous Sears tradition of good, better, best are offers for deluxe alternatives. A classic example would be a dictionary offered in a regular edition or in a thumb-indexed edition for $2 more. By giving the prospect the choice, the advertiser often increases total response and total dollars.

20. *Charters.* A charter offer, by its very nature, denotes something special. The offer plays on the human trait that many people want to be among the first to see, try, and use something new. The most successful charter offers include special rewards or concessions for early support.

21. *Guaranteed Buy-Back.* "Satisfaction guaranteed" is the heart of mail order selling. But the guaranteed buy-back offer goes much further. This guarantee pledges to buy back the product (if the customer so requests) at the original price for a period of time after original purchase.

22. *Multiproduct.* Multiproduct offers take the form of a series of postcards or a collection of individual sheets, each with a separate order form. Each product presentation is structured to stand on its own.

23. *Piggybacks.* These are "add-on" offers that ride along with major offers at no additional postage cost. The unit of sale is usually much smaller than the major offer. Testing is advocated to determine whether piggybacks add to or steal from sales of the major offer.

24. *Bounce-Backs.* Bounce-back offers succeed on the premise that "the best time to sell people is right after you have sold them." Bounce-back order forms are usually included in shipments or with invoices or statements. Bounce-backs can offer more of the same, related items, or items totally different from those originally purchased.

25. *Good-Better-Best.* The essence of this offer is to give the prospect a choice between something and something. For their State of the Union series, the

Franklin Mint gave the prospect three choices: 24k gold on sterling at $72.50 monthly, solid sterling silver at $43.75 monthly, and solid bronze at $17.50 monthly.

26. *Optional Terms.* The technique here is to give the prospect the option of choosing terms at varying rates. The bigger the commitment, the better the buy.

27. *Flexible Terms.* A derivative of optional terms is flexible terms. The potential subscriber to a magazine is offered a bargain weekly rate of, say, 25 cents a week for a minimum period of 16 weeks. But the subscriber may choose to enter the subscription for any number of weeks beyond the minimum at the same bargain rate.

28. *Exclusive Rights.* This is an offer made by publishers of syndicated newsletters. Under the term of such an offer, the first to order—an insurance broker, for example—has exclusive rights for his trading area so long as he or she remains a subscriber.

29. *Upgrade Offers.* Upgrade offers are particularly effective when applied to a customer base. Insurance companies are adept at applying this technique: "Double the daily benefits on your cancer policy for a small additional premium" is typical of upgrade offers by insurance companies. A response rate of 25–30 percent isn't unusual. Credit card companies have done a remarkable job of upgrading members based on their activities with existing card membership. American Express is a classic example, starting with its Green Card and moving up to its Gold and Platinum Cards.

30. *Promotional Videocassettes.* Direct marketers have been among the first to see the promotional opportunities through the medium of advertising videocassettes. It is estimated that by the end of this decade, 66 percent of television households will be equipped with a VCR. This gives the direct marketer the opportunity to use the demonstration power of TV without TV's time restraints. An offer to send a videocassette, either free or for a small charge, gives the marketer a unique opportunity for a professional, "live," in-depth, presentation of a product or service. Cruise lines, exercise equipment manufacturers, art galleries, and luxury apartment complexes are among business categories that are benefiting from the variety of videocassette offers being made.

Merchandising the Offer

Each of the offers we have just reviewed has wide application. As a matter of fact, many of the offers can be used successfully in combination. However, as powerful as many of these offers are, one must keep in mind that to maximize success the offers must be merchandised properly to target markets.

Free-Gift Offers

Giving free gifts for inquiring, for trying, and for buying is as old an incentive as trading stamps. It is not at all unusual for the right gift to increase response by 25 percent and more. On the other hand, a free-gift offer can actually reduce response or have no favorable effect on the basic offer. This is particularly true where the unit of sale or amount of sale consideration overshadows the appeal of the free gift.

What's more, there is a tremendous variance in the appeal of free gifts. For example, the Airline Passenger Association tested two free gifts along with a membership offer: an airline guide and a carry-on suit bag. The suit bag did 50 percent better than the guide. A fund-raising organization selling to schools tested three different gifts: a set of children's books, a camera, and a 30-cup coffee maker. The coffee maker won by a wide margin; the children's books came in a poor third.

Testing for the most appealing gifts is essential because of the great differences in pull. In selecting gifts for testing purposes, follow this rule of thumb: Gifts that are suited to personal use tend to have considerably more appeal than those that aren't.

There is yet another consideration about free gifts: Is it more effective to offer a selection of free gifts of comparable value than to offer only one gift? The answer is that offering a selection of gifts of comparable value usually reduces response. This is perhaps explained by the inability of many people to make a choice.

Adopting the one-gift method (after testing for the one with the most appeal) should not be confused with offering gifts of varying value for orders of varying amounts. This is quite a different situation. A multiple-gift proposition might be a free travel clock for orders up to $25, a free transistor radio for orders from $25 to $50, and a free Polaroid camera for orders over $50. Offering gifts of varying value for orders of varying amounts is logical to the consumer. The advertiser can afford a more expensive gift in conjunction with a larger order. The prime objective is accomplished by increasing the average order above what it would be if there were no extra incentive.

The multiple-gift plan works for many, but it can also boomerang. This usually happens when the top gift calls for a purchase above what most people can use or afford. The effect can also be negative if the gift offered for the price most people can afford is of little value or consequence. The multiple-gift plan tied to order value has good potential advantages, but careful tests must be conducted. An adaptation of the multiple-gift plan is a gift, often called a "keeper," for trying (free trial), plus a gift for keeping (paying for the purchase). Under this plan the prospect is told he or she can keep the gift offered for trying even if the product being offered for sale is returned. However, if the product being offered is retained, the prospect also keeps a second gift of greater value than the first.

Still another possibility with gift offers is giving more than one gift for either trying or buying. If the budget for the incentive is $1, for example, the advertiser can offer one gift costing $1, two gifts combined, costing $1, or even three gifts totaling $1. From a sales strategy standpoint, some advertisers spell out what one or two of the gifts are and offer an additional "mystery gift" for prompt response. Fingerhut Corporation of Minneapolis is a strong proponent of multiple gifts and "mystery gifts."

Free gifts are a tricky business, to be sure. Gift selection and gift tie-ins to offers require careful testing for best results. The $64,000 question is always: "How much can I afford to spend for a gift?" Aaron Adler, cofounder of Stone & Adler, maintains that most marketers make an erroneous arbitrary decision in advance, such as "I can afford to spend 5 percent of selling price." He maintains that a far more logical approach is to select the most appealing gift possible, without being restricted by an arbitrary cost figure, rather than to be guided by the net profit figures resulting from tests. For example, Exhibit 11–7 shows a comparison of net profits for two promotions on a $29.95 offer, one with a gift costing $1 and the other with a gift costing $2, given a 50 percent better pull with the $2 premium.

It is interesting to note that, in this example, when the $1 gift was offered, the mailing just about broke even. But when the cost of the gift was doubled, the profit jumped from $4.52 to $52.16 per thousand mailed. Another advantage of offering more attractive gifts (which naturally cost more) is to offer gifts of substantial value tied to cumulative purchases. This plan can prove particularly effective when the products or services being offered produce consistent repeat orders. A typical offer under a cumulative purchase plan might be, "When your total purchases of our custom-made cigars reach $150, you receive a crystal decanter absolutely free."

Get-a-Friend Offers

One overlooked and profitable offer is the get-a-friend offer. If you have a list of satisfied customers, it is quite natural for them to want to let their friends in on a good thing. The basic technique for get-a-friend offers is to offer an

Exhibit 11–7. Comparison of Profits from Promotions with Free Gifts of Different Costs

Item	$1 Gift	$2 Gift
Net pull of promotion	1%	1.5%
Sales per thousand pieces	$299.50	$449.25
Less		
Mailing cost	120.00	120.00
Merchandise cost (45%)	134.98	202.16
Administrative cost (10%)	30.00	44.93
Premium cost	10.00	30.00
Total costs	$294.98	$397.09
Profit per thousand pieces	4.52	52.16

incentive in appreciation for a favor. Nominal gifts are often given to a customer for the simple act of providing friends' names, with more substantial gifts awarded to the customer for friends who become customers.

Based on experience, here is what you can expect in using the get-a-friend approach: You will get a larger number of friends' names if the customers are guaranteed that their names will not be used in soliciting their friends. Response from friends, however, will be consistently better if you are allowed to refer to the party who supplied their names. To get the best of two worlds, therefore, you should allow customers to indicate whether their names may be used in soliciting their friends. For example: "You may use my name when writing my friends" or "Do not use my name when writing my friends."

Response from friends decreases in proportion to the number of names provided by a customer. One can expect the response from three names provided by one person to be greater than the total response from six names provided by another person. The reason is that it is natural to list the names in order of likelihood of interest.

Two safeguards should be applied to get the maximum response from friends' names: (1) limit the number of names to be provided, for example, to three or four, and (2) promote names provided in order of listing, such as all names provided first as one group, all names provided second as another group, and so forth. Those who have mastered the technique of getting friends' names from satisfied customers have found that, with very few exceptions, such lists are more responsive than most lists they can rent or buy.

Short- and Long-Term Effects of Offers

A major consideration in structuring offers is the effect a given offer will have on your objective:

- To get a maximum number of new customers for a given product or service as quickly as possible

- To determine the repeat business factor as quickly as possible

- To break even or make a profit in the shortest time

So, the key question to ask when designing an offer is "How will this offer help to accomplish my objective?" Say you are introducing a new hobby magazine. You have the choice of making a short-term offer (3 months) or a long-term offer (12 months). Because your objective is to determine acceptance as quickly as possible, you would decide on a short-term offer. Under the short-term offer, after 3 months you will be getting a picture of renewal percentages. If you have made an initial offer of 12-month subscriptions, you would have to wait a year to determine the publication renewal rate. In the interim, you would be missing vital information important to your magazine's success.

If the 3-month trial subscriptions are renewed at a satisfactory rate, you can then safely proceed to develop offers designed to get initial long-term subscriptions. It is axiomatic in the publishing field that the longer the initial term of subscription, the higher the renewal rate is likely to be. Circulation professionals know from experience that if they are getting, say, a 35 percent conversion on a 3-month trial, they can expect a conversion of 50 percent or more on 12-month initial subscriptions. This knowledge, therefore, can be extrapolated from the short-term objective to the long-term objective.

Sol Blumenfeld, a prominent direct marketing consultant, when addressing a Direct Mail/Marketing Association convention, made some pertinent remarks about the dangers of looking only at front-end response. Blumenfeld stated, "Many people still cling to the CPA (cost per application) or CPI (cost per inquiry) response syndromes. In their eagerness to sell now, they frequently foul up their chances to sell later."

He then asks, "Can the practice of those who concern themselves only with front-end response at least partially explain book club conversions of only 50 to 60 percent? Magazine renewal rates of only 30 percent? Correspondence school attrition factors of as much as 40 percent?"

Blumenfeld gives us a case in point. A control for the Britannica Home Study Library Service (a division of Encyclopedia Britannica) was run against several test ads developed by the agency. Control ads offered free the first volume of *Compton's Encyclopedia*. Major emphasis was placed on sending for the free volume; small emphasis was placed on the idea of ultimately purchasing the rest of the 24-volume set. Front-end response was excellent; the rate of conversion to full 24-volume sets was poor. Profitability was unacceptable. Against the control ad, the agency tested several new ads that offered Volume 1 free but also revealed the cost of the complete set in the headline. The cost per coupon for the new ads was 20 percent higher than for the control ad, but conversions to full sets improved a full 350 percent.

Ways to Hype Response

Once you have decided on your most appealing offer, either arbitrarily or by testing, you should ask a very specific question: How can I hype my offer to make it even more appealing? There are several ways: terms of payment, sweepstakes, umbrella sweepstakes, toll-free response, publisher's letters, and the guarantee.

Terms of Payment

Where a direct sale is involved, the terms of payment you require can hype or depress response. A given product or service can have tremendous appeal, but if payment terms are too stringent—beyond the means of a potential buyer—the offer will surely be a failure. Five general categories of payment terms may be offered: (1) cash with order, (2) cash on delivery (COD), (3) open account, (4) installment terms, and (5) revolving credit.

If a five-way split test were made among these categories, it is almost certain that response would be in inverse ratio to the listing of the five categories. Revolving credit would be the most attractive and cash with order the least attractive terms. With each loosening of terms, the appeal of the offer is hyped.

In a four-way split test on a merchandise offer, here's how four terms actually ranked (the least appealing terms have a 100 percent ranking): cash with order, 100 percent; cash with order—free gift for trying, 144 percent; bill-me offer (open account), 177 percent; and bill-me offer (open account) and free gift, 233 percent. As the figures disclose, the most attractive terms (bill-me offer and free gift) were almost two and one-half times more appealing than the least attractive terms (cash with order).

Although COD terms are generally more attractive than cash-with-order requirements, the hazard of COD terms is refusal on delivery. It is not unusual to sustain an 8 percent refusal rate when COD terms are offered. (Many COD orders are placed emotionally, and emotion cools off when the delivery person or letter carrier calls and requests payment.)

When merchandise or services are offered on open account, payment is customarily requested in 15 or 30 days. Such terms are naturally more appealing than cash with order or COD. Open-account terms are customary when selling to business firms. When used in selling to the consumer, however, such terms, while appealing, can result in a high percentage of bad debts, unless carefully selected credit-checked lists are used.

The best appeals lie in installment terms and revolving credit terms. Both mechanisms require substantial financing facilities and a sophisticated credit collection system. Installment selling in the consumer field is virtually essential for the successful sale of "big ticket" merchandise—items selling for $69.95 and up.

One can have the best of two worlds—most appealing terms and no credit risk—by making credit arrangements through a sales finance firm or commercial credit card operations, such as American Express, Diners Club, Discover, or one of the bank cards: Visa or MasterCard.

Banks cards and travel-and-entertainment cards have proved a boon to mail order operations, especially catalog operations. It is not unusual to hype the average order from a catalog by 15 percent when bank card privileges or travel-and-entertainment card privileges are offered. Not only do these privileges tend to increase the amount of the average order, but they also tend to increase the total response.

When arrangements are made through commercial credit card operations, any member may charge purchases to his or her card. The credit of all members in good standing is ensured by the respective credit card operations. The advertiser is paid by the agency for the total sales charged less a discount charge, usually about 1–3 percent for bank cards and 3–7 percent for travel-and-entertainment cards.

Sweepstakes

Perhaps the most hype available to direct marketers is the sweepstakes. (See Exhibit 11–8.) A sweepstakes overlaid on an offer adds excitement and interest. Two major direct marketers that have used sweepstakes through the 1960s and on into the 1990s are *Reader's Digest* and Publishers Clearing House. The techniques they use are the ultimate in sophistication.

Both *Reader's Digest* (RD) and Publishers Clearing House (PCH) use TV support as an integral part of their sweepstakes promotions. Success depends on the following:

1. Heavy market penetration of the printed materials

2. Time-controlled delivery of the printed offer to coincide with TV support

3. Sufficient TV impact to excite interest in the printed promotion

Careful testing is required to determine the most cost-efficient amount of TV laid over the print offer. "Keep TV commercials simple," cautions Publishers Clearing House. Current PCH commercials prove they practice what they preach: They feature the sweepstakes, using past winners to carry the message, leaving the magazine savings story to the mailing package.

Astute direct marketers like RD and PCH know incentives for prompt response tend to increase total response. Each has built incentives for prompt response into its sweepstakes contests. RD, for example, has offered the following bonus award incentive: "$1,000 a day for every day your entry beats the deadline of January 31." This means that, if the grand prize is $50,000 and your entry is postmarked before January 21, you, as the grand prize winner, will win an extra $10,000. Another technique is reader involvement. "Seven Chances to Be a Winner," PCH announced in promoting a $400,000 sweepstakes. The entrant was given seven prize numbers.

Umbrella Sweepstakes

A big sweepstakes requires a bushel of money for prizes and administration. Direct marketers, bottom-line people that they are, have found ways to overlay a major sweepstakes on more than one proposition. *Reader's Digest*, for example, can overlay the same sweepstakes on a magazine subscription offer, a book club offer, and a tape offer, each falling under the umbrella of one prize budget.

D.L. Blair, the largest sweepstakes judging agency in the country, points out that there are many questions to be answered for anyone contemplating a sweepstakes. Here are questions D.L. Blair has answered for us.

What are the most popular prize structures?

Cash, automobiles, travel, and home entertainment appliances—in that order—continue to be the most appealing and popular prize structures. According to

Exhibit 11–8.   Sweepstakes Offer

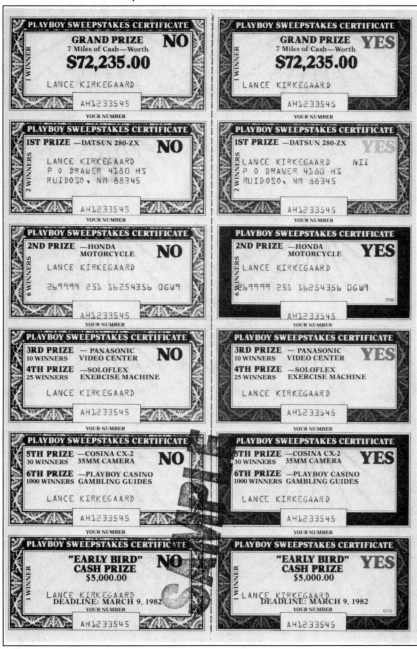

Playboy *Great Escape Sweepstakes offers a $72,235 grand prize and an array of lesser prizes on the front cover of a four-page folder and provides personalized entry coupons for the same group of prizes.*

our most recent research, apparel (fur coats, designer dresses) has virtually no appeal. As for other merchandise, we generally prefer to eschew the use of merchandise prizes except when we have conclusive research indicating greater consumer preference for the prize item than for its equivalent cash value.

When a sweeps is tested against a nonsweeps, what range of increase might be expected for a magazine subscription offer or catalog offer?

Using a sweepstakes overlay, we have never seen less than a 15 percent increase in orders for either a catalog or a magazine subscription. The greatest increase we have ever seen is 350 percent. Generally, the increment falls between 30 and 100 percent.

Can a low-budget sweeps be successful?

Though it is generally true that the success levels of any sweepstakes are importantly impacted by the prize budget, we have seen low-budget programs work extremely well when directed at special-interest groups. Thus, while a $3,500-value grand prize would provide little or no motivation to most broad audience segments, a $3,500 home flight simulator would be highly appealing to an audience comprised solely of private pilots; a $3,500 hunting carbine would be highly appealing to NRA members; a $3,500 one-of-a-kind Wedgewood bud vase would be extremely appealing to Wedgewood collectors.

From a legal standpoint, must all prizes be awarded in a sweepstakes offer?

Speaking solely from the narrow area of what is strictly legal, it is only necessary to award prizes to those who have submitted entry numbers that the judges have preselected as winning numbers. There are, however, very compelling business and ethical reasons that strongly suggest that any direct marketer would be ill-advised to consider awarding fewer than the full number of prizes that it has advertised.

Is the average order from a catalog, for example, likely to be smaller with a sweeps entry?

It depends on whether the order is from a former buyer or a new customer. The average order from former buyers tends to be larger. We've seen a sweepstakes increase the value of each catalog order by more than 40 percent. New-customer orders, on the other hand, tend to be lower than average, probably because these are fringe buyers coming in as a result of the sweepstakes overlay.

Having acquired a new customer with a sweepstakes contest, would you say that repeat business is likely to depend on additional sweepstakes contest?

Yes, to some degree it is true that continuing sweepstakes promotions might be necessary to maintain a normal level of repeat business. I would say this is true to the same extent that a customer first acquired with incentives such as price-off coupons, free gifts, discount offers, and the like would be conditioned to such offers in the future.

What is the profile of sweepstakes entrants?

It's becoming broader with more geographic, economic, and education homogeneity. This "flattening" process extends to the sex of respondents: men account for almost 47 percent of sweepstakes entrants.

Is the appeal of sweepstakes to direct marketing customers increasing, declining, or holding flat?

Almost without exception, our direct mail marketing clients are reporting greater new-customer and current-buyer penetration from their sweepstakes programs. Since we are seeing comparable response increases in programs run by our package-goods clients, it would appear that there is significantly more customer interest in sweepstakes than has ever been the case before.

Toll-Free Response

Toll-free telephone response (800 numbers) offers the opportunity to hype the response from just about any offer, particularly gifts involving free information or the sale of merchandise. (See Chapter 8, "Telemarketing.")

Publisher's Letter

Another innovative device that has been developed for hyping responses during the past decade is an extra mailing enclosure known as the "publisher's letter." It gets its name from its first usage—a short letter from a magazine publisher enclosed in the basic mailing package. The publisher's letter usually carries a headline: "If you have decided not to respond, read this letter." The letter copy typically reinforces the offer made in the basic mailing packages, assures the reader it is valid, and guarantees the terms. This extra enclosure often increases response by 10 percent and more. While the publisher's letter was originated for subscription letters, this device was soon adopted by other direct marketers selling goods and services. Results have been equally productive.

The Guarantee

No matter what the terms or basic offer may be, a strong guarantee is essential when selling products or services direct. For more than 95 years, Sears, Roebuck and Company has guaranteed satisfaction for every article offered (Exhibit 11–9). Over the years, no one else has ever succeeded in mail order operations without duplicating the Sears guarantee or offering a similar assurance. The importance of the guarantee is perhaps best understood by recognizing a fact

Exhibit 11–9.   Sears Guarantee

SEARS GUARANTEE

Your satisfaction is guaranteed or your money back.

We guarantee that every article in this catalog is accurately described and illustrated.

If, for any reason whatever, you are not satisfied with any article purchased from us, we want you to return it to us at our expense.

We will exchange it for exactly what you want, or will return your money, including any transportation charges you have paid.

SEARS, ROEBUCK AND CO.

---

of life: people are hesitant to send for merchandise unless they know that the product may be returned for full credit if it does not meet their expectations. Guaranteed satisfaction should be a part of any offer soliciting a direct sale.

Many marketers have developed unique guarantees that go beyond the trial period. Madison House, for instance, advertised a new fishing lure in a March issue of *Family Weekly*. The company knew, of course, that in northern areas, lakes were frozen over and that there would be no opportunity to test and use this lure before spring. Madison House overcame the problem beautifully by urging the fishing buff to send for the lure *now* with the provision that it could be returned any time within six months for a full cash refund. This guarantee had two advantages: It assured fishing buffs that, even though they were ordering the lure out of season, they could return it after they tried it in season; and it enabled Madison House to advertise and get business out of season.

Many marketers reinforce their own guarantees with a third-party guarantee. "Approved by Underwriters Laboratory" can make the difference where electrical appliances are concerned. The *Good Housekeeping* Seal of Approval has long been accepted as a guarantee of validity of claim.

Publishers Clearing House has made this statement: "In addition to the publisher's own warranties, Publishers Clearing House makes you this unconditioned guarantee: You may have a full cash refund at any time, or for any reason, on the unused part of any subscription ordered through the clearing house. This guarantee has no time limit. It is your assurance that you can order from Publishers Clearing House with complete confidence." In direct sales, the right proposition and the right terms of payment are only two-thirds of the impetus. A clear, strong guarantee completes the trio.

Danger of Overkill

The power of an offer cannot be overestimated. But there's such a thing as too much of a good thing—offers that sound too good to be true or that produce a great front-end response but make for poor pay-ups or few repeat customers. Here are two thought-provoking examples:

1. A comprehensive test was structured for a fund-raising organization to determine whether response would best be maximized by (a) offering a free gift as an incentive for an order, (b) offering a combination of free gift plus a cash bonus for completing a sale, or (c) offering a cash bonus only. The combination of free gift plus cash bonus pulled the lowest response by far; the free-gift proposition far outpulled the cash-bonus proposition.

2. A $200 piece of electronic equipment was offered for a 15-day free trial. This was the basic proposition. But half the people on the list also were invited to enter a sweepstakes contest. Those on the portion of the list not invited to enter a sweepstakes responded 25 percent better than those on the portion invited to enter.

In both these examples, the more generous offer proved to be "too much." One must be most careful not to make the offer so overwhelming that it overshadows the product or service being offered. Another important consideration in structuring offers is the axiom, "As you make your bed, so shall you lie in it." Here's what we mean. If you obtain thousands of new customers by offering free gifts as incentives, don't expect a maximum degree of repeat business unless you continue to offer free gifts. Similarly, if you build a big list of installment credit buyers, don't expect these buyers to respond well to cash-basis offers, and vice versa.

Making It Easy to Order

The structure of an offer should not be taken lightly. The impact an offer can have on immediate and long-term results can be tremendous. It is sad but true that some of the most brilliant offers fail not because the offers aren't appealing, but because they are poorly presented verbally, graphically, or both. The greatest sins of execution are to be found in coupon space ads.

Tony Antin, who directed creative services for *Reader's Digest*, laid down this mandate for coupon order forms: "A coupon (order form) should be— must be—an artistic cliché. Rectangular. Surrounded by dash lines. Not even dotted lines. Because one connects dots. One cuts along dashes. Moreover, the coupon should be where it belongs, at the lower outside. The coupon should stand out from the rest of the ad."

So, construction of offers boils down to this: Your primary job is to overcome human inertia. Your offers should relate to objectives. Consider the short- and long-term effects. And, by all means, make it easy to order!

SELF-QUIZ

1. List the ten basic factors to consider when creating a direct sale offer.

   a. _____   f. _____

   b. _____   g. _____

   c. _____   h. _____

   d. _____   i. _____

   e. _____   j. _____

2. Of the ten factors above, which one should always be applied to a direct sale offer?

   _____

3. What is a "till forbid" offer?

   _____

   _____

   _____

4. What is the difference between a negative option and a positive option?

   _____

   _____

   _____

5. What is the basic rule to follow in testing a variety of free gifts to determine which is most appealing?

   _____

   _____

6. Here are five terms of payment: (1) cash with order, (2) COD, (3) open account, (4) installment terms, and (5) revolving credit. Which is likely to have the most appeal?

7. Define *umbrella sweepstakes*.

8. What are the most popular prize structures for sweepstakes?

9. Define *publisher's letter*.

10. Why is the guarantee in direct sale offers so essential?

11. What is a third-party guarantee?

12. Under what conditions can an offer be too attractive?

13. Check the requirements for an effective coupon (order form):
Coupons should be ☐ rectangular   ☐ oval
and surrounded by ☐ dotted lines   ☐ dashed lines.

PILOT PROJECT

You have been given an important assignment: to launch a new publication called *Prime Time* for the over-50 market. This is to be a monthly publication carrying a cover price of $2.50, with a mail subscription rate of $24 a year. The publisher is anxious to: (1) reach a subscription base of 100,000 subscribers before the first issue appears and (2) determine the renewal rate as quickly as possible. There will be no newsstand distribution. Keeping the publisher's objectives in mind, develop three different offers that might be tested.

CHAPTER TWELVE

Selecting and Selling Merchandise and Services

The urge to enter the mail order business is an urge that just won't go away for thousands of entrepreneurs. Yet most who enter the arena fail miserably. The reasons for failure are many:

- A false belief one can get rich quick
- Lack of intuitive feelings about mail order products
- No sense of the required ratio of cost to selling price
- Failure to test properly
- A dearth of knowledge about appropriate media
- Poor merchandise sources
- Insufficient capital

Where to Find Mail Order Items

How then does one find hot mail order items? Where do you go? What do you look for? What should you avoid? How do you start? There is no greater authority to answer these questions than Len Carlson, who pioneered and marketed about 10,000 mail order items over the past 30 years. His first tip is to look for items whose benefits can be demonstrated with photos, graphics, and copy that dramatize the end use.

And where do you find such items? They are rarely found in general merchandise stores. More often they are found in boutiques—off-beat stores that offer the unusual—in this country and particularly abroad. Then there are the trade shows: the housewares show in Chicago, the hardware and stationery shows, the premium shows, and the foreign trade shows.

Carlson asks pointed questions at trade shows, such as the following:

- What items are you selling to mail-order companies now?

- Can you add this feature?

- What are the requirements for getting an exclusive on this item?

- What kind of a backup inventory can you guarantee?

- What do you have that doesn't sell well?

Most manufacturers' representatives are startled by this last question. Carlson often finds items that bombed out on retail shelves that he can bring to life in catalogs and promote with demonstrable benefits. Along the same line, he recommends resurrection of oldies but goodies, taking them out of mothballs for a new generation of buyers.

The tips for finding mail order items continue. "You have to become a great reader, subscribing to jillions of consumer and trade magazines," says Carlson, "Not only United States magazines, but foreign magazines as well." Many of the magazines are available in libraries. Then there is what he calls "the rule of two." Here's how it works. You religiously accumulate mail order catalogs. When you see a new item, you record it as a test. If you see the same item in a subsequent catalog, you assume the test worked and your interest should be piqued. If you don't see the item a second time, you can assume the item bombed.

One of the top mail order secrets Carlson learned years ago is the appeal of personalization. Few stores personalize. So a mail order operation can take a standard stock item, personalize it, and change the appeal from "ho-hum" to "exciting." Such mundane items as dog and cat dishes, floor mats, and paper napkins are good examples. Exhibit 12–1 lists the sources for discovering viable mail order items. Carlson's advice can be summarized as follows:

- Use your instincts.

- Keep your eyes open.

- Hustle! Work!

- Innovate.

- Think MERCHANDISE—all the time.

- The search never ends!

Exhibit 12–1.   Checklist of Sources for Mail Order Items

---

1. Study competitive catalogs and solo offers.

2. Read consumer magazines.

3. Subscribe to pertinent trade journals.

4. Cover U.S. trade shows.

5. Browse retail stores constantly.

6. Write to manufacturers listed in directories.

7. Talk to manufacturers' representatives.

8. Periodically visit book stores and libraries.

9. Attend foreign trade fairs; shop stores that carry foreign goods.

10. Read foreign magazines and catalogs.

11. Contact foreign commercial attachés.

12. Revive your old successes.

13. Set up and refer to your "idea file" frequently.

14. Add on features to existing items.

15. Personalize if pertinent to the product.

Exhibit 12–2 provides 34 important factors in selecting mail order items. Let's take No. 6, for example: Is the markup sufficient to assure profit? On this Carlson says, "The books say you need four or five times cost in order to sell profitably. I don't think that's necessarily true. Certainly you need to more than double the cost of an item to come out." Or No. 24, Will it lend itself to repeat business? "You should search for items that lend themselves to repeat business. Otherwise you've got to keep coming up with new items for repeat business. Consumable items are the idea." Knowing how to evaluate products is a key to mail order success, but not the only key. Finding a niche for yourself in the marketplace is at the top of the list.

"Your first question," says Carlson, "should be, 'What's missing from the market?'" When he launched Sunset House, he perceived a void in the marketplace that could be filled by bringing hundreds of gadgets together in one catalog. A multimillion-dollar business grew from the recognition of this void. Years later another entrepreneur perceived there was no one place in the market where one could buy hard-to-find tools. Thus the highly successful Brookstone Catalog operation was born.

Finding a void and the right items to fill that void are key. But even these steps are short of achieving success. The entrepreneur, in particular, must be a total businessperson. The final checklist from Len Carlson is the coup de grâce. It's the "moment of truth" for would-be mail-order millionaires. (See Exhibit

Exhibit 12–2.   Factors to Consider When Selecting Mail Order Items

1. Is there a perceived need for the product?
2. Is it practical?
3. Is it unique?
4. Is the price right for my customer or prospect?
5. Is it good value?
6. Is the markup sufficient to assure profit?
7. Is the market large enough? Does it have broad appeal?
8. Are there specific small segments of my list that have a strong desire for the product?
9. Is it new? Or will my customers perceive it to be new?
10. Will it photograph/illustrate interestingly?
11. Are there sufficient unusual selling features to make the copy exciting?
12. Is it economical to ship? Too fragile? Odd-shaped? Too heavy? Too big?
13. Can it be personalized?
14. Are there any legal problems to overcome?
15. Is it safe to use?
16. Is the supplier reputable?
17. Will backup merchandise be available for fast shipment on reorders?
18. Might returns be too huge?
19. Will refurbishing of returned merchandise be practical?
20. Is it, or can it be, packaged attractively?
21. Are usage instructions clear?
22. How does it compare to competitive products?
23. Will it have exclusivity?
24. Will it lend itself to repeat business?
25. Is it consumable (for repeat orders)?
26. Is it faddy? Too short-lived?
27. Is it too seasonal for mail-order selling?
28. Can an add-on to the product make it more distinctive and salable?
29. Will the number of stock-keeping units (sizes and colors) create inventory problems?
30. Does it lend itself to multiple pricing?
31. Is it too readily available in stores?
32. Is it like an old, hot item that guarantees its success?
33. Is it doomed because similar items have failed before?
34. Does my mother/wife/brother/husband like it? (If so, it probably should be discarded!)

12–3.) Careful study of this comprehensive checklist could lead many to conclude that mail order is not for me.'' And that could be good!

Case Study: The Peruvian Connection

With caution well established, it's time to give living proof that entrepreneurs can succeed in spite of the hazards involved. Annie Hurlbut is a classic example of getting into mail order by serendipity. A neophyte in every sense, she has performed as if she wrote Len Carlson's checklist! Hurlbut, an anthropologist, spent her sophomore summer vacation from Yale University working at an archaeological dig in Peru. There she encountered the alpaca, a cameloid animal related to the vicuna and the llama. Although the alpaca has an unpleasant disposition (it spits at people, Hurlbut says), it is the mainstay of the economy of the Andes, serving as food and, along with the llama, as beast of burden. (The alpaca can carry up to a 50-pound load. ''Put 51 pounds on it and it balks,'' she says.) But the alpaca is raised mainly for its extraordinary wool, which is lightweight, warm, and grows naturally in a variety of colors, from white to beige, brown and gray.

Hurlbut returned to Peru again as a graduate student in anthropology, but this time for her thesis research on women who sell in primitive markets. Among their wares were handloomed alpaca garments, which were warm and practical but not exactly stylish. So Hurlbut turned designer. She worked with the Peruvians to design sweaters with more flair so they would be more acceptable to North American women. With her first stock, Hurlbut returned to the family farm in Tonganoxie, Kansas, and started a mail-order catalog business called ''The Peruvian Connection'' with her mother as a partner. They produced a catalog and did some ads. And with this, Annie Hurlbut was in the mail order business.

Some of Hurlbut's early ads were primitive. And the first ''catalog'' was really no more than an amateurish flyer. But the first ads and catalogs sold enough merchandise to pay the bills, with some left over to reinvest. Clearly, alpaca styled by Peruvians overcame any lack of sophistication in mail order techniques. Hurlbut's sense of style, plus alpaca's uniqueness, worked. Hurlbut learned quickly that the secret to building a mail order business was to develop a customer file as quickly as possible and offer those customers other items.

The Peruvian Connection's first offering outside of apparel was pure alpaca blankets (See Exhibit 12–4.) There are a couple of other noteworthy tried-and-true mail order techniques that Hurlbut used in conjunction with this mailing. Enclosing a swatch of the blanket was a brilliant stroke. (I couldn't resist running my fingers over the swatch—it is really soft!) Also, Hurlbut encouraged ordering by phone and charging to a credit card. Would you like to guess what the pull was from the customer list? Five percent? No. Ten percent? No. Twenty-five percent? No. It pulled 43 percent—a pull the professionals would give their birthright for.

Exhibit 12–3.   Checklist for Mail Order Operation

Merchandise Selection and Product Development

1. Set marketing objective.
2. Select products.
3. Perform market research.
4. Evaluate potentials.

Media Selection

1. Make budget decisions.
2. Decide on direct mail circulation.
3. Select appropriate house list segments.
4. Arrange rental/compilation of outside lists (list brokers).
5. Decide timing of campaign.
6. Buy space/time (ad agencies, reps, media).
7. Arrange for inserts/co-ops/package inserts/other media.
8. Consider phone selling.

Creative Decisions

1. Develop the offers and formats.
2. Get copy prepared.
3. Arrange for photography/illustrations.
4. Determine typography, design, and layout.
5. Schedule production operations.
6. Set up printing and mailing program.
7. Buy envelopes.
8. Work with creative consultants.

Testing Projects

1. Offers
2. Prices
3. Lists
4. Geographic areas
5. Formats

Buying Procedures

1. Negotiate with vendors and purchase products.
2. Follow up vendors for delivery.
3. Re-buy.
4. Maintain inventory control.
5. Control inspection of incoming merchandise.
6. Dispose of inventory overstock.

Management Functions

1. Estimate costs, potentials, and profitability.
2. Analyze response and sales.
3. Check legal aspects of merchandising.
4. Double-check record-keeping and data-capture activity.
5. Decide whether credit/credit cards are to be offered.
6. Decide whether telephone orders should be accepted.
7. Determine whether foreign sales are possible.
8. Sell house products, wholesale, to others.
9. Maintain liaison with fulfillment, accounting, and customer service departments.

Exhibit 12–4.   The Peruvian Connection

Dear Special Customer:

   In early December, on a trip to Peru for Christmas orders,
I stumbled across some extraordinary 100% alpaca blankets, a
swatch of which I'm enclosing in this envelope. I was aston-
ished by the quality of the fibre used and impressed with the
workmanship, even to the blanket-stitched edges. When I heard
the prices (under half of what we pay for the $250 Mon Repos
blankets we import), I called the States to consult with my
partner, and bought up every one. A few hours later The Peruvian Connection was launched into the market of luxury blankets.
As far as I know, we are the first and only U.S. importers
of 100% alpaca blankets, although they have been exported to
Europe for some time.

   Our plan is to sell these blankets at direct-importer
WHOLESALE prices in order to compete with the $75 to $95 prices
of the 50%alpaca/50% sheep's wool blankets currently available
in stores and through catalogues such as Gumps, Brookstone,
Shopping International and others. These half alpaca blankets
are beautiful, warm and sturdy. We know, we've been importing
them for years. But for weightless warmth and silky softness,
no natural fibre-- not mohair, not angora, not even cashmere--
competes with pure alpaca. The secret lies in the high lanolin
content of this wool from the Andes.

   The reason you rarely see 100% alpaca blankets in this country
is simple: Alpacas, which live almost exclusively in the Andes,
produce a limited amount of wool (they are sheared only once
every two years during the rainy season). The global demand for
scarce alpaca fibre, however, is insatiable. In the four years

distributed in the united states by
canaan farm tonganoxie kansas 66086 (913) 845-2750

*This two-page letter gets attention at the outset and quickly establishes value through the technique of
favorable comparison.*

Exhibit 12–4 *(Continued)*.

of our import business, the Peruvian market price of alpaca has more than quadrupled.

Since Inca times, when by law only nobility could wear clothing of fine alpaca, alpaca has been valued over the hair of its coarser cousin, the llama. Now even lesser quality llama sells for astounding prices. In the December, '79 issue of Smithsonian, the domestic price of llama was quoted at $32 a pound, compared to the 75¢ a pound price quoted for sheep's wool. The article didn't mention alpaca, probably because even in Andean marketplaces, the latter sells for considerably more than the highest grade of llama. Predictions are that the price of this once royal fibre will continue to climb. Alpaca is, in effect, Peru's golden fleece.

The small number of blankets I brought back in December were bought just ahead of a substantial mid-December price rise. As a test market, between now and January 31st, we are offering 64 of these blankets at prices well below our own Wholesale prices. Because our supply at this price is limited, we are offering this special discount to only a fraction of our mailing list, most of whom are old customers. You are one of 100 people in on this sneak preview.

If you love alpaca, don't wait for the price rise to buy one of these blankets. As are all of our exotic exclusives from Peru, our new 100% alpaca blankets are fully guaranteed.

We at the Peruvian Connection send you our warmest, softest wishes for a Happy New Year.

WHOLESALE PRICES FOR 100% ALPACA BLANKETS:

SPECIAL PRICE THROUGH JAN 31st

Blanket (86"x65") .... $140.00 $125.
   (pictured, in natural alpaca stripes)

Throw Blanket   (75"x57") $103.50 $92.50
   (pictured, in natural alpaca stripes)

Lap robe (or child's blanket) (43"x35")...... $42.00 $37.50
   (not pictured, in solid color soft brown)

Exhibit 12–4 *(Continued).*

This four-color circular was included with the two-page letter.

Expanding Existing Mail Order Operations

It has been said that no mail order item or mail order line lasts forever. It is certainly true that every mail order item—not unlike items sold through traditional channels—is subject to product life cycles. (See Exhibit 12–5.) Hence there is the ever-present need to come up with new products and services. How does one do that?

When someone inquires of Aaron Adler, cofounder of Stone & Adler, how to determine what new product or service to offer, he asks, "What business are you in?" Nine times out of ten, the person will say, "Oh, I'm in the catalog business," or, "I sell collectibles," or "I sell books," or something similar. That type of answer is true, of course, so far as it goes. But it probably doesn't go far enough if you really want to explore all the possibilities of your operation.

Executives of companies who think of themselves as being in the "catalog business" or in the "tape business" limit their options severely. Their thinking is confined so narrowly that it becomes difficult to come up with new offers for customers. On the other hand, if they give serious thought to the total character of their business, new avenues of possibility are opened, perhaps leading to the development and promotion of a wider range of products and services.

To illustrate: Is a mail order insurance company in the business of merely selling insurance? Not at all. It is really in the business of helping to provide

Exhibit 12–5.   The Product Life Cycle

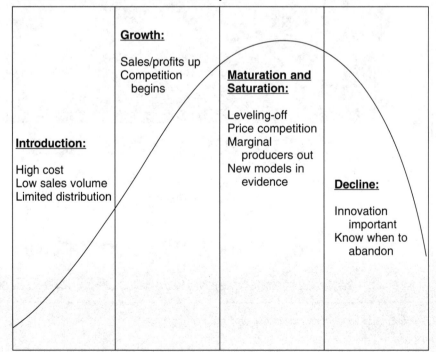

Growth:

Sales/profits up
Competition
  begins

**Maturation and
Saturation:**

Leveling-off
Price competition
Marginal
  producers out
New models in
  evidence

Introduction:

High cost
Low sales volume
Limited distribution

Decline:

Innovation
  important
Know when to
  abandon

financial security to its policyholders and prospects. From that perspective, management of an insurance company can rhink of offering not only other kinds of insurance policies but also financial planning services, loans, and the sale of mutual funds, assuming, of course, there is no conflict with insurance or investment laws and regulations.

More and more successful mail order companies have adopted this kind of thinking. A classic example is the Franklin Mint, whose management recognized that the company was not in the business of simply selling limited-edition medallions. The Franklin Mint was actually in the business of producing fine art objects on a limited-edition basis for those who enjoy the pleasure and status provided by owning handsome objects not available to the general public. In addition, the possibility existed that the value of these objects would increase as time went on. As a result, the company has successfully offered limited-edition art prints, books, glassware, porcelain, and a myriad of other items (See Exhibit 12–6.)

Another example is Baldwin Cooke Company. This firm for many years had offered an executive planner (desk diary) that businesspeople found made an excellent Christmas gift for their clients and friends. Then came the realization that the company was not simply in the business of selling desk diaries, but rather was in the business of selling executive gifts. This led to the development of a broad line of successful new products. The company's gift catalog today runs to 32 pages with a circulation of more than a million.

An outstanding example of this broad-based thinking is the Meredith Publishing Company, publishers of *Better Homes & Gardens*, among other publications. Recognizing that the company was not simply in the magazine-publishing business, but rather in the business of disseminating useful, helpful information to large segments of middle America, management moved into such product areas as geographic atlases, world globes, gardening books, cookbooks, and a whole range of similar materials.

Therefore, if you are looking for new products or services to offer your customers or to reach new prospects, think about what kind of business you are really in. When you make that determination, you'll find that many new areas will open up for you.

For the moment, let's pursue the idea that you are in direct marketing, that you have a list of customers built by offering products or services that they have found eminently satisfactory, and that you would like to expand your sales to those customers with new offerings. Let's also assume that you have answered the question of what business you are really in and have concluded that there are broader areas of endeavor available than you had previously realized. What then?

What Are Your Capabilities?

First, review your capabilities and those of your organization and, again, try to think in the broadest possible terms. For example, the G.R.I. Corporation,

Exhibit 12–6.   Expanding the Product Line

The renowned illustrator of "Little Women" creates her first porcelain sculptures . . .

Amy by Tasha Tudor

Inaugurating Tasha Tudor's first collection of porcelain sculptures. Individually crafted, hand-painted and issued in limited edition. Art of enchanting beauty, at the very attractive price of $75.

In today's world of fine book illustrators, there is one name that stands out among the rest—Tasha Tudor. An artist who, for almost fifty years, has been capturing the hearts of millions with art that is happy, innocent and filled with old-fashioned charm. With delicate use of colors and a wealth of detail, her illustrations create a magical world of make-believe with characters as loveable as they are unforgettable.

Now, to celebrate the 150th anniversary of author Louisa May Alcott's birth, Tasha Tudor has created her very first works in porcelain. A collection of limited edition "Little Women" sculptures that are sure to be of exceptional interest to collectors.

"Amy", portraying Louisa May Alcott's charming, blue-eyed beauty, inaugurates the collection. Crafted in fine, hand-painted porcelain, it is a thoroughly delightful work of art. And it will be issued at the very modest price of just $75—which may itself be paid in convenient monthly installments.

The figure that Tasha Tudor has designed is so vivid, so alive, it's as if "Amy" had invited you into the pages of "Little Women" to come pay a special visit. There she sits with dreamy eyes fixed on the sketchpad in her lap. From her cascading golden curls, to the ruffled pinafore she wears as an artist's smock—she's the very vision of loveliness. A captivating and compelling sculpture as charming and full of grace as Louisa May Alcott's young artist.

To ensure that every small detail of Tasha Tudor's art—every nuance of expression—is faithfully captured, each sculpture will be individually crafted by master porcelain artisans in Japan. Each sculpture will be hand-cast . . . hand-assembled . . . and hand-painted with uncompromising care.

In the tradition of classic works in fine porcelain, "Amy" will be issued in a single limited edition, reserved exclusively for those who order from the collection by November 29, 1982—the 150th anniversary of Louisa May Alcott's birth. When all valid orders from these individuals have been filled, the edition will be closed.

"Amy" will bring her own personality and charm to your home and any room in which you choose to display her. And in time to come, this engaging work of art is likely to become a treasured family heirloom, lovingly passed on from mother to daughter.

To acquire your own hand-painted fine porcelain sculpture of "Amy" by Tasha Tudor, it is important to act promptly. Please be sure to mail the accompanying advance reservation application by May 31, 1982.

- - - - - - - - - - - - ADVANCE RESERVATION APPLICATION - - - - - - - - - - - -

Figure shown actual size.

Amy by Tasha Tudor

Valid only if postmarked by May 31, 1982 · Limit: One sculpture per person.

Franklin Porcelain
Franklin Center, Pennsylvania 19091

Please accept my reservation for "Amy" by Tasha Tudor, to be handcrafted for me in fine, hand-painted porcelain.
   I understand that I need send no money now. I will be billed in four equal monthly installments of $18.75* plus 75¢ for shipping and handling, with the first payment due in advance of shipment.
      *Plus my state sales tax

Signature _____
ALL APPLICATIONS ARE SUBJECT TO ACCEPTANCE.

Mr.
Mrs.
Miss
   PLEASE PRINT CLEARLY

Address _____

City _____

State, Zip _____

3165

This ad from Franklin Porcelain typifies its new-product expansion program.

which originally launched the World of Beauty Club, decided to utilize the ability it had developed in working with cosmetic manufacturers to set up a similar arrangement of sampling with a group of food manufacturers. In this case, the market consisted of large numbers of people who wanted to sample new foods and save money on a regular basis.

Other companies that have looked at their own expertise and facilities to determine what new products and services they could develop range all the way from the Donnelley Company, which utilized its co-op mailings to include the sale of its own products, to Time-Life, which used its editorial and photographic expertise to produce probably the most successful series of continuity books in the publishing industry.

So along with determining the business you're in, probably the second most important factor to investigate is your company's capabilities. As you can see, determining the business you're in and examining your capabilities go hand in hand in helping you pinpoint new merchandise or service opportunities. There are significant differences between these areas, however, and they must be considered individually. By doing so, you will be able to broaden your horizons even more.

What Is Your Image with Your Customers?

A third area to consider in the process of expansion is one that, paradoxically, instead of expanding your horizons, is more likely to limit them, or at least put some boundaries on them. Unlike the first two considerations—determining the business you're in and examining your capabilities—this third area requires you to carefully analyze the image that customers have of your company. (See Exhibit 12-7.)

Every customer has an image of the company he or she deals with. This image may differ from customer to customer (and probably does in degree, if not in kind), based on the relationship each customer has had with that company. If one customer has had nothing but satisfactory dealings with a company, that customer's image would differ from that of one who has had an unsatisfactory experience, regardless of the cause. But the company's basic image will vary only slightly from customer to customer and will be essentially the same for all customers.

For example, General Motors has a particular image with most Americans. That image exists even for those who have never owned a GM car. The buyer of a GM car who was not happy with his or her purchase will have a somewhat different image of that company based on how his or her complaints were treated. But, in general, the American public believes that General Motors is a responsible, reputable company selling various forms of transportation among which are cars they enjoy using and driving.

Another example in an entirely different field is International Business Machines (IBM). Here is a company with which many Americans have never had direct contact. But the image of IBM with most people is probably that of a major multinational corporation with unsurpassed technical and scientific skill in the development of computers. As in the case of Henry Ford of an earlier day, IBM is probably regarded by most Americans as an advanced proponent of computing technology.

Although the perceived images of GM and IBM have stood the tests of time, it should be acknowledged that both images have become tainted in the past few years in particular: GM for the quality of its cars; IBM for failure to recognize the changing needs of computer users. This is fair warning to the rest of us that our images are subject to decay if we are not sensitive to consumer needs.

Exhibit 12–7. The Importance of Image

I don't know who you are.

I don't know your company.

I don't know your company's product.

I don't know what your company stands for.

I don't know your company's customers.

I don't know your company's record.

I don't know your company's reputation.

Now—what was it you wanted to sell me?''

MORAL: Sales start **before** your salesman calls—with business publication advertising.

McGRAW-HILL MAGAZINES
BUSINESS•PROFESSIONAL•TECHNICAL

This classic McGraw-Hill ad, directed to prospects for business publication advertising, applies with equal force to those who would enter the mail order field.

This perceived image is a vitally important factor when you are considering what new products or services to offer your customers or your prospects, if your company is sufficiently well known. It has been proved over and over in direct marketing as well as in other distribution channels that a company has great difficulty selling merchandise or services that do not fit the public's preconceived image of that company. This can be illustrated in the case of one company that built its customer list on the sale of power tools and then failed dismally in an offer of books of general interest to the same audience.

Let's take the case of the Minnesota-based Fingerhut Company. This firm has built a fine reputation by offering good values in medium- to low-priced merchandise ranging from power tools to tableware. While the company was able successfully to sell medium- to low-priced men's and women's wear to the same audience, it is highly doubtful that it could as successfully sell fine bound books or Yves St. Laurent clothing. This is true not only because the demographics of the Fingerhut list probably are not suited to the higher priced category, but also because the Fingerhut image does not conform to that high-priced merchandise.

Unless your customers or prospects believe that you are a qualified source for the products you are offering, they are unlikely to buy. But if those prospects expect certain products from you, because they fit your company image, your chances of success are vastly enhanced. Thus it is extremely important that you fully recognize the image you present to your customers and that you select offerings that are appropriate to that image. This recognition, as mentioned earlier, narrows your choices. But it narrows them to your ultimate advantage if it keeps you from going so far afield that what you offer will stand little chance of success.

At this point we might discuss the kinds of factors that tend to create a company's image. The combination of such factors consists of approximately equal parts of the following:

- The products or services offered in the past

- The style and quality of the new product itself

- The price level

- The presentation of the product, whether it is an ad, a commercial, or a mailing piece (The "sound" of the copy and the appearance of the graphics send a definite message to the prospect.)

- The "look" of the merchandise package received by the customer

- The "sound" and appearance of any other communication with your customer (e.g., the invoice, the way complaints are handled, and the way telephone communications are conducted)

- The "tone" of any publicity your company receives

An excellent example of the difference a company's image can make can be given in a comparison of two companies featuring outdoor products: L.L. Bean of Maine and Norm Thompson of Seattle, Washington. Just as they are at opposite ends of the country, both companies successfully present different, yet equally acceptable, images. L.L. Bean's image is that of an old-line, conservative company with the Yankee habit of underplaying its product, a company featuring timeless styles that appeal primarily to a mature audience. Norm Thompson, on the other hand, shows an image of a company that appeals to men and women with a more youthful lifestyle. The company prides itself on its ability to come up with interesting, often exotic new products from abroad.

What are the Characteristics of Your Customer List?

Another most important mine to explore for products or services is your own customer list. Study your list from a number of different perspectives, such as the following:

- How your list was developed

- How your customers have been "educated"

- What they are buying, if you give them choices

- The demographics and psychographics of your customers

- The "product experience" of your list

How Your List Was Developed. What type of merchandise have your customers been buying? At what prices? How have they paid: cash, charge, timepayment? These might appear to be obvious questions, but it is surprising how often they are overlooked when new product planning is under consideration.

Your customers are constantly telling you what they like and are interested in every time they make a purchase. Catalog companies are following this rule every time they analyze each product in their catalog for profitability. By doing this, they automatically determine which products are most popular and, as a corollary, which new products they should add to their line and at what prices.

If you are successfully selling a vacuum cleaner through direct marketing, it is likely your customers would be logical prospects for such products as sets of dishes, tableware, glassware, and similar items. If you are selling clothing through the mail, as do the Haband Company and New Process, your customers might well be tempted by offerings of economical housewares, luggage, towel sets, and the like.

Moreover, the price levels of your merchandise are standards by which to judge any new offering. There is one proviso: You should be constantly testing higher price levels to determine the upper pricing limits of your customer list.

Just a 10–15 percent increase in the price level your customers will accept may suggest many more profitable products or services for you to offer.

This, of course, raises the question of the methods of payment used by your customers. If they pay in cash or by credit card, they will probably prefer to continue to purchase on that basis. This will probably add to the difficulty of introducing a new item that requires a higher purchase price. On the other hand, if your customers are used to paying on the installment plan, they more likely will be willing to purchase higher-priced merchandise, especially if you can increase the number of installments. Customers who prefer to pay for their merchandise on a monthly basis are, generally speaking, more likely to be concerned with the amount of the individual payment rather than with the total price of the product.

How Have Your Customers Been Educated?   The way in which you first got your customers has an important influence on what they expect of you in future offers. An example of the power of this "educating" process is the Fingerhut Company, whose customers have been conditioned to expect a host of free gifts with every purchase. It is unlikely that Fingerhut would be successful with a new offering that did not include such free gifts.

The Grolier Corporation has built a large list of book customers by offering free the first volume of a set of books, whether or not the prospect decides to continue with the series. Again, an offering to these customers of a new series without the free volume would probably fail. At the same time, Time-Life Books has been extremely successful in a program of selling books with an offer that permits the prospect only to examine a new volume for a limited time, without getting it free.

Especially if you are just starting in business, give serious thought to your front-end offer. Be sure you are clear on how you want your customers "educated." The way you start out is probably the way you will have to continue. If you'd rather not adopt the pattern of free gifts, free volumes, and sweepstakes, you probably should not start with such offers.

What Are the Lifestyles of Your Customers?   Now we get to your customers themselves. What kind of a lifestyle do they have? If you haven't already, you should do a comprehensive analysis to develop a profile of your typical customer. More and more we are finding that the demographic profiles of customers combined with their psychographic (lifestyle) profiles give many clues to successful new-product development and sales.

With such a profile, you will find all kinds of "road signs" to new products or services. How your customers live, the kinds of vacations they take, the type of entertainment they enjoy, whether they prefer books to movies, as well as their income level, education, size of family, whether they live in a house or apartment, and other demographic characteristics—all are hints about the new products or services they might be interested in.

Obviously, people who live in an apartment are less likely to be prospects for a set of power tools than people who live in a house. Similarly, people who prefer movies to books are not very good prospects for a best-seller.

American lifestyles seem to be changing more rapidly all the time. The second wave of feminism initiated a continuing change in the lifestyle of many women that influence the lifestyles of a great many men as well. Over half of all women in American now work outside the home. Obviously, employed women have different needs from those who don't work outside the home. The number of unmarried women who head households also keeps growing. Their needs, too, are different. Their need for financial advice, for example, is certainly different from that of married women.

For many years, senior citizens have constituted a growing segment of U.S. society. Older people have many needs that differ from those of younger age groups. An example of how one group is addressing those needs is the American Association of Retired Persons. The association offers people over 55 years of age a wide variety of services, ranging from travel opportunities to insurance. Membership is in the millions. All of these groups have particular needs that frequently can be met by the perceptive direct marketer.

What New Products Are People Buying? When you want to determine whether an offering will work in direct marketing, review the products that people are currently buying at retail. Examples are costume jewelry and paperback books.

Formerly, direct marketers tended to shy away from products available at retail, but that is no longer true. A wide variety of products, ranging from Polaroid cameras to General Electric toasters, are being sold in increasing volume through the direct response method. Only a few years ago the Quality Paperback Book Club was started on a direct response basis to take advantage of the tremendous popularity of paperbacks. When you consider that paperbacks are sold in virtually every drugstore, cigar shop, candy store, railroad station, and airport—as well as every bookstore—QPB's success can be seen as a tribute to the convenience and acceptance of direct marketing.

Price/Value Relationships

Once you have selected your product or service, you are faced with the problem of pricing it. How much can you get for it? Whatever price you select, it must appear to the prospect to be the "right" price for that item. He or she must perceive your price as being a value. And that perception depends on the item and the person to whom you are appealing. A person earning $250 per week has one set of price/value relationships. Another earning $750 per week has a different set. To the first person, a $10 tie may have just the right price/value relationship. To the second, the tie might seem "cheap."

A piece of merchandise in itself has a perceived price/value relationship with the customer. One expects a set of cookware to cost less than a set of bone china dishes. A price of $49 for a set of cookware might sound just right. But $49 for a bone china dinnerware set sounds suspiciously inexpensive. As an example of how people establish a price/value relationship for a product, here's a test conducted by a direct marketer selling a set of four kitchen knives. Five offers were tested, with the results indicated.

1. Four knives at $19.95 plus $1 shipping and handling. Pull: 1.3 percent

2. Four knives at $19.95, plus hanging board at $1.50 (optional), plus $1 shipping and handling. Pull: 1.3 percent; 80 percent took the hanging board

3. Four knives, plus hanging board, plus shipping and handling at $24.95. Pull 0.9 percent

4. Three knives at $19.95, plus $1 shipping and handling. Pull: 0.8 percent

5. Five knives at $29.95, plus hanging board at $1.50, plus $1 shipping and handling. Pull: 0.7 percent

As you can see, the prospects saw Offer 2 as the best in terms of price and value, far better than Offer 3, which was only $2.50 more. We have been through this time after time, and we have found that the assumption that there is a right price for every item invariably holds true. Certain cookware sets can only be sold at $39.95. Certain clock radios can only be sold at $49.95. Certain sets of stainless tableware can only be sold at $24.95.

Conversely, we have also found that the customer will, in some cases, accept a higher price than you would have chosen as the proper price/value relationship. For example, a paint gun was tested at both $49.95, and $59.95, and sales at the $59.95 price were better. So although you might think you have a good idea what the right price for an item should be, you should test that price and also test at a higher and a lower price. You may be pleasantly surprised.

Price/value relationships change, too. Inflation has an effect on them. So does competition. And the relative popularity of the item is important. The same paint gun that sold successfully at $59.95 a few years ago now sells for $89.95 in about the same quantities as it did at the lower price. Remember when Sharp came out with the first electronic calculator? It was only a four-function model, but American Express sold thousands at $300. Today you'd be lucky to get $15 for it.

Others Areas to Consider

Finally, let's consider several other marketing factors apart from the product or service itself. These are such factors as the offer, the advertising medium to be used, how to use research in reaching your decision, finding reliable offers, and mining your customer base.

The Offer

The offer should be regarded as an opportunity to say to the prospect, "Here is a special reason for acting now rather than waiting to order at a future date." The best offers flow from the product or service being offered. A good example is the original Franklin Mint five-year buy-back guarantee, an offer that corresponded perfectly with the firm's assumption that its products might increase in value. Book club and tape club offers of X books or records for as little as ten cents are other examples. Free-gift offers, limited time or quantity offers, free-trial periods, and a wide variety of other offers can be useful. Try to develop an offer that relates to the general character of your merchandise. It can pay big dividends.

Determining the Media

When deciding which advertising medium to use, a number of basic factors must be considered. Generally speaking, if the product doesn't carry at least a $15 profit at a $29.95 retail price, you probably won't be successful in a solo mailing, unless the pull is really sensational. A further consideration in your decision about whether to use the direct mail system is the amount of copy and illustration you need. The more of both you require, the more likely it is that your product belongs in the mail. If your item is suited to a visual demonstration, television becomes a likely medium, especially if the item's price is under $29.95.

Newspaper inserts should not be overlooked as a viable medium today. Inserts have brought a new dimension that offers as much copy space as needed with a wide variety of interesting formats, plus a return envelope, quality reproduction, and, often, market segmentation. Newspaper inserts have opened opportunities for a wide range of offers, from insurance to limited-edition commemorative and free credit cards.

The Use of Research

In recent years, an activity that has been receiving more attention in determining product selection is market research. For many years, direct marketers believed that the only way to determine the appeal of a product or service was to put it in the mail or run an ad and see if it sold. Today, sophisticated direct marketers are more and more frequently turning to research as a means of helping to determine whether an item stands a chance of success. (See Chapter 21.)

Consider the various research techniques available to help in selecting your product or service to increase your prospects for success. Research such as focus group testing can give you valuable insights into the appeal (or lack thereof) of your offering. It can also help you determine which one or two or more items have the strongest appeal. Often this procedure can even help you add to the appeal of your product or service by suggesting benefits to be added.

Reliable Sources

Everything we've said so far presupposes that you have a dependable source of supplying your product or that you will have a supplier once you determine what you are going to sell. Seasoned direct marketers always make certain they are ready to deliver when they put a promotion in the mail, or advertise in a magazine, or offer the item via broadcast. A cardinal point to remember is that the product must be on hand before you start your promotion. Once you have mailed or placed your ad, you have committed yourself fully. You can't recall the mailing or magazine. And in the direct response business, if you can't deliver in a reasonable time, you will lose a large percentage of your orders. You will create much expensive, time-consuming correspondence. You will engender a lot of ill-will and undoubtedly lose the bulk of your investment.

Mining Your Customer Base

Direct marketers must be on a relentless, continuous search for new products and services. Nevertheless, there is the ever-present danger that the excitement of new-product development will take attention from the product or products that built the business in the first place. Established direct marketers cannot afford to overlook this danger, because their customer bases are the lifeblood of their businesses.

Promoting Services as "Products"

When one considers the idea of mail order, one thinks of products—merchandise, if you will. But the fact is that thousands of services are also sold via mail-order methods. The tenets that apply to products also apply to services. Indeed, most of the 34 factors to consider when selecting mail order items (Exhibit 12–2) are appropriate when considering services: perceived need, uniqueness, sufficient markup, large enough market, and so on.

SELF-QUIZ

1. The first tip in selecting mail order items is that you should select items whose benefits you can _____ with photos and graphics.

2. List ten sources for discovering mail-order items:

a. _____   f. _____

b. _____   g. _____

c. _____   h. _____

d. _____   i. _____

e. _____   j. _____

3. List ten factors to consider when selecting mail order items.

a. _____   f. _____

b. _____   g. _____

c. _____   h. _____

d. _____   i. _____

e. _____   j. _____

4. What are the four phases of the product life cycle?

a. _____   c. _____

b. _____   d. _____

5. In attempting to expand your business with new products or services, what is the first question you should ask yourself?

_____

_____

6. How does the image of your company influence your selection of products?

_____

_____

7. In determining what other products you might offer your customers, you should look at your house list from five different angles:

a. _____

b. _____

c. _____

d. _____

e. _____

8. Define price/value relationship.

_____

_____

_____

_____

9. The more copy and illustration you need to adequately present your product, the more likely it is that:
   ☐   Space is your best medium.
   ☐   Direct mail is your best medium.

10. A major source of gaining new customers is _____.

PILOT PROJECT

You are Annie Hurlbut. You have developed a customer base of 50,000 women who have purchased hand-loomed alpaca garments made in Peru. The question you face is, "What else might I offer to my customer list?" Make a list of ten products you think would be most attractive to this customer base.

CHAPTER THIRTEEN

Business-to-Business Direct Marketing

Consumer versus Business-to-Business Direct Marketing

The opportunities in business-to-business direct marketing are great: to get qualified leads, to screen leads, to sell by telephone, and to create catalogs and sales support material. Business-to-business direct marketing uses the same tools as consumer direct marketing, but significant differences separate the two (See Exhibit 13–1.) The major difference is an economic one.

The average order size of business-to-business direct marketing offers is large, and the lifetime value of a single customer can be enormous. For example, IBM sells $50,000 disk drives using direct marketing techniques. With order sizes of this type, the lifetime value of a business-to-business customer can be extremely high. It is not uncommon for a single business-to-business customer to represent millions of dollars in lifetime value. Although economic value is high, target market universes can be small. In some cases, this involves fewer than 100 companies. Therefore, the mass marketing techniques that work so well in consumer direct marketing are often not applicable to business-to-business.

Vic Hunter, founder and president of Hunter Business Direct, Inc., Milwaukee, Wisconsin, has developed an approach to business-to-business direct marketing that has proved highly successful for many *Fortune* 500 companies. He is developing a book that explains how his value-added approach to direct marketing significantly improves one's competitive position. This chapter is based on his ideas.

Exhibit 13–1. Consumer versus Business-to-Business Direct Marketing

Consumer Direct Marketing	Business-to-Business Direct Marketing
Individuals frequently buy for themselves	Individuals buy on behalf of an organization
Buying decision involves relatively few others	Decisions frequently involve multiple individuals
Single buyer groups	Multiple buyer groups
Informal buying process	Formal and informal buying process
Transaction-based	Relationship-based
Avearage order size is relatively small	Average order size tends to be large
Lifetime value is relatively low	Lifetime value can be very large
Easy to reach individuals	Difficult to reach individuals
Large target market universes	Small target market universes
Transaction-focused	Relationship process–focused

Source: Hunter Business Direct, Inc.

This means that businesses must invest far more in building and supporting a relationship with the customer—the loss of one customer can have a great economic impact on the business. As a result, direct marketing takes on new dimensions when used in business-to-business applications. No longer are its goals the capturing of an order or the acquisition of a new customer. Rather, the goals become increasing sales productivity while sustaining relationships with existing business customers. Instead of emphasizing new-customer acquisition, we "cultivate" existing customers and use that information to broaden our customer base.

Through this we begin to build a spirit of community among our customers. We want to leverage our relationship with the customer to build a bond that translates into a lasting relationship based on mutual interests, mutual trust, and healthy interdependence. We make the customer community economically desirable and stable through lowering selling costs for the seller and delivering higher product/service value to the customer.

Of course, this means that direct marketing processes look quite different in business-to-business marketing. For example, the functions or uses for direct marketing change. In business-to-business applications, direct marketing is used for such functions as reducing the number of face-to-face contacts with the customer, reaching marginal accounts that might not be profitable to contact through a face-to-face sales call, and building sustainable relationships with the customer.

Also, the measurements or metrics we use to evaluate results change. Rather than focusing on transaction- or campaign-based measurements, such as cost per thousand, number of calls per hour, response rates, etc., business-to-business direct marketing uses such qualitative measures as customer satisfaction, product penetration, account penetration, referrals, and loyalty.

Another difference is that we are dealing with individuals who represent economic value beyond themselves. They are the buyers, specifiers, approvers, etc., who influence or direct purchases for companies, institutions, or other organizations. As such, they are not spending their money but someone else's. As a result, this is a more complex buying process. Typically, more than one person is involved in a single buying decision, or there might be multiple buying groups within the same organizational buying the same type of product. With this complexity, it is difficult to find key buying influences and the purchasing patterns within an organization.

Value-Added Direct Marketing

In the early 1980s, Hunter Business Direct, Inc., began using and refining a highly effective business-to-business direct marketing technique called *value-added marketing*. The differences between traditional and value-added marketing are shown in Exhibit 13–2.

In value-added marketing, Hunter starts with the premise that they are dealing with a market size of a single individual. This is the key—marketing to individuals, not to accounts or organizations. Individualized messages go to target markets. Each has a size of one.

When one can make that paradigm shift from selling to accounts to selling to individuals who buy on behalf of others, the rest of the elements fall into place. For example, if you're selling to individuals, you can ask what their needs are and store them in a database. You don't have to guess. You can then look for product or service applications that meet their specific business needs.

In this approach, businesses manage contacts with the customer through a centralized operation, similar to a call center, called the *customer information center* (CIC). This gives them the ability to integrate direct marketing tools with field sales to provide the customer with a seamless flow of value-added information. That is, they ensure that every contact with the customer delivers value, as perceived by the customer.

A key concept here is to focus on retaining customers and building customer loyalties. In the past ten years, studies have shown that retaining existing customers is significantly less expensive and more profitable than acquiring new customers. So, direct marketing tools must focus on retaining customers, not simply getting them to place an order. This requires another paradigm shift, away from

Exhibit 13-2.   Traditional versus Value-Added Direct Marketing

Traditional Marketing		Value-Added Marketing
Mass marketing	→	$n = 1$
Projected needs	→	Actual needs
Product driven	→	Customer driven
Account focus	→	Individual focus
Activity based	→	Application based
Acquisition focus	→	Retention focus
Events and activities	→	Systems and procedures
Projected results	→	Actual results
Independent contacts	→	Integrated contacts
Impersonal communication	→	Personal communication
Supports traditional sales channels	→	Supports all sales channels

Source: Hunter Business Direct, Inc.

the transaction-based traditional approach to one that is focused on building long-term relationships.

A strategy of retention can build customer loyalty. This has distinct advantages: loyal customers are less likely to defect and more likely to become your "champions" within their organization and industry. Once we understand who our loyal customers are, it is only then that we can look at acquiring new customers. The reason is simple: we want new customers that look like and act like our best loyal customers. And we can't do that until we see who our best loyal customers are. If we blindly pursue an acquisition strategy designed to replace lost customers, we are likely to get some new customers that look like the customers we just lost. That's not smart marketing.

The principles and techniques of value-added marketing produce three major benefits:

1. Improved sales force productivity and reduced sales costs of up to 15 percent

2. Increased customer retention, which leads to customer loyalty

3. Sales revenue growth and increased profitability

These are dramatic benefits in today's highly competitive business-to-business world. They can be accomplished through a four-stage process. The major phases of this process include understanding the customer, developing a value-added communication strategy, using cultivation to build retention and loyalty, and acquiring new customers based on existing customer experience.

Listening to the Customer's Voice

Value-added marketing is built around the premise that all contacts with the customer deliver value. It is through this value-based approach that businesses can build long-lasting and sustainable relationships with customers. The first step in this process is understanding what the customer values in the relationship. As Stephen Covey noted in *The Seven Habits of Highly Effective People*, we must "seek first to understand." To accomplish this, first listen to the voice of the customer. Try to understand why customers buy from you, what needs your products or services fulfill, how you stack up against the competition, and how you can use this information for competitive advantage. Exhibit 13–3 summarizes the steps to take.

One of the most difficult aspects is identifying customer needs. Needs fall into three categories: basic, unfulfilled, and future needs. Basic needs are those you need to satisfy in order to be considered by the customer. These are needs that every entrant into the market must meet, or they become barriers to entry. If all competitors only satisfied basic needs, we would be dealing with a commodity-type product or service.

Unfulfilled needs are the path to competitive dominance. If you can uncover and meet needs that the competition is not meeting, that gives you a distinct advantage. At the same time, if you are not meeting unfulfilled needs, and the competition is, these become at-risk needs and can cause customer defections.

Exhibit 13–3.   Understanding the Customer

Task	Description	Implemented by	Information source
Customer needs assessment	Identify basic, unfulfilled, future, and at-risk needs	Marketing	Customer surveys
Attribute/feature analysis	Identify all attributes or features of your product or service	Marketing	Marketing
Competitive analysis	Compare attributes/features with competitors	Marketing	Competitive intelligence
External service values	Determine why customer buys product/service from you	Marketing	Attribute/feature and competitive analyses
Segment target markets	Group customers with common set of needs into target segments	Marketing	Database

Source: Hunter Business Direct, Inc.

By listening to the customer's voice, you can anticipate a customer's future needs. This requires a means of continuously monitoring a customer's changing needs. Businesses identify customer needs by determining external service values—the reasons that customers buy a product or service and buy from them.

Determining External Service Values

The step-by-step process used to uncover external service values starts with an understanding of the products and services. First, identify all of the product's features or attributes. In some cases, this can involve more than 100 attributes. Next, compare these attributes with those of competitive products or services. The result is a competitive analysis that helps to distinguish the product from competitive offerings and leads to defined external service values. Exhibit 13–4 shows a portion of a competitive attribute/feature analysis.

This type of analysis provides a clear picture of the competitive position. It shows a unique set of features or attributes that distinguish your product from the competition. However, this is strictly an internal analysis and must be tested against market realities by asking customers what's important. This can be accomplished in several ways. The simplest is to call the customer following receipt of the order and ask why they purchased. Then match that answer to the unique feature list.

A more systematic approach is to conduct periodic customer surveys. These surveys identify the key attributes/features and ask the customers to rate your

Exhibit 13–4. Competitive Attribute/Feature Analysis

Feature	Our Company	Competitors A	B	C
Time to ship	Same day	2 days	5 days	Same day
Guarantee	Unlimited	60	120	90
Handling charge	No	No	Yes	No
Quote turnaround	8 hours	2 days	24 hours	N/A
Volume pricing	Yes	Yes	Yes	Yes
Accuracy of order fulfillment	100%	98%	95%	100%
Recycled packaging	No	No	No	No
Price guarantee	90 days	No	30 days	No
Toll-free number	Yes	Yes	Yes	Yes
Customizing	5–10 days	6 weeks	5 weeks	No

Source: Hunter Business Direct, Inc.

unique value for that attribute compared to the competition's. Then ask them to rate each in importance in the buying decision. By multiplying the unique value by the level of importance in the purchasing decision, you have a quantitative measure of external service values. It's always good to go back and verify that this is why customers buy from you.

Another technique is to interview customers who defected or are no longer buying from you. By asking them why they are no longer buying, you can determine what external service values were not satisfied. This not only gives you valuable information about unfulfilled customer needs, but also can be an early warning system to help prevent additional defections.

A New Segmentation Tool

The external service value analysis enables you to group customers with like needs and reasons for buying. For example, when customers rank order the attribute/feature list, they are building a basis for target market segmentation. If no-cost shipping and handling, order turnaround time, and volume discounts are important to a select group of customers, they can represent an identifiable target segment.

Contact Channels and Communication Strategies

The successful businesses for the next decade and beyond will manage communications with their internal and external customers at every possible point of contact and use the knowledge gained from those contacts to create value in the relationship. Contacts are information pathways. Whoever owns these vital pathways owns the relationship with the customer.

There are two main objectives in developing specific communication strategies and plans. First, direct marketing enables you to leverage the high cost of field sales. For example, a typical business-to-business sales call averages more than $400. Therefore, direct marketing techniques should and can be used to support and leverage the field sales process. Second, studies have shown that frequency of contact is more important than contact media. Therefore, focus on the use of low-cost contact media if the same value-based communication can be made. Exhibit 13–5 summarizes the steps used in developing an effective contact plan and communication strategy.

First you need to know how, when, and about what customers contact you and you contact them. To do this, start by analyzing current contact practices. Identify every customer contact point within the organization, no matter how infrequent or at what location. Over a predetermined period, record all contacts with the customer. This is typically done using a contact log, which is shown

Exhibit 13–5.   Contact Plan and Communication Strategies

Task	Description	Implemented by	Information source
Contact analysis	Identify all contact points with customer by type and content	Marketing	Internal observation
Communication workshop	Identify customer contact preferences	Marketing	Customer
Grade customers	Determine which are most valuable customers (AA, A, B, C, D)	Marketing	Database
Customer contact matrix	Match customer contact preferences with contact media cost with economic value	Marketing	Database
Communication plan	Determine specific communication elements for contact matrix	Marketing	Marketing and sales
Develop offer	Base offer on external service values	Marketing	Database
Customer contact	Implement the communication plan	CIC	Database

Source: Hunter Business Direct, Inc.

in Exhibit 13–6. The contact log not only records the contact, but it also identifies the information content, the source of the contact (inbound or outbound), the contact owner, and the frequency of contact. You can then prepare a cumulative analysis that covers all contact points.

If you understand how customers want to receive certain types of information and then proceed to deliver it to them in that manner, this adds value to the relationship with the customer. This forms the base for the next step and helps in building the infrastructure for the customer information center.

Customer Contact Preferences

After you understand current contact practices and what the customer values, you need to ask customers what their contact preferences are:

- What types of information the customer considers important or value-based

- How the customer wants to be contacted on each (the medium)

Exhibit 13–6.   Sample Contact Log

Department (Group):	Key Contact:		Approvals:		
	Time Period				
Activity	Phone		Mail		Electronic	
	In	Out	In	Out	In	Out
A. Sales/revenue generation						
1. Orders/applications						
2. Contracts/confirmations/modifications						
B. Requests/exchange of information						
1. Product information						
2. Pricing/bid requests						
3. Literature/material						
4. Account related						
5. Special programs						
6. Other: _____						
C. Problems/customer service						
1. Shipment/completion status						
2. Problems/complaints						
3. Account corrections/adjustments						
4. Service related						
D. Messages/transfers						
E. Prospect/lead identification (solicited)						
F. Invoices/payments/claims/purchase orders						
G. Misdirected contacts/referrals						
H. Other: _____						

Source: Hunter Business Direct, Inc.

- When the customer wants contact
- How frequently the customer wants to be contacted

One way to gather this customer-specific information is to ask customers during the normal course of business. That is, during a phone call with the customer, the representative is prompted to ask specific questions related to communication preferences. A second way is to use a mail survey. Another technique is the customer communication workshop. Here, groups of customers, sales representatives, and product marketing representatives meet to:

1. Review the cumulative contact log.

2. Have each group identify the top 10–12 contact items.

3. Have each group present their selections and state reasons for the selection.

4. Resolve differences between groups.

This process has the customer define, together with the business, what contacts and what content are important, what contact medium the customer prefers, and how frequently the customer wants the information. From this a contact model can be developed for communication planning. Exhibit 13–7 shows a sample contact model. This model shows, for example, that for program specials, the customer is willing to have 12 notifications. They prefer to have this notification through e-mail, but consider mail, phone, and face-to-face notification acceptable.

Grading Customers

One mistake some companies make is to treat all customers equally when it involves direct marketing programs. This is highly ineffective—customers are not equal. They have different needs (market segment) and have different economic potential/value (grade). Some require more contact than others. Other customers cannot economically justify frequent contact. To avoid this mistake, it is wise to grade customers on an economic basis and develop direct marketing programs that specifically address the needs of each economic grade of customers.

Most marketers are familiar with the 20/80 form of segmenting customers: 20 percent of your customers account for 80 percent of your sales volume. Taking this a step further, you can segment customers into five categories—AA, A, B, C, D—to allow for a closer match of economic value to contact mix and fre-

Exhibit 13–7.   Value-Based Contact Model

Contacts	Frequency	E-Mail	Phone	Field	Mail
1. New-product announcements	4	P	A		A
2. Product application information	4	P	A	A	A
3. Product updates/new releases	4	P	A	A	

4. Case studies
   a. Product application
   b. Results
	4	P			A

5. Industry research	1	P			A
6. Article reprints	6	P			A
7. Program specials	12	P	A	A	A
8. Industry trends	2	P			A
9. Product uses/performance assessment	4		A	P	

P = Preferred medium   A = Acceptable medium

Source: Hunter Business Direct, Inc.

quency. The criteria used can include past sales history, profitability, and projected lifetime value. Typically, categories AA and A together correspond to the 20 percent in the 20/80 rule.

Creating a Customer Contact Plan

Once you have the customer contact preferences and have graded customers, you can build a contact plan that economically leverages sales contact costs in a highly effective manner. In essence, the plan delivers value, as defined by the customer, with every contact. Because the financial aspect is essential, you first need to set a budget. This includes setting a total budget and a budget for each customer grade. Next, establish costs for each type of media. Then generate a mix of media that satisfies the objectives of leveraging higher-cost media and being effective. From this, a customer contact plan is developed. Media costs can vary dramatically from medium to medium. Exhibit 13–8 shows the range of typical media costs.

The next step is to develop a mix of contact media that best fits your objectives and meets your budgets. Be advised that as you build a contact plan, you need to repeatedly adjust the mix until you reach the optimum plan.

Exhibit 13–9 shows a completed customer plan. This sample is derived from a base of 1,000 customers. To illustrate what each item represents, let's use Grade B customers. First, this group represents customers with $20,000–40,000 in annual sales. There are 250 customers in this category. According to the contact plan, this group is expected to generate about $7.5 million in sales revenue during the year. The plan is to invest approximately 13 percent of sales revenues, or $988,000, into communication and contact with the customer. This translates to 50 mailings (about one per week), 25 phone calls (about one every two weeks), and eight face-to-face sales contacts (about one every six weeks) for each customer in this buyer group.

Exhibit 13–8.   Comparative Costs of Contact Media per Contact

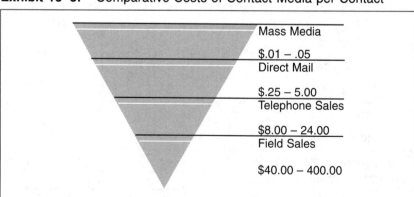

Mass Media
$.01 – .05
Direct Mail

$.25 – 5.00
Telephone Sales

$8.00 – 24.00
Field Sales

$40.00 – 400.00

Source: Hunter Business Direct, Inc.

Exhibit 13-9.   Customer Contact Plan Sample

Grade/Sales ($000)	1,000 = Buyer Groups	Mail Count	Phone Count	Field Count	Sales Cost ($000)	Percentage of Revenues
AA $60+	50	75 3,750	50 2,500	20 1,000	$ 469	13.4%
A $40–60	150	75 11,250	40 6,000	15 2,250	1,076	14.4
B $20–40	250	50 12,500	25 6,250	8 2,000	988	13.2
C $10–20	250	25 6,250	12 3,000	4 1,000	491	13.1
D > $10	300	25 7,500	10 3,000	1 300	218	14.5
Total	1,000	41,250	20,750	6,550	$3,242	13.6%

Source: Hunter Business Direct, Inc.

Marketing and Sales Communication Plan

Specific marketing communication and sales plans are now developed. First the 50 direct mail pieces must be developed: what each piece will consist of, its format, its content, and which external service values will be stressed. Because the customer's external service values are known, they are the basis for message content. Remember, these contacts are defined by the customer to have value if mailed to them with this frequency.

To show how this works in practice, let's assume you have a monthly newsletter that you send to customers. You plan the newsletter so that each issue includes information related to your core external service values. Then you use the cover letter to call attention to specific pieces of information within the newsletter that meet the individual customer's external service values. This adds value to your communication with the customer and delivers 12 mail contacts throughout the year.

Building the Customer Information Center

Because value-added direct marketing uses the full range of direct marketing and sales tools, you need a means to manage and monitor the process: the customer information center (CIC). All activities are coordinated, and flow through the CIC. Exhibit 13–10 shows the CIC model. The CIC's role involves

Exhibit 13–10.   Customer Information Center

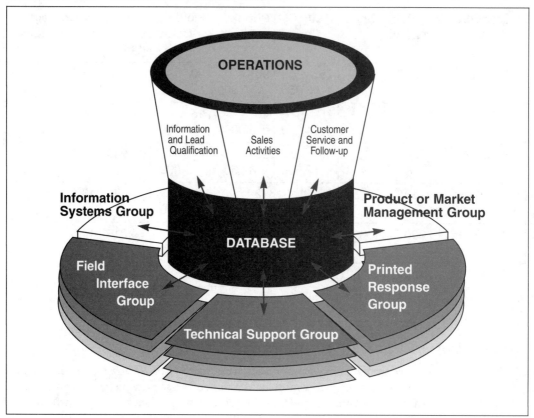

Source: Hunter Business Direct, Inc.

acquiring customer information and then using that information for marketing activities. It is the central contact point for customers and the place from which all outgoing contacts with the customer is initiated.

Database Is the Heart of the CIC

In direct marketing, the database is the heart of the process. It serves as the collective memory of all customer transactions and is the depository for customer attribute information. Because all customer information is contained in the database, it must be accessible to anyone who has contact with the customer. Through this, the business can achieve seamless, synchronized interaction with the customer.

For example, a salesperson could access the customer's file before making a sales call. Then the salesperson could review all contacts since the last sales call, review all actions taken on behalf of the customer, and access any specific interest areas the customer has identified. Equipped with this information, the salesperson has a more productive sales call and adds value to the relationship.

The database plays a critical role in many aspects of business-to-business direct marketing, such as the following:

- **Target market segmentation:** Use the customer attribute information for segmenting target markets.

- **Single source for customer inquiries:** Having access to the database enables fast answers to customer inquiries and eliminates unnecessary transferring of customer calls.

- **Product development:** By recording customers' changing needs, new product opportunities can be detected.

- **Analysis:** The information stored in the database can be used for analysis, such as expense to revenue ratios to determine customer profitability.

- **Metrics:** Database information facilitates a number of measurements, such as the effectiveness of lead-generation sources.

Operations for Customer Interface

The operations portions of the CIC is shown at the center of the model. This is the core set of functions that include information and lead qualification, sales activities, and customer service and follow-up. This typically is a centralized group of telemarketers that are the primary contact point for customers and field sales reps. The CIC phone reps input and extract data from the CIC database. Using telemarketing offers low-cost, high-frequency, two-way dialogue with customers that continually validates and refreshes the database.

Communication Management Group

This group plans and executes direct marketing campaigns. It controls the message being delivered to the customer. It designs campaigns and contact plans. A primary responsibility is to ensure that all communications with customers and prospective customers deliver value. Following are functions provided by the communications management group:

- **Design and develop direct mail pieces:** Communications managers are responsible for creating and producing direct mail items, generating and acquiring lists, and mailing.

- **Define telemarketing guides:** In business-to-business direct marketing, scripts are rarely used for outbound calling. In building a dialogue with the customer, the length of a call becomes a minor issue, because obtaining certain types of customer information will require lengthy conversations. The guides remind the telemarketing representative of the information needed.

- **Determine measures:** Develop methods to measure customer satisfaction, customer loyalty, profitability, lead sources, etc.

- **Develop lead-generation programs:** Create and execute advertising, direct mail, and telemarketing lead-generation programs. Set up lead-qualification and tracking programs.

- **Coordinate program training and instruction:** Provide training and instruction to keep telemarketing representatives current on product/service features and applications.

Printed Response Group

This group performs all mail room functions for printed material or personalized letters and responses. The group stocks, mails, and reorders literature supplies and other fulfillment material.

Technical Support Group

This group answers technically specific questions from customers, end users, or channel distributors that cannot be answered by the telemarketing representative.

Field Interface Group

This group provides a central, personal contact for dealers, jobbers, franchises, national accounts, sales reps, wholesalers, and retailers to interface with the CIC. It supports sales management functions to coordinate account planning activities between the customer, field sales reps, and telephone contact.

Information Systems Group

This group interfaces with electronic communication networks and the centralized database. It maintains the internal network linking together all functional groups with the database (e.g., inventory, order processing status, accounting). Obviously, the CIC involves a highly integrated process. To be effective, the processes leading up to the CIC must be completed. These enable businesses to better plan, design, and staff the CIC. Too often, companies make the mistake of starting with the CIC and ignoring the other processes. This leads to underutilizing the inherent power of the CIC and results in disappointment.

Cultivating Customers and Acquiring New Customers

The two major goals of direct marketing in a business-to-business environment are (1) to increase sales productivity (while reducing sales costs) and (2) to build customer relationships. The CIC is the tool used to accomplish these goals. The specific applications that lead to satisfying these goals are labeled *cultivation* and *acquisition*. The cultivation process is designed to build the customer relationship. Businesses must build a bond with the customer that leads to a long-term relationship that benefits both parties. Exhibit 13–11 summarizes the steps in the process.

An adage in business-to-business marketing is that your best source for new business is your current customers. Existing customers represent growth opportunities. The cultivation process takes advantage of this by actively searching out sales opportunities and by closely monitoring the relationship.

Increasing Sales Opportunities

After gaining a customer, businesses can use the CIC and direct marketing to pursue penetration strategies. They should penetrate the account to search

Exhibit 13–11. Cultivation Process

Task	Description	Implemented by	Information source
Product penetration	Determine which other products customer has application for	CIC	Database
Account penetration	Obtain customer referrals for others within buying group	CIC	Database
Location penetration	Obtain customer referrals for others within location and/or organization	CIC	Database
Complaint handling	Procedures for handling customer complaints	CIC	Marketing and database
Customer-at-risk	Determine which customers or target segments are at risk	CIC and marketing	Customer surveys and database
Measurements	Continuously monitor and measure the customer relationship	CIC and marketing	Database

Source: Hunter Business Direct, Inc.

out additional sales opportunities and strengthen relationships. They pursue this at several levels: the individual, the buyer group, the location, and the organization. Exhibit 13–12 illustrates an account model and the penetration strategy.

At the individual level (1) is the product penetration strategy. Businesses must ask customers what additional needs they have and what solutions might meet those needs. At the buyer group level (2), they will ask the customer to refer them to other people within the same function and at the same location with applications for our product or services. At the location level (3), they will find out whether the customer can lead them to other buyer groups within the customer's location. Here, the area sales manager introduces us to people in finance, manufacturing, and engineering located in the same area. Finally, they move to the account level (4) and determine whether there are other locations or operations within the organization with similar applications. The same area sales manager now introduces them to other area sales managers with the company or with affiliates.

Combined, these efforts enable businesses to build a stronger bond with the customer. By referring them to others within the organization, the customer takes a proactive role in the relationship. By focusing on delighting the sales manager, an apostle is created, more loyal to the company and helpful in growing the business profitably.

Exhibit 13–12.   Account Model with Penetration Strategies

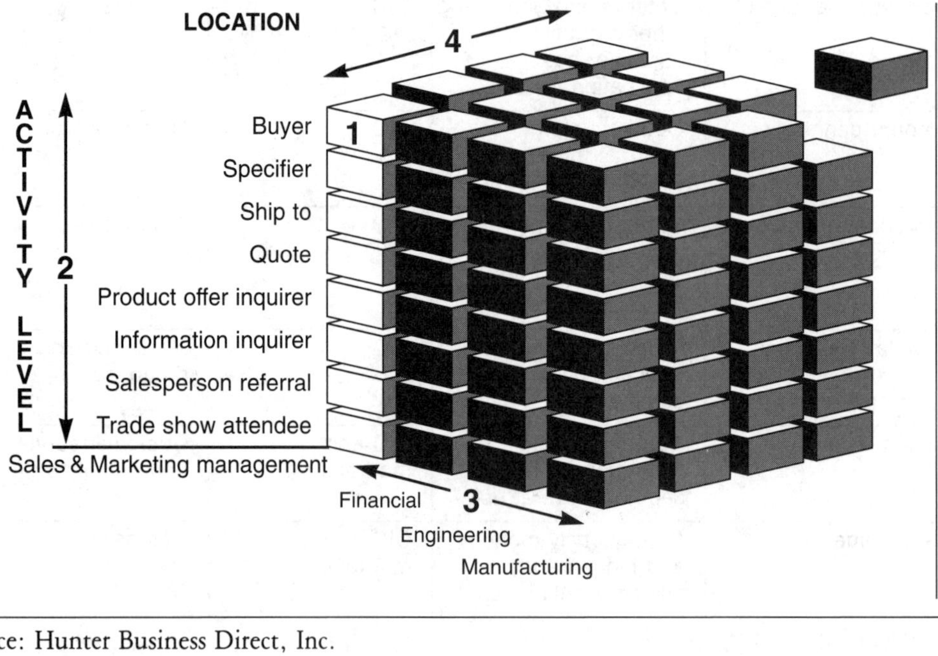

Source: Hunter Business Direct, Inc.

Protecting Your Customer Base

Although expanding your customer base is important, so is protecting this base. This involves customer-at-risk detection. Detecting customers at risk requires an ongoing program of monitoring the state of your customer relationships. This is an early warning system that detects changing customer needs, etc., and permits corrective actions before customers defect.

Acquiring New Customers

Acquiring stable, long-term customers is only possible if you know and retain your current customers. The most profitable new or prospective customers will look like your best current customers. The customer information gathered by the CIC will help you to acquire new customers. Exhibit 13–13 summarizes the steps in this process. Using the information in the CIC's database, you can identify attributes among your current customers that will help identify potential customers. From these attributes you can build a target segment, identify the unfulfilled needs or external service values of that segment, and determine how to position the product or service in respect to competitive products or services.

The next step in this process is lead qualification. The CIC is used to qualify leads before sending them to the sales force or other channel members. A communications plan is developed, similar to that used with current customers, for those qualified leads that express a current interest and have a customer buyer profile. This becomes the qualified prospect list and is managed through the CIC. The goal here is to advance the sales process so that the prospect is converted into a buyer.

Assimilation

Finally, new customers need to be assimilated into the customer community. Assimilation is the process of absorbing customers into the culture of the company—an initial "bonding" with the customer by acquiring and sharing valuable information. Think of it as welcoming a new employee into a company. It is the building of a "community of customers."

Meeting the Challenges of the '90s and Beyond

With rising sales costs, increased global competition, and rapid technological advances, business-to-business marketers need new tools to stay competitive in the 1990s and beyond. Value-added direct marketing provides the tools to increase sales productivity, build lasting customer relations, and improve revenues and profits. Let's close this chapter with a thumbnail case history that dramatizes the effects of value-added direct marketing.

Exhibit 13–13. Acquisition Process

Task	Description	Implemented by	Information source
Target segment attributes	Identify attributes for each target segment based on current customers	CIC	Database
Target segment needs	Identify unfulfilled needs of target segment based on current customers	CIC	Database
Competitive positioning	Determine positioning of product/service vis-à-vis competition	CIC	Database
Create the offer	Determine the offer based on current customer external service values	CIC	Database
Value-added communication plan	Determine the contact matrix to use with target segment	CIC	Database
Media selection	Determine media based on economics vis-à-vis contact plan	CIC	Database
Lead qualification	Qualify leads prior to distributing to field	CIC	Database
Advance the sales process	Develop and implement contact plan for prospects	CIC	Database
Measurements	Monitor and measure lead generation versus lead qualification	CIC	Database
New customer assimilation	Acclimate customer to customer community	CIC	Database

Source: Hunter Business Direct, Inc.

Case Study: Team TBA Program

Team TBA was set up as a separate company to market Shell Oil's non-petroleum products, which included tires, batteries, and accessories. Shell had not been satisfied with the sales they were achieving and chose to outsource the marketing of these products. The major objectives for Team TBA were to improve the profitability of the products and expand product penetration.

The first step Team TBA took was to put into place a value-added direct marketing program that combined mail, phone, and field sales contacts into a synchronized plan. The result reduced the number of field salespeople by 75 percent, going from 67 dedicated salespeople to 18. This saved more than $8 million in sales and marketing expenses.

Another important step was to shift the focus from selling to accounts to selling to individual service bay mechanics. Rather than focus on the dealership, the direct mail program concentrated on contact with individual mechanics. This not only increased product penetration, but also led to referrals to other mechanics at the Shell dealer level.

A major concern was the impact of a significantly reduced field sales force, because this would mean less frequent face-to-face contact. However, the synchronized program of mail and phone contacts, which produced more frequent contact, resulted in the customer's perception that field sales contact frequency had risen 17 percent. In fact, at the end of the first year of the program, customer satisfaction surveys showed increases in 30 of 31 categories.

SELF-QUIZ

1. What is the most significant difference between consumer direct marketing and business-to-business direct marketing?

   _____

   _____

   _____

2. Identify the five most important differences between the traditional approach to direct marketing and a value-added approach.

   a. _____

   b. _____

   c. _____

   d. _____

   e. _____

3. Define *external service values*.

   _____

   _____

   _____

4. What can customers who have defected tell a company that will help it to improve its marketing efforts?

_____

_____

_____

5. Explain the underlying reasons for grading customers.

_____

_____

_____

6. Describe how the customer contact plan is used.

_____

_____

_____

7. Identify the seven components of the Customer Information Center.

a. _____

b. _____

c. _____

d. _____

e. _____

f. _____

g. _____

8. What is the purpose of the cultivation process?

_____

_____

9. Explain how the account cube model is used.

_____

_____

_____

10. When acquiring new customers, what should they look like?

_____

_____

_____

PILOT PROJECT

You work for a quality-focused printer manufacturer with less than 10 percent market share. Your culture has been product and technology focused, but your vision station is customer focused. Your firm seems to exchange technology leadership every quarter, and margins continue to erode.

The chief operating officer came up through manufacturing but is "street smart." Budgeting is next month, and he has asked for a "white paper" to show how direct marketing can help the company grow and prosper by focusing on the customer. He and the president have asked you to address the following questions that were raised at a recent executive committee marketing:

1. What is special about integrated direct marketing?

2. What are the 3–5 key concepts the company must embrace to be successful in focusing on the customer?

3. How can you drive down sales costs and increase service levels?

4. Can you market or sell to individual customers even when you do a mailing?

5. What are the key steps you need to go through in building a pilot direct marketing program?

CHAPTER FOURTEEN

Retail Direct Marketing

Handbills. Flyers. Catalogs. Newspaper ads soliciting phone orders. Mailings to store credit card holders. Inserts in billing statements. All of these have been the tools of retailers for decades.

But, more often than not, the prime objective of retailers has been to create store traffic. There is nothing wrong with this, except that retailers have been hard put to accurately measure the cost-effectiveness of traffic-building material. The fact is that a retailer is rarely sure whether a particular promotion brought people into the store or whether the customers were shopping in the store anyway and discovered the promoted merchandise while browsing.

Today, all this is changing. Major retailers are rapidly embracing the sophisticated techniques now available to all who use the direct marketing discipline. And with this new sophistication retailers are discovering what mail order firms have known for decades: *All customers are not created equal*.

Identifying Heavy Users

The big breakthrough in direct marketing has been the ability to differentiate heavy users of package goods from average users and occasional users. Consider dog food as a category. Some customers purchase 20 pounds of dog food a week, as contrasted to an average of, say, 2 pounds a week. Good business dictates that the heavy user be cultivated.

Not only is it important to know who the heavy user is, but it is equally important to know which brand or brands the heavy user is buying. For if it is possible to identify heavy users with their names and addresses along with their brand preferences, then it is possible to persuade those customers either to switch brands or to buy more of a preferred brand.

The natural question is, How does one identify the customer by name, address, and brand purchased? That's where the computer comes into play. As a matter of fact, several systems have been developed that enable the package-goods company and/or the retailer to capture the necessary information. One such company is Schlumberger, of Chesapeake, Virginia. Its system is called the Smart Card.

In this system, retail chain store customers are given ID cards that provide "preferred customer" discounts. This gives each store the customers' names and addresses. Then bar codes on the packages identify brands purchased and the amount. All of this information is fed into the computer and stored. Thus cumulative purchases are recorded over time, making it possible to calculate average weekly purchases of given brands.

This type of information is invaluable for both the retailers and the package-goods companies, especially from a competitive standpoint. The package-goods company, for example, can send cents-off coupons or free samples to heavy users of competitive brands.

Case Histories

One person in particular has trumpeted the opportunities in direct marketing for retailers. That person is Peter Hoke, publisher of *Direct Marketing* magazine and publisher of a newsletter entitled *Promoting Store Traffic*. The case histories that follow have been gleaned from Hoke's extensive files.

IGA Supermarket Chain

This is the story of a segment of a supermarket chain that had never used direct mail but achieved a 63 percent return on its first mailing! The hero of the story is Orville Roth, who operates 12 IGA supermarkets in Oregon.

Roth decided to try direct mail, using one of its greatest strengths—testing. But first he had to build a database. Roth started to build a list with a sign-up-to-win sweepstakes promotion. The sign-up card included five household questions, so the database was enhanced by family size, ownership of a VCR, and similar information.

The sweepstakes offered four major prizes, but (this is the important part) everyone would win something. The number of households signing up was 2,786, creating a brand-new, clean, accurate database. Winners were drawn for the four major prizes; postcards were mailed to the remaining 2,782 people telling them they had also won something.

All the postcard recipients had to do was bring in the card for their free prize—a dozen eggs. The response was terrific: 1,752 people came into the store. This translates into a response rate of 63 percent. Cost per response was 66 cents. But what really counts is the bottom line: total store sales increased 43 percent the first day the postcards were received.

After these initial results, Roth made the understatement of the year, saying "I like this direct mail idea." Naturally, other direct mail promotions followed. One of Roth's unique promotions was his Leap Year Promotion. This was another fold-over mailer. (See Exhibit 14-1.) The headline—"A sale so great it happens once every four years—plus the four coupons formed the heart of this simple mailing. Results: an 18 percent redemption rate, with store sales increasing 17 percent over the same period in the previous year.

Exhibit 14-1. Leap Year Promotion

Saks Fifth Avenue Proprietary Charge Card

At one time, famous department stores like Neiman-Marcus, Marshall Field's, Macy's, Bloomingdale's, and Sears honored only one credit card—their own. But that has changed dramatically. Now Visa and MasterCard, in particular, are widely accepted by major department stores that also offer their own credit cards. This case history, however, proves conclusively that the house card customer is more loyal and spends more money.

Saks Fifth Avenue (SFA) uses its proprietary charge card to assess customer purchase habits, target direct mail promotions, and increase lifetime customer value. According to William Bloom, vice president for credit and services, private cards "give membership in a prestigious retail family. The loyalty generates a lot of business."

SFA found customers who charge purchases exclusively on its card spend an average of $554 annually, compared with $296 for American Express and $166 for bank cards. Among multicard users, the average is a whopping $1,834, remaining above $1,000 where SFA is one of two cards used. But bank card and American Express users spend just $245 on average. "It's the proprietary card that drives business into the store," states Bloom, "because we're in touch with them all the time."

With SFA's reliance on direct mail, Bloom says, "Knowing where customers live is almost as important as knowing what they buy. It enables you to target existing customers and find additional ones with similar characteristics." Bloom says in 1971 SFA realized it had 1.5 million charge customers "who are waiting to hear from you."

"You lose touch with your customers if you can't contact them," he notes. Without SFA's ability to track people, he says it wouldn't do as much repeat business. One recent 600,000-piece SFA mailing to active accounts offering a 10 percent discount on a day's purchases generated $18 million in incremental sales.

Many retailers that develop extensive catalogs do not accept mail orders. Their sole purpose is to excite interest in given products to induce prospects to come into the store to see, feel, and try on. The next case history is about such a retail operation.

When an established retailer with multiple locations recognizes the power of its database and decides it's time to release that static energy into the marketplace, it's opening the door to expansion. Helzberg Diamonds, Kansas City, Missouri, is a prime example of such a retailer.

Helzberg Diamonds

About 10 years ago, the 75-year-old specialty retailer decided to develop and use its customer database. At that time the company operated approximately

30 stores and had a database of about 25,000 names. In 8 years the company expanded to more than 70 stores while building a sophisticated database of almost 900,000 names.

In 1956 Barnett C. Helzberg, Jr., joined Helzberg Diamonds as the third generation in the family firm. He took the company into mail order sales of its nonjewelry product lines. In 1963 Helzberg took command of the 39-store firm. In 1967 Helzberg Diamonds opened its first corner store in a shopping mall. Success in the mall was immediate, and Helzberg continues to open more mall stores every year. In the mid-1970s Helzberg dropped its ancillary product lines and mail order operation to focus on diamonds, precious gemstones, and karat gold.

Then in 1979 a young journalism school graduate named John Goodman joined the firm. At that time the firm had about 40 stores and the beginnings of a database—some 20,000–30,000 names maintained in-house without the benefits of computerization. Goodman took some direct marketing lessons from Helzberg and from Martin Baier, who taught at the Center for Direct Marketing, University of Missouri at Kansas City. As vice president of advertising for Helzberg Diamonds and later as founder of Goodman Direct, Goodman helped Helzberg harness the power of the firm's database.

Helzberg Diamonds applied many of the same direct marketing principles it used in its mail order operations of the 1950s to generate store traffic in the 1980s. The major differences in its current mailings are that the prospect cannot order products by mail and that each mailing goes to a specific segment of the database residing within a certain distance of a shopping mall housing a Helzberg Diamonds shop.

The database is organized so that names can be selected by geodemographics, the amount of money a customer spends over a designated period, frequency of purchase, or method of payment. The names of proprietary charge card holders can be selected by active cards with no balance, active cards with a balance, or cards that have never been active. Other selections might be house names, seed names, and various rented files. Different selections are made to achieve different goals.

With almost 900,000 names in its database, Helzberg Diamonds uses an outside full-service direct marketing company, Marketing Communications Inc. (MCI), to maintain its database. Each week the 75 Helzberg Diamond shops in 30 markets send MCI data providing the name and address of each purchaser along with the date and amount of purchase.

MCI staffers then input the data into a single marketing database for all Helzberg Diamonds stores. Maintaining all of the firm's data in a single database provides several marketing benefits.

By monitoring and analyzing sales trends evidenced in this universal database, management can determine which markets require more promotional dollars and which markets could support an additional Helzberg Diamonds shop. If the company wants to do a promotional mailing to all customers who meet a certain criterion (e.g., first-time buyers, big spenders, or holiday purchasers), only one database need be accessed to select the appropriate names for all stores' customers. Another benefit of having all stores share a single database is that the addresses of customers who move from one market to another will be corrected during a national change of address (NCOA) pass. These customers will continue to receive mailings directing them to the Helzberg shop nearest their new residence.

According to Larry Hawks, vice president of development for MCI, the Helzberg database receives a thorough cleaning in the fall, just before the holiday mailings begin. The list is periodically passed against NCOA for address corrections. The Helzberg file is continually being cleaned to keep carrier route codes up to date and to eliminate duplications and therefore unnecessary mailings. Exhibit 14–2 shows the front cover of a Mother's Day catalog, a typical Helzberg Diamonds promotion.

Retail Direct Marketing Maxims

The thumbnail case histories we have reviewed are indicative of direct marketing opportunities for retailers. Those who have been at it for a long time have discovered certain principles, maxims that prove to be true time after time. Murray Raphel, an internationally respected consultant on retail direct marketing, has developed 30 maxims based on 30 years of experience.

1. **It's far, far easier to sell to the customer you have than to sell a new customer.** Most businesses spend six times as much money for new customers as they do for the customer they already have. Ridiculous. How do you overcome this wrong direction? Easy—direct mail.

2. **Limited time.** The tighter the time frame of the promotion, the more successful. We were so excited about the success of Neiman-Marcus "fortnight" promotions that we duplicated the idea for an Irish sale. We scheduled something every day for the two-week period including Atlantic City's first St. Patrick's Day parade. It was the biggest failure we ever had. Our analysis of why it failed narrowed down to its length. Three days would have worked. One day would have been terrific!

3. **Running a sale when other stores are closed brings in more customers.** We once ran a "Midnight Madness" sale for a supermarket. They worked with their wholesaler and came up with rock-bottom food prices. The crowds started forming at 10 p.m. By 11:00, all the shopping carts were gone and the just-arriving began to bid for carts held by others. By midnight, the carts were selling for $20 each, just to get into the store. This works as well with an "Early Bird Sale" that starts at 6 a.m. And remember our New Year's Day sale?

Exhibit 14–2.   Mother's Day Catalog Cover

4. **Running a sale with a sweepstakes increases traffic from 10 to 20 percent.** Or more. When we mailed a notice of a sale to customers on our mailing list, the average response was 8 percent. The first year we ran a sweepstakes, that jumped to 10–12 percent!

5. **Running a sale with a sweepstakes and the customer's name will increase response another 5–10 percent.** When we ran the sweepstakes, we told the customers to "fill out your name on this certificate and bring it to the store."

   We then preprinted each customer's name on the certificates and said, "This certificate is exclusively yours (your name is on the certificate). Just bring it to the store to be eligible for one of the 121 prizes." Response jumped from 10–12 percent to 15–18 percent.

6. **The mailer should "look" like your business.** Use the same typefaces consistently. If there is a color associated with your store (and if there isn't, there should be), use it. Our mailers for our shops became so identifiable that when we did a mailer for a local politician, most people thought it was from our store.

7. **Use your name as the name of your business.** Most people are uncomfortable using their own name. It's like looking at yourself in a mirror. It's okay to do if you're alone, but not if others are watching. Putting your own name for everyone to see is too much "exposure" for most. They tell you, "It won't work." And I tell them, "You're right. But don't tell that to Mr. Macy, Mr. Nordstrom, John Wanamaker, L. L. Bean. . . ." Your name is your name. Through the years it will achieve its own recognition and reputation. And you can avoid the cute names like "The Shop on the Corner" (I hope you never move), or the shoe store called "A Step in Time," or, well, walk through your nearest mall and you'll see what I mean.

8. **Give the customer a choice between something and something, not something and nothing.** When was the last time you received a catalog with only one item? Even the covers of most catalogs have a selection of the most-wanted items. Our mailers listed at least six popular items in each of the shops.

9. **A guaranteed winner guarantees more customers.** We posted "lucky" numbers on all our mailers. (The word "lucky" is powerful.) Every single number won at least something. Most were $2 winners. Even though we told the customers (at least six times) in each mailer that everyone was a winner, customers would come in the store and see their "lucky" number as a $2 winner and scream, "I won! I won!" And no, we never said, "Hey, didn't you read the mailer—everybody won!"

10. **Guarantee your merchandise.** Guarantee everything you sell. Regular price merchandise. Sale merchandise. Anything and everything they buy in your

store. Each mailer has a "guarantee" that the customer must be satisfied with what they buy. Not just the usual guarantee against wear and tear, but guaranteed to make them happy. Greenwich Workshop is the nation's finest distributor of signed limited edition prints. Many of their dealers increased sales dramatically when they told customers to take the prints home, hang them, and if they didn't like them on the wall, bring them back for another print or their money back. The point: A print looks different on a gallery wall than on your living room wall.

11. **If a headline works, repeat it.** I really don't know why a certain combination of nouns, verbs, adjectives and/or prepositions makes a customer stop what they are doing and run to buy from you. Every once in a while it just happens. Through the years there are a handful of headlines that worked every time they were used. Here's one:
    - "Would you buy a $50 Yves St. Laurent shirt on sale for $29?" You can substitute the original price, the name, the sale price for whatever you want to sell and it brings in customers. We've used it successfully for clothing, stationery shops, supermarkets, and a dozen other businesses.
    - "The name is Mañana. But at $25, you'd better buy it today." This was for a woman's jacket made in Mexico. We sold out of the 48 pieces the same day the ad ran. We reordered and (with trepidation) ran the exact same ad only ten days later. And sold out again! We reordered again and ran the same ad two weeks later. Sold out again.

    Moral: If a headline works, repeat it. There are those who never saw it the first time. There are those who saw it and are reminded. There are those who will tell others.

12. **Cross-sell in your mailer.** If you are a supermarket selling seafood, mention lemons. If you are a clothing store selling snowsuits, mention scarfs, gloves, and hats. Things that go together are natural add-ons.

13. **Repeat your main offer many times.** You, your wife or husband, people who work with you and your parents will read every word you write. Your customer does not. They scan quickly. Take your biggest value and repeat it often. If you say it ten times, the first time the customer sees it might be the last time you wrote it.

14. **Co-op with other stores.** Two reasons for this: 1. It gives your customer additional reasons for coming to the sale. 2. It cuts your cost of mailing, because your noncompetitors will pay their share of printing and mailing.

    We have done many mailings for no printing or mailing costs. We supplied the artist and layout to give the mailer a total overall "look."

15. **It's far easier to sell more at busy times than at slow times.** Those hard-to-beat figures for Christmas, Easter, and Back to School are the best times to do more business. People expect to spend money at certain times of the year. Give them reasons to come to you at that time. Creating a Millard

Fillmore Birthday sale is unusual, but it will be tough to get customers to leave the house and open their wallets. When you fish, you go where the fish are.

16. **Mail customers ahead of time.** Customers want to feel important and receive something special. Telling them to shop the sale before it's advertised in other media is a good move. We once persuaded a stationery retailer to send a mailer to his customers telling them of the "private sale for our customers only." Then he became nervous no one would show up.

    He placed a large newspaper ad and ran several radio commercials to announce the sale to the public for the same day. Later he told me hardly anyone from his mailing list showed up. "I guess direct mail doesn't work," he said. And we explained, "No, it doesn't work if you tell someone the sale is for them and then tell everyone else to come the same day!"

17. **Mail more often than you think is acceptable.** We started out sending mailings to our customer list twice a year for winter and summer sales. Then we went to six times a year. Then we went to every month for our Gold Card customers. Then we sent this select group something twice a month. The percentage of returns always related more to the offer than the frequency of the mailing. I still like the story about when Leon Gorman, grandson of founder L. L. Bean, took over the operation and decided the customer should make the decision when to buy instead of him making the decision when to sell. So he increased his catalog mailings and did more business.

18. **Calling after a mailing increases store traffic the day of the sale.** A simple "Did you receive our mailer? We wanted you to know before anyone else . . . ." Take your key customers. Give their names and phone numbers to your staff. They call during "down times" when they are not waiting on customers or working on stock. An automatic, never-fails, guaranteed way to bring in more business from your mailing piece.

19. **Write four notes a day.** Each of your staff should have "key" customers. In slow times, have them drop a note to their best customers about new merchandise that has just arrived or for any other plausible reason. The owner of a diner put the postcard received from a salesman in our men's shop on her front cash register. She pointed it out to her customers as "the first time anyone ever wrote me from a store." Yes, she also came in and bought. Would you believe $654.13? Believe it. It happened.

    Make four phone calls a day. Reread #19 and substitute the word "phone" for "notes." It works as well.

20. **Make sure the story isn't better than the store.** Vrest Orton, founder of the Original Vermont Country Store in Weston, Vermont (pop. 400), made a success sending his homespun catalog of turn-of-the-century artifacts (Bon Ami soap, corncob holders, Walnetto candies). When he began, he went to L.L. Bean in Freeport, Maine, and asked for advice. Bean said, "Just

remember one sentence: Make sure the story isn't better than the store." His point: Don't exaggerate what you are selling. Use the ancient and honorable technique of "Promise a lot—but deliver more." I once saw an appliance store advertise a TV set with an outline of a man next to the set. The TV set was as tall as the man! I called and asked how this could be, and the store owner answered, "Well, the man is only three feet tall."

21. **Have an in-store display of what you featured in your mailer.** Put it in your store where you put it in your mailer. Up front. We once visited a supermarket in Alabama that mailed 20,000 flyers to customers for a giant "Buy One, Get One Free" sale. We walked all around the store and asked, "Where are the specials you advertised?"

    "On the shelves where they usually are," said the store manager. "When the customer asks, we tell them to pick out the items in the mailer and bring them to the front counter and we'll give it to them on sale at that time."

    The store owner later told me, "You know, that's the best pulling headline in supermarketing, but it didn't work for me." Really?

22. **Send your mailer to the postmaster in every ZIP code you mail.** Enclose a note that explains this is your mailing piece that must arrive at your customer's house before the date shown. Otherwise, who comes to your sale? Ask them to please call you when the mailers are mailed. Most will not. And so, you make phone calls to each postmaster after your advertisement is mailed. Did they receive the mailer yet? Was it sent out yet? Are there any problems?

23. **Have extra copies of your mailer available.** If you're running a sweepstakes, a certain percentage of your customers will come and say, "I left my mailer at home. How do I know if I won anything?" You quickly give them another mailer with its lucky number and sweepstakes for them to fill out and enter in the store.

    The importance of reminding the customers what you have to sell with extra mailers reminds us of the time we did an attractive four-color brochure for a supermarket on their attractive sandwich trays. They printed 5,000 to mail and give customers while shopping. When the job was finished, I visited the market and couldn't find the brochures. I asked for the owner and they sent me to his office.

    I asked him where he was keeping the brochures. He took keys from his pocket, unlocked a cabinet, and there were the 5,000 brochures.

    "Why don't you have these on counters for customers to pick up?" I asked.

    "Are you kidding?" he answered. "They cost me 50 cents apiece. If I put them on the counters, people will just pick them up and take them away!" (Now, you can't make up stories like that. . . .)

24. **Don't make customers mad.** If you run out of an item, offer them a rain check or something not on sale for the same price. Whatever it takes. Stew Leonard, owner of two of the world's highest-volume supermarkets in Danbury and Norwalk, Connecticut, knows the average person spends $246,000 in a lifetime at a supermarket.

He told me, "Every time I see someone coming through the front door, I see stamped on their forehead in big red letters: $246,000. Nothing I'm going to do to have them get mad at me."

25. **Steal!** Everyone in business receives dozens of mailing pieces every day. Which ones made you stop and, better yet, open what you received? Save that mailer! And ask yourself, "How can I use this idea in MY business?" There are no new ideas, just new ways of using the successful ones.

26. **Fear of loss is far more powerful than promise of gain.** Those letters you receive in the mail every January from magazine publishers headlined "you have won $10 million" found their sales increased when they changed the words to "you have lost $10 million" (if you did not enter the contest).

27. **Use the word "gift certificate" instead of "coupon."** Coupons are for supermarket ads.

28. **Use testimonials.** Once, during our New Year's sale, we hired a radio station to come and ask people their thoughts about the sale while they were shopping.

The station had release forms signed so we could use the commercials at a later date. We did use them for radio commercials in future sales and about 20 of them for the cover of the following year's New Year's Day sale mailer. If you say something nice about your business, that's you saying it. If a customer says something nice about your business, that carries a lot more believability and is a "makes me want to go there and shop" attraction.

29. **Involve your staff.** Show the folks that work with you a "rough" of your mailer before it is printed. You'll receive valuable advice. In the past, employees have noticed the following: "You have the wrong date." "The markdown isn't large enough to make anyone come." "I've spotted four misspellings so far."

In addition, you are accomplishing what people want most from their jobs. When he was a professor at Ohio State University, Ken Blanchard (of *One Minute Manager* fame) did a comprehensive survey on "What Workers Want from Their Jobs." Higher wages came in fifth. "Being appreciated" was first and "a feeling of being 'in' on things" was second. Involve your people if only because your mailer will be more successful.

30. **Give the customer what they want to buy, not what you want to sell.** Too many retailers think a sale is having huge markdowns on merchandise that

doesn't sell. Your mailer should offer your best-selling items on sale! When they come to the store they'll also buy what you want them to buy. Especially if the store is crowded. That's why casinos bring busloads of senior citizens to play the slot machines. The cost of the trip to the seniors: nothing, plus a chit for lunch. But when others arrive, they see the huge crowds and say, "Wow! I've come to the right place!"

SELF-QUIZ

1. What is the prime objective of most retailers? _____

_____

2. What lessons have retailers learned that mail order firms have always known? _____

_____

3. When package-goods companies use direct marketing, their primary objective is to identify _____

_____

4. Describe how a supermarket might record customer names and what those customers purchase over time. _____

_____

_____

_____

5. If a package-goods company has access to names of heavy users of competitive brands, how might it induce consumers to switch brands? _____

_____

_____

_____

6. For a department store, what are the advantages of a house credit card over a bank credit card such as Visa or MasterCard?

a. _____

b. _____

7. Why would a retailer send out a catalog but refuse to accept mail orders?

   _____

   _____

   _____

   _____

8. Complete this direct marketing principle: If you know the profile of your customer base, your objective should be _____

   _____.

9. Running a sale with a sweepstakes increases the traffic from _____ percent to _____ percent.

PILOT PROJECT

You work for a chain of four supermarkets. You don't know who your regular customers are by name and address, yet you believe that direct marketing could increase traffic, sales, and profits.

Prepare a letter to your management outlining how you would proceed to build a database, what incentives you would employ to increase store traffic, and what tests you would make.

CHAPTER FIFTEEN

Managing a Lead-Generation Program

Not long ago, the "face" a company had to its customers was the sales force. They represented the company in every way. In fact, to customers they *were* the company. Remember the blue-suited image of IBM? The sales force answered questions, demonstrated the product, offered solutions to problems, and established loyal relationships. Nowadays, the sales force is still vitally important, but their job is different. Instead of "cold canvassing" to solicit interest, "appointment selling" is preferred when a face-to-face visit is needed to sell the product—usually a product with a high-ticket price tag.

For many products, communications takes on the role once served by salespeople. These communications can take many forms: direct mail, catalogs, infomercials, the Internet, and traditional advertising media such as print, radio, and TV. Every contact a customer has through these vehicles, whether requested or not, serves to establish and build on a relationship that customer has with the company. So, these communications not only sell products, but they also support the brand image of the company and are inextricably linked to long-term customer loyalty.

Lead-generation programs are a method devised to bring leads to the sales force and classify those leads so that the sales force knows which lead is "hot,"

Bette Anne Hutchings, a partner and management supervisor at Ogilvy and Mather Direct, is a self-proclaimed technophile, representing the new breed of thinking and application. Her credentials include marketing assignments for both AT&T and IBM. This chapter is based on her ideas.

"warm," or "cool." Thus, they can prioritize their efforts and focus on closing more sales, more often.

Technology and Time

The Technology Age has made marketing and advertising even more critical to the sales process. Everything moves faster today than it did ten years ago. Product information is required sooner, and buying decisions are made more quickly.

Don't forget that a prospect inquiry is a signal of buying interest. If there is no fulfillment, or if fulfillment is delayed, prospects will make their decisions without information on your products. In a more general sense, you've made a promise to each prospect answering your ad: "If you contact me, I will send you information." If you don't follow through promptly, you've broken your promise, and might have created a negative image of your company. A well-run inquiry-management system ensures that the right material goes out to every prospect every time, thus keeping your promises and enhancing your image.

The sooner information can be delivered or fulfilled, the higher the odds of closing the sale. The smartest marketers will use lead-generation programs to preempt an inquiry and send information and/or pertinent offers at the precise moment the prospect is ready to receive them. This demonstrates the symbiotic relationship between lead generation and database marketing.

But how does one know what customers or prospects want and when they are ready to buy? The key: leverage every contact with customers or prospects to learn more about them. Asking the appropriate questions will lead to highly profitable answers. To demonstrate this approach, we need to start at the very beginning.

Types of Lead-Generation Programs

There are three overall types of lead-generation programs. Although the principles that govern them are the same, the needs that dictate the programs differ.

Business-to-Business

The primary objective in business-to-business lead generation is to get qualified leads from prospects who, in effect, raise their hands and say, "I'd like more information about your proposition." The thrust of the promotion can be as simple as encouraging prospects to request literature with an inducement to order by mail. Telephone follow-ups of those who request literature are often an integral part of the lead-generation program. For more complex propositions requiring interaction with a live salesperson, the objective is to get a request for a salesperson to call. However, the cost of an industrial sales call being what it is today, mail and phone follow-up is more and more becoming the norm, rather than the exception.

Business-to-Consumer

The feasibility of lead-generation programs for consumer products is usually dictated by price point and available channels of distribution. The unit of sale inherent in package goods, for example, obviates the practicality of a lead-generation program, except in the case of a cents-off coupon co-op. (See Chapter 7, "Co-Ops.") However, lead-generation programs do make eminent sense for the likes of a lawn care service where the expenditure is around $700 a year. Or for refrigerators, air conditioning, freezers, or insulation—each a considered purchase of magnitude for the consumer.

Some manufacturers sell major equipment directly to the consumer. Most sell through traditional retail channels. In the former, the objective is to get qualified leads and to complete the transaction by mail, phone, or salesperson.

Public Relations

A third type of lead-generation program uses public relations as the medium for getting leads. Done right, PR is an extremely effective method of producing leads in both the consumer and business field.

As a matter of fact, more often than not, editorial mention of a free booklet offer for a new product is likely to produce more leads than a space ad. The theory is that the reader puts more stock in editorial mentions than in ads. The other side of the coin is that conversion to orders is more likely from space ads than from editorial mentions.

Publishers' policies vary when it comes to giving free editorial mention. Some publishers give editorial mention only if an ad is placed; others give editorial mention irrespective of space advertising. Many firms prepare and distribute their own news releases to likely publications. However, there is no substitute for a good public relations agency in getting news releases placed.

Essential Elements of Successful Lead-Generation Programs

Implementation involves consideration of eight key areas: involving the sales force, determining objectives, planning capacity and lead flow, promotion strategy, creative strategy, media strategy, fulfillment strategy, and measuring results.

Involving the Sales Force.   When planning a promotion, marketers often overlook the most valuable tie to their customer base—the sales force. No source will be able to relate to the specific needs and product application for a market as well as the sales force. They are on the "firing line." They know what's going on out in the territory, who their competition is, and the spheres of influence among their prospects. Even the message in your communications can be influenced in both tone and content by the sales force.

Front-end involvement is essential, but don't overlook the sales force's ability to judge the effectiveness of the promotion. A feedback loop should be established for a qualitative assessment of positive and negative results.

Determining Objectives.   The special need for objectives in a lead-generation program relates to the quality of leads. An abundance of leads can be meaningless if an insufficient number convert to sales. The key question is, "What ratio of sales to inquiries do we need to make this program profitable?" This must be spelled out when setting objectives.

Planning Capacity and Lead Flow.   Lead flow is not a faucet that can be turned on or off at will. Lead flow must be planned so that leads come in at a rate equal to the sales force's capacity to handle them. Although there will be more on this subject later in this chapter, the key point to remember is that either too few leads or too many leads will work to the detriment of the program.

Promotion Strategy.   Strategies should identify the steps required for accomplishing the program's objectives. They are the road map for getting from where you are to where you want to be. In addition, they should mesh with the strategies being applied by the sales force and other distribution channels. For example, if the sales force's strategy is to sell more computers by targeting the legal profession, then the promotion's strategy could be to develop a direct mail/lead-generation campaign directed to that same target audience. This, in turn, would provide qualified leads from the legal profession for the sales force to convert into sales.

Creative Strategy.   Creative strategy for a lead-generation program should reflect the creative strategies applied for other advertising efforts, including general advertising. The look and feel of the communication should be consistent with the overall image of the company to leverage the full benefits of an integrated campaign.

Media Strategy.   The key question is, given the target market and the product offering, what media will most effectively accomplish the task? Whether it be mail, print, broadcast, cable—whatever the medium—considerations such as penetration, key prospects reached, number of contacts, and so forth, must be considered.

Fulfillment Strategy.   As simple as it sounds, one must know exactly what will happen to a lead once it's received. If there is to be a brochure, for example, ample quantities must be in stock before the initial communication occurs. Measurement systems must be in place for scheduling sales calls, referring leads to the field, call-back programs, and so forth. Failure to be ready to fulfill promptly can kill the best of promotions.

Results Measurement.   It is imperative that the lead-generation effort be measurable and accountable. Success and failure factors must be identified before the program is developed to ensure that these determinants are tracked and analyzed appropriately once the program is in place.

Let's look at some of these essentials in greater detail.

Using the Ingredients of an Effective Inquiry-Handling System

To develop a successful marketing program, you have to know what you're up against. Here are a few eye-opening facts from the Advertising Research Foundation:

- Up to 60 percent of all inquiries are made with a view to purchase within one year.

- Up to 25 percent of those with a purchase in view will have an "immediate need" and will purchase the product or service advertised from the company of which they inquired or from a competitor.

- Up to 10 percent of those with a purchase in view will be "hot" leads.

- Up to 60 percent of the inquirers who contact you also contact your competitor.

- In 20 percent of all prospects' requests for information, the respondents never received any material.

- In 43 percent of those inquiries, the material was received too late to be of any use.

- 59 percent stated that they threw away one or more pieces of the response material as being valueless.

This data suggests that there is a substantial waste of communications expenditures, which results in disenchantment for large numbers of people because of unresponsive companies. So how does one overcome these hurdles?

Start at the End.   Determine the measurements for success up front. How will the program be measured? Gross sales? Revenue? Cost per order? Starting here will help in the design of systems and management processes to meet those objectives. It's extremely inefficient—and sometimes impossible—to change objectives midstream. Ask yourself these questions:

- What constitutes a good/bad lead?

- How many leads are enough?

- Which is worse: no leads, or too many?

- How will we track leads? Who will be responsible for them?

- How will we automate our processes for secure data flow?

- How will we report our progress to management?

The inquiry system will survive only if emphasis is placed on the ability of the system to measure effectiveness and identify its contribution to sales.

Understand the Nature of the Beast.   A good inquiry follow-up system should address the interaction problem often associated with the activities of the salespeople, the marketing manager, and the advertising manager.

Sales representatives in general loathe and avoid paperwork. They often resent any intrusion in their territory and scorn measurement and control. A good inquiry-handling system must be simple to use, easy to work with, and not looked on by salespeople as a burden.

Sales representatives typically do not supply the total feedback necessary for proper evaluation. A smart system must be able to supply the necessary analysis without total reliance on the sales representative.

The Inquiry System Does Not Exist without an Offer.   Communications objectives should be inquiry-oriented. The creation of advertising that employs known response techniques should be the mission of agency and/or staff copywriters and art directors. The advertising produced should be measured against response-oriented goals.

The offer must be in line with program objectives and with the company's operational ability to follow up on responses. If the objective is to generate leads, make an offer that will generate only as many as you can effectively handle. Too many leads can be even more destructive to the program than not enough. Lead quantity is not as important as lead quality.

When testing a less expensive offer against your control offer, don't assume that a lower response rate is necessarily less effective. Include the fulfillment costs for the offer and then review the total direct marketing costs per respondent and per order. You might find that the less expensive offer produces a more valuable customer (over time), thus producing a more profitable program.

Do Not Be Afraid to Mention the Price.   Even if the price is prohibitive, this will immediately weed out those that cannot afford your product. They are unqualified. You should spend most of your time talking to prospects who have the money, authority, need, and desire to purchase what you have to sell.

Ask the Prospect Some Leading Questions.   The questions you ask will allow you to determine where the prospect falls in the purchase decision process. Use every available opportunity, but don't turn your qualification effort into market research. There's no need to overload a single contact with a customer or prospect by asking lots of questions. Spread them out. Use several contacts. This will not only improve the probability that you'll get all the answers, but it also will provide a reason to keep communicating. After all, don't forget the out-of-sight, out-of-mind rule. Stay in your prospect's field of vision at all times. Sample questions and their implications are shown in Exhibit 15–1.

   Note that the answers can feed some important learning that you can capitalize on. Use all this data to build a rich database from which to develop ongoing

Exhibit 15–1.   Questions for Sales Prospects

Authority in the buying decision	How would you describe your involvement in the decision to purchase our product? • You make the decision. • You investigate and recommend. • The decision is made elsewhere in the company. (*Make sure to get the name of that person.*)
Monetary resources	How much are you willing to spend?
Potential sales volume	How many people in your company could benefit from our product(s)? How will you put our product to use?
Predisposition to buy from you/ customer loyalty	Have you purchased any of our products in the past? Which ones? Would you like to remain on our mailing list?
Immediacy of need/desire	Are you ready to buy now? In 3–6 months? 6–12 months? Over 12 months? Would you like a salesperson to call/visit?

marketing communications. Constantly add new data to the old. And refresh worn-out data. If, in your database, you find that a prospect who already has experience with your company is the decision-maker in the buying process and has an immediate need, make sure you get to him/her quickly. You're about to close a sale!

Incorporate a Bounce-Back Card in Your Fulfillment Follow-up.   This is the key to the whole system. Add a card that poses some of the questions above into your fulfillment offering. This allows you to qualify the lead after they've had a chance to review the information requested.

Monitor the time from the shipment date of the fulfillment package. If the bounce-back card is not returned within a specified time, send another one. After three unsuccessful efforts however, you can call it quits. Additional follow-up is unproductive. Analyze and compile the data from the bounce-back card and the original inquiry to classify the lead as qualified or unqualified.

Some inquiry management systems use the telephone to qualify inquiries. However, the telephone is costly when the volume of inquiries is extensive. A preferred method is to use the telephone for upgrading promising bounce-back respondents. The quantity is lower, and the success rate is higher.

Understanding the Art of Communication

Hierarchy of Effects

Any purchase decision is an evolutionary process. The advertising industry has accepted a model developed by researchers Lavidge and Steiner to explain how advertising works. (See Exhibit 15-2.) Their model is based on a hierarchy of effects in the communication process that move the prospect from awareness to purchase.

Before purchasing action occurs, an evolution takes place; mentally, the prospect moves through a series of steps starting with awareness and ending in the purchasing action. Within these stages of involvement, different modes of communication play different roles. Although responsibility overlaps, it's clear to see how direct marketing plays a significant role in the selling process.

General advertising is most efficient in generating awareness, knowledge, and interest. Direct marketing's strength lies in encouraging evaluation, preference, conviction, and ultimately purchase. These steps often require more information, whether that is delivered in a one-on-one conversation (in person or on the telephone), a product demonstration, an information-rich brochure, or a World Wide Web home page on the Internet.

To increase efficiency and cut costs, marketers should insist that each mode of communication is accountable for what it does best. General advertising should be measured on its ability to generate awareness and consideration;

Exhibit 15–2. Hierarchy of Effects

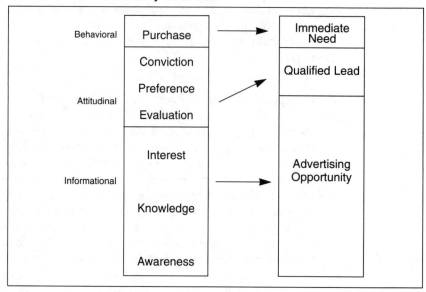

direct marketing should be evaluated on its ability to move the prospect from consideration to purchase and beyond. An effective inquiry system assigns specific roles to both and leverages the strengths inherent within each. Working seamlessly together, they comprise a communications program that's unbeatable.

Checks and Balances

Multimedia synergy (the combination of two or more forms of communication) can dramatically affect results and productivity. For example, if you are running TV advertising in a market and simultaneously mail within that market, you will see lifts in response. But there's another benefit to integrated marketing programs: checks and balances.

Advertising is expensive. You need tools to measure and compare results in order to focus your resources on the most effective channels and activities. The inquiry management system should provide reports of inquiries by source, media, product, and sales territory. Not only for results analysis, but also as a valuable aid in advertising planning.

Adjusting Quality and Quantity of Leads

No matter what the type of lead-generation program, all marketers have an option to produce what are commonly referred to as ''soft'' or ''hard'' leads.

Soft lead offers can be expected to produce a higher front-end response; hard lead offers can be expected to produce a lower front-end response, but a higher closure percentage. Exhibit 15–3 shows ten examples of lead "softeners" and ten lead "hardeners."

The decision about whether you want soft leads or hard leads must be dictated by experience. If salespeople close only one out of ten soft leads, for example, they might become discouraged and abandon the program. On the other hand, if salespeople close three out of ten soft leads versus five out of ten hard leads with twice as many leads to draw from, they (and management, too) might opt for the soft lead program.

Capacity Planning

Let's take a closer look at capacity planning. We said that it was a critical component of the up-front planning process, but it is also key to managing the program on an ongoing basis. No matter how carefully planned, a program can change because of internal and external variables.

For instance, postal deliveries might be slower or faster than anticipated, a computerized customer file might malfunction, a new product could take twice as much time to sell to a lead as anticipated. The possibilities are endless, but the point is simple: *Plan your capacity to be flexible to change.* Exhibit 15–4 is a typical capacity planning chart, which indicates an optimum lead flow.

Assuming a salesperson can average one cold prospect call a day, Exhibit 15–4 shows how many calls each office can make in a working month of 20

Exhibit 15–3.   Lead Softeners and Hardeners

Softeners:	Hardeners:
1. Tell less about the product.	1. Mention a price.
2. Add convenience for replies.	2. Mention a phone or sales call.
3. Give away something.	3. Tell a lot about the product.
4. Ask for less information.	4. Ask for a lot of information.
5. Highlight the offer.	5. Specify terms for the offer.
6. Make the ad "scream."	6. Ask for postage on the reply.
7. Don't ask for the phone number.	7. Bury the offer in the copy.
8. Increase the offer's value.	8. Tie the offer to a sales call.
9. Offer a contest or sweepstakes.	9. Change the offer's value.
10. Run in more general media.	10. Ask for money.

Exhibit 15–4.   Capacity Planning Chart

District Offices	No. of Salespeople in Each	Total Qualified Calls Needed Each Month	Total Leads Required (at 20% Qualified)	Mailings Required (at 5% Return)
Indiana	10	200	1,000	20,000
Tennessee	14	280	1,400	28,000
Virginia	10	200	1,000	20,000
Michigan	10	200	1,000	20,000
Illinois	16	320	1,600	32,000
West Virginia	13	260	1,300	26,000
New Jersey	5	100	500	10,000
San Francisco	8	160	800	16,000
Maine	9	180	900	18,000
Seattle	9	180	900	18,000
New York City	10	200	1,000	20,000
Ohio	10	200	1,000	20,000
Texas	7	140	700	14,000
Utah	3	60	300	6,000
Connecticut	6	120	600	12,000
Pittsburgh	9	180	900	18,000
Philadelphia	11	220	1,100	22,000
Miami	3	60	300	6,000
Des Moines	7	140	700	14,000
Los Angeles	2	40	200	4,000
Denver	2	40	200	4,000
Atlanta	3	60	300	6,000
Totals	**177**	**3,540**	**17,700**	**354,000**

days (20 calls per person). This information determines what quantity of mail is required at a 5 percent return to furnish leads for these calls, given that probably 20 percent of them will be qualified calls and the rest will be screened out prior to a sales call.

Thus, control can be exercised over mailings so that the two salespersons in Denver, for example, will not suddenly be swamped by scores of sales leads. In their district, 4,000 mailing pieces would be needed to furnish them with

40 qualified leads, as many as the two salespersons can follow up in one month. ZIP code selectivity helps to target mailings within a district.

To keep a constant flow of leads moving to the field at an average of 3,500 a month would require 70,000 mailing pieces per month. A year's campaign (12 months multiplied by 70,000) requires 840,000 mailing pieces.

Of course, all of this up-front planning and development is directed toward providing the sales center with an even flow of qualified leads. In simple terms, the sales center is a centralized location that houses your telemarketing sales force. This subject was covered in detail in Chapter 8.

Lead Flow Monitoring and Contingency Planning

As mentioned earlier in this chapter, the more quickly a lead is acted on, the higher the likelihood of conversion. The theory behind this is that the interest is highest when a prospect has first responded to an offer. The longer that lead sits, the "colder" the prospect becomes. (It differs by offer, but a rule of thumb is that a lead should be acted on within 10 days *maximum*. Sooner, if possible.) But, as anyone who has worked with a lead-generation program will tell you, sometimes leads come in at a greater rate than anticipated. The latter will not cause "cold" leads, but they could have impact on sales force morale, overhead costs, and so on. Whether too high or too low, it pays to have contingency systems in place. Let's look at a typical lead flow planning model to see the normal distribution of leads into a sales center. (See Exhibit 15–5.) In the case of this illustration, we have learned over time that the response to mailings will almost always follow this response curve, with 50 percent of total responses in the first four weeks, and the balance over the next six weeks. Exhibit 15–6 is a series of these response waves, each representing mailings. If print or broadcast were being used, a different formula for each would have to be developed.

At best, our planning will keep us within 90–110 percent of the dotted line, our stated capacity. But what if some of the internal or external events mentioned earlier should change our response curve and create a shortfall? There are two basic systems that can be employed to effectively manage around this: in queue (or lead bank) and shelf contingency systems.

In Queue (Lead Bank) System

Many companies create a "lead bank" system, which is a purposeful manner of always being above capacity. When a lead enters the sales center, it first enters the lead bank before being dispatched for follow-up. If there is always an extra week's worth of leads, and they are handled first in, first out, no leads are penalized or allowed to get "cold." Naturally, the "lead bank" would be stocked with mail responses. You must handle telephone responses immediately.

Exhibit 15-5. Typical Distribution of Leads

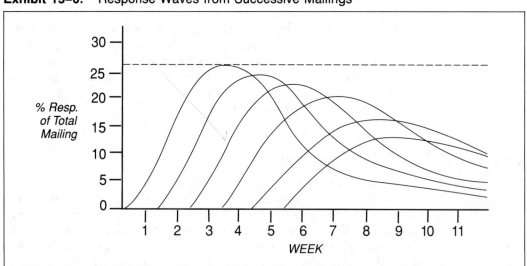

If and when there is an underdelivery of leads, the lead bank is drawn down until additional leads can be driven into the center. Or the bank can be increased temporarily when an overdelivery occurs until the up-front solicitation can be decreased.

Exhibit 15-6. Response Waves from Successive Mailings

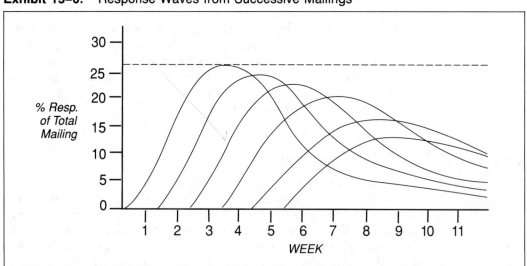

Shelf Contingency

It is always wise to have additional up-front communications "on the shelf"— that is, produced and ready to go—in the event of an underdelivery. If the lead-generation program is direct mail, for example, two weeks of additional mail packages in reserve will assure a timely response to an underdelivery problem. And after normal capacity resumes, the lead bank can be replenished.

Lead Classification and Scoring

It is no secret that in any lead-generation program lead quality varies a great deal. In fact, generally speaking, about 20 percent of total leads will result in about 80 percent of total sales revenue. Given this, it makes sense to optimize time and effort with a good lead classification system. There are two good reasons for optimizing time and effort:

1. **Time is money:** Given the cost of an industrial sales call, it costs too much to have a salesperson call on unqualified prospects.

2. **Good leads get "cold":** While salespeople are pursuing low-quality leads, high-quality leads get "cold." Each day a lead is not acted on makes the likelihood of sales conversion less likely.

How can leads be qualified? The best way is to build screening devices into the up-front media selection. Lists in the business field, for example, can be selected by sales volume, number of employees, or net worth. It must be recognized, however, that although such selectivity can produce a better-qualified lead, it can also reduce the number of leads, sometimes significantly. If a product or service tends to have more of a mass application, this might not be desirable. So not all leads are created equal. A classification system is needed to prioritize which ones to respond to first, assuming that they have an immediate need and will close most quickly.

ABC Classification

ABC classification is a one-dimensional approach to lead classification. (See Exhibit 15–7.) It's based on categorizing leads by likelihood of when that lead is expected to convert to a sale. When a salesperson is requested, or any other clues are given that the prospect is ready to buy, the lead is classified as "A," and sent to the sales force for immediate follow-up. This "A" will be used for forecasting sales potential and generating management reports. Leads that are analyzed as having a continuing interest are classified as "B." They are qualified leads and need to be developed either through personal contact with a salesperson or by sending more information. All other inquiries are classified as "C." They are the emerging market and a very responsive mailing list for future

Exhibit 15–7. One-Dimensional Inquiry Classification

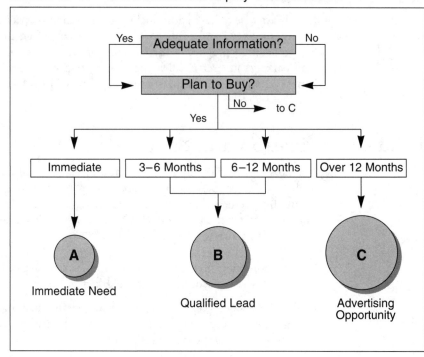

efforts. It is this group that represents the advertising opportunity. The goal here is to drive the group up the purchasing-decision hierarchy through a combination of media. Keep an eye on this group. Too often, companies discard inquiry names if they are not immediately productive. This is a major error and a waste of excellent business potential.

Three-Dimensional Scoring

The previous model assumed that every lead generated by the system, if closed, would become a profitable customer. That's not always the case. Which would you rather have, a sale to a one-time customer or a sale to a customer who would continue to buy from you over time? Of course, you want to close both sales, but it would be wise to focus your effort on the latter first. In order to factor other elements into the lead classification process, you need to evaluate those factors in three dimensions:

- **Speed of action.** How quickly will the buying decision be made?

- **Closing potential.** How well can we satisfy the consumer's need?

- **Account value.** What is the total anticipated amount of the purchase or the projected value of the customer to your company?

A three-dimensional model scores the relative value of leads compared to one another and provides learning that will allow you to appropriate the best communication treatment plans. (See Exhibit 15–8.)

To rank the prospect on three dimensions, you need to assign values that will classify each component. For the purposes of illustration, let's assign the value 3 as "high," 2 as "medium," and 1 as "low." This allows a potential for 27 possible scores, where the best lead is classified as a "333," and the poorest lead a "111." This model will help to determine the best next steps: determination of your allowable spending per lead, when to time the communications, and the basis for evaluation pre- and post-contact.

Inquiry Processing Cost Analysis

We've been looking at inquiry management effectiveness, but it's also very important to consider how much your company is spending to manage inquiries. There isn't any "right" amount to spend. You can spend too little as well as too much. If your company isn't spending enough to make full use of the inquiries generated, you aren't saving money on inquiry fulfillment—you're wasting money on advertising.

The real questions are what level of service you want to provide and how much that level should cost. Setting levels of service is always difficult, and

Exhibit 15–8.   Three-Dimensional Scoring

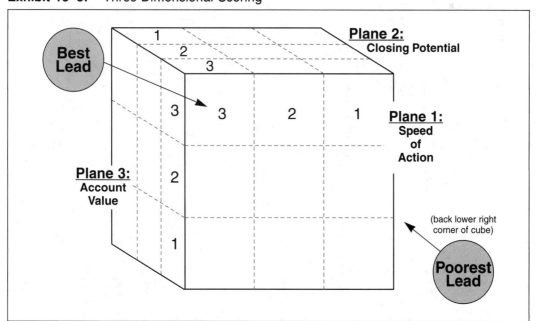

it's particularly difficult in inquiry management. Wide fluctuations in inquiry volume (see Exhibit 15–9) caused by sudden surges in the number of calls can jeapordize the desired level of service.

If you have enough people, machines, and other facilities to handle your peak volumes with a high level of service, you'll have unused capacity (and high cost) when volumes fall. But lower capacity can lead to poor response times when volumes are high, which, in turn, can waste advertising investment. The trick, of course, is to organize your operation to minimize fixed costs so that costs will vary with volume.

The use of temporary labor and shared facilities can help, but more management time will be required to ensure that service is maintained. Another solution is to obtain inquiry management from outside sources, which can level the peaks and valleys among many customers, providing universal cost-effectiveness, without adversely affecting service levels.

Tracking and Results Reporting

Tracking and results reporting are as important as management of leads in the sales center. These activities will result in quantification of the actual effort, relating the success of the program to its objectives, and making management aware of the degree of efficiency, market penetration, and revenue streams.

Exhibit 15–9. Sales Inquiry Volume

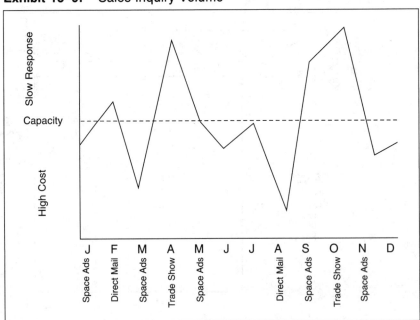

Tracking

Which information an advertiser decides to track is largely a function of individual needs. However, the following data be will be essential.

Number of Leads by Effort. Whether for a mailing, print ad, or broadcast spot, the number of leads responding to each effort should be captured. This is usually handled by a specific code for each. For instance, a mailing with a split copy test is actually two mailings. Therefore, each response device should have a specific code so when it's received at the sales center, the proper mailing can be credited. If telephone response is encouraged, as it should be, a unique phone number or extension should be given for each mailing, thus making it possible to credit the proper promotion effort. By capturing information by code, the winning test promotions will emerge.

Quality of Lead/Conversion Information. The mailing or ad that pulls the most responses is not always the most successful, for it is conversion to sales that is the true measure of success. The comparison of two mailing packages in Exhibit 15–10 illustrates the point. As you can see, package A would seemingly be the more successful package if response were the sole measure. But when conversion is factored in, the greatest number of sales actually came from package B. This is the more successful effort.

Results Reporting

There's little question that an efficient lead-generation program will increase sales and cut sales costs. But it is essential that results be measured and reported. Documentation of results is essential for three basic reasons: (1) to measure against original objectives of the lead-generation program, (2) to prove value to the sales force, and (3) to prove value to management.

Reporting Results to Management

Information generated in any phase of a lead-generation program provides a database from which a wealth of useful information is available. Once the results

Exhibit 15–10. Comparison of Two Mailing Packages

	No. Mailed	Percentage Response	No. of Responses	Percentage Conversion	No. of Sales
Package A	20,000	2.0%	400	6%	24
Package B	20,000	1.0	200	15	30

of advertising and sales efforts are summarized, it can be sorted in countless ways. The resulting information can help provide advertising accountability. Reports prove useful in researching and evaluating new markets. They can evaluate publication effectiveness and provide insight into the value of various creative appeals. Some reports can be used to evaluate the effectiveness of sales follow-up activity and even the equity of sales territory assignments.

Sample Reports for Sales Managers

The Purchase Potential Report.   Closing potential numbers assigned by the salespeople establish a ratio norm against which other programs are evaluated. These norms are useful in comparing current month activity against previous month activity and comparing achievements against year-to-date objectives. Because this report identifies the volume of potential sales, it's also useful for manufacturing planning. (See Exhibit 15–11.)

The Product Inquiry Report.   This report maintains a running record of the numbers of inquiries for each product in the line. Quite often, there is a correlation between product inquiries and product sales volume. It can also highlight those areas where more advertising is needed to increase the number of inquiries. (See Exhibit 15–12.)

Exhibit 15–11.   The Purchase Potential Report

National Potential for Lead Closing							
						Date:	June
						Page:	1
Name	**Company**	**City**	**State**	**POT**	**PROD**	**TER**	**REG**
R P Sloane	Honeywell	Phoeniz	AZ	1	E2	RK	DW
A P Masino	Hansens Lab Inc	Rochester	NY	1	V0	CD	PC
D Halpern	Easton Corp	Murray Hill	NH	1	U1	JX	PC
C A Chang	Wyeth Labs	Toledo	OH	1	I3	LL	HD
G Larson	A W Lyons	Raritan	NJ	1	L0	LC	PC
C K Kim	Ortho Pharm Corp	Spring House	PA	1	I9	JC	TM
J R Breco	Sherwin Williams	Philadelphia	PA	2	N8	CJ	TM
C T Kitchen	Kitchen Microtech	Morgan Town	WV	2	L9	GC	HD
F Randa	Parker Corp	Des Plaines	IL	2	G1	GD	HD
S G Weber	Pennwalt Corp	Aurora	IL	2	V0	DC	TM
D Jung	General Grain	Cranbury	NJ	2	V0	JK	PC
R La Corte	Smith Kline & French	Pittsburgh	PA	2	V0	DC	TM
B Peppe	Univ Pittsburgh	Pittsburgh	PA	2	V0	DC	TM
E N Plosed	S C Johnson Co	Racine	WI	2	I3	GO	HD

The Regional Inquiry Report.   This report compares the effectiveness of one region with another in scoring inquiry potentials. A similar report can compare sales representatives' effectiveness within a region against their record. (See Exhibit 15–13.)

Sample Reports for Advertising Managers

The Daily Flash Report.   This report identifies the daily status of each promotion. The daily mail count is recorded by a bar chart that records the total inquiries for the campaign. As time progresses, the bar chart forms a bell-shaped

Exhibit 15–12.   Product Inquiry Report

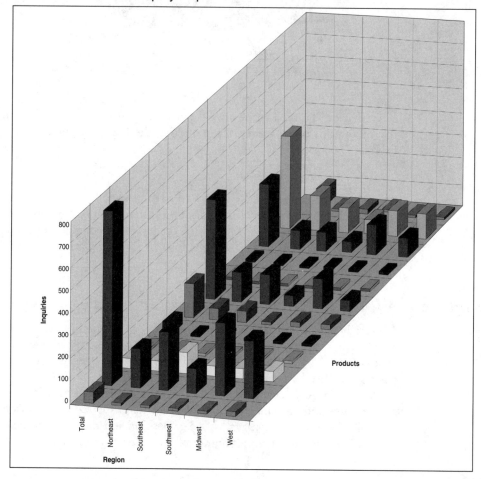

Exhibit 15–13. Regional Inquiry Report

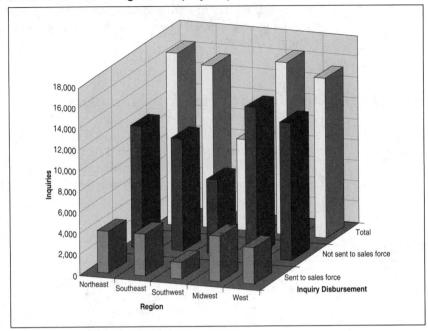

curve that can be used to identify the halfway point of the inquiry returns. Identifying this point is useful in projecting the life of the promotion. (See Exhibit 15–14.)

The Media Effectiveness Report. This report lists the various media employed and identifies the total expenditure of the promotion. This report should also include measures of cost per inquiry, the percentage of qualified inquiries, the cost per qualified inquiry, and the forecast revenue-to-expense ratio.

A Picture is Worth a Thousand Words (or Figures)

Charts add a dimension to the meaning of a report. Responsible managers who need to know the progress of inquiry promotion programs generally have limited time to review results. Submitting hard copy reports loaded with columns of figures is a mistake.

Most managers manage by comparison. Graphic charts present easy-to-see relationships and encourage deeper involvement in the report. It is easier to compare a present position against a past position and the intended objective with a chart than it is with a printout of hundreds of numbers.

Exhibit 15–14. Daily Flash Report

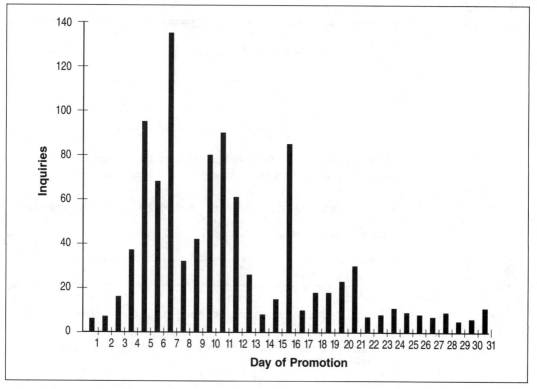

Summary

The efficient handling and managing of inquiries in business-to-business marketing is a major problem for many companies. An inquiry-management system can be a solution and also become a valuable company asset.

- An inquiry system helps advertising to become more accountable for its expenditures; it integrates the advertising and selling functions into a unified whole.

- The system can increase sales productivity by eliminating unproductive follow-up calls; it is an aid in finding prospects ready to buy.

- The application of an inquiry system to the advertising and marketing functions can become a valuable management tool, one that is useful in assessing progress toward objectives.

   In summary, an inquiry-management system works because it measures results—the ingredient most wanted in marketing activity today.

SELF-QUIZ

1. Name the three types of lead-generation programs.

   a. _____

   b. _____

   c. _____

2. Editorial mention of a free booklet offer is likely to produce more leads than a space ad making the same offer. ☐ True ☐ False

3. Why is it important to get the sales force involved in the development of a lead-generation program? _____

   _____

   _____

4. The inquiry system doesn't exist without an offer. ☐ True ☐ False

5. Too many leads can be even more destructive to a program than not enough. ☐ True ☐ False

6. Name at least one way to qualify a lead as ''hot,'' ''warm,'' or ''cool.''

   _____

   _____

   _____

7. Define the *hierarchy of effects* in the communication process. _____

   _____

   _____

8. If you are after ''soft leads,'' it is important that you mention price in your solicitation. ☐ True ☐ False

9. If you are soliciting leads, you can expect to receive 50 percent of total response in the first _____ weeks.

10. Generally speaking, _____ percent of sales will come from _____ percent of the leads you receive.

PILOT PROJECT

You work for a firm that manufactures central air-conditioning systems for the home. A minimum sale comes to $5,000. All sales are handled through a sales force. The target market is home owners with a median income of $50,000.

Your firm has decided to test the viability of a lead-generation program and has selected Milwaukee, Wisconsin, as a test market. Your assignment is to develop a marketing plan for management review.

In preparation for actually writing the marketing plan, answer the following questions.

1. What information will you need from the sales force?
   Examples might be: (a) Who is the firm's competitor? (b) Who is the decision maker in the home? (c) What are the major objections the sales force has to overcome?

2. What objectives will you set for the program?
   For example, how many leads per day will you propose to furnish each salesperson? How would you propose to screen leads so you could distinguish between high potential and low potential? What other objectives would you set?

3. What would your strategies be for obtaining highly qualified leads?
   One strategy, for example, might be an offer to conduct a free survey to determine the cost of central air-conditioning in a home. Another strategy might be a special promotion, aimed at customers in Milwaukee, asking them to provide names of friends whom they consider most likely to have an interest in central air conditioning. What other strategies might you employ?

4. How will you implement your lead-generation program? Here are some key questions you should answer in your marketing plan:
   a. Will you ask your sales force to provide names of key prospects? How else will you involve the sales force?
   b. What media strategies will you employ?
      • Will you use direct response lists? If you will, what kinds of direct response lists? (Lawn care subscribers, for example?)
      • Will you use newspapers? Which ones?
      • Will you use magazines? Which ones?
      • Will you use radio? Which stations?
      • Will you use TV? Which stations?
      • Will you use cable TV? Which stations?

Managing the Creative Proccess

CHAPTER SIXTEEN

Creating Direct Mail Packages

Direct mail is an expensive advertising medium. It costs 15 to 20 times as much to reach a person with a direct mail package as it does to reach him or her with a 30-second TV commercial or a full-page ad in a newspaper. But direct mail has certain unique advantages that more than compensate for its higher cost. If you understand what these advantages are and use them properly, you will be able to bring in orders or responses at a cost equal to or below that of space or broadcast. And, as a general rule, customers acquired by direct mail are better customers in terms of repeat business than those acquired by space or broadcast advertising.

Advantages of Direct Mail

Selectivity

Through careful list selection and segmentation, direct mail can give you pinpoint selectivity unmatched by any other advertising medium (with the exception of the telephone). You can literally pick out households one by one, mailing only to those that are the best prospects for your offer.

Virtually Unlimited Choice of Formats

In direct mail, you are not restricted to 30 seconds or a 7" × 10" page. You can use large, lavishly illustrated brochures. You can have any number of inserts. You can use pop-ups, fold-outs, swatches, or even enclose a computer diskette. What you can do is limited only by your imagination and budget.

Personal Character

Even though you mail in the millions, you are still mailing individual pieces to individually addressed human beings. Every recipient knows that an ad or a TV commercial was not created specifically for him or her but for a mass audience. Direct mail approaches the prospect on a personal level that, with personalized letters, even extends to a greeting by name. As any salesperson will agree, you can sell much better when you are talking to an individual rather than to people en masse.

No Competition

In most advertising media, the advertising is an adjunct, not the main reason the person is watching the TV channel or reading the magazine. In direct mail, advertising arrives all by itself to be opened and read at the recipient's leisure. When it is read, there is nothing to compete with it for your prospect's attention.

Most Testable Medium

With direct mail you can virtually simulate laboratory conditions for testing. You control exactly when the mail is dropped, and you control exactly who gets which test package. Many magazines and newspapers can give you an A/B split, but direct mail will give you as many splits as you care to have.

Unique Capability to Involve the Recipient

Direct mail offers a wide choice of devices that involve the recipient, such as tokens, stamps, questionnaires, and quizzes. And with direct mail, you can literally get the recipients to "talk back" to you—to open a dialogue—by asking them questions and giving them space to respond via the reply format.

Selecting the Format

Because direct mail offers an unlimited choice of formats, a good place to start is deciding which basic format to use. There are three basic formats to choose from: the classic format, the self-mailer, and the catalog.

Classic Format.   The classic format utilizes a separate mailing envelope. The size of that envelope, the material from which it is made (paper, plastic, foil) and the number of colors in which it is printed can vary widely. What goes inside that envelope can vary even more widely. Classic formats range from simple, dignified, businesslike letters (Exhibit 16–1) to lavish packages stuffed with brochures, inserts, gifts circulars, pop-ups, and computer diskettes. (See Exhibit 16–2.) The classic format is the most personal of the direct mail formats.

Exhibit 16–1.   Classic Direct Mail Format

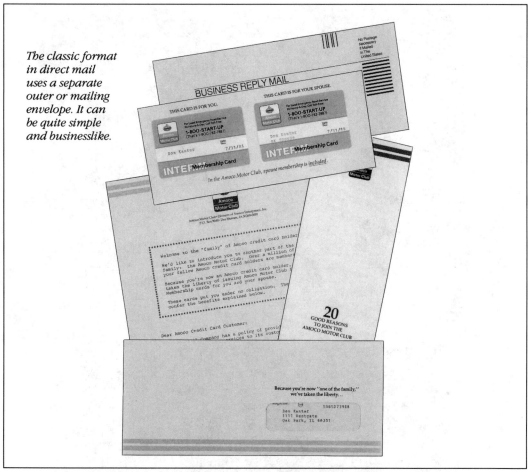

The classic format in direct mail uses a separate outer or mailing envelope. It can be quite simple and businesslike.

The classic format in direct mail uses a separate outer or mailing envelope. It can be quite simple and businesslike.

For this reason, it almost always includes a separate letter, either preprinted or personalized.

Self-Mailer.   The self-mailer does not have an outer envelope. These mailers vary from a single sheet of paper folded once for mailing to wonderfully complex pieces with multiple sheets and preformed reply envelopes. (See Exhibit 16–3.) Generally, a self-mailer comes off the press complete, ready to address and mail. As a rule, self-mailers are less expensive than classic mailing packages. There is only one component to produce and no inserting is needed because the piece is completed on-press.

Exhibit 16–1   (Continued).

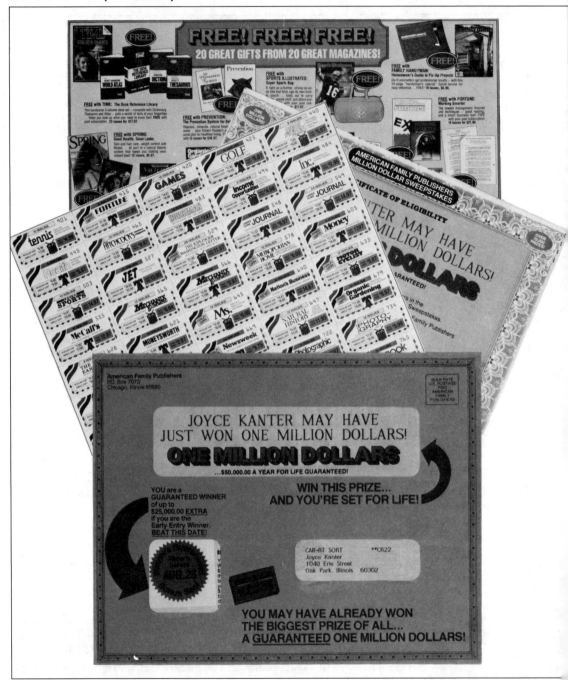

The classic format can also be lavish, exciting, and packed with different pieces, as illustrated by the mailing by American Family Publishers.

Exhibit 16–2. Expanded Classic Direct Mail Format

A variety of enclosures enhances interest in the total mailing package.

Exhibit 16–3. Self-Mailer

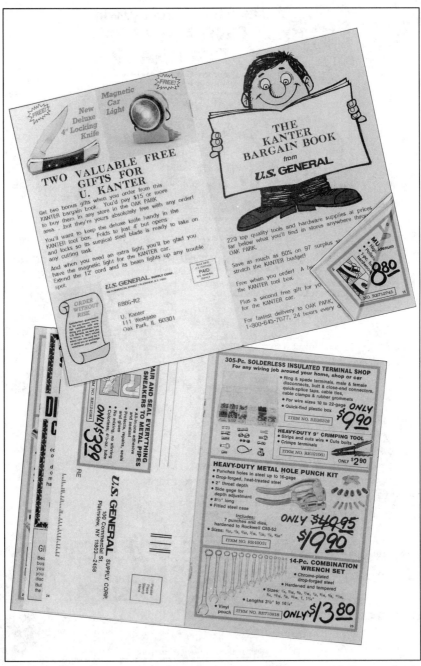

A self-mailer is produced on one pass through the press. When opened, it contains individual, personalized premium (gift) slips, order form, and bound-in 44-page catalog. Even a preformed order envelope is included!

Catalog.   The catalog is literally a magazine, with up to many hundreds of pages, stitched, glued, or perfect-bound. Catalogs require a highly specialized format, and their use is subject to many important guidelines. Catalogs are discussed in detail in Chapter 17.

No discussion of direct mail formats would be complete without mentioning some of the specialized devices that are used regularly in direct mail. Involvement devices include stamps, tokens, rub-offs, and sealed envelopes—one company used a jigsaw puzzle that the recipient had to put together. Regardless of the format, reader involvement can make it dramatically more effective. If you get the reader involved with your offer and message, you're well on your way to a sale. (See Exhibit 16–4.) A most effective way to get the reader involved is to include a product sample or swatch in the mailing. Obviously, this device is not suitable for all types of merchandising, but nothing beats letting somebody touch, feel, and try what you're selling.

Specialized devices include die-cut shapes, tip-ons, and pop-ups. These can be great attention-getters. But be careful: You don't want to let the gimmick take the reader's attention from your basic sales message. One company tested an elaborate (and expensive) pop-up device and found that the mailing actually pulled better without it! The pop-up was stealing attention from the mailer's message.

In connection with formats, there are several tried-and-true variations you should consider for your mailing package.

The second letter, or "publisher's letter," has become almost a must in direct mail today. Repeated testing indicates that such a letter boosts response 10 percent or more. The letter is either a folded letter or a letter in a separate sealed envelope that warns sternly: "Open this letter *only* if you have decided not to respond to this offer." Of course, everybody opens it immediately. This gives you the chance to do a little extra selling, primarily in reassuring the prospects that they really have nothing to lose and everything to gain in accepting your offer.

The closed-face envelope has the name and address of the recipient "typed" right on the envelope; there is no window or slot through which the name shows. Inside there are two or three other pieces (letters, applications) on which the recipient's name, address, and other information are also "typed." The mailing looks like it was typed individually, but this is not so: These ingenious mailings are run on computer, then the outer envelope is matched to the pieces inside. Because they look so personal, closed-face packages are rarely discarded without opening.

Invitation formats have been around for a long time. They are very effective, especially for publishers, club memberships, and credit card solicitations. The format simulates a formal invitation ("You are invited to accept . . ."). The outside of the invitation usually carries a letter explaining the offer. Naturally, an RSVP—a call to action—is included in the mailing.

The simulated telegram is less formal but carries a lot of urgency. It's been popular as a follow-up mailing or part of a renewal series and has worked well for credit card solicitation, insurance, and loan offers. However, with the decline

Exhibit 16–4.   Involvement Device

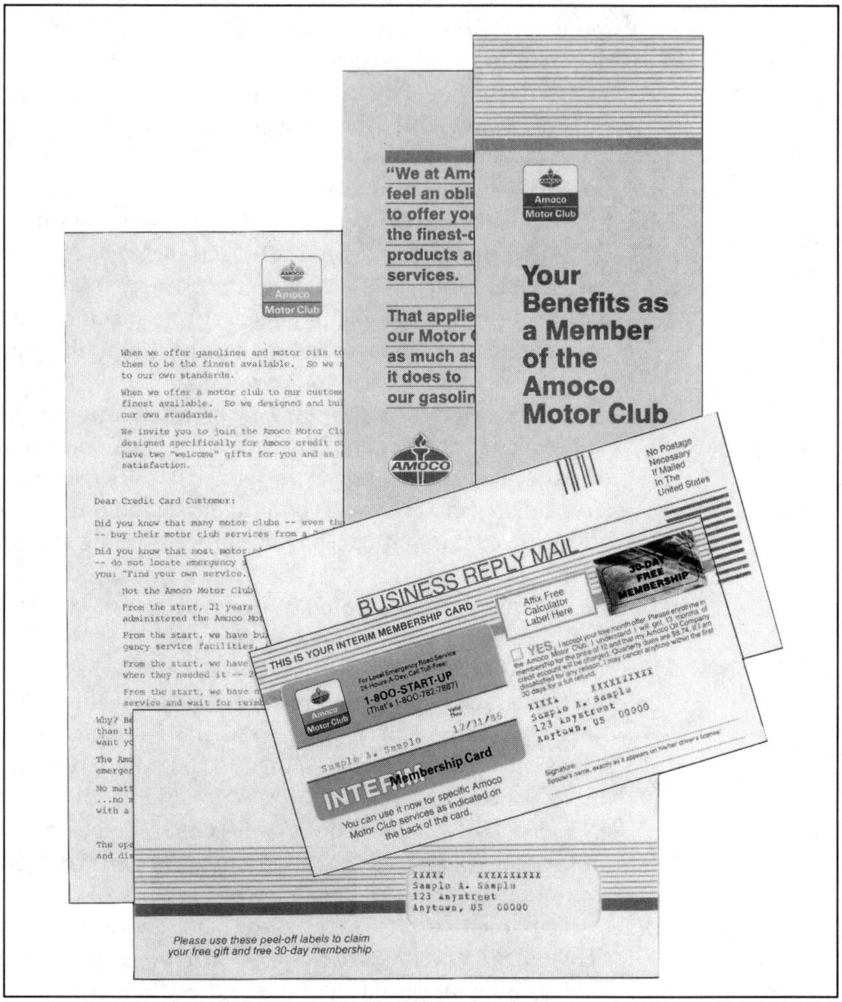

A typical involvement device: The reader is asked to lift the peel-off stickers from the outer envelope and affix them to the order form, thereby "validating" the free gift and free trial membership.

in the use of real telegrams, the simulated telegram is being used less and less. The simulated telegram is usually printed on yellow stock and, more often than not, is computer-filled. (Caution: the basic telegram format is copyrighted by Western Union. You are not allowed to use it.)

Personalization is common today, regardless of what format you use. Personalization is done by computer, by ink-jet imaging, or by laser printing. Each method has its advantages and its particular requirements. Each method requires specific preparation of materials, so you would be well advised to seek professional production help if you are planning a personalized mailing.

When you run into somebody who tells you that personalized letters "always" outpull nonpersonalized ones, be skeptical. In my experience, personalized letters *usually* outpull nonpersonalized ones, but not always. Also, they have to outpull by enough to pay for the extra cost of personalization. When you use personalization, use all the information you can. But don't scatter the person's name indiscriminately throughout the letter. A good rule to follow is to write a personalized letter as you would write a letter to any person you know fairly well.

Which format should you choose for your mailing piece? That depends. It depends on your budget. It depends on who you're trying to reach. Do you want a package that will stand out on the businessperson's desk? Or is it something designed for leisurely reading by the consumer at home? If you're not sure, you should use the classic format with a separate outer envelope and a separate letter. Most direct mail today uses this format, and although it is more expensive than a self-mailer, it will usually pull better.

One further caution on formats: Postal regulations, which govern the mailability of any given piece, change regularly. You should check the layout of your mailing piece with your local post office before you produce it. There are few things in life more disheartening than a phone call that begins: "This is the post office, and we're holding your mailing because . . ."

Creative Strategy

Now that we have the product or service, our offer (proposition), and our format, we're ready to create the mailing piece. Right? Wrong. And therein lies a basic failing in a lot of direct mail produced today. The writer is too anxious to dash to the word processor, and the artist is too anxious to get to the drawing board. Why does this occur? Marketing is "work," but creative effort is fun, and we all tend to do what we like to do. But unless the creative work is strategically grounded, it will not work—or, at least, not as well as it should.

As one sage observed: "If you don't know where you're going, any road will take you there." Advertising, general or direct response, has to know exactly where it is going, and the road map that points the way is called *creative strategy*.

Every large advertising agency and virtually every large company has its own creative strategy, under one name or another. They all share a common objective: They focus the efforts of the creative personnel. It is the discipline of creative strategy that prevents advertising from trying to be all things to all people— and, in reality, being nothing to any of them.

Following is an outline for a typical creative strategy that organizes the information about the product or service into a disciplined format. Remember: To be useful, this outline must be *written*.

- **The product.** What it is, what it does, how it works, what it costs, what its features are, what its benefits are, what makes it different, what makes it better—even what its weaknesses are.

- **Competitive products.** How they compare with ours in terms of features, benefits, and price.

- **The market.** How big is it and what share of it do we have? Who buys the product today and why? Who else *should* buy it and why? Who are our present customers and future prospects in terms of demographic characteristics, such as age, sex, marital status, income, and education? Who are they in psychographic terms? Are they liberal or conservative, avant-garde, or traditional?

- **The media.** What's going to carry our message? If space or broadcast media are to be used, which ones, how often, and in what space or time units? If direct mail is the only medium, what lists will we be using—specifically or in general? What do we know or assume about quantities, formats, colors?

- **The budget.** What limitations should govern our creative thinking in terms of creative staff time, layout costs, photography, illustrations, production costs?

- **Objective.** As specifically as possible, what are we trying to do in terms of overall goals and specific goals, in accordance with the total program, and in line with specific components within the program? Among all possible goals, what are our priorities? Which ones are primary and vital; which are secondary and merely desirable; which are nice but expendable?

- **Creative implementation.** How do we propose to organize what we know or assume about the product, the competition, and the market to achieve our stated objectives? How will we position the product? What relative emphasis will we give to product features and product benefits? What do we anticipate as our central copy theme? How will it be executed visually? And how will it be orchestrated among various elements of the program? Most important of all from a response standpoint, what will our offer be and how will it be dramatized?

How your creative strategy document addresses these questions, the order in which you address them, and the format in which you cast them are all minor matters. They can be varied according to circumstances. When the creative strategy is thoroughly digested by both the writer and the artist, they both have a good idea of what the mailing package should accomplish, how, and why.

Precreative Work

With a creative strategy in place, you're ready to start creative work. Well . . . almost ready.

First, there are some important "precreative" matters to be take care of before one word of copy is written or one piece of the mailing is designed. Listen to Gene Schwartz, a professional direct response writer, as he describes how he listens first with his ears and then with his eyes:

1. Sit down with the owner of the product or service—the man who's hiring you—and pump hell out of him. Put it on a tape recorder and have him talk for three or four hours.

    Ask him where the product comes from, what it does, what are its problems and how he's tried to cure them, why it's better than its competitors, who likes it, who doesn't like it, what proof he's got that it works, what strange uses people have got out of it, what funny stories he has accumulated in regard to its manufacture or use, what problems he was trying to solve when he created it, how he would improve it if he had unlimited money, what causes most of his refunds, who works for him to help him make it, how it is made, how he keeps up the quality, who writes him what about it, etc.

2. Talk to his customers. Do it in person, or on paper. See if they agree with him. If they don't, find out why.

3. Listen to his competitors. They often tell you more about the opportunities they're missing in their ads than the opportunities they're seeing and therefore seizing. Let them write a possible head or two for you—out of the body copy of their ads.

4. Then put all the material down, in one big pile, and underline it. Start blending it together, like you'd make a cake. Give first priority to your head and subheads, then the body claims. And then type it up, preferably adding little of yourself except as selector and condenser.

Direct response creative pros use a variety of techniques for approaching the moment of truth. But they all have one thing in common: They dig, dig, dig. The hack, on the other hand, just sits down to write. Miracle performances don't happen by accident—they're created.

The Copywriter as Salesperson

Listen to Don Kanter, long-time vice president of Stone & Adler, who now owns his own direct response creative service. He has a unique way of describing some copywriters. "The trouble with many copywriters," he says, "is that they think their job is to write copy." Kanter quickly explains this by adding:

That is equivalent to a salesperson saying, "My job is to talk." The job is not to "talk." For a writer, the job is not to "write." For both, the job is to *sell*. Selling is the end result; writing is merely the means a copywriter uses to reach that end. This is true of all advertising copywriting; it is especially true of direct response copywriting because the writer is usually the only salesperson with whom the prospect will ever come in contact. If he or she doesn't make the sale, there is nobody else to do it.

The Benefit/Price/Value Equation

To sell effectively, the direct response writer must know why people buy. They buy, essentially, when they consider something to have value. This is often expressed in a simple equation: Benefit divided by price equals value. In other words, every time individuals are confronted with a buying decision, they subconsciously assign a worth to the benefits they perceive. At the same time, they assign a worth to the price they must pay. And subjectively, very subconsciously, they divide one into the other to reach their buying decision. If they believe the benefits outweigh the price, they will buy. If the price outweighs the benefits, they will not buy.

What Is Price?

To most people, *price* is the monetary amount asked for the goods or services being sold: the $29.95, or $39.95, or $5 per month, or whatever. But there is more to price than that. There's time. We are asking customers to wait before they can enjoy the benefits of what they buy. There's the factor of buying the product sight unseen (unlike retail purchasing, where customers can see, touch, and often try what they are buying). There's a factor of buying from a company the customers might not know. There's the risk that the product or service might not deliver the benefits that have been promised. In direct marketing, all of these are part of the price that must be paid. While we might not be able to do much about the actual price (the $29.95, or $39.95, or $5 a month), we can (and we must) do everything possible to reduce the other factors of price to the minimum.

How? By using the proven techniques that direct marketing has pioneered:

- Testimonials
- Guarantees
- Free-trial offers or cancellation privileges
- Reassurance about the stature and reliability of the selling company

What Is a Benefit?

Let's assume we are selling a stereo system. This system has two three-way speakers, each with a big "woofer" and "tweeter" and a midrange. That's a benefit. Right? Wrong. That's a selling point or product feature. It's a distinction that every writer must recognize and keep in mind. A benefit is something that affects customers personally. It exists apart from the merchandise or service itself. A selling point or product feature is something in the product or service that makes possible and supports the benefit. Our stereo system with two three-way speaker systems is a selling point. It is a quality in the product itself. That customers can enjoy lifelike, three-dimensional sound is the benefit. It is this benefit that affects them personally. This benefit is made possible by the fact that this stereo system has two three-way speakers. Remember, it is the benefit that customers really want to have. It is the selling point that proves to them that they can really have it.

Translate Selling Points into Benefits

Before you write any copy, therefore, it is very important to dig out every selling point you can and translate each selling point into a customer benefit. The more benefits customers perceive (i.e., the more benefits you can point out to them), the more likely they will buy. Here's an example: Suppose you're writing copy to sell a portable countertop dishwasher. Below are listed some of the selling points for this merchandise, and alongside each is the benefit that the selling point makes possible:

Selling Point	Benefit
1. A 10-minute operating cycle	1. Does a load of dishes in 10 minutes; gets you out of the kitchen faster
2. Measures 18 inches in diameter	2. Is small enough to fit on a countertop; doesn't take up valuable floor space
3. Has a transparent plastic top	3. Lets you watch the washing cycle; you know when the dishes are done
4. Has a universal hose coupling	4. Fits any standard kitchen faucet; attaches and detaches in seconds

Copy Appeals and Basic Human Wants

With your benefits down on paper, you now have to decide on the appeals that will do the best selling job. Creative people refer to this in different ways. Some talk about how you "position" the product in the prospect's mind. Others refer to "coming up with the big idea" behind the copy. What is it about your offer and benefit story that is most appealing? When you stop to think about it, people respond to any given proposition for one of two reasons: to gain something they do not have or to avoid losing something they now possess.

Exhibit 16–5 shows how basic human wants can be divided into these two categories. Professional copywriters carefully sift and weigh the list of basic human wants to determine the main appeal of their proposition. (In Chapter 18 you'll see how the same product can be slanted to employ many different appeals just by changing your headline.)

Exhibit 16–5.   Two Categories of Human Wants

The Desire to Gain	The Desire to Avoid Loss
To make money	To avoid criticism
To save time	To keep possessions
To avoid effort	To avoid physical pain
To achieve comfort	To avoid loss of reputation
To have health	To avoid loss of money
To be popular	To avoid trouble
To experience pleasure	
To be clean	
To be praised	
To be in style	
To gratify curiosity	
To satisfy an appetite	
To have beautiful possessions	
To attract romantic partners	
To be an individual	
To emulate others	
To take advantage of opportunities	

Eleven Guidelines to Good Copy

Does your proposition offer the promise of saving time and avoiding hard or disagreeable work? Most people like to avoid work. Saving time is almost a fetish of the American people. Appeal to this basic want, if you can.

Does your proposition help people feel important? People like to keep up with the Joneses. People like to be made to feel that they are a part of a select group. A tremendous number of people are susceptible to snob appeal. Perhaps you can offer a terrific bargain by mail and capitalize on the appeal of saving money. The desire to ''get it wholesale'' is very strong.

Don Kanter uses these guidelines as checkpoints for good, professional copy:

1. Does the writer know the product? Has he or she dug out every selling point and benefit?

2. Does the writer know his or her market? Is he or she aiming the copy at the most likely prospects rather than at the world in general?

3. Is the writer talking to the prospect in language that the prospect will understand?

4. Does the writer make a promise to the prospect, then prove that he or she can deliver what was promised?

5. Does the writer get to the point at once? Does he or she make that all-important promise right away?

6. Is the copy, especially the headlines and lead paragraphs, germane and specific to the selling proposition?

7. Is the copy concise? There is a great temptation to overwrite, especially in direct mail.

8. Is the copy logical and clear? Does it flow from point to point?

9. Is the copy enthusiastic? Does the writer obviously believe in what he or she is selling?

10. Is the copy complete? Are all the questions answered, especially obvious ones like size and color?

11. Is the copy designed to sell? Or is it designed to impress the reader with the writer's ability? If somebody says "that's a great mailing," you've got the wrong reaction. What you want to hear is, "That's a great product (or service). I'd love to have it."

The Changes in Direct Mail

Only a few years ago, direct mail was a "set" medium, with its own rules that you broke at your peril. A direct mail package had—at the minimum—an outer envelope, a reply envelope, a letter (at least two pages and probably more), a brochure, and an order form.

But change is coming. In fact, it's here, according to Don Kanter, who has been doing direct response creative work for 20 years. The changes, he says, are focused on one objective: faster, stronger, more telegraphic communication with the prospect.

Why? Two reasons, Kanter says. First, "mailbox clutter" is becoming real, just as TV clutter did some years ago. Only a direct mailing that grabs and holds the prospect's attention—from the envelope through every component— has a chance of working. Second, we are now talking to the TV generation, which grew up with visual symbols. Unlike older people who grew up reading books, the TV generation is less inclined to stay with you if you don't get your message across very quickly. Basically, the specific changes are in two areas: shorter and better copy and quicker communication through graphics.

Shorter Copy and Better Copy. Kanter believes that direct mail historically has been overwritten, because direct mail does not impose the discipline for tight, concise writing that space or broadcast does. Now that discipline is being imposed by outside factors, it means that the direct mail writer must edit and polish copy, making every word justify its existence. A four-page letter (or longer) might still be the best way to go, but it must be a beautifully written, meticulously polished, and lovingly edited four-page letter.

Quicker Communication through Graphics.   At long last, the designer is becoming an equal partner in the direct mail creative process, as we learn what our counterparts in general advertising have always known: Graphics communicate more quickly and more forcefully than words. An added benefit of the designer's involvement is that we are improving the appearance of direct mail, as well as the level of taste. The old "direct mail look" that was distinguished by type piled up on virtually every component, is slowly disappearing.

Creating the Classic Mailing Package

Now that we've looked at formats and discussed copy, let's turn to the individual pieces in a so-called classic mailing package.

The Outer Envelope

The outer envelope, or carrier envelope has one job: to get itself opened. To accomplish this, the envelope can use several techniques:

- It can dazzle recipients with color, with graphics, and with promises of important benefits (including wealth, in the case of sweepstakes offers) if they will only open it.

- It can impress recipients with its simplicity and lead them to believe that the contents must be very important.

- It can tease recipients and so excite their curiosity that they simply must open it.

To help accomplish its purpose, the envelope can be the traditional paper envelope (perhaps with extra cut-outs or "windows"), or it can be made of transparent polyethylene or foil. Whatever it's made of and whatever it says, the outer envelope sets the tone of your mailing. It must harmonize with the materials inside.

The Brochure

As noted, most mailing packages require a good brochure or circular in addition to a letter. It can be a small, two-color affair or a beautiful, giant circular that's almost as big as a tablecloth. But the job it has to do is the same, and it deserves your best creative effort. One way or another, your circular has to do a complete selling job. To give yourself every chance for success, review the appearance, content, and preparation of your circular. Exhibit 16–6 is a handy checklist for this purpose.

The Order Form

If Ernest Hemingway had been a direct response writer, he probably would have dubbed the order form "the moment of truth." Many prospects make a final decision on whether to respond after reading it. Some even read the order form before anything else in the envelope, because they know it's the easiest way to find out what's being offered at what price. The best advice I can offer on order forms comes from Henry Cowen, a direct marketing specialist:

> There are direct mail manuals around that recommend simple, easy-to-read order forms, but my experience indicates the mailer is far better off with a

Exhibit 16–6. Brochure Checklist

Appearance

1. Is the circular designed for the market you are trying to reach?

2. Is the presentation suited to the product or service you are offering?

3. Is the circular consistent with the rest of the mailing package?

Content

4. Is there a big idea behind your circular?

5. Do your headlines stick to the key offer?

6. Is your product or service dramatized to its best advantage by format and/or presentation?

7. Do you show broadly adaptable examples of your product or service in use?

8. Does your entire presentation follow a logical sequence and tell a complete story—including price, offer, and guarantee?

Preparation

9. Can the circular be cut out of standard-size paper stock?

10. Is the quality of paper stock in keeping with the presentation?

11. Is color employed judiciously to show the product or service in its best light?

busy, rather jumbled appearance and plenty of copy. Formal and legal-looking forms that appear valuable, too valuable to throw away, are good.

The key words in Cowen's statement are "too valuable to throw away." The order form or reply form that appears valuable induces readership. It impels the reader to do something with it, to take advantage of the offer. High on the list of devices and techniques that make order forms look valuable are certificate borders, safety paper backgrounds, simulated rubber stamps, eagles, blue handwriting, seals, serial numbers, receipt stubs, and so on. And sheet size alone can greatly add to the valuable appearance of a response form. (You've seen examples of many of these techniques on the order forms shown in Chapter 11.)

Above all, don't call your reply device an order form. Call it a Reservation Certificate, Free-Gift Check, Trial Membership Application, or some other benefit heading. It automatically seems more valuable to the reader.

Getting back more inquiry and order forms starts with making them appear too valuable to throw away. But to put frosting on the cake, add the dimension of personal involvement. Give readers something to do with the order form. Ask them to put a token in a "yes" or "no" slot. Get them to affix a gummed stamp. Have them tear off a stub that has your guarantee on it. Once you have prodded the prospect into action, there is a good chance you will receive an order.

Finally, the order form should restate your offer and benefits. If a prospect loses the letter or circular, a good order form should be able to stand alone and do a complete selling job. And if it's designed to be mailed back on its own (without an envelope), it's usually worthwhile to prepay the postage.

Gift Slips and Other Enclosures

In addition to the letter, brochure, and order form, one of the most common enclosures is a free-gift slip. If you have a free-gift offer, you'll normally get much better results by putting that offer on a separate slip rather than building it into your circular.

If you insert an extra enclosure, make sure it stands out from the rest of the mailing and gets attention. You can often accomplish this by printing the enclosure on a colored stock and making it a different size from the other mailing components. Most free gifts, for example, can be adequately played up on a small slip that's 3½" × 8½" or 5½" × 8½".

Another enclosure that's often used is a business reply envelope. This isn't essential if the order form can be designed as a self-mailer. But if you have an offer that the reader might consider to be of a private nature, an envelope is usually better. Buying a self-improvement book, for example. Or applying for an insurance policy, where the application asks some personal questions. Also, the extra expense of a reply envelope is often justified if you want to encourage more cash-with-order replies.

The Seven-Step Formula for Champion Letters

If any one piece in a direct mail package is key, that piece is the letter. One of the prime advantages of direct mail is its capacity for personal, one-on-one communication, and the letter provides that personal communication. It's no wonder, then, that more has been written about how to create a good direct mail letter than about any other part of the direct mail package.

Here's a letter-writing formula that has served me well. I believe it follows a more detailed route than most formulas. And, used wisely, it should not stifle your creativity.

1. *Promise your most important benefit in your headline or first paragraph.* You simply can't go wrong by leading off with the most important benefit to the reader. Some writers believe in the slow buildup. But most experienced writers favor making the important point first. Many writers use the "Johnson Box": short, terse copy that summarizes the main benefits, positioned in a box above the salutation.

2. *Immediately enlarge on your most important benefit.* This step is crucial. Many writers come up with a great lead, then fail to follow through. Or they catch attention with their heading, but then take two or three paragraphs to warm up to their subject. The reader's attention is gone! Try hard to elaborate on your most important benefit right away, and you'll build up interest fast.

3. *Tell readers specifically what they are going to get.* It's amazing how many letters lack details on such basic product features as size, color, weight, and sales terms. Perhaps the writer is so close to the proposition that he or she assumes the readers know all about it. A dangerous assumption! And when you tell the reader what they are going to get, don't overlook the intangibles that go along with your product or service. For example, they are getting smart appearance in addition to a pair of slacks, knowledge in addition to a 340-page book.

4. *Back up your statements with proof and endorsements.* Most prospects are somewhat skeptical about advertising. They know it sometimes gets a little overenthusiastic about a product. So they accept it with a grain of salt. If you can back up your own statements with third-party testimonials or a list of satisfied users, everything you say becomes more believable.

5. *Tell readers what they might lose if they don't act.* As noted, people respond affirmatively either to gain something they do not possess or to avoid losing something they already have. Here's a good spot in your letter to overcome human inertia—imply what could be lost if action is postponed. People don't like to be left out. A skillful writer can use this human trait as a powerful influence in his or her message.

6. *Rephrase your prominent benefits in your closing offer.* As a good salesperson does, sum up the benefits to the prospect in your closing offer. This is the proper prelude to asking for action. This is where you can intensify the prospect's desire to have the product. The stronger the benefits you can persuade the reader to recall, the easier it will be for him or her to justify an affirmative decision.

7. *Incite action. Now.* This is the spot where you win or lose the battle with inertia. Experienced advertisers know that once a letter is put aside or tossed into a file, they're out of luck. So wind up with a call for action and a logical reason for acting now. Too many letters close with a statement like "supplies are limited." That argument lacks credibility. Today's consumer knows you probably have a warehouse full of merchandise. So make your reason a believable one. For example, "It could be many months before we go back to press on this book." Or "Orders are shipped on a first-come basis. The sooner yours is received, the sooner you can be enjoying your new widget." (See Exhibit 16–7.)

Strategic Writing

The seven-step sales letter formula provides a route to follow when constructing a letter. Another way to approach the task is to review the problems you face and then come up with strategic solutions to those problems. Expressed as a formula: Problems ÷ Strategies = Solutions.

A dramatic example of the application of this technique involves the launch of a certificate program in direct marketing at the University of Missouri–Kansas City (UMKC). I accepted the assignment of doing a direct mail package to be tested against a traditional package prepared by a local agency in Kansas City.

Example: The UMKC Certificate Program

In preparing to write the sales letter, I first listed the problems I faced:

1. To enroll, the applicant would have to have a degree from an accredited college or university.

2. The applicant would have to have two or more years' experience as a professional direct marketer.

3. The applicant would have to agree to spend three weeks on campus at UMKC.

4. The student would be subjected to 14-hour days on campus.

5. Each student would be required to take three written examinations as well as participate in team assignments.

Exhibit 16–7.   The Kiplinger Letter

STANLEY R. MAYES   *ASSISTANT TO THE PRESIDENT*

THE KIPLINGER WASHINGTON EDITORS, INC.
1729 H STREET, NORTHWEST, WASHINGTON, D. C. 20006   TELEPHONE: 887-6400

THE KIPLINGER WASHINGTON LETTER   THE KIPLINGER TAX LETTER
THE KIPLINGER AGRICULTURAL LETTER   THE KIPLINGER FLORIDA LETTER
THE KIPLINGER CALIFORNIA LETTER   THE KIPLINGER TEXAS LETTER
CHANGING TIMES MAGAZINE

<u>More Growth and Inflation Ahead</u>...
<u>and what YOU can do about it.</u>

      The next few years will see business climb to the highest
level this country has ever known. And with it...inflation.

      This combination may be hard for you to accept under today's
conditions. But the fact remains that those who do prepare for both
inflation AND growth ahead will reap big dividends for their foresight,
and avoid the blunders others will make.

      You'll get the information you need for this type
of planning in the Kiplinger Washington Letter...
and the enclosed form will bring you the next 26
issues of this helpful service on a "Try-out" basis.
The fee: Less than 81¢ per week...<u>only $21 for the
6 months just ahead</u>...and tax deductible for business
or investment purposes.

      During the depression, in 1935, the Kiplinger Letter warned
of inflation and told what to do about it. Those who heeded its advice
were ready when prices began to rise.

      Again, in January of 1946, the Letter renounced the widely-
held view that a severe post-war depression was inevitable. Instead
it predicted shortages, rising wages and prices, a high level of
business. And again, those who heeded its advice were able to avoid
losses, to cash in on the surging economy of the late '40s, early '50s
and mid '60s. It then kept its clients prepared for the swings of the
'70s, keeping them a step ahead each time.

      Now Kiplinger not only foresees expansion ahead, but also
continuing inflation, and in his weekly Letter to clients he points
out profit opportunities in the future...and also dangers.

      The Kiplinger Letter not only keeps you informed of present
trends and developments, but also gives you advance notice on the
short & long-range business outlook...inflation forecasts...energy
predictions...housing...federal legislative prospects...politics...
investment trends & pointers...tax outlook & advice...labor, wage
settlement prospects...upcoming gov't rules & regulations...ANYTHING
that will have an effect on you, your business, your personal finances,
your family.

      To take advantage of this opportunity to try the Letter and
benefit from its keen judgments and helpful advice during the fast-

(Over, please)

One of the most famous letters in direct mail, the Kiplinger letter. With minor changes, it beat
all tests against it for almost 40 years! Notice how it follows the seven-step formula for writing
sales letters.

Exhibit 16–7   *(Continued).*

changing months ahead...fill in and return the enclosed form along
with your $21 payment. And do it with this guarantee: That you may
cancel the service and get a prompt refund of the unused part of
your payment any time you feel it is not worth far more to you than
it costs.

I'll start your service as soon as I hear from you, and
you'll have each weekly issue on your desk every Monday morning
thereafter.

Sincerely,

Stanley Mayes
Assistant to the President

SAM:kga

P. S.   More than half of all new subscribers sign up for a full year
at $42. In appreciation, we'll send you FREE five special Kiplinger
Reports on receipt of your payment when you take a full year's service,
too. Details are spelled out on the enclosed slip. Same money-back
guarantee and tax deductibility apply.

6. Each student would be required to complete assignments between intervening on-campus periods.

7. The company sponsoring the applicant had to pay a tuition fee of $4,500.

These problems called for strategic solutions. Here is how each problem was dealt with.

Problem 1.   Will a professional direct marketer accept the word of a college administrator over a professional colleague?

Strategic solution.   Write the letter printed on my personal letterhead and use the salutation "Dear Colleague."

Problem 2.   Is it better to bury the stiff requirements in the body of the letter or to get major negatives out of the way in the first paragraph?

Strategic solution.   Get the negatives out of the way immediately.

> If you accept this proposal, it will cost your firm $4,500. Not an insignificant sum. And there's more. If you accept this proposal, you or your designate will submit to a series of 14-hour days on campus. So much for the agony: now for the ecstasy!

The ecstasy paragraph expounded on these benefits:

> If you accept this proposal, you or your designate will be one of 35 nationwide who will be eligible to receive certification as a PROFESSIONAL DIRECT MARKETER (PDM).

Problem 3.   Because most of the prospects probably had attended only one- or two-day seminars, they might therefore construe these to be adequate.

Strategic solutions.   Promote the advantage of the longer time required.

> But the lasting impact might be compared to taking a cortisone shot to relieve a current problem as contrasted to a life-long infusion of healthy knowledge. The difference: night and day.

Problem 4.   The prospect might wonder if there is any precedent for education of this nature.

Strategic solution.   Put the UMKC program at the same level as similar programs at other prominent universities.

Actually there is strong precedent to recommend the UMKC Professional Direct Marketing Certification Program. It's in exactly the same mode as programs conducted at Harvard, Stanford, and Northwestern's Kellogg School. America's major corporations send their brightest to the on-campus management programs of these distinguished universities.

Problem 5.   There is an unexpected fear of "going back to college." So how can this fear be alleviated?

Strategic solution.   Point out the advantages of the professional over the college student—experience.

To catch up with professionals, college students would have to attend two classes a week for 15 consecutive weeks.

Problem 6.   If I ask the prospect to return the enrollment form to UMKC, I might break the colleague-to-colleague relationship.

Strategic solution.   Have the applicant return the enrollment form to me.

Because I am personally responsible for 17 of the 35 applications, I want to maintain tight control. To accomplish this, I've enclosed a stamped envelope addressed to me at my study at home. I'd appreciate your decision as quickly as possible.

Problem 7.   There is a need to speed up the response process and play on the one-on-one relationship I've tried to establish.

Strategic solution.   Use a postscript to give the prospect an opportunity to contact me directly and engage in a personal conversation.

P.S.: Let me give you my unlisted phone number. It is: 1–847–251–XXXX.

Once the problems had been faced and the strategies for dealing with them had been established, I proceeded to write the six-page proposal letter that is presented in Exhibit 16–8.

Results.   This package—six-page letter, application form, and reply envelope—produced some remarkable results. Here are the details:

1. 3,500 packages were mailed to Direct Marketing Association members at a cost of $1 each.

Exhibit 16–8.   Certification Program Proposal Letter

BOB STONE

1630 SHERIDAN ROAD #8G   •   WILMETTE, ILLINOIS 60091

Dear Colleague:

If you accept this proposal it will cost your firm $4,500. Not an insignificant sum. And there's more. If you accept this proposal you or your designate will commit to a series of 14-hour days on a college campus.

So much for the agony: Now for the ecstasy!

If you accept this proposal you or your designate will be one of 35 nationwide who will be eligible to receive certification as a **PROFESSIONAL DIRECT MARKETER (PDM)**. This certification will come from the University of Missouri-Kansas City -- the first university in the nation to establish a Direct Marketing Center.

The significance of being certified probably won't strike home at first. For the opportunity never existed till now. But, to put certification into perspective, it's comparable to an accountant studying for CPA certification. Or, an insurance executive going back to college to become a chartered life underwriter (CLU).

CPA, CLU, PDM. Each certification tells the world the possessor is at the top of a chosen profession.

But you might rightly point out, "I've been to college. That's behind me. And I am a professional." Right on all counts! That's precisely why I'm writing you.

Take college background. If your experience is anything like mine, your major was in marketing. And what did marketing texts teach us about direct marketing? Nothing. Oh, there may have been a page or two about "sales letter writing." Maybe.

Contrast our college background and that of some of your people with collegiate marketing curriculums today. Over 160 colleges and universities teaching one or more courses in direct marketing. Graduate programs at UMKC, Northwestern University, University of Cincinnati, and others. Hundreds are entering the direct marketing

Exhibit 16–8   (Continued).

2

profession with foreknowledge we never had.

The first day on the job these "kids" sit down with an incredible body of knowledge.   Databases.   Market segmentation. Socio-economic influences. Positioning. Pricing models. Operations research. Life-time value. Theories   of   productivity.   Statistical   theory. Quantitative methods. Consumer behavior. --- And more.

All these students are computer smart.   Their PC's are to them what our slide rules were to us.

As one who has had the privilege of teaching Direct   Marketing   at   both   UMKC   and Northwestern   University,   I've   seen   the advantages of a combination of academic theory and practical skills. They're inseparable. I've learned, without doubt, that <u>degree of skills</u> <u>is</u> <u>in</u> <u>direct</u> <u>ratio</u> <u>to</u> <u>acquired</u> <u>knowledge.</u>

The bottom line is that after only a few years I'm maintaining   a   lively   correspondence   with   former students.   The letterheads upon which they write speak volumes.   **L. L. Bean, Hewlett-Packard, Spiegel, Allstate, Mayo Clinic, AT&T.** Their acquired knowledge has paid off. Big.

But what about the professionals? You. Me. Our brethren?

What are our avenues of continuing education? Chances are, like me, you've attended one-day, two-day seminars.   You may even have enrolled in continuing education programs over several weeks. Most of these programs are excellent.

But the lasting impact might be compared to taking a cortisone shot to relieve a current problem as contrasted to a life-long infusion of healthy knowledge. The difference : night and day.

Now, for the first time, college education is available for the professional. End result: **certification**.

Actually there is strong precedent to recommend the UMKC Professional Direct Marketing Certification Program. It's in exactly the same mode as programs conducted at Harvard, Stanford and Northwestern's   Kellogg   School. America's major corporations send

Exhibit 16–8   (Continued).

3

their brightest to the on-campus management programs of these distinguished universities.

What the Chief Executive Officers of these leading corporations have learned is that the brightest of people become even brighter and more productive when academic knowledge is melded with practical skills. As one educator put it to me - "An astronaut can have all the technical skills needed, but he can't fly to the moon if he doesn't have the knowledge of the physicist."

So it is with direct marketing. A copywriter, for example, can't become a true wordsmith unless he or she clearly understands consumer behavior. No way. The need for knowledge to implement experience is doubly important for the professional direct marketing manager.

The advantage of the professional: <u>Experience</u>

As bright as these college kids are today, we have an advantage that no <u>magna cum laude</u> can come close to matching - **experience.** That's why UMKC has developed a concentrated program that will lead to certification in three weeks of on-campus time with several week intervals between each of the three weeks. To catch up with professionals, college students would have to attend two classes a week for 15 consecutive weeks over several semesters!

Here are the specific dates for on-campus course work:

Week One: October 30 thru November 3, 1989
(Mon.-Fri.)

Week Two: February 26 thru March 2, 1990
(Mon.-Fri.)

Week Three: April 30 thru May 4, 1990
(Mon.-Fri.)

Classes will begin each day at 8:00 a.m. and conclude at 10:00 p.m. (Remember, I warned you about those 14-hour days!) But the pros get a break on Fridays: classes conclude at 4:00 p.m.

Over the three one-week periods participants will be graded on three examinations. Plus -- they will be evaluated by their peers for excellence in team assignments. A minimum of 85 percent attendance is

Exhibit 16–8   (Continued).

4

<u>mandatory.</u>

There are just two other requirements:

1) To be eligible you or your designate must have two or more years experience as a direct marketer and 2) the enrollee must have completed a degree at an accredited college or university. (Special consideration will be given to applicants not fulfilling the college degree requirement provided they have a minimum of seven years of work experience.)   That's it.

A word about UMKC.

University of Missouri-Kansas City School of Business - world renowned - is enshrined in a beautiful tree-lined campus in the cultural center of Kansas City, Missouri.   The number of UMKC students and faculty who have moved on to become Fulbright scholars is legend.

Classes in the Professional Certification in Direct Marketing program will be held in the magnificent new $8 million Henry W. Bloch School of Business and Public Administration. State-of-the-art in every way, including satellite communication.

Knowing that the 35 students in residence will all be mature professionals, the administration of UMKC has made some important concessions.

- **Housing.** PDM students won't be subjected to bare-bones college dormitories. Instead they will be housed at the Residence Inn Kitchenette Apartments, just a few blocks off campus. (The group can have their own "beer busts" - if they're up to it!)

- **Breakfast** will be provided with housing. Casual lunches will be provided at the Henry Bloch School.

- **PDM** students will have full access to the famed UMKC library, housing what many believe to be the most complete library of direct marketing books, tapes, videocassettes in the world.

- **And** for exercise buffs, UMKC will provide a <u>free</u> membership in the new multi-million dollar Swinney Recreation Center. The center is just across from the Bloch School.

Exhibit 16–8   *(Continued).*

5

About the Curriculum.

The curriculum will enhance all aspects of the direct marketing discipline. Strategy. System. Planning. Communication. Evaluation. There will be independent research, field study and team project development during the intervening time prior to Week Two and Week Three.

For a detailed outline of the on-campus curriculum, see separate sheet enclosed. It's all one could dream of - and more. I guarantee it.

About the faculty.

The UMKC faculty is the priceless ingredient that makes the Professional Direct Marketing certification program possible. The faculty is distinguished.

Among the faculty members who will instruct is **William B. Eddy**, Interim Dean of the business school. Then there's **Richard A. Hamilton**, Associate Professor of Direct Marketing, along with professors of finance, of quantitative analysis, of business operations, of organizational behavior, of operations management. A core of **49** professors in all. And most with a Ph.D. after their names.

This group will be reinforced by direct marketing professionals with extensive teaching experience. **Martin Baier**, for one, who pioneered the Direct Marketing Center at UMKC. And I will complete the faculty by teaching various aspects of direct marketing. (I'm thrilled to be asked.)

Why I am so excited.

Excited really isn't a strong enough word to describe how I feel about the Professional Direct Marketing Program. **Enthralled** comes closer. Enthralled that for the first time in our exciting history full-scale college education is available to professionals. Enthralled that for the first time in history certification (PDM) is available.

Because I believe so strongly in what this program will do for our profession, I made an unusual request of the UMKC administration. I asked if I could be personally responsible for **17** of the **35** students to be accepted nationwide. To my complete delight the response was, **"permission granted!"**

Exhibit 16–8 *(Continued).*

6

The bottom line is - I **want your firm to be one of the 17 accepted.**

A challenge to you or your designate.

Because of your experience and stature you may choose to forego the college experience in deference to a designate of your choice. This would be the person in your organization who you single out to be capable of a quantum leap in knowledge and skills.

There is just one thing. To be accepted, your designate must meet both the academic and experience requirements set forth. And this person must be personally sponsored by you.

How to lock-up an enrollment.

$500 will lock-up an enrollment. (But as the S&L's put it - "Certain restrictions apply.") After **35** applications are received, additional applications will be put on a waiting list. Unfortunately there will be no exceptions to the maximum class size of **35**.

Because I am personally responsible for **17** of the **35** applications, I want to maintain tight control. To accomplish this, I've enclosed a stamped envelope addressed to me at my study at home. I'd appreciate having your decision as quickly as possible.

I'll put your application through the moment I receive it. For sure. Sending the application in guarantees a once-in-a-lifetime experience that will pay off for decades to come!

Sincerely,

Bob Stone

Bob Stone

P.S. Let me give you my unlisted phone number. It is: **1-312-251-**xxxx. You can reserve by phone, if you wish.

2. Although originally the class was limited to 35 students, response was so strong that the class was expanded to 42 students.

3. Total revenue came to $168,000; promotion cost came to $3,500.

4. This package outpulled by 5 to 1 the traditional package, which consisted of a two-page letter, circular, application form, and reply envelope.

5. All but three of those who responded to this package called the unlisted number to make their reservation.

Choosing the Lead

Whatever formula or philosophy you adopt, the first task is to decide on the lead for the letter. Nothing is more important. Numerous tests have shown that one lead in a letter can pull substantially better than another. Let's look at six of the most common types of leads used in sales letters. To help you compare them, let's take a sample product and write six different leads for that product. The product we'll use is a business self-improvement book, which includes biographical sketches of a dozen prominent business leaders.

1. *News.* If you have a product that is really news, you have the makings of an effective lead. There is nothing more effective than news. If you have a product or service that's been around a while, perhaps you can zero in on one aspect of it that's timely or newsworthy.

    Examples: Now you can discover the same success secrets that helped a dozen famous business leaders reach the top!

2. *How/What/Why.* Any beginning newspaper reporter is taught that a good story should start out by answering the main questions that go through a reader's mind: who, what, when, where, why, and how. You can build an effective lead by promising to answer one of these questions and then immediately enlarging on it in your opening paragraphs.

    Examples: How successful people really get ahead; what it takes to survive in the executive jungle; or why some people always get singled out for promotions and salary increases.

3. *Numbered Ways.* This is often an effective lead because it sets the stage for an organized selling story. If you use a specific number, it will attract curiosity and usually make the reader want to find out what they are.

    Examples: Seventeen little-known ways to improve your on-the-job performance—and one big way to make it pay off!

4. *Command.* If you can use a lead that will command with authority and without offense, you have taken a big step toward getting the reader to do what you want.

    Examples: Don't let the lack of education hold you back any longer!

5. *Narrative.* This is a difficult type of lead to write, but it can prove to be one of the most effective. It capitalizes on people's interest in stories. To be effective, a narrative lead must lead into the sales story in a natural way and still hold the reader's interest. Ideally, the lead should also give the reader some clue to where the story is going or why he or she should be interested.

Examples: When he started in the stockroom at IBM, nobody ever thought Tom Watson would someday be president of this multibillion-dollar corporation.

6. *Question.* If you start with the right type of question, you can immediately put your reader in the proper frame of mind for your message. But be sure the question is provocative. Make it a specific question, promising benefits— one that's sure to be answered in the affirmative.

Examples: If I can show you a proven way to get a better job, without any obligation on your part—will you give me a few minutes of your time?

It is impossible to put too much emphasis on the importance of working on your leads. The lead is the first thing your reader sees. Usually he or she makes a decision to read or not read at this point. I always write out at least three or four different leads, then choose the one I think will do the best job of appealing to the reader's basic wants.

Make a Letter Look Inviting

Here's a final, important tip from top professional writers. They try to make their letters look attractive, and easy to read (See Exhibit 16–9.) The pros keep paragraphs down to six or seven lines. They use subheads and indented paragraphs to break up long copy. They emphasize pertinent thoughts, knowing that many readers will scan indented paragraphs before they decide whether to read a letter clear through. They use underscoring, CAPITAL LETTERS, and a second ink color to make key words and sentences stand out. And they skillfully use leader dots and dashes to break up long sentences.

Scan the two versions of the AMA letter in Exhibit 16–9. Notice how much more inviting the second letter is compared to the original typewritten version. Same copy, but one letter encourages reading and the other doesn't.

Letter Length and the Postscript

"Do people read long copy?" The answer is "Yes!" People will read something for as long as it interests them. An uninteresting one-page letter can be too long. A skillfully woven four-pager can hold the reader until the end. Thus a letter should be long enough to cover the subject adequately and short enough to retain interest. Don't be afraid of long copy. If you have something to say and can say it well, it will probably do better than short copy. After all, the

Exhibit 16-9. Effective Letter Design

This November, you're invited to take an exciting look at what computers can do for you...

...at the landmark course that will give you--as it's given thousands of executives--the confidence and know-how you need to:

* Clear up the mystery and confusion of data processing!
* Make your computer work harder for you!
* Tell your systems people what you want--instead of the other way around!
* Make computers your partner in management

Dear Executive:

If you're baffled by computers...baffaloed when systems people use words like "byte" and "nanosecond"...if you're tired of the data processing department telling you what can be done, because you don't know enough to give the orders...

...it's time you took the American Management Associations' course that's cured thousands of "computer phobia"...

FUNDAMENTALS OF DATA PROCESSING FOR THE NON-DATA PROCESSING EXECUTIVE

Not for programmers or DP professionals...this 3-day course is one of the few computer seminars just for you, the data processing user! One at which you'll take a fascinating look at what computers can do for you...and learn how to utilize them to become a more effective manager...

...And this November, you can attend any of 12 sessions in 10 major cities across the country--including a city near you!

Thousands of managers and executives have attended this landmark course and, without hesitation, many have called it "the best course they've ever taken." Here's what just a few of the recent attendees had to say:

"I got terrific ideas and concepts that I can implement and

(inside...)

American Management Associations · 135 West 50th Street · New York, N.Y. 10020 · (212)586-8100

Notice how much more inviting the letter on page 348 is, even though the letters have identical copy.

Exhibit 16–9   *(Continued)*.

```
* * * * * * * * * * * * * * * * * * * * * * * * * * * * * * * *
*                                                             *
*       This November, you're invited to take an exciting look  *
*             at what computers can do for you...             *
*                                                             *
*  ...at the landmark course that will give you--as it's given  *
*  thousands of executives--the confidence and know-how you need to: *
*                                                             *
*     * Clear up the mystery and confusion of data processing!  *
*     * Make your computer work harder for you!               *
*     * Tell your systems people what you want--instead of the  *
*       other way around!                                     *
*     * Make computers your partner in management             *
*                                                             *
* * * * * * * * * * * * * * * * * * * * * * * * * * * * * * * *
```

Dear Executive:

    If you're baffled by computers...buffaloed when systems people use words like "byte" and "nanosecond"...if you're tired of the data processing department telling you what can be done, because you don't know enough to give the orders...

...it's time you took the American Management Associations' course that's cured thousands of "computer phobia"...

        FUNDAMENTALS OF DATA PROCESSING
    FOR THE NON-DATA PROCESSING EXECUTIVE

        Not for programmers or DP professionals...
        this 3-day course is one of the few computer
        seminars just for you, the data processing
        user! One at which you'll take a fascinating
        look at what computers can do for you...and
        learn how to utilize them to become a more
        effective manager...

        ...And this November, you can attend any of
        12 sessions in 10 major cities across the
        country--including a city near you!

    Thousands of managers and executives have attended this landmark course and, without hesitation, many have called it "the best course they've ever taken." Here's what just a few of the recent attendees had to say:

      "I got terrific ideas and concepts that I can implement and

                                    (inside...)

longer you hold a prospect's interest, the more sales points you can get across and the more likely you are to win an order.

Regardless of letter length, however, it usually pays to tack on a postscript. The P.S. is one of the most effective parts of any letter. Many prospects will glance through a letter. The eye will pick up an indented paragraph here, stop on an underlined statement there, and finally come to rest on the P.S. If you can express an important idea in the P.S., the reader might go back and read the whole letter. This makes the P.S. worthy of your best efforts. Use it to restate a key benefit. Or to offer an added inducement, like a free gift. Even when somebody has read the rest of the letter, the P.S. can make the difference between whether or not the prospect places an order. Use the P.S. to close on a strong note, to sign off with the strongest appeal you have.

The Value of Versioned Copy

Suppose, just suppose, that instead of sending exactly the same letter to all your prospects, you could create a number of versions for each major segment of your market. Then rather than talking about all the advantages and benefits of the product, you could simply zero in on those that fit each market segment. Sounds like a logical idea that should increase response, doesn't it?

Yet my own experience with versioned or segmented copy has been mixed. Sometimes I've seen this technique work effectively; other times it's a bomb. So I suggest that you test it for yourself. If your product story should be substantially different for certain audience segments—and you can identify and select them on the lists you're using—develop special versions of your regular copy and give the technique a try.

One type of versioned copy that generally does pay off is special copy slanted to your previous buyers. Customers like to think a firm remembers them and will give them special treatment. In going back to your satisfied buyers, there's less need to resell your company. You can concentrate on the product or the service being offered.

How to Improve a Good Mailing Package

So far we've been talking about how to create a new mailing package. Let's suppose you've done that, and you want to make it better. Or you've got a successful mailing package you've been using for a couple of years (your control) and you want to beat it. How do you go about it? One of the best ways I know is to come up with an entirely different appeal for your letter. For instance, suppose you're selling an income tax guide and your present letter is built around saving money. That's probably a tough appeal to beat.

But to develop a new approach, you might write a letter around a negative appeal, something people want to avoid. Experience with many propositions has proved that a negative appeal is often stronger than a positive one. Yet it's frequently overlooked by copywriters. An appropriate negative copy appeal for our example might be something like, "How to avoid costly mistakes that can get you in trouble with the Internal Revenue Service." Or, "Are you taking advantage of these six commonly overlooked tax deductions?"

Another good technique is to change the type of lead on your letter. Review the examples of six common types of leads given earlier. If you're using a news lead, try one built around the narrative approach. Or develop a provocative question as the lead. Usually a new lead will require you to rewrite the first few paragraphs of copy to fit the lead, but then you can often pick up the rest of the letter from your control copy.

A creative professional with a well-organized approach for coming up with new ideas is Sol Blumenfeld. He uses the additive approach, the extractive approach, and the innovative approach, among others.

The Additive Approach

The additive approach adds something to a control package that can increase its efficiency in such a way as to justify the extra cost involved. Usually, this entails using inserts. Inserts that can be used to heighten response include testimonial slips, extra discounts, a free gift for cash with order, and a news flash or bulletin. Other additive ideas include building stamps or tokens into the response device. And, if you have a logical reason to justify it, add an expiration date to your offer.

The Extractive Approach

The extractive approach requires a careful review of your existing mailing package copy. You often can find a potential winning lead buried somewhere in the body copy.

The Innovative Approach

Unlike the extractive approach, the innovative approach is designed to produce completely new ideas. If you are testing three or four new copy approaches, at least one of them should represent a potential breakthrough, something that's highly original, perhaps even a little wild. I encourage writers to let themselves go, because we've seen them produce real breakthroughs this way: dramatic new formats, exciting copy approaches, and offers that have really shellacked the old control!

When you create your own direct mail, consider the checklist in Exhibit 16–10. Remember that these are guidelines, not rigid rules, and that when I say "X will usually outpull Y," that means every so often X will not outpull Y.

Exhibit 16–10.   Checklist for Direct Mail Packages

Mailing format

- The letter ranks first in importance.
- The most effective mailing package consists of outside envelope, letter, circular, response form, and business reply envelope.

Letters

- Form letters using indented paragraphs usually outpull those in which paragraphs are not indented.
- Underlining important phrases and sentences usually increases results slightly.
- A letter with a separate circular generally does better then a combination letter and circular.
- A form letter with an effective running headline ordinarily does as well as a filled-in letter.
- Authentic testimonials in a sales letter ordinarily increase the pull.
- A two-page letter ordinarily outpulls a one-page letter.

Circulars

- A circular that deals specifically with the proposition presented in the letter is more effective than a circular of an institutional character.
- A combination of art and photography usually produces a better circular than one employing either art or photography alone.
- A circular usually proves to be ineffective in selling news magazines and news services.
- In selling big-ticket products, deluxe, large-size, color circulars virtually always warrant the extra cost over circulars 11″ × 17″ or smaller.

Outside envelopes

- Illustrated envelopes increase response if their message is tied into the offer.
- Variety in types and sizes of envelopes pays, especially in a series of mailings.

Reply forms

- Reply cards with receipt stubs usually increase response over cards with no stub.
- "Busy" order or request forms that look important usually produce a larger response than neat, clean-looking forms.
- Postage-free business reply cards generally bring more responses than those to which the respondent must affix postage.

Reply envelopes

- A reply envelope increases cash-with-order response.
- A reply envelope increases responses to collection letters.

Exhibit 16–10 *(Continued).*

Color

- Two-color letters usually outpull one-color letters.
- An order or reply form printed in colored ink or on colored stock usually outpulls one printed in black ink on white stock.
- A two-color circular generally proves to be more effective than a one-color circular.
- Full color is warranted in the promotion of such items as food products, apparel, furniture, and other merchandise if the quality of color reproduction is good.

Postage

- Third-class mail ordinarily pulls as well as first-class mail.
- Postage-metered envelopes usually pull better than affixing postage stamps (and you can meter third-class postage).
- A "designed" printed permit on the envelope usually does as well as postage metered mail.

SELF-QUIZ

1. What unique advantages permit direct mail to do a better selling job than any other advertising medium?

   a. _____

   b. _____

   c. _____

   d. _____

   e. _____

2. What are the three basic formats of direct mail?

   a. _____

   b. _____

   c. _____

3. Personalized letters will always outpull nonpersonalized ones.
   ☐ True ☐ False

4. A "publisher's letter" will usually boost response 10 percent or more.
   ☐ True ☐ False

5. A pop-up device is a sure-fire way to increase response.
   ☐ True   ☐ False

6. Invitation formats are outmoded.
   ☐ True   ☐ False

7. Complete this equation for making a sale.
   Benefit ÷ _____ = _____.

8. What is the difference between a benefit and a selling point?

   _____

   _____

   _____

   _____

9. What are some of the basic wants inherent in most people?

   a. _____   f. _____

   b. _____   g. _____

   c. _____   h. _____

   d. _____   i. _____

   e. _____   j. _____

10. What do most people want to avoid?

    a. _____   d. _____

    b. _____   e. _____

    c. _____   f. _____

11. Name 11 guidelines for good direct mail copy.

    a. _____   g. _____

    b. _____   h. _____

    c. _____   i. _____

    d. _____   j. _____

    e. _____   k. _____

    f. _____

12. The key objective in preparing an order form is to make order forms look

_____

_____.

13. Name four typical involvement devices.

a. _____

b. _____

c. _____

d. _____

14. Name the six mot common types of leads used in sales letters.

a. _____ d. _____

b. _____ e. _____

c. _____ f. _____

15. List the points in the seven-step letter-writing formula in sequence.

a. _____ e. _____

b. _____ f. _____

c. _____ g. _____

d. _____

16. What are the two best applications of a postscript?

a. To restate _____.

b. To offer an added _____.

17. Define each of these approaches for improving a good mailing package:

a. The additive approach _____

_____

_____

b. The extractive approach _____

_____

_____

CREATING DIRECT MAIL PACKAGES   355

    c. The innovative approach _____

_____

_____

18. Complete this formula: Problems ÷ Strategies = _____.

PILOT PROJECT

You are the advertising manager of a major national chain store group (e.g., Sears, Montgomery Ward's, J.C. Penney). Your company wants to get more of its credit cards in the hands of qualified persons. Your assignment is to prepare a direct mail package to ''sell'' your store's credit card. Use these assumptions:

- The credit card is free; there is no yearly fee for it.

- It is honored in your company's stores from coast to coast for anything sold in those stores.

- In addition to your company's own credit card, your company's stores also accept Visa, MasterCard, and Discover.

The objective of your direct mail package is to get creditworthy persons to fill out an application for the card. They will be credit-checked, and a certain number of persons will be turned down. Another obvious objective is that, when a person has applied and been approved for the card, you want him or her to use it.

Here are some steps to guide you through the decisions you will have to make:

1. Write a creative strategy. Pay particular attention to competitive products, market, and creative implementation.

2. Which format would you select: classic or self-mailer. Why?

3. Here are some selling points (or product features) of the card. Below each one, list the customer benefit made possible by that selling point. (To get started, the first one is filled in.) Note: More than one benefit can usually be derived from a single selling point.

    a. Lets you charge purchases.

    You don't need to carry cash. _____

b. Card is good nationwide.

_____

c. Card is good for anything sold at our stores.

_____

4. What is the ''big idea'' behind your mailing package? How will you implement this theme in the letter? Circular? Outer envelope? Order form (application)?

5. Will you use any additional pieces, such as free-gift slips or a publisher's letter?

6. Write your sales letter. Pay particular attention to the seven-step formula.

7. How could you use versioned copy in your letter?

CHAPTER SEVENTEEN

Creating and Managing Catalogs

America's longest-standing love affair may well be with the catalog. The reasons for catalog shopping have changed drastically over the past century, but the love affair goes on unabated.

Back in the late 1880s and for decades thereafter, the foremost reason for catalog shopping was to find items not readily available in areas in which millions of Americans lived. But in the World War II period, when shopping centers sprang up even in small towns, two major reasons for catalog shopping emerged: (1) to save time and (2) to find unusual and exclusive items not generally available in retail channels. Business-to-business cataloging also emerged as companies sought new distribution channels and less expensive ways to reach and sell to business firms.

The catalogs that succeed today, both customer and business to business, rely on feasibility studies, business planning, niche marketing, customer tracking, product analysis, and all of the other sophisticated tools available to direct marketers in general.

With this sophistication has come a body of catalog specialists who serve mature catalog operations as well as catalog start-ups. The right catalog specialists are worth their weight in gold.

Jack Schmid, of Shawnee Mission, Kansas, heads J. Schmid & Associates, Inc. He has served such consumer and business-to-business clients as Hershey Foods, Hewlett-Packard, Anheuser-Busch, Sara Lee, and Hallmark Cards. This chapter is based on his ideas.

Key Catalog Trends and Issues

From the early 1980s on, catalog mailings grew dramatically. Exhibits 17–1 through 17–3 show how dramatic mail-order growth has been. Sales nearly tripled—and catalogs have been a prime contributor to this growth. Mail order sales represent a significant portion of the overall economy: 1.9 percent of gross national product (GNP), 4 percent of retail sales, and 11.1 percent of general merchandise sales (1994 data).

Trends of the 1990s

One might expect the catalog business to be dominated by huge companies each annually mailing millions of catalogs. But that is not the case. *Catalog Age's* 1995 annual survey confirms that smaller-sized companies tend to be the norm:

- 51.7 percent reported annual sales under $1 million.

- 17.5 percent reported annual sales of $1–3 million.

- 10.3 percent reported annual sales of $3–5 million.

- 6.8 percent reported annual sales of $5–10 million.

- 13.7 percent reported annual sales of over $10 million.

Another surprise is that 74.6 percent of catalog distributors indicate that they mail fewer than 500,000 catalogs each year. These statistics demonstrate

Exhibit 17–1.   Sales via Mail ($ Billions)

	Consumer		Business to	Charitable
	Products	**Services**	**Business**	**Contributions**
1994	$78.5	$51.2	$71.1	$52.0
1993	71.6	47.0	67.7	50.5
1992	67.5	45.5	57.3	49.7
1991	64.9	43.0	54.1	49.0
1990	57.5	40.7	53.5	49.0
1989	54.0	33.0	50.4	45.9
1988	48.0	29.0	45.6	41.8
1987	43.4		43.6	37.6
1986	29.4		37.6	33.6
1985	27.0		32.4	31.4
1984	24.8		27.5	30.0
1983	22.5		23.1	25.8
1982	41.5		24.4	24.4
1981	31.0		19.5	21.6

Source: Arnold L. Fishman, *The Guide to Mail Order Sales, 1994* (Chicago, Ill.: Marketing Logistics, Inc., 1994).

Exhibit 17–2. Catalogs Mailed per Year: 1983–1994 (Thousands)

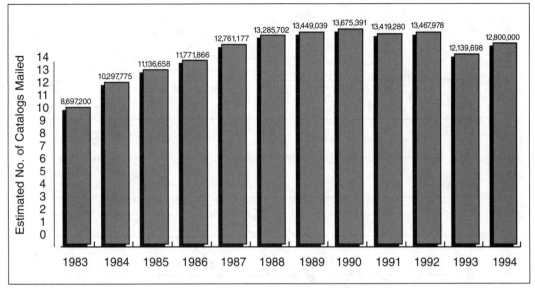

[a]Extrapolated from the USPS *Revenue, Pieces and Weight by Classes of Mail Report*, based on the following assumptions, which have been agreed upon by both the USPS and DMA and further substantiated by the findings of the USPS *Household Diary Study*:

- 18% of all third-class mail is catalogs (including nonprofit mail). (NOTE: Prior to 1993, the percentage used to calculate the number of catalogs comprising third-class mail was 21%.)

- 85% of all fourth-class bound printed matter is catalogs

Source: Direct Marketing Association, *1994/95 Statistical Fact Book.*

the entrepreneurial nature of cataloging and indicate that its roots have come from small, innovative, niche-driven companies and individuals:

- 74.6 percent mail fewer than 500,000 catalogs annually.

- 10.6 percent mail 500,000–1 million catalogs annually.

- 8.0 percent mail 1–5 million catalogs annually.

- 3.0 percent mail 5–10 million catalogs annually.

- 3.8 percent mail more than 10 million catalogs annually.[1]

What factors have contributed to the dramatic growth of direct marketing and, in particular, of catalog mailings and sales? Following are some of the business, social, and economic trends responsible for the increase:

[1] "Annual Analysis of Trends and Practices in the Catalog Business," *Catalog Age* (December 1994).

Exhibit 17–3.   Direct Marketing Sales ($ Billions)

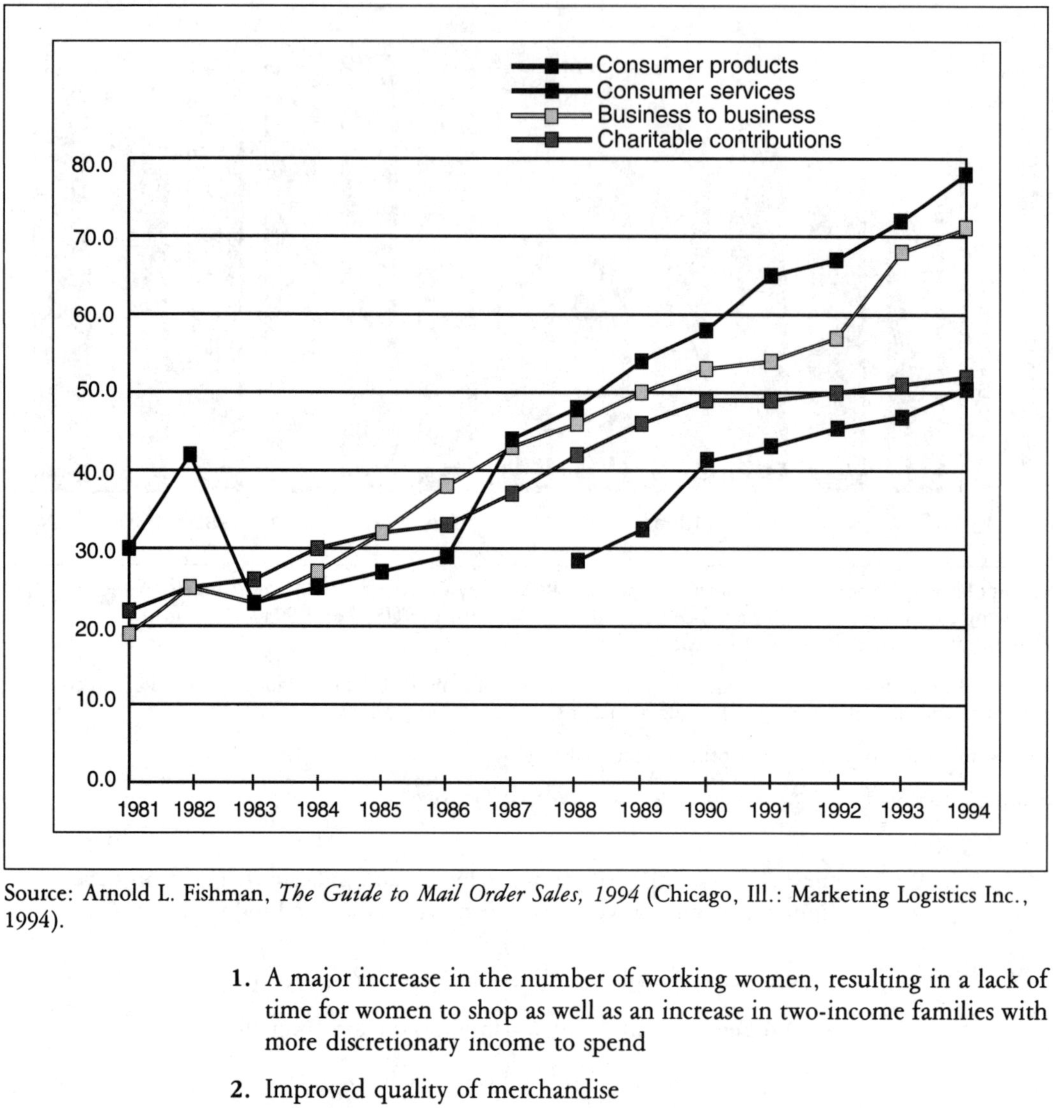

Source: Arnold L. Fishman, *The Guide to Mail Order Sales, 1994* (Chicago, Ill.: Marketing Logistics Inc., 1994).

1. A major increase in the number of working women, resulting in a lack of time for women to shop as well as an increase in two-income families with more discretionary income to spend

2. Improved quality of merchandise

3. Improved creative presentation of merchandise

4. Consumers turning away from retail shopping

5. Increased use of credit cards for everyday shopping

6. Increased use of the telephone and fax in the ordering process

7. Increased targeting/specialization of products and markets

8. Improved fulfillment and customer service

9. Better color separations, printing, and paper

10. The computer and its steadily decreasing costs of storing and retrieving information

11. Development of sophisticated customer databases

12. Scarcity of quality salespeople, both retail and business

13. High cost of making a sales call

14. Diminished return of cold sales calls

15. New catalog formats such as tabloid size on newsprint, square, oversized, "slim-jim" (under $6^{1}/_{8}"\times 11^{1}/_{2}"$, unbound multiproduct promotions in an envelope, and the like

16. The demand for measurable and accountable advertising

Issues of the Future

Presented here are a number of issues that will affect cataloging into the next century:

Maturity of the Catalog Business.   All the signs point to cataloging having reached a level of maturity, at least on the consumer side. The market is not growing at nearly the dramatic rate it did in the past. For years direct marketers have talked about "catalog glut." At the same time, only slightly over half of the households in the United States regularly use mail-order buying. Business-to-business cataloging, however, remains on a strong growth curve for the future. This is due, in large part, to business catalogs usually being a new marketing channel.

Greater Competition.   It's a fact: Consumer, business, and retail catalogs are facing more competition from other mailers. This underscores the importance of differentiating one catalog's products and positioning from those of other catalogs.

Niche-Driven Catalogs.   Greater specialization and narrower niches will be a hallmark of catalogs in the next decade. Much like the magazine industry, which evolved from general to highly targeted editorial content, specialized catalogs are not part of the future—they are here today.

Fewer Start-ups.   It is increasingly difficult to launch a new catalog that quickly generates a profit. Unless companies are prepared to look at new start-ups as long-range investments (and have the capital to support them), many new catalogs will die in the planning stages.

Stronger Customer Service and Fulfillment.   It is no longer acceptable to *think about* improving customer service in the future. The industry standard is being set by catalog leaders like Lands' End and Quill, which have superb telephone operations, on-line customer databases and inventory information, and 24-hour turnaround in shipping. These companies have set a standard that customers now expect. If a catalog doesn't meet this standard, it will have a more difficult time staying in business.

New Technology.   Catalogers are developing new ways to design, print, and mail catalogs that reduce production costs. Desktop publishing, digital photography, Scitex-type color separations, selective binding, personalized ink-jetting of special messages, improved papers (i.e., recycled and recyclable), and improved printing are only a few. It's now possible to reduce creative and prepress costs and ultimately the cost in the mail.

The Global Village.   One can no longer think about cataloging as just an American phenomenon. U.S. mailers such as L.L. Bean and Sharper Image are mailing into Japan. A host of American catalogs are mailing in the United Kingdom and Europe. Canadian markets are being tested by scores of U.S. catalogers, and Canadian catalogers are turning an eye to the United States. International ownership of U.S.–based catalogs is a fact; America's largest cataloger, Spiegel, for example, is owned by Otto Versand of Germany. Japan's interest and investment in catalogs is growing.

Consolidation.   Another development that started in the 1980s and has continued into the 1990s is the consolidation of catalog efforts. Companies like Hanover Direct, CML Group, Spiegel, Arizona Mail Order, Williams Sonoma, Sara Lee, Campbell Soup, and Rivertown Trading are all owners of multiple catalogs. They have either acquired existing catalogs or started new ones that complemented their other product offerings and offered seasonal, financial, or recessionary stability.

Greater Use of Catalogs by Nontraditional Marketers.   Traditionally, catalogs are thought of as direct-to-the-consumer items. But business-to-business cataloging has become very strong in the past two decades. An interesting trend of the 1990s is the use of catalogs by fund raisers, professional associations, publishers, speakers' bureaus, seminar companies, financial service companies, and even travel companies. Any business that has multiple products or services to sell can do so through cataloging.

Concern for the Environment.   There are no direct marketers more visible in the environmental arena than catalogers. With coated paper that is difficult to recycle, packing materials like styrofoam peanuts, and general consumer concern about overuse of paper, catalogers are the target of environmentalists across the country. Smart catalogers are responding to environmental concerns. Many catalog marketers are using biodegradable materials for packaging. Even though it is more expensive, more and more catalogs are being printed on recycled paper and are using soy-based ink.

Paper and Postage Costs.   Today the largest parts of any catalog mailing budget are paper and postage. Both of these factors have had dramatic increases in recent years and have become a major concern, especially if increases follow in size and frequency as they occurred in the mid-1990s.

Sales/Use Taxes.   An issue on which catalog companies are in the forefront is the collection of sales or use taxes. The Supreme Court ruling on National Belles Hess (1967) established "nexus," or physical presence in a state, as the criterion for determining whether a company is required to collect and remit sales taxes to a state. The *Quill v. North Dakota* ruling (1992) throws the ball back to Congress, stating that this is an interstate commerce issue. Because so many states are financially strapped and eager to find sources of new revenue, it is unlikely that this issue will go away.

Privacy.   Although privacy is more of a list or database issue, its concerns will dramatically affect catalogers because of the prevalence of multiple mailings. Consumers object to having corporations know too much about them. Catalogers, on the other hand, want to have every possible piece of information to help them better target their mailings. These two objectives are clearly conflicting.

The Catalog Process and Strategies

The rest of this chapter is devoted to the catalog process and the strategies used to build and manage a winning catalog company. We will consider the key ingredients of catalog success and the strategies smart catalogers are applying in merchandising, positioning of the catalog, building and using the customer database, creative execution, catalog fulfillment, and analysis of results. The catalog process chart shown in Exhibit 17–4 identifies the components of a winning catalog. Refer to this chart as you read the rest of this chapter.

Merchandising

Catalogs are a blend of merchandise and audience. Most catalogs are merchandise-driven, that is, they start from a merchandise point of view and address

Exhibit 17-4. The Catalog Process

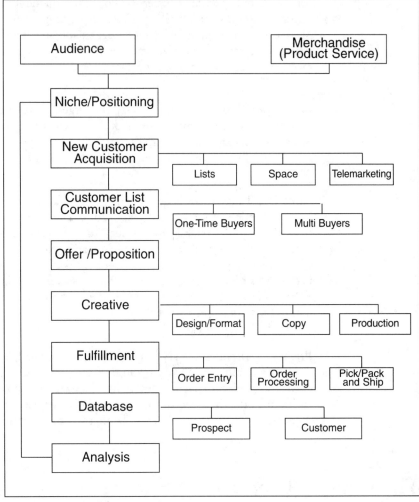

Source: © J. Schmid & Associates Inc.

the purchaser of the product. Many of the pioneers in cataloging were first and foremost merchandisers who had a product idea. People like Roger Horchow of the Horchow Collection, Chuck Williams of Williams Sonoma, Manny Fingerhut of Fingerhut, and many others started with a solid product concept and from that concept built a growing business.

Even if a catalog is market- or audience-driven (that is, if it starts with an audience and then determines what products can be sold), merchandising is of vital importance. The familiar adage "Nothing comes before the product," simply stated, means that if catalogers desire to build repeat buyers—a prime goal for profitability—then they must start with and build a strong merchandising program that will continue to attract customers over time.

Understanding the psychology of the catalog buyer is essential to catalog merchandising. (See Exhibit 17–5.) If the goal of a catalog is to build repeat buyers, then understanding who those customers are and why they come back

Exhibit 17–5.   The Psychology of the Catalog Buyer

Frequent Buyers	Infrequent Buyers
Convenience	
A quick and easy way to shop	Hassles in dealing with the PO
A comfortable alternative to retail shopping	Waiting for an order
A way to avoid crowds	Returning merchandise
Merchandise	
Unusual merchandise	Cannot see or feel merchandise
New products and style	Hard to judge quality
Found merchandise that fits	Problems with fit, color, etc.
Consumer's Outlook	
Confident	Skeptical
In control	Afraid of losing control
Excited, anticipation	Fear of "rip-offs"
Dream fulfillment	
Value	
Lower prices on special promotions	Can shop around at retail
Added value from not having to drive to store	More sales at retail
Can comparison shop by using multiple catalogs	Can control bills
Brand	
Expertise in dealing with companies in direct mail selling uncommon brand names	Lack of expertise in buying unknown brands
Trust direct mail companies	Uncertain about the reputation of direct mail companies
Need	
Can wait for a number of products	Want immediate gratification at time of purchase
Order well in advance of special need	Waiting time is frustrating

is paramount. Exhibit 17–5 also differentiates between frequent mail order buyers and "touch-and-feel shoppers" who prefer to shop in retail stores and who distrust catalog shopping.

Know Thy Customer.   Know thy customer is the first rule of catalog merchandising. A catalog product buyer must understand why and how people use the catalog. A classic mistake made by those who select products for catalogs is putting their own tastes and preferences first and paying little heed to what they know about the ultimate consumers.

How do you get to know your customers? Listed here are techniques used by successful catalogs.

- A demographic survey that rides along in the box shipment to first-time customers

- Annual demographic surveys to repeat buyers, seeking information on who the customers are and what additional products they might like to see in the catalog

- Phone contact with customers through telemarketing representatives or a phone survey

- Regular dialogue (i.e., taking phone calls or orders) between key people in the company and customers regarding how various aspects of the catalog might be improved.

- Customer focus groups

- Customer advisory boards

The key is to listen to what customers are saying in research surveys and phone conversations.

Build on Your Winners.   Issuers of successful catalogs watch what their customers buy and listen to what they say. The worst catalog from a merchandise sales standpoint is the first catalog. With each succeeding mailing, a catalog should build on the merchandise categories and the price points that the customer is buying. Analysis of catalog sales results is essential, especially in the merchandise area.

A favorite example of a company that has listened to its customers is Lands' End. (See Exhibit 17–6.) This successful cataloger started in the retail business selling sailing gear. Over several decades, it listened and watched as its customers bought more and more soft-sided luggage, sportswear, and nonsailing items. Its merchandise mix evolved into men's, women's, and children's clothing, soft goods, and luggage. Could it have experienced outstanding growth to an $800 million public company had it not listened to its customers and built on its winning merchandise?

Exhibit 17–6.   Lands' End Catalog Cover

Other Merchandise Strategies.   What other merchandise strategies are smart catalogers using? Here are several that have proved to be successful.

Improve product quality while reducing cost.   Customers are concerned about the value of products they buy through a catalog. Value is a price/quality relationship. Smart catalogers constantly try to improve product quality while improving their margins. Whether through importing, buying in larger quantities as the catalog grows, or improving vendor relationships, a catalog's challenge is to buy better and at the same time give customers more for their money. Surely that will keep them coming back.

Strengthen new-product development efforts.   During recessionary times, it is common for companies to cut back or discontinue new-product development. New-product development, however, is the lifeblood of the catalog. Winning catalogers keep it at the forefront of their minds and budgets at all times.

Strengthen inventory control systems.   A merchandising area that has been a major pitfall for many catalogers is inventory control. One major difference between retailing and cataloging is exemplified by the statement: "Retailers sell what they buy, and catalogers buy what they sell." Retailers buy merchandise for an entire season. If a woman comes into a shop to buy an advertised dress and finds her size is unavailable, the shop owners will try to sell her another dress in her size. They are "selling what they bought." A catalog, however, normally will commit for only 40–50 percent of its anticipated needs for a season. Then it will read the selling results early in the season and reorder ("buying what they are selling").

It is vital for catalogs to have reliable vendors who can back them up in merchandise and turn around reorders quickly. It is also crucial to have a buying and rebuying staff as well as computer systems that can help forecast product needs down to the last stockkeeping unit (SKU).

Imagine the task of controlling inventory for the women's shoes shown on the catalog page from the Bloomingdale's catalog that appears in Exhibit 17-7. One style, the Amalfi pump, comes in 5 colors, 17 shoe lengths, and 5 widths. Guess how many SKU's are involved here? Over 350! And look again—it comes in three different heels!

The final aspect of catalog inventory control is disposing of leftover merchandise at the end of a season. There are a number of options:

- Repeating the item in a future catalog

- Special sales pages

- Package inserts of remainder products

- An outlet store

- An annual warehouse sale for local people

Exhibit 17–7.   SKUs and Cataloging

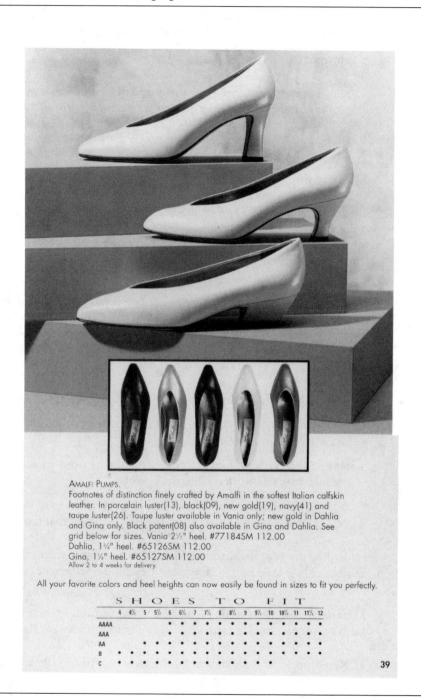

AMALFI PUMPS.
Footnotes of distinction finely crafted by Amalfi in the softest Italian calfskin
leather. In porcelain luster(13), black(09), new gold(19), navy(41) and
taupe luster(26). Taupe luster available in Vania only; new gold in Dahlia
and Gina only. Black patent(08) also available in Gina and Dahlia. See
grid below for sizes. Vania 2½" heel. #77184SM 112.00
Dahlia, 1¾" heel. #65126SM 112.00
Gina, 1¼" heel. #65127SM 112.00
Allow 2 to 4 weeks for delivery.

All your favorite colors and heel heights can now easily be found in sizes to fit you perfectly.

SHOES TO FIT

	4	4½	5	5½	6	6½	7	7½	8	8½	9	9½	10	10½	11	11½	12
AAAA					•	•	•	•	•	•	•	•	•	•			
AAA					•	•	•	•	•	•	•	•	•	•	•	•	
AA			•	•	•	•	•	•	•	•	•	•	•	•	•	•	•
B		•	•	•	•	•	•	•	•	•	•	•	•	•	•		
C	•	•	•	•	•	•	•	•	•	•	•	•					

39

- A special sale at the state fair or other event where thousands of people are present

- Telephone specials during the life of the catalog

- Remainder merchants

Most successful catalogs have fine-tuned their remainder systems so that they minimize the markdown expense that haunts retail stores.

Positioning the Catalog

As catalog firms strive to set themselves apart from the competition, most seek to define a niche, or a unique positioning, for their catalog. A niche is both a unique identity and a special place in the market where there is a void that is not being met by the competition. A catalog can be unique, or set apart from its competition, by its merchandise, creative style or format, offers, and customer service.

Defining the Catalog's Niche.   What does a cataloger need to think about before beginning creative execution? Often catalogers, particularly first-time catalogers, jump right into the creative process without first thinking through some very basic issues. Here's a checklist of some key questions that must be answered:

1. Who is the company and the catalog? What product or service does it sell?

2. To whom does it sell? Who are its primary customers, secondary customers, and even tertiary customers?

3. How is the catalog unique? What sets it apart from its competitors? Its products? Its service? Its offers? Its pricing?

4. Who is the competition? What is their niche? What are their strengths? Weaknesses? Do they have a serious void or weakness that can be exploited?

One good way to articulate the catalog's niche is through a mission statement. Exhibit 17–8 is an example of a strong positioning statement.

Differentiating the Catalog from the Competition.   There are innumerable ways to set a catalog apart. Five variables to consider are the following:

1. **Merchandise.** This is a vital area in which to be different. Perhaps it is acceptable to be No. 2 in the auto rental area, as Avis has shown, but to be No. 2 in a catalog niche and not have a defined difference in product can be financially disastrous.

Exhibit 17-8.   Lands' End Principles of Doing Business

1. We do everything we can to make our products better. We improve material, and add back features and construction details that others have taken out over the years. We never reduce the quality of a product to make it cheaper.

2. We price our products fairly and honestly. We do not, have not, and will not participate in the common retailing practice of inflating markups to set up a phony "sale."

3. We accept any return for any reason, at any time. Our products are guaranteed. No fine print. No arguments. We mean exactly what we say: GUARANTEED. PERIOD.

4. We ship faster than anyone we know of. We ship items in stock the day after we receive the order. At the height of the last Christmas season the longest time an order was in the house was 36 hours, excepting monograms, which took another 12 hours.

5. We believe that what is the best for our customer is best for all of us. Everyone here understands that concept. Our sales and service people are trained to know our products, and to be friendly and helpful. They are urged to take all the time necessary to take care of you. We even pay for your call, for whatever reason you call.

6. We are able to sell at lower prices because we have eliminated middlemen; because we don't buy branded merchandise with high protected markups; and because we have placed our contracts with manufacturers who have proved that they are cost conscious and efficient.

7. We are able to sell at lower prices because we operate efficiently. Our people are hard working, intelligent, and share in the success of the company.

8. We are able to sell at lower prices because we support no fancy emporiums with their high overhead. Our main location is in the middle of a 40-acre cornfield in rural Wisconsin. We still operate our first location in Chicago's Near North tannery district.

2. **Pricing or use of credit.** A pricing method can help set a catalog apart. Current Inc.'s catalog is an excellent example. It uses a three-part pricing strategy that basically says to the customer: "The more items you buy, the better the price." Discounters like Damark or Viking are also good at using pricing to help build a unique identity. Fingerhut sells only on credit (its own) and establishes a niche in doing so.

3. **Catalog format and creative presentation.** Besides merchandising, the catalog's creative format, design, and copy can make a tremendous difference in establishing its niche. Examples are catalogs like Patagonia with its unique in-use photography (all supplied by readers and customers); J. Peterman with its unique catalog size, copy, and use of illustrative art; and L.L. Bean with its square shape, cover art, and catalog layout.

4. **Offer.** An offer, or proposition, is what the cataloger is willing to give to customers in return for their response. What catalog has a unique offer that sets it apart? Hammacher Schlemmer consistently offers a special in its catalog: "Buy two items and get a third free." Nordstrom's offers free pick-up on any return.

5. **Customer service/fulfillment.** Here is an ideal way to set a catalog apart: Service so good that it is the envy of every competitor. It starts with the phone people and a database system that allows real-time access to customers' records while they are on the phone. Next is on-line inventory so that customers know before hanging up whether the size and color of the item is in stock and can make a decision about alternatives. Then it's the delivery time of the product. Finally comes the handling of returns and inquiries. Without a doubt, customer service can set a catalog apart.

Building and Using the Customer Database

The catalog process chart in Exhibit 17–4 identifies the next series of tasks in building a successful catalog business: targeting media. It is critical for a catalog to build a buyer list—a group of people or companies that will keep coming back again and again to order from it.

When a new catalog starts, it has no buyers and probably no affinity names—names of potential buyers who have some relationship to your company or catalog. For example, Hershey Foods Inc. has about 1.8 million people visit Hershey Chocolate World every year. Some sign up to receive a catalog during the holiday season. Although these are not proven catalog buyers, they represent a list of prospects with whom the company has had some relationship. There is a good chance that a catalog will be received, read, and, if it has the right items, there will be orders.

If a company has no affinity names, then it must rely on building its customer list from list rentals, space ads, and various other media that can be targeted to its audience. It is not unusual for the buyer list to outperform an outside list or nonaffinity names many times over. This is why it usually takes a new catalog three years to break even and about five years to recapture its initial investment.

Front-end/Back-end Marketing. A concept well understood by veteran catalogers is front-end and back-end marketing. (See Exhibit 17–9.) *Front-end marketing* refers to prospecting or new-customer acquisition. Few catalogers make money on prospecting; it is a cost-related activity. The objectives of front-end marketing are to acquire new first-time customers, or to acquire leads and inquiries that can be converted into first-time buyers, and to acquire the most names at the least cost. Smart catalogers measure precisely what it costs to acquire a

Exhibit 17–9.   Front-end/Back-end Concept of Marketing

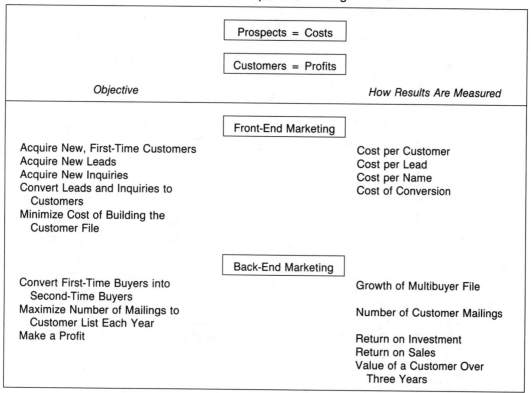

	Prospects = Costs
	Customers = Profits
Objective	*How Results Are Measured*

Front-End Marketing

Objective	How Results Are Measured
Acquire New, First-Time Customers	Cost per Customer
Acquire New Leads	Cost per Lead
Acquire New Inquiries	Cost per Name
Convert Leads and Inquiries to Customers	Cost of Conversion
Minimize Cost of Building the Customer File	

Back-End Marketing

Objective	How Results Are Measured
Convert First-Time Buyers into Second-Time Buyers	Growth of Multibuyer File
Maximize Number of Mailings to Customer List Each Year	Number of Customer Mailings
Make a Profit	Return on Investment
	Return on Sales
	Value of a Customer Over Three Years

new, first-time buyer and are tenacious about tracking where the name came from.

Back-end marketing refers to working the customer list. This is where the profitability for a catalog must come from. The objectives of back-end marketing are to convert first-time buyers into second-time buyers, to maximize the number of profitable mailings to this list each year, and to determine where the best long-term customers come from so that the catalog can change or modify its front-end media. A winning catalog carefully observes the month-to-month growth of its buyer file, watching especially for buyers who have purchased more than twice. Large catalogers often divide the marketing functions by front end and back end. The small cataloger must understand and play both roles within the company.

The Customer Hierarchy.   More than any other type of direct marketer, the cataloger has to understand the hierarchy of a customer. (See Exhibit 17–10.) Because the primary goal of a catalog is to get repeat orders from its customer list, a successful catalog must build trust, credibility, and confidence. In this

Exhibit 17–10.   The Customer Hierarchy

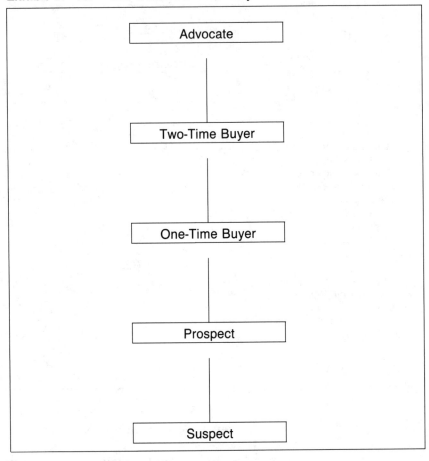

process, there are three distinct hurdles to be surmounted. The first is converting prospects to first-time buyers. Perhaps these first-time buyers can be called "triers." They are cautious, have a low response rate, have a lower average order size, and expect the catalog to prove itself worthy before ordering again.

What message do buyers give when they purchase a second time? Generally, it's this: "You're okay. I like your products, and your service is acceptable." Average order value goes up. A higher response rate develops.

A further step is building the multibuyers into advocates. These buyers will recommend the catalog to others. They will peruse the catalog carefully, and they usually respond at many times the rate of first-time buyers. This phenomenon is what makes a successful, profitable catalog.

New-Customer Acquisition Strategies.   Historically, catalogs have relied heavily on rented lists to develop their customer base. But this isn't the only method. Because of rising postal and mailing costs, catalogers are seeking alternative ways to obtain new buyers. Innovation is the name of the prospecting game. Here are 15 options, other than list rentals, that catalogs are using today:

1. *Customer referrals.* These are very good quality names. Ask "advocate" customers for names of friends, relatives, co-workers, and the like.

2. *Space advertising.* Many of today's large catalogs built their buyer lists through space advertising. There are many options: small space ads (one-sixth page) versus large space ads (full page), and the direct sales of a product versus generating a lead or inquiry.

3. *Magazine catalog sections.* Many consumer and some business magazines publish an annual or a biannual catalog lead-generation section.

4. *Free-standing newspaper inserts (FSIs)*

5. *Package inserts.* These ride along in the box shipment of another mailer. The promotion could be a catalog or a lead-generation flyer.

6. *Co-op mailings.* Carol Wright is an example.

7. *Trade shows.* These are especially effective for business catalogs.

8. *Television*

9. *Catalog shoppers.* Today there are several lead-generation publications, such as *Shop-at-Home Directory* and *The Best Catalogs in the World*, that exclusively promote catalogs.

10. *Card decks*

11. *Credit card or billing inserts*

12. *Doctor's or dentist's office "take-ones"*

13. *Back panels of cereal boxes*

14. *Public relations*

15. *Gift recipients*

What are the innovative strategies for acquiring new customers that winning catalogs use today? Consider the following list:

1. Aggressively source coding every new-customer acquisition effort and tracking results and capturing original source codes on the customer database

2. Seeking as much publicity (PR) as possible by creating events (e.g., marathon races sponsored by marketers of health-related products)

3. Measuring the cost of acquiring names by each type of medium and determining what the catalog can afford to spend for a new customer.

4. Developing customer referral programs such as those used by book clubs

5. Carefully watching the seasonality of mailings and concentrating prospecting in the prime season

6. Targeting, targeting, targeting mailings, especially when using list rentals

7. Telephoning to prequalify names before mailing a business-to-business catalog and sending a postcard before the catalog mails to prequalify the name

8. Keeping names of old buyers and inquiries that are no longer mailed and putting them into merge-purge

9. Establishing and maintaining a detailed prospect database of inquiries, gift recipients, people who paid for a catalog, and the like and capturing original source codes and dates of inquiry.

10. Getting the catalog to the prospect who requests it as fast as possible and letting the prospect know that ''this is the catalog you requested.'' (Maximum turnaround time should be no more than a week.)

11. Correlating back-end customer name value with front-end name source to maximize quality of names over quantity of names

12. Watching the aging of buyers, inquiries, and catalog requests. (People who have not purchased in over 12 months need a special message or incentive to remind them that they asked for the catalogs they receive.)

The Customer List: A Catalog's Most Important Asset

Even though few catalogs identify their customer list on the company's balance sheet, it is their most important asset. The buyers are their major source of revenue through sales of merchandise or list rentals. To maximize the use of this asset, however, the list must be maintained and mailed. Let us further discuss these two factors.

List Maintenance.   Most catalogers will include an ''address correction'' postal endorsement at least once or twice a year. In this way they can update the names of people or companies that have moved and eliminate catalogs being discarded for insufficient address. The use of the Postal Service's National Change of Address program (NCOA) during the merge-purge of the customer list with outside lists is well worth the cost and effort in ensuring better delivery.

Mailing the Customer List.   Mailing catalogs is expensive. Also, too often companies tend to undermail their best customers. During the mid-1970s, for example, Fingerhut was mailing its customer list 20 times a year. By using simple segmentation techniques such as recency, frequency, monetary, and product category, the company was able to test and ultimately increase its mailings to 30 times a year. Most catalogers probably underutilize or undermail their customer list. One reason is that they tend to treat all customers alike.

Using the Customer List More Effectively.   The following how-to tips are suggestions for a more effective and efficient use of the customer list:

1. The customer list is a catalog's most important asset. Track buyers by source. Track growth of the customer list on a weekly or monthly basis.

2. Know who the best customers are. Survey them. Ask them for help. Research them. Talk to them on the phone.

3. Mail the best customers more often.

4. Build a simple segmentation system to prioritize the buyer file. All customers are not created equal.

5. Keep track of:
   When customers buy
   What customers buy
   How customers respond (phone/fax/mail/e-mail)
   How customers pay (check/cash/credit card/purchase order)
   How and why customers return merchandise

6. Invest in a catalog fulfillment database system that allows tracking, measuring, and segmenting of the customer list.

7. Maintain the list and keep it updated. Remember that 20 percent of the list changes each year.

8. Rent the buyer list for extra income.

9. Reactivate former-year buyers.

10. Treat buyers like good friends.

Circulation Planning.   *Circulation* is a word that is very familiar to magazine publishers. It is also a word that is starting to mean more to catalogers. It means: "When are you mailing which catalog and to whom?" At a catalog conference, a forum of small catalogers identified circulation as the most important marketing skill for profitable growth.

Catalog Creative Execution

The challenge in catalog creative execution is in differentiating the catalog from its competition. There are six aspects of the creative process:

- Pagination

- Design and layout

- Color as a design element

- Typography as a design element

- Copy

- Photography or illustrative art

Pagination.   Many catalog experts think pagination, or planning the overall scheme of the catalog, is the most important aspect of the creative process. Pagination determines the catalog's organization (i.e., by product category, mixing product, product function, theme, color, or price). And pagination determines exactly what product goes where in the catalog. It is the master plan for the catalog.

With a new catalog, there are a number of decisions that have to be made before beginning overall design and layout. Here is a checklist of items to be considered:

1. Catalog size

2. Postal requirements

3. Items per page

4. One-color, two-color, or four-color

5. Space mix among photos, copy, and white space

6. Amount of copy

7. Position of copy

8. Method of layout

9. Method of organization

10. Use of photography and/or illustrative art

11. Type size, type face, use of reverse type in headlines or body copy

12. Color as a design element

The most important thing to keep in mind in pagination is knowing who the customers are and how they will use the catalog. Sound pagination puts the best-selling products in the ''hot spots'' of the catalog and thereby maximizes sales. Another consideration of pagination is the niche, or positioning, of the catalog. A catalog must provide the ambience that its audience expects. Pagination ensures that there is "flow" from page to page and from product category to product category.

Design and Layout.   If pagination is the master plan, then design and layout is the blueprint that will guide the creative construction process. Unlike many direct mail creative projects that are directed by the copywriter, the catalog is clearly design-driven. Two critical areas of design are covers and page or spread layouts.

Catalog covers.   The front and back covers have the following roles:

- Attracting the customer's attention
- Telling what the catalog is selling
- Reinforcing the catalog's niche
- Attracting the reader inside the catalog
- Offering a benefit
- Selling products
- Getting the catalog mailed
- Offering service information such as the telephone/fax, guarantee, and credibility information

Preliminary design of a new catalog concentrates a lot of effort on getting the right "feel" on the cover. To illustrate the feel of a catalog cover, note in Exhibit 17–11 how Handshake's cover illustrates the feel of business greeting cards.

Page or spread layouts.   The second critical area of catalog design is page or spread layout. (Most professionals advocate spreads because the eyes tend to scan two facing pages.) Layout options break into five categories:

- Grid layout
- Free form (asymmetrical)
- Single item per page
- Art and copy separation
- Product grouping

Exhibit 17–11.   Catalog Copy That Creates Appropriate "Feel"

Because the layouts provide the blueprint for copy and photography, it is important that they reinforce the image of the company selling the products. Successful catalogers:

- Make the product the hero. The product is what's being sold, not the models, the props, or the backgrounds.

- Use "hot spots" (front and back covers, inside front cover and inside back cover spreads, the center of a saddle-stitched catalog, the order form, additional spreads in the front of the catalog, i.e., pages 4–5, 6–7) effectively in promoting winning products—those with the best margins.

- Remember their customers and how they will use the catalog.

- Use a logical eye flow within a spread from the right-hand page to the left-hand page and back again to the right-hand page.

- Use the telephone/fax number and other information such as testimonials, technical specifications, and the like as part of the design of the catalog.

- Strive for consistency in layout from catalog to catalog so that the customer will not be confused.

Color as a design element. People react differently to the use of color in catalogs. Red and yellow are strong colors that attract attention. Blue is seldom used with food. Research shows that people prefer the use of white, beige, or gray for backgrounds. Catalog readers like contrast between the product and the background. White space is clearly a design element. Too much of it and layouts appear to have gaping holes; too little and it's confusing. Care in the use of color in cataloging is especially important in page backgrounds, photo backgrounds, headlines, and screens for special sections.

Typography as a design element. Everyone learns to read black on white, left to right, left-justified columns, top to bottom, with short column length, reasonably sized type, and a serif type face. There needs to be a good reason for an art director to vary from these patterns, otherwise readability is affected and so is customer response. Attractive type helps readability and ease of catalog use. Unattractive type can actually turn off the reader and result in lost sales. Catalogers must remember their catalog's positioning and target audience in selecting the appropriate type. Art directors should be careful not to overuse reverse type, overprint type on a busy photo, or use all capital letters, extended line length, and type or calligraphy that is difficult to read.

Catalog Copy: Your Salesperson

When we state that a catalog tends to be layout-driven, we do not mean to imply that copy is unimportant. The layout helps to attract and direct the reader's attention, but it is the copy that closes the sale. Catalog copy must perform these functions:

- Reinforce the catalog's niche or positioning

- Inform

- "Grab" the reader with headlines

- Educate

- Entertain

- Give reassurance

- Build credibility and confidence

- Describe the product

- Close the sale

It is not unusual to have a number of writers working on catalog copy. It is therefore important for all of the writers to understand the positioning of the catalog, to know precisely who the target customer is, and to have agreed on a copy style. Many catalogs have even developed style manuals to achieve consistency. There are many copy styles from which to choose. The right one is selected with the customer in mind.

Photography or Illustrative Art

The catalog is a visual format, and one of the key elements of the design is photography or artwork. Photography helps attract the reader's attention to the product. It also shows product features and color differences. Photography or artwork builds credibility for the product and romances the product. But, most importantly, the photo or illustrative art makes the product the hero.

The photographer, art director, and photo stylist together can make products come alive with effective use of propping, accessorization, lighting, and level of contrast. Whatever the photo style or type of camera and whether or not models are used, photography is a vital part of the catalog creative process. Illustrative art is also used in catalogs to promote greater understanding of hard-to-shoot subjects, to be different from other catalogs, or, sometimes, to effect a cost savings.

Catalog Fulfillment

After the catalog has been targeted, created, and mailed, you are ready to take orders. Fulfillment is an essential element of a profitable catalog. It closes the loop with the customer. During the 1970s there was no urgency to improve catalog customer service, but in the 1980s this function became a "must have" for catalogers. Order entry by phone, mail, and fax; data entry and fulfillment systems; warehousing and pick, pack, and shipping; credit handling; return handling; and customer communications—all have become essential to the fulfillment function. Today's customers demand quality service in every aspect of the catalog operation.

Catalog Database Strategies

The fulfillment function provides information about prospects and customers. Catalogers relish having information about their customers that will help them improve the response percentage, obtain a larger average order, and get customers to buy more frequently. With today's improved computer hardware and software, the arduous task of maintaining critical customer purchase information and demographic data has become very manageable. Computer costs are one of the few costs that have been significantly reduced in the last decade. There are good custom-designed PC-based (micro-computer) software packages available. And they are affordable! There is no excuse for a catalog of any size not to have a state-of-the-art fulfillment and database system to track customer activity.

Analysis—The Numbers Side of Cataloging

Closing the loop. Ensuring that every catalog is better than the last one. Making sure that catalog promotions are measurable. This is what analysis is all about. Analysis helps critique each mailing and therefore makes the next one better.

There are few prosperous catalogs that don't devote a lot of effort and staff time to the numbers side of the business. Here is a checklist of the typical analyses that catalogers perform:

1. List/source/media analysis

2. Merchandise analyses:
   Price points analysis
   Square-inch analysis
   Product category analysis
   Sales by catalog item, page, and spread

3. Inventory analyses:
   Product returns
   Cancellations
   Back orders
   Remainders/markdowns of merchandise

4. Analysis of tests such as offers, covers, seasonality, and lists

5. Mailing plan: actual results versus projection

6. Profit and loss: actual results versus plan

7. Lifetime value of customers

The Catalogs of Tomorrow

The buzzword in cataloging is the Internet, and there are concerns among printers and mailers alike that it will replace the printed word as we know it today. The Internet might become a major new source of generating new catalog prospects, rather than selling product. Others suggest that the printed catalog be replaced by a catalog on video or computer disc. Although interactive, electronic marketing is surely gaining acceptance, it is unlikely that it will make enormous in-roads before the next decade. Electronic catalogs should show greater acceptance by business-to-business companies. Many direct marketing futurists suggest that consumer acceptance of interactive marketing will not become a reality until people can order through their own television, from their own living room, and from electronic catalogs of every specialty niche.

Catalogs of the twenty-first century will continue to be more and more targeted. They will become more personalized and use more techniques like selective binding to present specialized merchandise to individuals rather than large groups.

One thing is certain: The catalog process that we have looked at in this chapter will not go away, even though it will change. To survive and prosper in the 2000s, catalogs cannot do well some of the tasks mentioned in the catalog process and leave others to chance. Winning catalogs must be able to perform every task well. That's the challenge and the opportunity.

SELF-QUIZ

1. Identify five key issues that catalogers will face in the next decade.

   a. _____   d. _____

   b. _____   e. _____

   c. _____

2. What are the two primary things the cataloger must consider when starting a new catalog?

   a. _____

   b. _____

3. What are the key merchandise strategies that successful catalogs employ?

a. _____

b. _____

c. _____

4. Define *niche* as it applies to a catalog.

_____

_____

5. What do catalogers mean by front-end marketing? Back-end marketing?

_____

_____

_____

_____

6. Why is the customer list so important to a cataloger?

_____

_____

_____

7. Identify six vital aspects of the catalog creative process.

a. _____   d. _____

b. _____   e. _____

c. _____   f. _____

8. What are the ''hot spots'' of a catalog?

_____

_____

9. What type of analyses do catalogers perform, and how is each analysis used?

_____

_____

_____

_____

PILOT PROJECT

You have been asked by a leading brewery to do a feasibility study concerning a new gift catalog. There are two key audiences for the product that the catalog might promote:

- **Primary audience:** Young men and women, age 21–35, who consume more beer than the average American. This audience tends to be middle-American, blue-collar, and with a high school rather than a college education.

- **Secondary audience:** Men and women, age 35–60, who are collectors of various beer paraphernalia—beer glasses, steins, mugs, trays, and the like.

With this background, develop a feasibility plan and a strategic business plan that would include answers to the following questions:

1. What might be an appropriate name for the catalog?

2. How could this catalog be unique? What niche could this catalog fill to be successful?

3. Identify 20 items that might be appropriate for this catalog to promote.

4. What mailing lists should the catalog rent for an initial test?

5. What publications might be used to obtain catalog requests and inquiries?

6. How would you treat the front cover of the catalog to maximize the appeal of the first catalog and attract the reader's attention?

CHAPTER EIGHTEEN

Creating Print Advertising

Many of the creative techniques needed in creating a successful direct mail package (Chapter 16) are also necessary in creating productive direct response ads in magazines and newspapers. But here the space available for words and pictures is much more severely limited, and most of the gimmicks, gadgets, showmanship, and personal tone of direct mail do not apply. This throws a heavy load of responsibility for the success of the ad on a carefully worded headline, a compelling opening, tightly structured copy, and appropriate visual emphasis.

Before the actual work of creating an ad begins, two important questions should be answered: Who is the prospect? What are the outstanding product advantages or customer benefits?

Often there is no single clear answer, but rather several distinct possibilities. Then the profitable course of action is to prepare ads embodying all your most promising hypotheses and split-test as many of them as your budget permits.

Visualizing the Prospect

Every good mail-order or direct mail piece should attract the most attention from the likeliest prospects, and capable creators of direct response advertising visualize their prospects with varying degrees of precision when they sit down at the computer or drawing board.

Good direct response advertising makes its strongest appeal to its best prospects and then gathers in as many additional prospects as possible. And who are the prospects? They are the ones with the strongest desire for what you're selling. You must look for the common denominators. For instance, let's say you are selling a book on the American Revolution. Here are some of the relevant common denominators that would be shared by many people in your total audience:

1. An interest in the American Revolution in particular

2. An interest in American history in general

3. A patriotic interest in America

4. An interest in history

5. An interest in big, beautiful coffee-table books

6. An interest in impressing friends with historical lore

7. A love of bargains

8. An interest in seeing children in the family become adults with high achievement

Now, out of a total audience of 1,000, some readers would possess all 8 denominators, some would possess some combination of 6, some a different combination of 6, some just one of the 8, and so on.

If you could know the secret hearts of all 1,000 individuals and rank them on a scale of relative desire to buy, you would place at the very top of the list those who possessed all 8 denominators, then just below them those who possessed just 7, and so on down to the bottom of the scale, where you would place those who possessed none.

Obviously, you should make as many sales as possible among your hottest prospects first, for that is where your sales will be easiest. Then you want to reach down the scale to sell as many of the others as you can. By the time you get down to the people possessing only one of the denominators, you will probably find interest so faint that it would be almost impossible to make your sales effort pay unless it were fantastically appealing.

Obvious? Yes, to mail-order professionals who learned the hard way. But to the novice it is not so obvious. In an eagerness to sell everybody, he or she might muff the easiest sales by using a curiosity-only appeal that conceals what is really being offered.

On the other hand, the veteran but uninspired pro might gather up all the easy sales lying on the surface but, through lack of creative imagination, fail to reach deeper into the market. For instance, let's say that of 1,000 readers, 50 possess all 8 denominators. A crude omnibus appeal that could scoop up many of them would be something like "At last—for every liberty-loving American family, especially those with children, whose friends are amazed by their understanding of American history, here is a big, beautiful book about the American Revolution you will display with pride—yours for only one-fifth of what you'd expect to pay!'' A terrible headline, but at least one that those possessing the denominators of interest would stop to look at and consider. You might get only 5 percent readership, but it will be the right 5 percent.

On the other hand, suppose you want to do something terribly creative to reach a wider market. So you do a beautiful advertising message headed ''The Impossible Dream,'' in which you somehow work your way from that starting point to what it is you're selling. Again, you might get only 5 percent readership, but these readers will be scattered along the entire length of your scale of interest. Of the 50 people who stopped to read your message, only 2 or 3 will be prime prospects possessing all 8 denominators. Many people really interested in books on the American Revolution, in inspiring their children with patriotic sentiments, and in acquiring big impressive books at big savings will have hurried past unaware.

The point: Don't let prime prospects get away. In mail order you can't afford to. Some people out there don't have to be sold; they already want what you have, and if you tell them that you have it, they will buy it. Alone they will not constitute enough of a market to make your selling effort pay, but without them you haven't got a chance. So, through your clarity and directness, you gather in these prime prospects; then through your creative imagination you reach beyond them to awaken and excite mild prospects as well.

Once the prospect is clearly visualized, a good headline almost writes itself. For example, here is an effective and successful headline from an ad by Quadrangle/New York Times Book Company. It defines the prospect so simply and accurately that the interested reader feels an instant tug:

> For people who are almost (but not quite) satisfied with their house plants . . . and can't figure out what they're doing wrong . . .

A very successful ad for the Washington School of Art, offering a correspondence course, resulted from our bringing the psychographic profile of our prime prospect into sharp focus. We began to confront the fact that the prospect was someone who had been drawing pictures better than the rest of us since the first grade. Such people are filled with a rare combination of pride in their talent and shame at their lack of perfection. And their goal is not necessarily fame or fortune, but simply to become a ''real artist,'' a phrase that has different meanings for different people. The winning headline simply reached out to the right people and offered them the right benefit:

> If you can draw fairly well (but still not good enough), we'll turn you into a real artist.

Of course, a good headline does not necessarily present an explicit definition of the prospect, but it is always implied. Here are some classic headlines and the prospects whom the writer undoubtedly visualized:

> Can a man or woman my age become a hotel executive?

The prospect is, probably, a middle-aged man or woman who needs, for whatever reason, an interesting, pleasant, not too technically demanding occupational skill such as hotel management and is eager for reassurance that you *can* teach an old dog new tricks. Note, however, how wide the net is cast. No one is excluded. Even people who worry they are too young to be a hotel executive can theoretically read themselves into this headline.

Don't envy the plumber—be one.

The prospect is a poorly paid worker, probably blue-collar, who is looking for a way to improve his lot and who has looked with both indignation and envy at the plumber, who appears not much more skilled but earns several times as much per hour.

How to stumble upon a fortune in gems.

The prospect is everybody, all of us, who all our lives have daydreamed of gaining sudden wealth without extreme sacrifice.

Is your home picture-poor?

The prospect is someone, probably a woman, with a home, who has a number of bare or inadequately decorated walls, and who feels not only a personal lack but also, perhaps more importantly, a vague underlying sense of social shame at this conspicuous cultural "poverty." Whether she appreciates it or not, she recognizes that art, books, and music are regarded as part of the "good life" and are supposed to add a certain richness to life.

Become a "non-degree" engineer.

This is really a modern version of "Don't envy the plumber." The prospect is an unskilled or semiskilled factory worker who looks with a mixture of resentment and grudging envy on the aristocracy in his midst, the college grads who earn much more, dress better, and enjoy special privileges because they are credentialed engineers. The prospect would like to enjoy at least some of their job status but is unwilling or unable to go to college and get an engineering degree.

Are you tired of cooking with odds and ends?

The prospect is that Everywoman, or Everyman, who has accumulated over the years an enameled pan here, an aluminum pot there, an iron skillet elsewhere, and to whom a matched set of anything represents neatness, order, and elegance.

Can you call someone a failure at 30?

The prospect is a young, white-collar worker, 25–32 years old, who is deeply concerned that life isn't turning out the way he or she dreamed and that he or she is on the verge of failing to "make it"—permanently.

Selecting Advantages and Benefits

Advantages belong to the product. Benefits belong to the consumer. If the product or service is unique or unfamiliar to the prospect, stressing benefits is important. But if it is simply a new, improved model in a highly competitive field where there already exists an established demand, the product advantage or advantages become important.

When pocket electronic calculators were first introduced, such benefits as pride, power, and profit were important attributes. But as the market became flooded with competing types and brands, product advantages such as the floating decimal became more important.

There are two kinds of benefits, the immediate or obvious benefit and the not-so-obvious ultimate benefit—the real potential meaning for the customer's life of the product or service being sold. (See Exhibit 18–1.) The ultimate benefit often proves to have a greater effect, for it reaches deeper into the prospect's feelings.

Victor Schwab, one of the great mail order pioneers, was fond of quoting Dr. Samuel Johnson's approach to auctioning off the contents of a brewery: "We are not here to sell boilers and vats, but the potentiality of growing rich beyond the dreams of avarice."

It pays to ask yourself over and over again, "What am I selling? Yes, I know it's a book or a steak knife, or a home study course in upholstering—but what am I *really* selling? What human values are at stake?"

For example, suppose you have the job of selling a correspondence course in advertising. Here is a list of ultimate benefits and the way they can be expressed in headlines for the course. Some of the headlines are patently absurd, but they illustrate the mind-stretching process involved in looking for the ultimate benefit in your product or service:

- *Health:* "Successful ad people are healthier and happier than you think— and now you can be one of them."

- *Money:* "What's your best chance of earning $50,000 a year by the time you are 30?"

- *Security:* "You are always in demand when you can write advertising that sells."

- *Pride:* "Imagine your pride when you can coin a slogan repeated by 50 million people."

- *Approval:* "Did you write that ad? Why, I've seen it everywhere."

- *Enjoyment:* "Get more fun out of your daily job. Become a successful ad writer!"

- *Excitement:* "Imagine working until 4:00 a.m.—and loving every minute of it!"

Exhibit 18–1. Classic Direct Response Ad

"Can he really play?" a girl whispered. "Heavens no!" Arthur exclaimed. "He never played a note in his life."

They Laughed When I Sat Down At the Piano But When I Started to Play!—

ARTHUR had just played "The Rosary." The room rang with applause. I decided that this would be a dramatic moment for me to make my debut. To the amazement of all my friends, I strode confidently over to the piano and sat down.

"Jack is up to his old tricks," somebody chuckled. The crowd laughed. They were all certain that I couldn't play a single note.

"Can he really play?" I heard a girl whisper to Arthur.

"Heavens, no!" Arthur exclaimed. "He never played a note in all his life... But just you watch him. This is going to be good."

I decided to make the most of the situation. With mock dignity I drew out a silk handkerchief and lightly dusted off the piano keys. Then I rose and gave the revolving piano stool a quarter of a turn, just as I had seen an imitator of Paderewski do in a vaudeville sketch.

"What do you think of his execution?" called a voice from the rear.

"We're in favor of it!" came back the answer, and the crowd rocked with laughter.

Then I Started to Play

Instantly a tense silence fell on the guests. The laughter died on their lips as if by magic. I played through the first few bars of Beethoven's immortal Moonlight Sonata. I heard gasps of amazement. My friends sat breathless — spellbound!

I played on and as I played I forgot the people around me. I forgot the hour, the place, the breathless listeners. The little world I lived in seemed to fade — seemed to grow dim — unreal. Only the music was real. Only the music and visions it brought me. Visions as beautiful and as changing as the wind blown clouds and drifting moonlight that long ago inspired the master composer. It seemed as if the master

musician himself were speaking to me—speaking through the medium of music—not in words but in chords. Not in sentences but in exquisite melodies!

A Complete Triumph!

As the last notes of the Moonlight Sonata died away, the room resounded with a sudden roar of applause. I found myself surrounded by excited faces. How my friends carried on! Men shook my hand — wildly congratulated me—pounded me on the back in their enthusiasm! Everybody was exclaiming with delight—plying me with rapid questions. "Jack! Why didn't you tell us you could play like that?"... "Where did you learn?"—"How long have you studied?"—"Who was your teacher?"

"I have never even seen my teacher," I replied. "And just a short while ago I couldn't play a note."

"Quit your kidding," laughed Arthur, himself an accomplished pianist. "You've been studying for years. I can tell."

"I have been studying only a short while," I insisted. "I decided to keep it a secret so that I could surprise all you folks."

Then I told them the whole story.

"Have you ever heard of the U. S. School of Music?" I asked.

A few of my friends nodded. "That's a correspondence school, isn't it?" they exclaimed.

"Exactly," I replied. "They have a new simplified method that can teach you to play any instrument by mail in just a few months."

How I Learned to Play Without a Teacher

And then I explained how for years I had longed to play the piano.

"A few months ago," I continued, "I saw an interesting ad for the U. S. School of Music—a new method of learning to play which only cost a few cents a day! The ad told how a woman had mastered the piano in her spare time at home—and without a teacher! Best of all, the wonderful new method she used, required no laborious scales—no heartless exercises — no tiresome practising. It sounded so convincing that I filled out the coupon requesting the Free Demonstration Lesson.

"The free book arrived promptly and I started in that very night to study the Demonstration Lesson. I was amazed to see how easy it was to play this new way. Then I sent for the course.

"When the course arrived I found it was just as the ad said — as easy as A.B.C.! And, as

the lessons continued they got easier and easier. Before I knew it I was playing all the pieces I liked best. Nothing stopped me. I could play ballads or classical numbers or jazz, all with equal ease! And I never did have any special talent for music!"

Play Any Instrument

You too, can now teach yourself to be an accomplished musician—right at home—in half the usual time. You can't go wrong with this simple new method which has already shown 350,000 people how to play their favorite instruments. Forget that old-fashioned idea that you need special "talent." Just read the list of instruments in the panel, decide which one you want to play and the U. S. School will do the rest. And bear in mind no matter which instrument you choose, the cost in each case will be the same—just a few cents a day. No matter whether you are a mere beginner or already a good performer, you will be interested in learning about this new and wonderful method.

Send for Our Free Booklet and Demonstration Lesson

Thousands of successful students never dreamed they possessed musical ability until it was revealed to them by a remarkable "Musical Ability Test" which we send entirely without cost with our interesting free booklet.

If you are in earnest about wanting to play your favorite instrument—if you really want to gain happiness and increase your popularity—send at once for the free booklet and Demonstration Lesson. No cost — no obligation. Right now we are making a Special offer for a limited number of new students. Sign and send the convenient coupon now — before it's too late to gain the benefits of this offer. Instruments supplied when needed, cash or credit. **U. S. School of Music, 1831 Brunswick Bldg., New York City.**

— — — — — — — — — — — —

U. S. School of Music,
1831 Brunswick Bldg., New York City.

Please send me your free book, "Music Lessons in Your Own Home," with introduction by Dr. Frank Crane, Demonstration Lesson and particulars of your Special Offer. I am interested in the following course:

....

Have you above instrument?.................

Name.....................................
(Please write plainly)

Address..................................

City..................State...........

Pick Your Instrument

Piano, Organ, Violin, Drums and Traps, Banjo, Tenor Banjo, Mandolin, Clarinet, Flute, Saxophone, 'Cello, Harmony and Composition, Sight Singing, Ukulele, Guitar, Hawaiian Steel Guitar, Harp, Cornet, Piccolo, Trombone, Voice and Speech Culture, Automatic Finger Control, Piano Accordion

This ad, written by John Caples, a member of the Direct Marketing Hall of Fame, is considered one of the classics of direct response writing.

- *Power:* "The heads of giant corporations will listen to your advice—when you've mastered the secrets of advertising that works." (Just a wee bit of exaggeration there, perhaps.)

- *Fulfillment:* "Are you wasting a natural talent for advertising?"

- *Freedom:* "People who can get million-dollar advertising ideas don't have to worry about punching a time clock."

- *Identity:* "Join the top advertising professionals who keep the wheels of our economy turning."

- *Relaxation:* "How some people succeed in advertising without getting ulcers."

- *Escape:* "Hate going to work in the morning? Get a job you'll love—in advertising!"

- Curiosity: "Now go behind the scenes of America's top advertising agencies—and find out how multimillion-dollar campaigns are born!"

- *Possessions:* "I took your course five years ago—today I own two homes, two cars, and a Chris-Craft."

- *Sex:* "Join the people who've made good in the swinging advertising scene."

- Hunger: "A really good ad person always knows where his or her next meal is coming from."

Harnessing the Power of Semantics

A single word is a whole bundle—a nucleus, you might say—of thoughts and feelings. And when different nuclei are joined together, the result is nuclear fusion, generating enough power to move the earth.

Semantics is the hydrogen bomb of persuasion. In politics, for example, entire election campaigns sometimes hinge on the single word "boss." If one side manages to convince the public that the other side is controlled by a boss or bosses, but that the first side has only "party leaders," the first side will probably win the election.

In direct marketing, clear understanding and skillful use of semantics can make a powerful contribution to ad headlines. (See Exhibit 18–2.) Here are a few examples.

What do you think when you read the word *Europe?* Perhaps there are certain negative connotations: constant military squabbles, lack of Yankee know-how, and so on. But far more important in the psyche of most Americans are the romantic implications: castles, colorful peasants, awesome relics of the past, charming sidewalk cafes, all merging into the lifelong dream of making the Grand Tour of Europe.

Exhibit 18–2.   The Power of a Strong Headline

At 4½ she's reading 3rd grade books

a child prodigy? not at all! your child, too can be reading one, two or three years beyond his present age level...even if he's a "poor" reader now

Prove it to yourself...with this 10 day free trial!

Reading is fun for Sarah—as it *should be* for every child. At age four and a half, she's already choosing her own books at the San Diego, Cal. library.

She reads books many third graders find "hard going." Yet she won't enter first grade for another year.

Sarah is typical of thousands of children who learned to read with "Listen and Learn with Phonics"—a reading kit that actually makes reading fun.

"Listen and Learn with Phonics" was developed by a reading expert. It has been endorsed, after extensive testing by teachers, schools, and educators.

This practical (and inexpensive) home-learning kit *fascinates* eager young minds from three to ten. The child *hears* the letters or sounds on the phonograph record, *sees* them in his book and repeats them himself. This makes an absorbing *game* of better reading—with amazing results!

FOR EXAMPLE:

- Slow or average readers show sudden, often spectacular improvement in reading, in spelling, in understanding.

- Older children often advance their reading skills several years beyond their age levels.

- Young "pre-schoolers" actually *teach themselves to read* by this simple but startlingly effective phonics method of words, pictures, and records.

6 TEACHING GAMES INCLUDED FREE
Set includes six separate "word building" games. All six are sent with your Listen and Learn Phonics Set FREE of charge!

TEACHERS & PARENTS ACCLAIM RESULTS
"I received your Combination Teaching Set and am positively delighted with it! . . . your marvelous approach to reading is just what we need."
Mrs. Rogavin, Central High School, Snyder, N.Y.

"We purchased 'Listen and Learn With Phonics' . . . for our nine year old son . . . within two weeks his reading had improved 100%."
Mrs. Gregory Knight, San Leandro, Cal.

4-MONTH UNCONDITIONAL GUARANTEE
If not delighted with the progress shown by your child—just return the set for complete refund.

These "Learning Tools" Simple to Use!
You don't need special teaching skills to use this program. Nor do you need any special knowledge of phonics.

In fact, your child needs no special supervision on your part. This set is so simple, so fascinating, he can learn "on his own" *without help.*

10-DAY FREE TRIAL—PLUS 4-MONTH MONEY-BACK GUARANTEE!
Results are so dramatic, the publishers will make the complete kit available to your child with an equally dramatic FREE trial and guarantee.

Under the terms of this unusual offer you can test the kit free of charge for ten days. Moreover you may use the kit for four months and then return it for *full refund* if you're not completely satisfied with your child's progress!

See for yourself how fast your child can learn to read. Just fill out and mail the coupon below. There's no obligation, and six teaching games are included free—yours to keep whether you buy or not. Americana Interstate, a division of Grolier, Inc., publishers of Book of Knowledge, Mundelein, Ill.

THE RED WORD BOX

THREE UNBREAKABLE 33⅓ RPM RECORDS

LETTER AND WORD STRIPS

FOUR ILLUSTRATED WORD BOOKS

TURN-A-WORD GAME

Good Housekeeping

MAIL COUPON FOR 10-DAY FREE TRIAL!

CAREER INSTITUTE, MUNDELEIN, ILL. 60060 P2-593

Send me for Free Examination, complete Listen and Learn with Phonics plus Free Educational Games. If not satisfied at the end of 10 days, I may return the $19.95 set and owe nothing. Otherwise, I'll send a first payment of $5.90 and then 3 monthly payments of $5 each which includes shipping and handling.

Name_____
Address_____
City_____State_____Zip_____
Child's Grade Level_____ Your Phone No._____

☐ SAVE! Enclose check or money order for $19.95 and we pay shipping and handling. Same free trial privilege with full immediate refund guaranteed. (Illinois residents add $1.00 Sales Tax.)
   This offer available in Canada. Canadian residents mail coupon to Illinois address. Shipment of books and all services will be handled within Canada.

This classic ad, appearing in scores of publications over a period of years, consistently outpulled all ads tested against it. Its success may well be attributed to the major headline's strong appeal to parental pride.

Another semantically rich word is *shoestring*. You'd be a fool to start a business with inadequate capital, but if you succeed, you are a *wizard*, and your inadequate capital is seen in retrospect as a *shoestring*. Harian Publications got the idea of linking these two words with a couple of modest connectives and achieved verbal nuclear fusion that sold thousands of books on low-cost travel: "Europe on a Shoestring."

Because there is no copyright on semantic discoveries, Simon & Schuster could capitalize on Harian's discovery and publish its *$1 Complete Guide to Florida*. In fact, it was so successful it broke the mail-order "rule" that a product selling for only $1 cannot be profitably sold in print ads.

For the word *Europe*, Simon & Schuster simply substituted another semantically rich word, *Florida*, and came up with another powerful winner. A one-inch advertisement using this headline drew thousands of responses at a profitable cost per order, even when the tiny ad appeared to be completely lost on a 2,400-line page filled with larger ads screaming for attention.

The fascinating thing about this kind of verbal nuclear fusion is that once it has been achieved it can be repeated almost endlessly—not only in the same form, but in other forms as well. For example, a real breakthrough in selling *Motor's Auto Repair Manual* was achieved many years ago with the headline, "Now You Can Lick Any Auto Repair Job." Every single word made a contribution to the power of the headline, as indeed each word always does in an effective headline. *Now* made the ad a news event, even after it had been running for years. *You*, perhaps the sweetest word ever sounded to the ears, made it clear that the benefit included the reader and not just professional auto mechanics. *Can*, another great word, promises power, achievement. *Lick* promises not only sure mastery but sweet triumph. Notice how much richer it is than *do*. *Any* increases the breadth of the promise to the outermost limit. *Auto* selects the prospect and defines the field of interest. *Repair* defines the proposition, and *job* emphasizes the completeness of its scope.

Once this breakthrough had been achieved, it was possible to make the same statement in many different ways with equal success. "Now Any Auto Repair Job Can Be 'Duck Soup' for You." "Now Any Auto Repair Job Can Be Your 'Meat,'" and so on.

Engineer is a rich many-faceted word. To an artist or a writer the word can connote a literal-minded square. To an engineer's prospective mother-in-law, it can connote a good provider. To an engineer, it means a degree in engineering and professional standing earned by hard study at college. But to the manual and semiskilled workers in an electronics plant, our agency reasoned, in developing appeals for the Cleveland Institute of Electronics, the word *engineer* suggests the college-educated know-it-alls in the plant—an object of envy on the part of the worker and of secret derision born of that envy. We couldn't promise, "You too can be an engineer," because *engineer* by itself is taken to mean a graduate engineer, and completion of CIE courses doesn't provide college credits or a college degree. However, many of the job titles in our promotion, such as *broadcast engineer*, *field engineer*, or *sales engineer*, have the word *engineer* in them without requiring a college degree. So we were legitimately able to promise prospective enrollees the prestige and other rewards of being an engineer in an ad headed, "Become a 'Non-Degree' Engineer." (See Exhibit 18–3.)

Semantic considerations like these cause mail order people to spend hours discussing and tinkering with a single headline or even a single word in the headline. It will pay you to study the mail order headlines you see used over and over again and try to analyze and apply the semantic secret of their success.

Building In the "Hook"

A successful direct marketing ad must compete fiercely for the reader's time and attention. No matter how great the copy is, it will be wasted if the headline does not compel reading. Most successful headlines have a "hook" to catch readers and pull them in. The most common hooks are such words as *why, how, new, now, this, what.* They make the reader want to know the answer, *Why* is it? *How* does it? *What* is it?

Consider the flat statement:

Increasing your vocabulary can help you get ahead in life.

This is merely an argumentative, pontifical claim. It doesn't lead anywhere. But notice how the addition of just one word changes the whole meaning and the mood:

How increasing your vocabulary can help you get ahead in life.

This unstylish, uncreative headline, and the copy that followed sold hundreds of thousands of copies of a vocabulary book. It selected the prospects (people who were interested in larger vocabularies), it promised an ultimate benefit (success), and it built in a hook (how).

Of course, the hook can be merely implied. There is no hook word in the headline "Become a 'Non-Degree' Engineer." But there is a clear implication that the copy will tell you how to achieve this.

Writing the Lead

Perhaps the most troublesome and important part of any piece of mail order copy is the lead, or opening. A lead that "grabs" readers doesn't guarantee that they will read the rest of the copy. But one that fails to grab them does guarantee that they won't read the rest.

Always remember in writing or judging a lead that your readers have better things to do than sit around and read your advertising. They don't really want to read your copy—until you make them want to. And your lead must make them want to.

A common error in writing leads is failure to get to the point immediately— or at least to *point* to the point. Haven't you had the experience of listening

Exhibit 18–3.   The Power of Semantics

How to Become a "Non-Degree" Engineer in the Booming World of Electronics

Thousands of real engineering jobs are being filled by men without engineering degrees. The pay is good, the future bright. Here's how to qualify...

By G. O. ALLEN

President, Cleveland Institute of Electronics

THE BIG BOOM IN ELECTRONICS—and the resulting shortage of graduate engineers—has created a new breed of professional man: the "non-degree" engineer. He has an income and prestige few men achieve without going to college. Depending on the branch of electronics he's in, he may "ride herd" over a flock of computers, run a powerful TV transmitter, supervise a service department, or work side by side with distinguished scientists designing and testing new electronic miracles.

According to one recent survey, in military-connected work alone 80% of the civilian field engineers are not college graduates. Yet they enjoy officer status and get generous *per diem* allowances in addition to their excellent salaries.

In TV and radio, you qualify for the key job of Broadcast Engineer if you have an FCC License, whether you've gone to college or not.

Now You Can Learn at Home

To qualify, however, you do need to know more than soldering, testing circuits, and replacing components. You need to really know your electronics theory—and to prove it by getting an FCC Commercial License.

Now you can master electronics theory at home, in your spare time. Over the last 30 years, here at Cleveland Institute of Electronics, we've perfected AUTO-PROGRAMMED™ lessons that make learning at home easy, even if you once had trouble studying. To help you even more, your instructor gives the homework you send in his undivided personal attention—it's like being the only student in his "class." He even mails back his corrections and comments the same day he gets your work, so you hear from him while everything is still fresh in your mind.

Does it work? I'll say! Better than 9 out of 10 CIE men who take the U.S. Government's tough FCC licensing exam *pass it on their very first try.* (Among non-CIE men, 2 out of 3 who take the exam *fail.*) That's why we can promise in writing to refund your tuition in full if you complete one of our FCC courses and fail to pass the licensing exam.

Students who have taken other courses often comment on how much more they learn from us. Says Mark E. Newland of Santa Maria, Calif.:

"Of 11 different correspondence courses I've taken, CIE's was the best prepared, most interesting, and easiest to understand. I passed my 1st Class FCC exam after completing my course, and have increased my earnings by $120 a month."

Mail Coupon for 2 Free Books

Thousands of today's "non-degree" engineers started by reading our 2 free books: (1) Our school catalog "How to Succeed in Electronics," describing opportunities in electronics, our teaching methods, and our courses, and (2) our special booklet, "How to Get a Commercial FCC License." To receive both without cost or obligation, mail coupon below.

CIE   **Cleveland Institute of Electronics**
1776 E. 17th St. Dept. PS-6, Cleveland, Ohio 44114

Cleveland Institute of Electronics
1776 East 17th Street, Dept. PS-6, Cleveland, Ohio 44114

Please send me without cost or obligation:
1. Your 40-page booklet describing the job opportunities in Electronics today, how your courses can prepare me for them, your methods of instruction, and your special student services.
2. Your booklet on "How to Get a Commercial FCC License."

I am especially interested in:
☐ **Electronics Technology**   ☐ **Electronic Communications**
☐ **First Class FCC License**   ☐ **Industrial Electronics**
☐ **Broadcast Engineering**   ☐ **Advanced Engineering**

Name................................... Age ......
        (Please print)

Address......................................

City .... State .... Zip.......

Present Job Title ....

Accredited Member National Home Study Council
A Leader in Electronics Training...Since 1934

The power of semantics is shown in this strong headline. It incorporates many favorable connotations in the promise to become a ''non-degree engineer.''

to a friend or associate or public speaker who is trying to tell you something but is not able to get to the point? Remember how impatient you felt as you fumed inwardly, "Get to the point!" Your readers feel that same way about copy—and can very easily yawn and turn away. A good roundabout lead is not impossible, but it takes a brilliant writer.

A good principle to follow is that the copy should proceed from the headline. That is, if your headline announces what you are there to talk about, then you should get down to business and talk about it. Although it is true that some successful advertising merely continues the message started by the headline or display copy, there is far less danger of confusion if the copy repeats and expands the headline message, exactly the way a good news item does.

Notice how marvelously these leads from the *Wall Street Journal* news columns form a bridge between the headlines and the rest of the stories:

NEW POSTAGE-STAMP INK TO SPEED MAIL PROCESSING
NEW YORK—U.S. postage stamps will soon be tagged with a special luminescent ink that will permit automatic locating and canceling of the stamps to speed processing of the mail.

AFFLUENT AMERICANS AWASH IN DOCUMENTS SNAP UP HOME SAFES
NEW YORK—There's a popular new home appliance that won't wash a dish, dry a diaper, or keep a steak on ice. It's a safe. And it's being propelled into prominence by a paperwork explosion.

Notice, too, that although the lead restates the thought of the headline, it does it in a different way, recapping the thought but also advancing the story.

Classic Copy Structure

In a classic mail order copy argument, a good lead should be visualized as the first step in a straight path of feeling and logic from the headline or display theme to the concluding call for action. In that all-important first step, the readers should be able to see clearly where the path is taking them. Otherwise they might not want to go. (This is the huge error of ads that seek to pique your curiosity with something irrelevant and then make a tie-in to the real point. Who's got time for satisfying that much curiosity these days?)

The sections of a classic copy argument can be labeled *problem, promise of solution, explanation of promise, proof,* and *call to action*. However, if you're going to start with the problem, it seems like a good idea at least to hint right away at the forthcoming solution. Then the readers won't mind your not getting to the point right away, as long as they know where you're going. A generation ago, when the pace of life was slower, a brilliant copywriter could get away with spending the first third of his copy leisurely outlining the problem before finally getting around to the solution. But in today's more hectic times, it's riskier.

Here is an ad seeking Duraclean dealers in which the problem lead contains the promise of solution:

I found the easy way to escape from being a ''wage slave.''

I kept my job while my customer list grew . . . then found myself in a high-profit business. Five years ago, I wouldn't have believed that I could be where I am today.

I was deeply in debt. My self-confidence had been shaken by a disastrous business setback. Having nobody behind me, I had floundered and failed for lack of experience, help, and guidance.

The copy could have started out simply, ''Five years ago, I was deeply in debt,'' and so on. But the promise of happier days to come provides a carrot on a stick, drawing us down the garden path. You could argue that the headline had already announced the promise. But in most cases, good copy should be able to stand alone and make a complete argument even if all the display type were removed.

Here, from an ad for isometric exercises, is an example of the flashback technique referred to earlier:

[*Starts with the promise*]

Imagine a 6-second exercise that helps you keep fit better than 24 push-ups. Or another that's capable of doubling muscular strength in 3 weeks!

Both of these ''quickie'' exercises are part of a fantastically simple body-building method developed by Donald J. Salls, Alabama Doctor of Education, fitness expert, and coach. His own trim physique, his family's vigorous health and the nail-hard brawn of his teams are dramatic proof of the results he gets—not to mention the steady stream of reports from housewives, athletes, even school children who have discovered Dr. Salls' remarkable exercises.

[*Flashback to problem*]

Most Americans find exercise a tedious chore. Yet we all recognize the urgent personal and social needs for keeping our bodies strong, shapely, and healthy. What man wouldn't take secret pride in displaying a more muscular figure?

What woman doesn't long for a slimmer, more attractive figure? The endless time and trouble required to get such results has been a major, if not impossible hurdle for so many of us. But now [*return to the promise*] doctors, trainers, and physical educators are beginning to recommend the easy new approach to body fitness and contour control that Dr. Salls has distilled down to his wonderfully simple set of 10 exercises.

Of course, a really strong, exciting promise doesn't necessarily need a statement of the problem at all. If you're selling a ''New Tree That Grows a Foot a Month,'' it could be argued that you don't actually have to spell out how frustrating it is to spend years waiting for ordinary trees to grow; this is well known and implied.

Other Ways to Structure Copy

There are as many different ways to structure a piece of advertising copy as there are to build a house. But response advertising, whether in publication or direct mail, has special requirements. The general advertiser is satisfied with making an impression, but the response advertiser must stimulate immediate action. Your copy must pile up in your readers' minds argument after argument, sales point after sales point, until their resistance collapses under the sheer weight of your persuasiveness, and they do what you ask.

One of the greatest faults in the copy of writers who are not wise in the ways of response is failure to apply this steadily increasing pressure. This may sound like old-fashioned "hard sell," but, ideally, the impression your copy makes should be just the opposite. The best copy, like the best salesperson, does not appear to be selling at all, but simply to be sharing information or proposals of mutual benefit to the buyer and seller.

Of course, in selling certain kinds of staple merchandise, copy structuring is not important. There the advertising can be compared to a painting in that the aim is to convey as much as possible at first glance and then convey more and more with each repeated look. You wouldn't sell a 35-piece electric drill set with a 1,000-word essay, but rather you would sell it by spreading out the set in glowing full-color illustrations richly studded with "feature call-outs." But where you are engaged in selling intangibles, an idea or ideas instead of familiar merchandise, the way you structure your copy can be vitally important.

In addition to the classic form mentioned above, here are some other ways to structure copy. With the "cluster-of-diamonds" technique, you assemble a great many precious details of what you are selling and present them to the reader in an appropriate setting. A good example is the "67 Reasons Why" subscription advertising of *U. S. News & World Report*, listing 67 capsule descriptions of typical recent news articles in the magazine. The "setting"—the surrounding copy containing general information and argumentation—is as important as the specific jewels in the cluster. Neither would be sufficiently attractive without the other.

The "string-of-pearls" technique is similar but not quite the same. Each "pearl" is a complete little gem of selling, and a number of them are simply strung together in almost any sequence to make a chain. David Ogilvy's "Surprising Amsterdam" series of ads is like this. Each surprising fact about Amsterdam is like a small-space ad for the city, but only when all these little ads are strung together do you feel compelled to get up from your easy chair and send for those KLM brochures. This technique is especially useful, by the way, when you have a vast subject like an encyclopedia to discuss. You have not one but many stories to tell. If you simply ramble on and on, most readers won't stay with you. So make a little list of stories you want to tell, write a tight little one-paragraph essay on each point, announce the subject of each essay in a boldface subhead, and then string them all together like pearls, with an appropriate beginning and ending.

The "fan dancers" technique is like a line of chorus girls equipped with Sally Rand fans. The dancers are always about to reveal their secret charms, but they never quite do. You've seen this kind of copy many times. One of the best examples is the circular received in answer to an irresistible classified ad in *Popular Mechanics*. The ad simply said "505 odd, successful enterprises. Expect something odd." The circular described the entire contents of a book of money-making ideas in maddening fashion. Something like: "No. 24. Here's an idea that requires nothing but old coat hangers. A retired couple on a Kansas farm nets $240 weekly with this one." "No. 25. All you need is a telephone—you don't call them, they call you to give their orders. A bedridden woman in Montpelier nets $70 a week this way." And so on.

With the "machine gun" technique, you simply spray facts and arguments in the general direction of the reader, in the hope that at least some of them will hit. This is called the *no-structure stucture*, and it is the first refuge of the amateur. If you have a great product and manage to convey your enthusiasm for it through the sheer exuberance of your copy, you will succeed, not because of your technique, but despite it. And the higher the levels of taste and education of your readers, the less chance you will have.

Establishing the Uniqueness of Your Product or Service

What is the unique claim to fame of the product or service you are selling? This could be one of your strongest selling points. The word *only* is a great advertising word. If what you offer is "better" or "best," this is merely a claim in support of your argument that the reader *should* come to you for the product or services offered. But if what you are offering is the "only" one of its kind, then readers *must* come to you if they want the benefits that only you can offer.

Here are some ways in which you might be able to stake out a unique position in the marketplace for the product or service you are selling: "We're the largest." People respect bigness in a company or a sales total. They reason that if a product leads the others in its field, it must be good. Thus "No. 1 Best-Seller" is always a potent phrase, for it is not just an airy claim but a hard fact that proves some kind of merit.

But what if you're *not* the largest? Perhaps you can still establish a unique position, as in "We're the largest of our kind." By simply defining your identity more sharply, you might still be able to claim some kind of size superiority. For example, there was the Trenton merchant who used to boast that he had "the largest clothing store in the world in a garage!"

A mail order photo finisher decided that one benefit it had to sell was the sheer bigness of its operation. It wasn't the biggest—that distinction belonged, of course, to Eastman Kodak. But it was second. And Eastman Kodak was involved in selling a lot of other things, too, such as film and cameras and chemicals. Its photo-finishing service was only one of many divisions. So the advertiser was able to fashion a unique claim: "America's Largest *Independent* Photo Finisher."

"We're the fastest-growing." If you're on the way to becoming the largest, that's about as impressive a proof of merit as being the largest. In fact, it can be even more impressive, because it adds the excitement of the underdog coming up fast. *U.S. News & World Report* used this to good effect during the 1950s while its circulation was growing from approximately 400,000 to about three times that figure: "America's Fastest-Growing News-magazine." Later, the same claim was used effectively for Capitol Record Club, "America's Fastest-Growing Record Club."

"We offer a unique combination of advantages." It could be that no one claim you can make is unique, but that none of your competitors is able to equal your claim that you have *all* of a certain number of advantages.

In the early 1960s, the Literary Guild began to compete in earnest with the Book-of-the-Month Club (BOMC). The Literary Guild started offering books that compared very favorably with those offered by BOMC. But the latter had a couple of unique claims that the Guild couldn't match—BOMC's distinguished board of judges, and its book-dividend system, with a history of having distributed $375 million worth of books to members.

How to compete? The Guild couldn't claim the greatest savings; one of Doubleday's other clubs actually saved the subscriber more off the publisher's price. It couldn't claim that it had books offered by no other club; some of Doubleday's other clubs were offering some of the same books, and even BOMC would sometimes make special arrangements to offer a book being featured by the Guild.

But the Guild was able to feature a unique set of advantages that undoubtedly played a part in the success it has enjoyed: "Only the Literary Guild saves you 40–60 percent on books like these as soon as they are published." Other clubs could make either of these two claims, but only the Guild could claim both.

"We have a uniquely advantageous location." A classic of this was James Webb Young's great ad for "Old Jim Young's Mountain Grown Apples—Every Bite Crackles, and the Juice Runs Down Your Lips." In it Jim Young, trader, tells how the natives snickered when his pappy bought himself an abandoned homestead in a little valley high up in the Jemes Mountains. But "Pappy" Young, one of the slickest farmers ever to come out of Madison Avenue, knew that "this little mountain valley is just a natural apple spot—as they say some hillsides are in France for certain wine grapes. The summer sun beats down into this valley all day, to color and ripen apples perfectly; but the cold mountain air drains down through it at night to make them crisp and firm. Then it turns out that the soil there is full of volcanic ash, and for some reason that seems to produce apples with a flavor that is really something.''

Haband Ties used to make a big thing out of being located in Paterson, New Jersey, the silk center of the nation. Even though most of the company's ties and other apparel were made of synthetic fibers, somehow the idea of buying ties from the silk center made the reader feel he was buying ties at the very source. In the same way, maple syrup from Vermont should be a lot easier to sell than maple syrup from Arizona.

Finally, suppose you believe that you have something unique to sell, but you hesitate to start an argument with your competitors by making a flat claim that they might challenge. In that case, you can imply your uniqueness by the way in which you word the claim. ''Here's one mouthwash that keeps your mouth sweet and fresh all day long'' doesn't flatly claim that it's the only one. It simply says, ''at least *we've* got this desirable quality, whether any other product does or not.'' *Newsweek* identified itself as ''the news magazine that separates fact from opinion—a powerful use of that innocent word *the* that devastates the competition.

''Versatility'' Campaign: Apple Computer

The computer market is huge, and the competition is fierce. Among the unquestioned leaders is Apple Macintosh Computer Systems.

Situation.   The small-business market includes over 22 million desk workers. This group's aggregate expenditures for personal computers come to $12 billion. This market had generated sizable revenue prior to the ''Versatility'' campaign. However, Apple's position was eroding at the time.

Strategy.   Apple developed a three-year plan, designed to capitalize on the small-business market opportunity. A direct response print ad was developed to qualify high-potential prospects. (See Exhibit 18–4.) The ad was directed to any small-business owner who might come upon it in general business publications. The same ad appeared in vertical publications directed to such fields as accounting, law, real estate, engineering and design, architecture, communications, advertising, and publishing.

Results.   When Wunderman Worldwide, the agency, saw the results, it noted that the ad appealing to all small businesses did very well in general business publications but not so well in vertical publications. So the agency developed a new strategy for vertical publications: version copy to each category of business being pursued. Responses doubled! (See Exhibit 18–5 for versioned copy targeted to the communications field.)

Exhibit 18–4.   Direct Response Ad

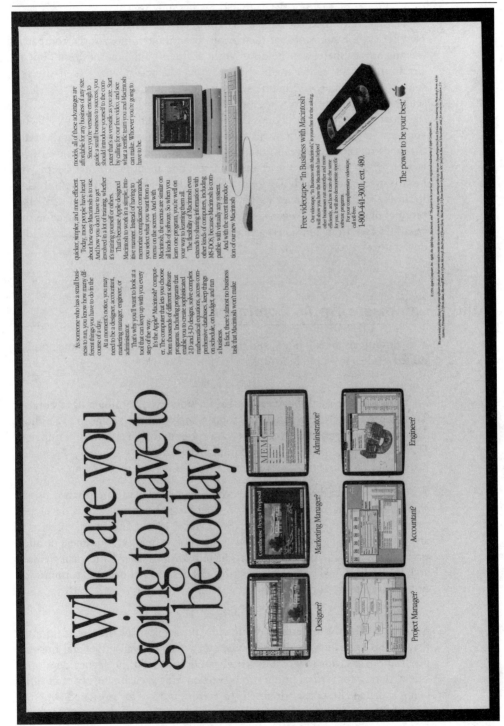

General ad directed to small businesses in all categories.

Exhibit 18–5.   Category Direct Response Ad

Versioned ad directed to the communications field.

A final note: The lack of a coupon was purposeful. It was learned that specifying an 800 number as the only means to respond had a positive effect in qualifying leads. Dealers were sent only qualified leads—small businesses that indicated they were in a position to act immediately.

Effective Use of Testimonials

If you have a great product or service, you have an almost inexhaustible source of great copy practically free—written by your own customers. They will come up with selling phrases straight from the heart that no copywriter, no matter how brilliant, would ever think of. They will write with a depth of conviction that the best copywriters will find hard to equal.

The value of testimonials in mail order advertising has been recognized for nearly 100 years, is generally taken for granted, and nonetheless is frequently overlooked. If a survey were conducted of companies dependent on responses by mail, the survey would undoubtedly reveal that a shockingly high percentage of those companies have no regular, methodical system of soliciting, filing, and using good testimonials. Yet a direct marketing enterprise often stands or falls on whether it makes a good use of testimonials.

Many years ago the Merlite Company was founded to sell the Presto midget fire extinguisher entirely through agents. The advertising job was to pull inquiries from prospective agents, who were then converted to active salespeople by the follow-up direct mail package. One of the first efforts for Merlite was the creation of a testimonials-soliciting letter.

From this letter, which was mailed to a fair number of Merlite's agents, came the story that formed the basis for a successful small-space ad that ran for years and resulted in the sale of thousands of units. The headline: "I'm Making $1,000 a Month—and Haven't Touched Bottom Yet!" In those days, $1,000 a month was big money. It represented just about the wildest dreams of people of modest means. If the ad had claimed, "Make $1,000 a month selling this amazing little device," it would have sounded like a hard-to-believe get-rich-quick scheme. But the fact that an actual agent said it (his name and picture appeared in every ad) made the possibility a fact, not a claim. And the "haven't touched bottom yet" was a homey additional promise that probably no city slicker copywriter would have thought of if he or she were creating a fictional testimonial.

Many U.S. School of Music ads in the past were built around testimonials. Being able to play a musical instrument has a deep meaning for people that could best be expressed by the students themselves. One ad bore a headline extracted from an ecstatic student's comments: "I Can't Believe My Ears—I'm Playing Music! My friends all think it's me, but I keep telling them it's your wonderful course."

You might have received some unsolicited testimonials that you have received permission to use and are already using. But if you expand this collection by setting up a methodical testimonial-soliciting program, you can increase tenfold your effective use of testimonials. Because the quality and usefulness of testimonials vary widely, the more testimonials you pull in, the more pure gold you should be able to pan from the ore.

Of course, it's important to get the testimonial donor's signature on some kind of release giving you permission to use his or her comments, name, and photo, if any. The wording of the releases varies. Some companies are content with a very simple "You have my permission" sentence; others use a more elaborate legal form. Consult your attorney about the kind you choose to use.

Your testimonial-soliciting letter should drop a few gentle hints about your interest in hearing of actual benefits and improvements from your product. Otherwise you'll get too many customers writing similar lines of empty praise such as "it's the greatest" and "it's the finest."

Justify the Price

"Why Such a Bargain? The Answer Is Simple." These eight magic words constitute an important building block in the mail order sale. They have been expressed hundreds of different ways in the past and will appear in hundreds of new forms in the future. But whether in the mail order ads of magazines and direct mail yesterday and today, or the televised, home-printed facsimile transmission of tomorrow, the price justification argument will always be with us. It does an important job of making the low price seem believable and the high price not really so high.

Here are a number of examples of price justification from the past. As you read through them, ask yourself if it isn't likely that similar arguments will still be used in the year 2010.

- *Doubleday Subscription Service:* "How can the Doubleday Subscription Service offer these extremely low prices? The answer is really quite simple. Not everyone wants the same magazines. By getting all the publishers to allow us to make their offers in one mailing, each subscriber has a chance to pick and choose; each magazine gets its most interested readers at the lowest possible cost. The savings are passed on to you in the lowest possible prices for new, introductory subscriptions."

- *Reader's Digest (Music of the World's Great Composers):* "How is this low price possible? Without the great resources of RCA and the large 'audience' of *Reader's Digest*, such a collection would have to cost about $60.00. This sum would be needed to cover royalties to musicians, the cost of recording, transferring sound from tape to records, manufacturing and packaging. But because a single large pressing of records brings down the cost of manufacturing, and because the entire edition is reserved in advance for *Digest* subscribers, you can have these luxury-class records now at a fraction of the usual price for records of such outstanding quality!"

- *Singer (socket wrench and tool set):* "This set is not available in stores but sets like these sell regularly in stores at a much higher price. You save the difference because unlike the usual store which sells just a few sets at a time, we sell many hundreds, thus enabling us to purchase large quantities at big savings which we pass on to you."

Visual Reinforcement of Words and Ideas

Our powers of comprehension are largely built on our earliest sensations and associations. First comes touch, but that won't be much help to advertising until Aldous Huxley's "Feelvision" is invented. Next, when we are several months old, comes image, as we learn to associate Mama's smiling face with getting fed, burped, and changed. Then comes the spoken word, when we learn to call Mama by name. This early experience with the image and the spoken word is what makes television such a potent advertising force.

Our earliest experience with the printed word is usually in our heavily illustrated first reader (or preschool picture book). It is printed in large clear serif type, in lowercase. This is why serif body types seem more readable than sans serif, and lowercase more comfortable than upper. And when the book says, "Oh! See the boy!" sure enough, there is usually a picture of a boy. This makes it less likely that we would stand up in class and read aloud, "Oh! See the dog!"

Advertising has seized on this fact of human development and developed it into an astonishingly effective tool of communication. It has learned, probably far more than ever before in human history, to team words and pictures for greater impact than either alone can achieve. Sometimes it's a rebus in which a picture is substituted for some of the words. For instance, instead of saying "(a summons, a will, a deed, a mortgage, a lease) are a few of the reasons why every family should have a lawyer," an ad for New York Life Insurance Company substituted pictures of documents, such as a will and a mortgage, for the words in parentheses.

Sometimes, it's a pantomime, with the words providing only the necessary minimum of explanation. An Itkin Brothers office furniture ad showed in four pictures what the subhead promised: "In less than 45 minutes you can have four new offices without changing your address, increasing rent, or interrupting work." The pictures were the headline, and the four captions under the photos of the partitions being installed simply read: "8:45 . . . 8:50 . . . 9:15 . . . and 9:25.

Sometimes, it's a visual literalism. For instance, our small-space ad for the U.S. School of Music, headed "Are You Missing Half the Fun of Playing the Guitar?" showed only half a guitar. The instrument was literally sawed in half. Sometimes, it's an abstract picture. How can you picture the abstract concept "two," for instance? Avis made it literal with a photo of two fingers.

Also, the overall appearance of the ad provides visual reinforcement. Even if there are no illustrations, which is often the case, the typography and design can convey a great deal about the kind of company behind the advertising. For decades most mail order advertising was notorious for being less attractive than general advertising; much of it still is. Whether this helps or hurts results is hotly debated. It might be that a certain homey or buckeye look adds an air of unsophisticated honesty and sincerity. But for any company involved in starting an ongoing relationship with a customer, the appearance of its direct marketing advertising should convey that it is a responsible, tasteful, and orderly company with which to do business.

The Response Device

Most direct response ads carry a reply coupon or card for ease of responding. The significant exception is small-space ads. A two-inch ad would have to be about twice as big to accommodate a coupon. Many advertisers find that it does not produce twice as many results.

A black-and-white page with an insert card (a postpaid reply postcard inserted next to the ad) costs about two and a half times more than a black-and-white page alone but usually pulls at least four times as much as a page without coupon. (Advantages of insert cards were explored in Chapter 4.)

There are many variations of the postpaid reply envelope, depending on cost and publication policy: oversize card insert, full-page insert with detachable card, four-page card stock insert with detachable card, eight-page newspaper advertising supplement with bound-in or stuck-on card or envelope, loose envelope (such as for film processing) inserted in Sunday newspapers, and so on.

The creative problem in preparing coupon or card copy is to summarize the message from the advertiser to the prospect as clearly, succinctly, and attractively as possible. Many readers tear out a card or coupon and leave it in a pocket or drawer for days or even weeks before deciding to send it in. At that point, the reader wants to know what this minicontract entails. It is important to provide as much resell and reassurance as possible.

If the advertiser is a club, the coupon copy should clearly spell out terms of membership. Check boxes, numbers to be circled, and other aids to make completing the form easy should be provided wherever possible. Any money-back guarantee, whether already mentioned in the adjoining copy or not, should be clearly stated.

Telescopic Testing

For many years it has been standard practice in direct mail to test simultaneously as many as 5–6 or even 10–12 different copy appeals, formats, or offers. Giving each package equal exposure over a representative variety of lists is probably the most scientifically precise research method in advertising. But this practice has not been as common in publication advertising. There, for a long time, advertisers were limited to the simple A/B split-run test, in which every other copy of a given issue of a publication would contain Ad A and every other copy Ad B (separately keyed, of course). (See Exhibit 18–6.) This too is very precise. The main thing is to make sure that the circulation purchased is large enough to provide a statistically significant variation in results between the two ads. But for testing your way to a breakthrough, it can be slow.

If you test two ads, wait for the results, then test two more, and so on, a year or so could pass before you discover the "hot button." On the other hand, if you test the control against one ad in Publication A and another in Publication B (we often do), it is useful, but it does introduce another variable, the difference in the two publications. A truly scientific test has only one variable.

All our experience and common sense tell us that 6–8 tests are far more likely to produce a hit than only two. To solve this problem, direct marketing advertisers are turning increasingly to multiple ad testing. We call it *telescopic testing*, because it permits the advertiser to telescope a year's testing experience into a single insertion. Telescopic testing simply applies the direct mail principle of multiple testing to publication advertising. But it requires publications or formats with the mechanical capability of running such tests.

Perhaps the first magazine to offer this capability was *TV Guide*. Because television programs are different in each region, *TV Guide* publishes over 80 different regional editions. Theoretically, you could do over 80 different split-runs, one in each regional edition, in a single week. (But you wouldn't, because the circulation for each test would be too small.) By testing Ad A versus Ad B in the first region, Ad A versus Ad C in the next region, and so on, it is possible to test as many as 10 or 15 different ads or ad variations simultaneously. By assigning to Ad A results the numerical value of 100, we can give the other ad results proportionate numerical values and rank them accordingly.

An easier way to do multiple testing is by intermixed card stock inserts bound into a magazine so that Ad A appears in Copy 1, Ad B in Copy 2, Ad C in Copy 3, and so on.

Advertisers began testing new appeals and offers by doing A/B regional splits of black-and-white pages and even half-pages in the local program section of *TV Guide*. The following examples illustrate what can be done:

- A book series achieved a 252 percent improvement.

- A correspondence course inquiry ad was improved 209 percent.

- A name-getting giveaway program brought its advertising cost per coupon down to 19 cents.

The technique of applying telescopic testing is discussed in Chapter 20. Today there are three basic methods of running multiple tests:

Exhibit 18–6.   A/B Copy Test

ADD THIS PRODUCT TO
ANY MOTOR OIL
FOR MORE POWER WITH LESS GAS

Sluggish motors get a new lease on life with Wynn's Friction Proofing Oil. This new chemical compound added to your present brand of motor oil every 1000 miles, bonds a super-slick surface to engine parts. This virtually eliminates the friction drag that wastes up to half your car's power, and gives you so much extra mileage from gasoline that it's like getting one gallon free with every ten you buy. Besides paying for itself in gasoline savings, Wynn's cuts carbon and sludge, frees sticky valves, reduces wear and repairs. Try Wynn's for new pep, power, economy from your car. We're so sure you'll continue to use it that we make this special introductory offer of a regular 1000-mile size 95¢ can of Wynn's for only 10¢. Just send your name and address, enclosing 10¢ in coin or stamps. By return mail you'll get a certificate entitling you to a 95¢ can of Wynn's without additional charge at any Wynn dealer. Limit one. Offer expires April 30. Write today—Wynn Oil Company, Dept. A-4, Azusa California.

AT SERVICE STATIONS, GARAGES, NEW CAR DEALERS

CAR OWNERS! SAVE ONE
GALLON OF GAS IN EVERY TEN

Sluggish motors get a new lease on life with Wynn's Friction Proofing Oil. This new chemical compound added to your present brand of motor oil every 1000 miles, bonds a super-slick surface to engine parts. This virtually eliminates the friction drag that wastes up to half your car's power, and gives you so much extra mileage from gasoline that it's like getting one gallon free with every ten you buy. Besides paying for itself in gasoline savings, Wynn's cuts carbon and sludge, frees sticky valves, reduces wear and repairs. Try Wynn's for new pep, power, economy from your car. We're so sure you'll continue to use it that we make this special introductory offer of a regular 1000-mile size 95¢ can of Wynn's for only 10¢. Just send your name and address, enclosing 10¢ in coin or stamps. By return mail you'll get a certificate entitling you to a 95¢ can of Wynn's without additional charge at any Wynn dealer. Limit one. Offer expires April 30. Write today—Wynn Oil Company, Dept. C-12, Azusa, California.

AT SERVICE STATIONS, GARAGES, NEW CAR DEALERS

The makers of Wynn's Friction Proofing Oil wanted to test two different sales appeals: (1) get more power with less gas; (2) save one gallon of gas in every ten. These two "reader ads" were written to test the appeals. The second appeal brought twice as many sample requests as the first one.

1. Simultaneous split-runs in regional editions of a magazine that offers such a service, with one ad used as a control in all the splits

2. Free-standing stuffers or loose newspaper preprints, intermixed at the printing plant before being supplied to the publication

3. Full-page card inserts in magazines, intermixed at the printing plant

It's a rather expensive game to play, but major direct marketers today are playing for multimillion-dollar stakes. All it takes is one breakthrough to pay for all the necessary research in a very short time.

A dramatic example of the application of telescopic testing is provided by a series of six ads created for *Consumer Reports* and tested simultaneously against the control ad via intermixed bound-in inserts in *TV Guide*. Shown in Exhibit 18–7 is the first page of the seven insert tests. Study each carefully and see whether you can give ratings for Ads A through G.

Have you rated the ads? Now let's review the actual results by coupon count. Ranking Ad A—the control ad—as 100, here is the relative pull of each ad, courtesy of Joel Feldman, director of marketing/circulation for the magazine at the time:

Ad A—100 (control)	Ad E—65
Ad B—107	Ad F—61
Ad C—101	Ad G—33
Ad D—82	

Although the 7 percent gain scored by the winner, Ad B, might not seem like a startling improvement, it is important to keep in mind that this 7 percent was on top of the impressive gains scored by Ad A, the winner in previous tests. And the circulation of 500,000 given to each ad resulted in a sufficiently large number of responses to make the results highly significant statistically. So thanks to this test, the client could be confident that future publication advertising would be 7 percent more efficient—a substantial gain when applied to millions of dollars worth of advertising.

Creating "Stopping Power" for Your Ads

As a final thrust toward getting more of your ads read and acted on, let's explore some unique techniques for stopping the reader as he or she flips through a magazine or newspaper. These techniques were developed by creative directors of the far-flung Young & Rubicam network of agencies around the world. The premise of "stopping power" is that if you can stop a person long enough to read an intriguing headline, your chances of getting the person to read and act on the rest of the ad are greatly enhanced.

Hanley Norins, a former creative director at Young & Rubicam West, put the entire Y&R training program into perspective in a remarkable book, *The*

Exhibit 18–7.   Control Ads in Insert Test

A.

B.

C.

D.

Exhibit 18–7   (Continued).

E.

F.

G.

Young & Rubicam Traveling Creative Workshop.[1] He devoted one chapter to direct marketing and direct response advertising. The seven principles of "stopping power" are detailed as follows:

1. Attracts the defined target audience, plus an audience beyond

2. Demands participation

3. Forces an emotional response by touching on a basic human want or need

4. Creates a desire to know more

5. Surprises the reader

6. Exposes expected information in an unexpected way

7. Breaks with the personality and rules of the product category

These seven principles give the creative person a "cafeteria list" of guidelines, any of which may be selected as appropriate for a given headline. The techniques of applying "stopping power" give the creative person eight different options for applying the principles:

1. Open-minded narrative (picture or thought) in which the resolution is not presented

2. Ironic twists on ordinary behavior

3. Play on words in the headline

4. Incongruity of visual elements and/or words by unusual juxtaposition of elements

5. Exaggeration

6. Simplification

7. Shocking visual and/or headline

8. Participation visuals (e.g., tests, games, multiple visuals)

SELF-QUIZ

1. Good direct response advertising should make its strongest appeal to

_____

_____

[1] Prentice Hall, 1990.

2. Who are the best prospects?

_____

_____

_____

3. In print advertising, advantages belong to the _____

_____

Benefits belong to the _____

_____

4. When are benefits more important?

_____

_____

5. When are advantages more important?

_____

_____

6. Fill in this list of ultimate benefits:

a. _____   j. _____

b. _____   k. _____

c. _____   l. _____

d. _____   m. _____

e. _____   n. _____

f. _____   o. _____

g. _____   p. _____

h. _____   q. _____

i. _____

7. Semantics is the hydrogen bomb of _____.

8. Most successful headlines have a "hook" to catch the reader and pull him or her in. The most common hooks are such words as:

a. _____   b. _____

c. _____   e. _____

d. _____   f. _____

9. A common error in writing leads is that the writer _____

_____

10. A good writing principle is that body copy should _____

_____

11. What labels may be applied to the sections of a classic copy argument?

    a. _____

    b. _____

    c. _____

    d. _____

    e. _____

12. Name four other ways to structure copy.

    a. _____

    b. _____

    c. _____

    d. _____

13. What four-letter word is a great advertising word?

    _____

14. Name five unique claims to fame that can prove to be the strongest selling
    points for a product or service.

    a. _____

    b. _____

    c. _____

    d. _____

    e. _____

15. What is the major advantage of using testimonials in direct response
    advertising?

_____

_____

_____

_____

16. Name an important building block in the mail order sale.

_____

_____

_____

_____

17. Name four ways you can give visual reinforcement to words and ideas.

    a. _____

    b. _____

    c. _____

    d. _____

18. When is a coupon not indicated for a direct response ad?

_____

_____

_____

_____

19. Define *telescopic testing*.

_____

_____

_____

_____

20. What are the three basic methods of running multiple tests?

    a. _____

    b. _____

    c. _____

21. Define *stopping power*.

_____

PILOT PROJECT

You are a copywriter by profession. You have just been employed by a direct response advertising agency. The agency has been appointed by a home study school offering a course in accounting. Your copy supervisor has asked you to come up with headlines designed to get inquiries. Develop one headline for each of these ultimate benefits:

Health: _____

_____

Money: _____

_____

Security: _____

_____

Pride: _____

_____

Approval: _____

_____

Enjoyment: _____

_____

Excitement: _____

_____

Power: _____

_____

Fulfillment: _____

_____

Freedom: _____

_____

Identity: _____

_____

Relaxation: _____

_____

Escape: _____

_____

Curiosity: _____

_____

Possessions: _____

_____

Sex: _____

_____

Hunger: _____

_____

SECTION V

Testing and Measuring

CHAPTER NINETEEN

Mathematics of Direct Marketing

The Basic Strands

The mathematics of direct marketing is a high-tension web of interacting revenues and costs supported by three strands: sales, marketing cost, and contribution to marketing cost and profit. There is no single balance of the strands that is right for all direct marketing businesses, but similar threads exist in all direct marketing programs. Direct marketers need to learn the elements in general, quantify them for their specific situation, and then determine which can be tuned to create a stronger business. (See Exhibit 19–1.)

The unique ability to track and measure results of specific marketing decisions supports a high level of analysis. The belief that the future will be somewhat similar to the past supports reasonable forecasting of the probable results from marketing decisions. The availability of individual specific databases, computers, and statistics supports differential marketing investment at the customer level.

The challenge to the direct marketer is to identify, evaluate, and respond to the vast amount of available marketing information without drowning in

We are indebted to Bob Kestnbaum, founder of Kestnbaum & Company, and to Pamela Ames, his vice president of 14 years, for this chapter. The Kestnbaum organization has as clients all the major general mail order houses, leading specialty firms like L.L. Bean and Bear Creek, and telephone companies, banks and insurance companies, automotive manufacturers, and major airlines.

Exhibit 19–1.   Three Strands Support the Web of Direct Marketing
Arithmetic

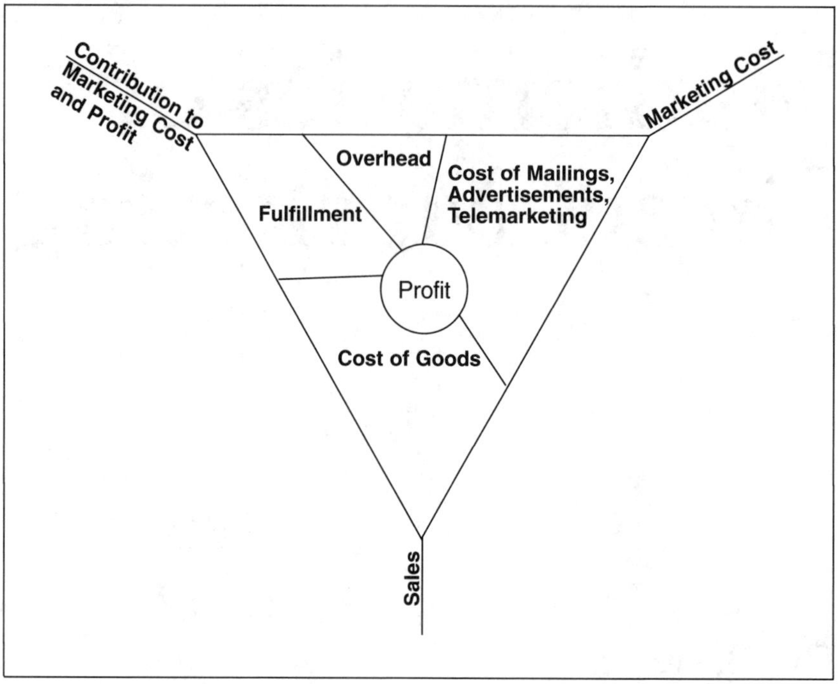

the flow. The decision to spend marketing money is applied at the individual customer level, but in actuality, the marketer usually keeps the number of decisions within reason by identifying groups of customers with similar propensities to buy. The marketer never bets on an individual's buying behavior, but willingly bets on the combined buying behavior of sets of people, usually thousands at a time.

Single Transaction Costs and Contribution to Marketing Costs and Profit

A convenient starting point for understanding any direct marketing activity is to determine the amount of money from a single transaction that is available for marketing costs and profit after direct costs associated with the transaction are subtracted. This entails working with averages, cost allocations, and the cost structure of the full business. These direct costs are known before marketing decisions and are often relatively stable over long periods. If different marketing programs have different average transaction sizes and cost structures associated with them, then each must be analyzed separately.

At a very high level, the direct costs can be classified into three categories: merchandise or service, fulfillment, and direct overhead. The merchandise or service costs should include all expenses and staffing related to purchasing, making, transporting, and storing the product(s) or service(s) being sold, often including warehouse costs. Fulfillment costs should include all costs and people related to processing, filling, and delivering an order. Usually such diverse items as customer service, bad debt, costs of returns and exchanges, and charges for payment by credit card are included in fulfillment. Direct overhead can include costs associated with computer services, finance/accounting, office space, and a charge for some management and staff.

Exhibit 19–2 shows a very simple example of this idea. This company has two quite different products or buying levels with average transaction sizes of $50 and $80. Notice that we have chosen to treat shipping and handling charges paid by the customer as an offset to fulfillment costs. Some companies list shipping and handling revenues as other income that would increase both the average order and the fulfillment costs but not change the contribution to marketing costs and profit. However, all of the percentages would change. Notice in the exhibit that the fulfillment cost of $6 is the same for both orders. If the nature of transactions in a given business is reasonably similar, fulfillment tends to be a constant cost per transaction or a fixed cost plus a variable component for each line item in the transaction.

As a reminder that this is a very high level view, Exhibit 19–3 shows a possible breakdown of this $6 fulfillment cost. Even this list is simplified, but it shows that considerable analysis can be applied to determine reasonable values for each of the direct cost elements. Usually companies perform these analyses over a long time, as much as a year. If there is a strong seasonality to the business, it might be better to work in seasons or half years.

It might seem strange to exclude all marketing costs from these calculations, but the goal is to understand the share of revenue committed to "fulfilling the promise" if a customer makes a purchase. These costs are relatively fixed, predictable, and stable. The revenue remaining after covering these direct costs can be applied to paying marketing costs and obtaining some profit. Exhibit 19–4 shows how this approach divides revenue into these direct costs and the contribution to marketing cost and profit.

Exhibit 19–2. Contribution to Marketing Cost and Profit

	Offer A	Offer B
Average transaction (goods only, no S&H)	$50.00	$80.00
Cost of goods	20.00 (40.0%)	36.00 (45.0%)
Fulfillment (after S&H revenue offset)	6.00 (12.0%)	6.00 (7.5%)
Overhead	5.00 (10.0%)	8.00 (10.0%)
Contribution to marketing cost and profit	$19.00 (38.0%)	$30.00 (37.5%)

Exhibit 19–3.   Cost Detail for Fulfillment of Transaction during Fall Season

Cost Center	Assumptions	Cost per Transaction
Transaction processing	All transactions	$3.53
Inbound phone	70% of transactions at $3.50/call	2.45
Credit card discount	75% of transactions at 2.5%/transaction	1.65
Customer service	6% of transaction at $8/case	0.48
Returns and exchanges	3% of transactions at $15/case	0.45
Collections and bad debt	0.5% of transactions at $88/case	0.44
Pick and pack	All transactions	1.75
Postage	All transactions	2.91
Management	All transactions	0.09
S&H revenue	All transactions	− 7.75
Net cost per transaction		$6.00

Exhibit 19–4.   Where the Dollars Go

Marketing Costs

In direct marketing, the costs of placing advertisements, making mailings, or selling by telephone are really selling expenses rather than advertising. The messages, delivered by the chosen media, are the salespeople of direct marketing. We refer to them as *marketing costs*. They are highly controllable. Very importantly, they are committed to a given program before any sales are obtained.

When catalogs or other mailed materials are used, it is customary to express their costs on the basis of each thousand pieces mailed or otherwise distributed. When an advertisement is placed in a magazine or electronic medium, the cost of each advertising appearance or group of appearances is used. Telemarketers usually work with cost per completed call or one thousand completed calls.

Often it is advisable to test variations in advertisements and/or mailing packages. Because variations are tested in small quantities, extra costs are incurred for printing and additional creative efforts. It would be misleading to include these one-time extra costs as part of the regular profitability calculation. It is generally preferable to include the added costs of creative and small printing quantities associated with testing as a budgeted part of overhead expense. Evaluation of potential profitability of a total direct marketing effort should be computed on the basis of marketing costs one expects to encounter in an ongoing larger-scale program of the size normally conducted in the business.

Exhibit 19–5 provides a simplified marketing cost worksheet for a cataloger. It shows how direct marketers think in costs per thousand people contacted as well as total costs of the program. Many direct marketers choose to think in terms of $0.55 per name contacted instead of $550 per thousand contacts, but for reasons that will become apparent below, many of us prefer thinking in "units" of one thousand. Several items are interesting to note: 600,000 names were processed to obtain 500,000 contacts; creative, testing, and the cost of the marketing department staff are carried as a lump sum, possibly a budget line item; two sharply different promotion costs are computed to account for whether the name was owned or rented.

Exhibit 19–5. Marketing Cost Worksheet

	Quantity	Cost	Cost per 1,000
Catalog	500	$110,000	$220
Transaction form	500	16,000	32
List unduplication	600	4,200	7
Address/mail	500	12,000	24
Postage	500	115,000	230
Creative/testing/overhead		16,000	32
		$273,200	$545
House list preparation	150	750	5
Rented names	450	45,000	100
		$318,950	

Total cost per thousand: house names, $550; rented names, $645

Response Rate

Once you know the promotion costs and the contribution to marketing costs and profit associated with each transaction, it is possible to begin to discuss the response rate or transaction levels required to achieve a given level of profitability. One can think of the promotion costs as the money invested at the beginning of the program and the contribution per transaction multiplied by the number of transactions as the return on that investment.

Using the current examples, one question for Offer B from Exhibit 19–2 might be how many net transactions contributing $30 each are needed to recover marketing costs of $550 per thousand? The answer, shown in Exhibit 19–6, is 550/30 or 18.33, a 1.83 percent net response with product sales of $1,467 per thousand contacted (18.33 × 80). For Offer A, how many completed transactions contributing $19 each are needed to recover marketing costs of $550 per thousand? The answer is 28.95 or a 2.90 percent response with product sales of $1,447 per thousand contacted (28.95 × 50).

However, these calculations merely find break-even, the sales needed to cover selling costs but make zero profit. If the goal were 10 percent pretax profit, we must set aside the target profit and use the remainder of contribution to cover marketing cost. For the $80 transaction, a 10 percent profit target of $8 must be deducted from contribution. The questions would become how many transactions contributing $22 ($30 − $8) or $14 ($19 − $5) each are needed to recover marketing costs of $550 per thousand.

Note that these calculations are based on completed transactions or net revenue. If returns are 5 percent of gross orders, each of the preceding answers

Exhibit 19–6. Break-even to a Goal

	Offer A (Zero Profit)	Offer A (10% Profit)	Offer B (Zero Profit)	Offer B (10% Profit)
House transactions				
Response percentage	2.90%	3.93%	1.83%	2.50%
Average transaction	$50	$50	$80	$80
Sales per 1,000	1,447	1,964	1,467	2,000
Contribution per 1,000				
(38%, 37.5%)	550	746	550	750
Promotion cost per				
1,000	550	550	550	550
Profit		196		200
Rental transactions				
Response percentage	3.39%	4.61%	2.15%	2.93%
Average transaction	$50	$50	$80	$80
Sales per 1,000	1,697	2,304	1,720	2,345
Contribution per 1,000				
(38%, 37.5%)	645	875	645	880
Promotion cost per				
1,000	645	645	645	645
Profit		230		235

would need to be divided by $1 - (5/95)$, or $.947$. Also, these sales per thousand are product revenues, which are less than the actual revenue received when shipping and handling is included.

Setting the Marketing Investment

Long-term or Lifetime Value of a Customer

In a typical direct marketing business, 40–60 percent of customers who buy once will purchase again. Some two-time buyers will buy a third time, and so on. The first transaction should be the beginning of a long-term, repeat buying relationship for many customers. The greater the average value of new customers acquired, the more a company should be willing to spend to acquire those customers so as to reap future revenues and profits from the repurchases. This concept is known as the lifetime or long-term value of a customer (LTV).

The LTV of a new customer is the net present value of all future revenues minus all attributable costs that are associated with an average customer. Note that it is based on profits, not revenue. A discount factor is used to recognize that money earned in the future is worth less than money earned today. Some offsprings of the LTV idea are the remaining value of an established customer and the value of a reactivated dormant customer. Also, some businesses are trying to estimate different LTVs for groups of customers who start in different ways or who have different characteristics, such as inquirers or rented names or buyers with high-dollar first orders.

We suggest that you not include profit or loss earned on the first purchase as part of the long-term value calculation. The first transaction is best thought of as an acquisition investment. Future purchases begin to offset that investment and contribute to the long-term value.

Marketing costs themselves have a major impact on LTV: too few contacts will certainly lower LTV, but too many will lower it even faster.

LTV can be estimated by extrapolating current customer performance under "business-as-usual" assumptions. There are numerous approaches to estimating LTV, which probably suggests that there is no one "right" way. Most approaches eventually derive a table like the one shown in Exhibit 19–7. Notice how the same principles that have already been developed are used, except now the numbers represent multiple contacts over multiple years.

The LTV calculation is based on all activity from a group of new customers subsequent to their acquisition. Because fewer and fewer customers buy in each succeeding year, sales decline each year, even if remaining customers increase their purchases. In this example, the LTV is $3.31 per new customer if profits are discounted at 15 percent, or $2.77 if a 25 percent discount factor is used. If another year were added, the LTV would increase by less than $0.10. The combination of customer attrition and the effect of discounting make it mean-

Exhibit 19-7.   Six-Year Value of 1,000 New Buyers

	Year 1	Year 2	Year 3	Year 4	Year 5	Year 6
Purchase transactions	279	233	168	132	100	79
Average transaction size	$51.22	$51.35	$51.60	$51.75	$52.01	$52.06
Gross product sales	$14,296	$11,940	$8,659	$6,834	$5,200	$4,101
Returns	572	478	346	273	208	164
Net sales	13,724	11,462	8,313	6,561	4,992	3,937
Merchandise costs	6,213	5,189	3,763	2,970	2,260	1,783
Operating costs	1,381	1,153	836	660	502	396
Overhead	2,041	1,704	1,236	975	742	586
Contribution	4,089	3,416	2,477	1,956	1,488	1,172
Selling cost	2,687	2,608	1,799	1,495	1,146	911
List rental income	311	111	84	65	50	39
Cash flow	1,713	919	762	526	392	300
Discounted at 15 percent	1,490	695	501	301	195	130
Cumulative present value	1,490	2,184	2,685	2,986	3,181	3,311
Discounted at 25 percent	1,370	588	390	215	128	79
Cumulative present value	1,370	1,959	2,349	2,564	2,693	2,771

ingless in most businesses to carry out the calculation for more than 5–7 years. That is why we prefer the description *long-term value* over *lifetime value*.

If a business can develop an estimated LTV for new customers, this can be used to establish how much to spend on acquiring them. Given the uncertainty of the future and the ability to do "business as usual," many companies prefer to invest only 30–40 percent of the expected LTV in acquisition, or to apply a 25–30 percent hurdle rate as a discount. Either way, LTV is primarily used to help set an allowable cost or loss for acquiring customers and quantify the return on that investment. It also can be used to estimate the value of a current house file and to set an appropriate level of ongoing marketing expense.

Customer Groups and Targeting within Customer Groups

One key to successful contact planning is divide and conquer. That is, potential buyers should be separated into large groups with some natural affinity and marketing potential. Each of these groups would be evaluated separately. For example, past buyers can be separated into one-time and multibuyers and rental lists can be grouped by list categories. This supports marketing contact decisions at a finer level.

Buying potential within each group can be further differentiated using RFM or statistical models that estimate likelihood of purchase from a given contact. These estimates will be based on historic buying rates and patterns. They need to be adjusted for changes in the offer, the competition, or the economy.

The goal of all this division is to forecast buying levels and resulting profitability in order to identify which customers or potential customers to contact, given specific marketing goals. The aim is to create a hierarchy of expectations, establish profitability at each level, and find the "margin," the edge or last set of people who should be contacted. Exhibits 19–8 and 19–9 provide examples of estimated performance for representative groups, but they do NOT make the contact decision.

Contact Goals

The contact decision must be made relative to established business goals. These should vary by group and should provide not only desired performance on average, but also desired performance at the margin. Often the most difficult and at the same time the most important goals are those that state profitability

Exhibit 19–8. Historic Performance for One-Time Buyers

Recency of Last Purchase	Response Percentage	Sales per 1,000	Profit per Buyer at Promotion Costs of		
			$450/K	$500/K	$550/K
Less than 6 months	4.2%	$2,520	$9.09	$7.90	$6.70
6–12 months	3.5	1,995	5.95	4.52	3.10
12–24 months	2.4	1,248	– 1.59	– 3.67	– 5.76
24–36 months	1.8	900	– 8.50	– 11.28	– 14.06
36–48 months	1.2	564	– 21.99	– 26.16	– 30.32
48 + months	0.9	405	– 35.15	– 40.71	– 46.26

Exhibit 19–9. Historic Performance for Rental List 506

Select	Response Percentage	Sales per 1,000	Profit per Buyer at Promotion Costs of		
			$550/K	$600/K	$650/K
Buyers in last three months	2.8%	$1,596	– $0.83	– $2.62	– $4.40
4–12 month multibuyers	3.5	1,995	3.10	1.67	0.24
12–24 month multibuyers	2.1	1,092	– 9.03	– 11.41	– 13.79
4–12 month single buyers	2.6	1,482	– 2.34	– 4.27	– 6.19
12–24 month single buyers	1.7	884	– 15.19	– 18.13	– 21.08

of the weakest cells you elect to contact. If the worst cell contacted breaks even, the whole program will be profitable. However, even if the poorest cell contacted shows a loss, the whole program still could be highly profitable.

Depending on overall business needs, it is reasonable to set different marginal goals at different times. When near-term profit is crucial, the goals can be set very high. When volume, expansion, and growth are important, the marginal goals can be lowered as the business elects to invest in the future. This could entail acquiring new customers as well as reactivating stagnant customers, both at a short-term loss. Never should the immediate loss be greater than the long-term value of the expected repeat transactions.

Exhibit 19–10 provides a simplified mail plan that uses the three key strands of promotion cost, purchase size, and single-order contribution to marketing cost and profit, plus marginal profit per buyer goals to establish minimal performance to meet the goals. Considering the interactions of these multiple elements, the required purchase rate from the "last" or marginal cells varies from barely 1 percent to more than 2.4 percent, while the sales per thousand varies within a much tighter band. Can you imagine some of the thinking that went into establishing these groups and setting such varied goals? Can you believe that each group has been differentiated so that only those customers and prospects who might be expected to meet the minimal standards could be chosen for contact?

Special Programs

Continuities

Programs where the initial purchase is the first in a defined series of transactions are called *continuities*. In addition to the traditional direct marketing product continuities such as a book series and monthly coffee or tape shipments, this

Exhibit 19–10. A Sample Mail Plan

	Promotion Cost/K	Average Transaction	Contribution Percentage	Goal for Marginal Profit/Buyer	Required to Reach Marginal Goal	
					Sales/K	Response
House file						
Big spenders	$400	$100	33%	– $5	$1,052	1.05%
Middlers	400	75	33	– 2	1,121	1.50
Pikers	400	50	33	0	1,212	2.42
Inquirers	400	60	33	– 3	1,053	1.75
External lists						
MO rental	525	75	33	– 5	1,324	1.76
Subscribers	475	60	33	– 4	1,197	2.00
Compiled	450	50	33	– 3	1,154	2.31

includes businesses such as long-distance telephone, credit cards, and insurance. These programs can be quantified using the same principles, but quantifying the "average order" and contribution to marketing costs and profit become more difficult.

The dynamics of continuities are such that, while each payment in the revenue stream might be small, the total revenues from one customer are high. This usually justifies spending much larger amounts to acquire the customer, including sweeteners and signing bonuses. Cancellation, return, and bad debt risks often are high, especially at the beginning of the series. The need to estimate applicable rates, revenue, and costs for each transaction in the series contributes to the difficulty in estimating the overall future revenues and costs from a group of customers.

Inquiry Conversion Programs

Up to this point, we have assumed that the first transaction is a purchase triggered by advertisements or direct contacts. Sometimes the difficulty in targeting possible buyers makes it more profitable to generate inquiries using various low-cost methods and then convert those inquiries into sales by using one or more mailings, telephone calls, and/or sales visits. This usually is advantageous when selling high-ticket items, when prospects need pre-qualification or cultivation, when personal contact is needed to close the sale, or when the same inquirers become good prospects for multiple additional offers.

Inquiries can be generated through any of the media available to the direct marketer. For example, if an advertisement costing $5,000 placed in a magazine produces 1,000 inquiries, the cost per inquiry would be $5. In addition, there will be a cost of perhaps $75 per thousand to process inquiries into a usable mailing list. This processing should be done promptly and the promotion activity taken immediately, because studies have shown that the sooner the response to an inquiry is received, the higher is the likelihood of response. In addition, the marketer has the right to repromote these inquirers as many times as is profitable.

Varying the media, kinds of advertisements, appeals, and offers will affect the cost of generating inquiries and possibly the rate at which they convert to buyers. Typically, the more highly qualified an inquiry, the more costly it will be to generate, but the higher the conversion rate will be. The thoughtful direct marketer will experiment continuously with various ways of producing inquiries and various means of converting them in order to fine-tune a program and to maximize profits.

Most companies find that an inquiry list will support repeated conversion contacts. There is likely to be a fall-off in response to each successive effort, but it is profitable to continue making conversion contacts until the incremental cost of the last one is greater than the contribution it generates.

Exhibit 19-11 shows a typical set of inquiry conversion results when multiple contacts are used. The costs of acquiring the inquiry and making repeated conversion efforts are the marketing investment. As inquirers are converted to buyers, the quantity available for subsequent contacts goes down. The likelihood of response goes down very quickly as the best prospects are captured and removed from the group. The true measure of performance is the cumulative cost and profit associated with the series of contacts including acquisition costs. At some point, repeat contacts will become unprofitable. Did they go one contact too far here, should they go one more, or did they do it just right?

Engineering a Direct Marketing Business

Spreadsheet-based computer models can be used to simulate a direct marketing business quite accurately. Usually these use monthly time frames and spread both response and costs so that the final model provides a reasonable set of expectations for cash flow. Many companies have found these extremely useful for long-term planning and identifying the profit sensitivity to key parameters.

In addition, these models can be used to assess the consequences of changes in strategy or policy. Exhibit 19–12 illustrates the impact on return on investment of the pursuit of three different strategies to build a catalog mail order business.

The model assumes that the same amount of money is invested in each strategy.

The strategies are to:

1. Mail more catalogs to rented lists to acquire more customers.

2. Expand the catalogs by adding more products and increasing the number of pages.

3. Create an extra catalog to be mailed to better customers during the fall season.

Exhibit 19–11.   Inquiry Conversion with Multiple Follow-up Contacts

	Inquiry Acquisition Cost	Contact #1	Contact #2	Contact #3	Contact #4	Total Program
Quantity mailed		1,000	940	912	898	3,750
Response percentage		6.0%	3.0%	1.5%	0.6%	2.9%
Net transactions		60	28	14	5	107
Net sales		$9,000	$4,200	$2,100	$750	$16,050
Contribution		3,600	1,680	840	300	6,420
Selling cost	$5,075	400	376	365	359	6,575
Profit	–5,075	3,200	1,304	475	–59	–155
Cumulative profit	–5,075	–1,875	–571	–96	–155	
Cumulative profit per buyer		–31.25	–6.49	–0.94	–1.45	

Exhibit 19–12.   Return on Investment Index

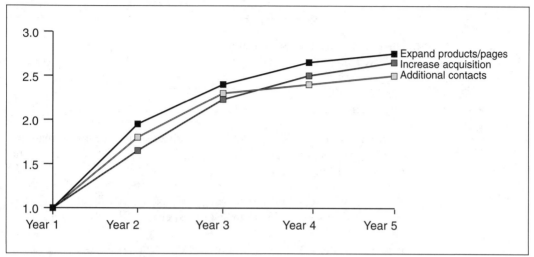

Over the five-year horizon for which results are simulated, the company in question would invest most advantageously in expanding its product line. Notice, however, that the customer acquisition strategy appears to be closing the gap quickly at the end of the period and might be expected to outperform the product line expansion strategy in the sixth or seventh year. Further study might indicate that this particular company could blend the two approaches by expanding the size of some of its catalogs and also enlarging its customer acquisition activities.

This example shows one reason why so many of us truly enjoy direct marketing. It is accountable marketing where the impact of specific marketing actions can be estimated, tested, and evaluated. If the marketer is willing, able, and persistent, the potential exists to understand the impact of decisions and make significant, measurable contributions to the profitability of the business. The web of interacting costs and profit drivers is remarkably resilient, rebounding and adjusting to small pressures. Sharp blows or inordinate forces can cause great damage, but the web glistens in the morning dew and has singular attractive powers.

SELF-QUIZ

1. The three major strands that support the web of direct marketing arithmetic are:
   a. Contribution to selling costs and profit

b. _____

c. _____

2. Direct costs can be classified into three categories:
   a. Merchandise or service

   b. _____

   c. _____

3. In direct marketing, the costs of placing advertisements, making mailings, or selling by telephone are really _____ expenses rather than advertising.

4. The costs of creative and testing (one-time extra costs) should be charged to overhead expense rather than selling expense. ☐ True ☐ False

5. In a typical direct marketing business, 40 percent to _____ _____ percent of customers who buy once will buy again.

6. Lifetime value or long-term value (LTV) usually requires an investment (loss) to acquire a new customer. In computing long-term value of a customer, a discount factor should be used to recognize that money earned in the future is worth less than money earned today. ☐ True ☐ False

7. The economics of direct marketing dictate that not all customers are equal in value. For example, past buyers can be separated into one-time and multibuyer, multibuyers being a more profitable group. Name three other ways to further differentiate buyers.
   a. By using RFM

   b. _____

   c. _____

8. Inquiry-conversion programs are often advisable when selling high-ticket items.
   ☐ True ☐ False

9. It makes economic sense to continue to try to convert inquiries to sales until the cost is greater than the _____.

PILOT PROJECT

1. A test mailing of 15,000 pieces with a total promotion cost of $4,500 generated $13,500 net sales. The average order size was $50, and each order

contributed $20 to promotion costs and profit after paying for the cost of goods, fulfillment, and an overhead allocation. Compute the following:
a. Total orders
b. Total contribution
c. Total profit
d. Profit as percentage of net sales
e. Response percentage
f. Orders/thousand
g. Promotion cost/thousand
h. Contribution/thousand
i. Profit/thousand

2. A company has the following cost profile:

Cost of goods	40.0% of net sales
Operating expenses	11.6% of net sales
Overhead expenses	14.4% of net sales

a. What is the contribution to promotion costs and profit?
b. Find the sales/thousand break-even if:
   (1) Promotion cost is $425/thousand.
   (2) Promotion cost is $425/thousand and there is a targeted profit of 9 percent.

3. A firm has two different methods by which it can generate average orders of $80 with a contribution to promotion costs and profit of $32. Complete the break-even analysis.

	Magazine Space Ad	Small Catalog
Promotion cost/thousand	$12	$360

Breakeven:
   Orders/thousand
   Response percentage
   Sales/thousand

Break-even given a 15 percent profit target:
   Orders/thousand
   Response percentage
   Sales/thousand

Answers to Pilot Project

1. a. 270
   b. $5,400
   c. $900
   d. 6.67%

e. 1.80%
f. 18
g. $300
h. $360
i. $60

2. a. 34% of net sales
   b. (1) $1,250
   c. (2) $1,700

3.

	Magazine Space Ad	Small Catalog
Promotion cost/thousand	$12	$360
Breakeven:		
Order/thousand	0.375	11.25
Response percentage	0.0375%	1.125%
Sales/thousand	$30	$900
Break-even given a 15 percent profit target:		
Orders/thousand	0.6	18
Response percentage	0.6%	1.8%
Sales/thousand	48	$1,440

CHAPTER TWENTY

Creativity and Testing

"We've got to develop ideas with breakthrough potential and test their validity" is an oft-repeated statement in direct marketing circles. The never-ending quest for the breakthrough is motivated by fantastic payoff potential. "Book-of-the-Month Club" was a breakthrough concept, leading to billions of dollars in book sales. Newspaper and magazine inserts. The "Gold Box" concept. TV support for other media. Ink-jet imaging. Each a gigantic breakthrough.

But how does one develop breakthrough ideas? Are there techniques to be applied? Yes.

Urgent Need for Creativity

The major breakthroughs of past decades all came about as a result of brilliant creativity. But, sad to say, a strong case can be made for the widespread belief that there is a dearth of breakthrough ideas today as compared to the recent past. Two reasons are given for this condition: (1) the tendency to "play it safe" to protect the bottom line, and (2) not enough way-out testing to lead to creative new breakthroughs. In short, creativity is deteriorating.

To illustrate what I mean by creativity, let me share the following story with you.

The Yamaha Piano Story

Situation Analysis. Yamaha had succeeded in capturing 40 percent of the global piano market. Unfortunately, just when Yamaha became market leader, the overall demand for pianos started declining by 10 percent a year.

Around the world, in living rooms, dens, and concert halls, there are some 40 million pianos. For the most part, the pianos just sit and gather dust. As head of Yamaha, what do you do?

Some American analysts would advise: "Get out of the piano business!"

Solution.   Yamaha's marketers determined that one possible way to solve the problem was to add value to the millions of pianos already out there. In this exercise they remembered the old player piano—a pleasant idea with a not very pleasant sound.

Using a combination of sophisticated digital and optical technology, they developed a "player" program that can distinguish 92 degrees of speed and strength of key touch. With this technology, piano owners could now record live performances by the pianists of their choice, or they could buy such recordings on a computer disk–like cartridge. So now, for an expenditure of around $2,500, piano owners could retrofit their idle, untuned, dust-collecting pieces of over-sized furniture and have great artists play for them in the privacy of their homes.

End Result of the Value-Added Concept.   Owners of 40 million mostly idle pianos became a vibrant market for $2,500 retrofitting sales. Yamaha started marketing this technology in April 1988, and sales since then have been explosive. This very technology has created a new interest in learning to play the piano. After reading about Yamaha's success, we should all ask ourselves these questions:

- Do we have products or services that have become obsolete?

- By thinking in terms of "value added," can we create whole new markets?

It's been said that creativity is something everyone talks about but few can define. To determine your creative ability, I urge you to review these 16 traits of successful creative people:

- Curiosity
- Sense of humor
- Independence
- Observation
- Persistence
- Motivation
- Eclectic taste
- Love for reading

- Good imagination
- Energy
- Hard work
- Ambition
- Visual thinking
- Originality
- Self-confidence
- Awareness of the "big picture"

Rate yourself on a scale of 1–10 for each trait. 160 points = creative genius; 120–160 = brilliant; 80–120 = need counseling; under 80 = stick to bean counting.

Regardless of what your score is, you can improve. Consider taking these steps to improve your personal creativity:

1. Block out the time.

2. Get comfortable.

3. Eat something healthful.

4. Stock up lots of background.

5. Experience the world.

6. Be ready when the ideas strike.

7. Use a "don't disturb" sign.

8. For "blue-sky" projects, have a glass of wine.

9. Let your work rest before evaluation.

10. Enjoy the process.[1]

Brainstorming

Brainstorming, first popularized in the 1950s by Alex Osborne of BBD&O, continues to be an effective method of finding new creative solutions to difficult problems. Brainstorming is part of a three-phase process:

1. Before starting, create an agenda and carefully define problem(s) in writing.

2. Set quotas for ideas and a time limit for each section of the agenda.

3. Review the house rules with participants before each brainstorming session.

Let's look at some rules for brainstorming, then consider a few examples of breakthroughs that have emerged from the process.

Selecting a Leader

Select a leader, and have him or her take all responsibility for contact with reality. Everyone else in the brainstorming meeting is to "think wild." In the

[1]Susan K. Jones, *Creative Strategy in Direct Marketing* (Lincolnwood, Ill.: NTC Business Books, 1991).

brainstorming meeting, the leader plays a low-key role. It's important to avoid influencing the participants. The duties of the leader are as follows:

- To see that detailed notes are taken on all ideas expressed

- To see that the agenda and time schedule are adhered to

- To admonish any critical thinkers in the group—no negative thinking is allowed during the brainstorming session

- To see that the group takes time to "build up" each idea

- To keep all participants involved and contributing

House Rules during Brainstorming

1. Suspend all critical judgment of your own—or other people's—ideas. Don't ask yourself if this is a *good idea* or a *bad idea*. Accept it and rack your brain for ways to improve the concept.

2. Welcome freewheeling, off-the-wall thinking. Wild, crazy, funny, far-out ideas are important. Why? Because they frequently shock us into a totally new viewpoint of the problem.

3. Quantity, not quality, is the objective during the brainstorm session. This sounds contradictory—it's not. Remember, every member of the group has been briefed on the problem in advance. You have a carefully planned agenda of material to cover. Consequently, your group is well directed toward the right problem. Therefore we can say, "Go for quantity in the idea session."

4. Build up each idea. Here's where most brainstorming sessions fail. They just collect ideas as fast as they come and let it go at that. The leaders should carefully slow the group down so they stop with each idea and help build it up. Enhance each idea, no matter how crazy or offbeat it seems.

It's the leader's responsibility to see that these four guidelines are adhered to in every meeting, but he or she should do this in a very low-key, informal manner. It is important that the leader not become a dominant authority figure in meetings.

When the session is over, then—and only then—use your normal everyday judgment to logically select ideas with the most potential from all of the available alternatives.

Brainstorming Examples

Example 1. *The problem:* Insurance companies are not allowed to give free gifts as an incentive for applying for an insurance policy. How can we offer a free gift and stay within the law? Sounds like an impossible problem, right? Wrong. Brainstorming participants broke through with a positive solution, a blockbuster.

The breakthrough: The brainstorming idea that hit pay dirt was to offer the free gift to everyone, whether they apply for the policy or not.

The result: A 38 percent increase in applications.

Example 2.   *The problem:* How can we avoid paying postage for sending prizes to "no" entrants in an "everybody wins" sweepstakes? (Possible savings in postage to the marketer if the problem could be solved was about $250,000.)

The breakthrough: We asked "no" entrants to provide a stamped, self-addressed envelope. We included a prize in the shipping carton for those who said "yes." (The Postal Service approved the requirement at the time.)

The result: This was the most successful sweepstakes contest the sponsor ever conducted. The sponsor also enjoyed savings of $250,000 in postage.

Example 3.   *The problem:* We have 36 competitors selling to schools. They all promise "prompt shipment" of their pompons. How can we dramatize the fact that we ship our pompons in 24 hours and thus capture the bulk of the market?

The breakthrough: We inserted a Jiffy Order Card in the catalog, in addition to the regular order form, featuring guaranteed shipment within 24 hours.

The result: Pompon sales increased 40 percent!

Example 4.   *The problem:* As a leading agricultural chemical company, we manufacture both a corn herbicide and corn insecticide. Each product has its own positioning in the farm market, and each product has a different share of market in various geographic areas across the nation. How can new users for each product be won over from the competition?

The breakthrough: We created a combination rebate program. Because the ratio of herbicide to insecticide remains relatively constant regardless of size, we offered a rebate on both products when purchased at the same time.

The result: A significant number of farmers who had planned to purchase the two products from different manufacturers took advantage of the rebate offer and purchased both products from the sponsor, with an average order of $25,000.

Creative Stimulators

The degree of truly creative output is directly related to two factors: clear and specific definitions of problems to be solved and the right "atmosphere" for developing creative solutions.

Frank Daniels, a former creative director with Stone & Adler, has a system for stimulating creative people. Using a long-established technique for idea stimulating, he provides creative people with eight "stimulators" designed to expand their thinking. The examples that follow were applied to the Lanier Company, manufacturers of dictating equipment. Creativity was being stimulated for promoting a minirecorder, Lanier's Pocket Secretary. Each of the eight stimulators is accompanied by a key thought and a series of questions designed to promote creative solutions.

Can We Combine?

Combining two or more elements often results in new thought processes. The following questions are designed to encourage brainstorming participants to think in terms of combinations.

Key Thought. Combine appropriate parts of well-known things to emphasize the benefits of our product. "Think of owning a Rolls-Royce the size of a Volkswagen" (Lanier Pocket Secretary).

- What can be combined physically or conceptually to emphasize product benefits?

- Can the product be combined with another so that both benefit?

- Where in the product offer would a combination of thoughts be of most help?

- What opposites can be combined to show a difference from competitive products?

- What can we combine with our product to make it more fun to own, use, look at?

- Can part of one of our benefits be combined with part of another to enhance both?

- Can newness be combined with tradition?

- Can a product benefit be combined with a specific audience need through visual devices? Copy devices?

- What can we combine from the advertising and sales program to the benefit of both? Can salespersons' efforts be combined into advertising?

- Can we demonstrate product advantages by using "misfit" combination demonstrations?

- Can we combine manufacturing information performance tests with advertising to demonstrate advantages?

Time Elements

Saving time and having extra time are conventional human wants. This series of questions is designed to expand one's thinking toward making time a plus factor in the product offer.

Key Thought. Alter time factor(s) in present offer, present schedules, and present product positioning to motivate action.

- Does seasonal timing have an effect on individual benefits?

- Can present seasonal timing be reversed for special effect?

- Can limited offers be effective?

- Can early buyers be given special consideration?

- Can off-season offers be made?

- Are there better days, weeks, or months for our offers?

- Can we compress or extend present promotional sequencing?

- Can our price be keyed to selected times of the week, month, year?

- Can we feature no-time-limit offers?

- Can we feature limited-time offers?

- Can we feature fast delivery or follow-up?

Can We Add?

An axiom of selling is that the customer often unconsciously compares the added benefits of a competitor's product with those of your product. The product with the most added benefits traditionally sells better. These questions are designed to ferret out added benefits for a particular product.

Key Thought. Look for ways to express benefits by relating functional advantages of unrelated products or things. "We've taken all the best cassette recorder features and added one from the toaster" (pop-out delivery).

- What has been added to our product that's missing from others?

- Do we have a deficiency due to excess that can be turned into advantage?

- Is our product usable in many different ways aside from the intended use?

- Is our product instantly noticeable? Is it unusual in terms of size, shape, color? What unrelated symbols can we use to emphasize this unique characteristic?

- Does our product make something easier? What have we added by taking this something away?

- Does our product make order out of chaos or meaningful chaos out of total chaos? What have we added by taking this something away?

- What does the purchase of our product add to the buyer's physical condition, mental condition, subconscious condition, present condition, future condition?

- Where will the buyer be if he or she does not purchase? What will be missing from the buyer's life?

- Does our product give its full benefit to the buyer immediately, or does the buyer build up (add to) his or her well-being through continued possession?

Can We Subtract?

Taking away can often be as appealing as adding to. Less weight, less complexity, less fuss, less bother are fundamental appeals. These questions steer brainstorming participants in that direction.

Key Thought.   Subtract from the obvious to focus attention on the benefits of our product or service. ''We've weighed all the minirecorders and made ours lighter.''

- What deficiencies does our product have competitively?

- What advantage do we have?

- What features are the newest? The most unusual?

- How can our product use/cost be minimized over time?

- Can a buyer use less of another product if he or she buys ours?

- Can the evidence of total lack of desire for our product be used to illustrate its benefits?

- Can the limitations of our benefits be used as an appeal?

- What does lack of our product in the buyer's living habits do to him or her?

- Does our product offer a chance to eliminate any common element in all competitive products?

- Does our product reduce or eliminate (subtract) anything in the process of performing its work?

- Will our product deflate (subtract from) a problem for the buyers?

Can We Make Associations?

Favorable associations are often the most effective way to emphasize product benefits. "Like Sterling on silver," a classic example of a favorable association, is a comment that accrues to the benefit of the product being compared with other products.

Key Thought.   Form a link with unrelated things or situations to emphasize benefits.

- Can we link our product to another, already successful product to emphasize benefits?

- Can we appeal to popular history, literature, poetry, or art to emphasize benefits?

- What does the potential buyer associate with our product? How can we use this association to advantage?

- When does the potential buyer associate our product with potential use?

- Can associations be drawn with present or future events?

- Can associations be made with abstractions that can be expressed visually, musically, with words, and so forth?

- Can funny, corny, challenging associations be made?

- Can associations be made with suppliers of component parts?

- Is our product so unique that it needs no associations?

- Can our product be associated with many different situations?

Can We Simplify?

What is the simple way to describe and illustrate our major product benefit? As sophisticated as our world is today, the truism persists that people relate best to simple things. These questions urge participants to state benefits with dramatic simplicity.

Key Thought.   Dramatize benefits individually or collectively with childishly simple examples, symbols, images.

- Which of our appeals is strongest over our competition? How can we simplify to illustrate?

- Is there a way to simplify *all* benefits for emphasis?

- Where is most of the confusion about our product in the buyer's mind?

- Can we illustrate by simplification?

- Is our appeal abstract? Can we substitute simple, real visualizations to emphasize?

- Could a familiar quotation or picture be used to make our appeal more understandable?

- Is our product complex? Can we break it up (literally) into more understandable pieces to emphasize benefits?

- Can we overlap one benefit with another to make product utility more understandable?

- Can we contrast an old way of doing something with the confusing part of our product to create understanding?

- Is product appeal rigidly directed at too small a segment of the market? Too broad a segment?

- Can we emphasize benefits by having an unskilled person or child make good use of the product in a completely out-of-context situation?

Can We Substitute?

The major product benefit for our product is often so similar to major product benefits of competitive products that it is difficult for the consumer to perceive the difference. Substituting another theme, such as Avis did when the company changed its theme to ''We Try Harder,'' can often establish a point of difference. These questions inspire participants to think in terms of substitution.

Key Thought. Substitute the familiar for another familiar theme for emphasis; substitute the unfamiliar for the familiar for emphasis.

- Can a well-known theme for another product be substituted for our theme, or can a well-known benefit for another product be substituted for our benefit?

- Can an incongruous situation be used to focus emphasis on our theme or benefits?

- Can a series of incongruous situations be found for every benefit we have? Can they be used in one ad? Can they form a continuity series of ads?

- What can be substituted for our product appeal that will emphasize the difference between us and our competitors?

- Can an obviously dissimilar object be substituted for the image of our product?

- Can a physical object be used to give more concrete representation of a product intangible?

- Is our product replacing a process rapidly becoming dated? Can we substitute the past for the present, or the future for the past or the present?

- Can we visualize our product where the competitor's product is normally expected to be?

- Can we visualize our product as the only one of its kind in the world, as if there were no other substitutes for our product?

Can We Make a Reversal?

The ordinary can become extraordinary as usual situations are reversed. A man wearing a tennis skirt. A woman wearing a football helmet. A trained bear pushing a power mower. These questions are designed to motivate participants to think in terms of reversing usual situations.

Key Thought.   Emphasize a benefit by completely reversing the usual situation.

- What are the diametrically opposed situations for each of our product benefits?

- For each copy point already established, make a complete reverse statement.

- How would a totally uninformed person describe our product?

- Can male- and female-oriented roles be reversed?

- Can art and copy be totally reversed to emphasize a point?

- How many incongruous product situations can be shown graphically? Verbally?

- Can we find humor in the complete reversal of anticipated product uses or benefits?

Test the Big Things

Whether testable ideas come out of pure research, brainstorming, or self-developed creativity, the same picture applies: *Test the big things*. Trivia testing (e.g., the tilt of a postage stamp or the effects of various colors of paper) are passé. Breakthroughs are possible only when you test the big things. Following are six big areas from which breakthroughs emerge:

1. The products or services you offer

2. The media you use (lists, print, and broadcast)

3. The propositions you make

4. The copy platforms you use

5. The formats you use

6. The timing you choose

Five of the areas for testing appear on most published lists these days. But testing new products and new product features is rarely recommended. Yet everything starts with the product or service you offer.

Many direct marketers religiously test new ads, new mailing packages, new media, new copy approaches, new formats, and new timing schedules season after season with never a thought to testing new product features. Finally, the most imaginative of creative approaches fails to overcome the waning appeal of the same old product. And still another product bites the dust.

This need not happen. For example, consider the most commonplace of mail order items, the address label. Scores of firms offer them in black ink on standard white stock. Competition is keen: Prices all run about the same. From this variety of competitive styles, however, a few emerge with new product features: gold stock, colored ink, seasonal borders, and so forth. Tests are made to determine appeal. The new product features appeal to a bigger audience.

Projectable Mailing Sample Sizes

Some direct marketers live by probability tables that tell the mailer what the sample size must be at various response levels within a specified error limit, such as 5 or 10 percent. No one argues the statistical validity of probability tables. Although probability tables can't be relied on too heavily because it is impossible to construct a truly scientific sample, such tables, within limits, can be helpful. Exhibit 20-1 is based on a 95 percent confidence level at various limits of error.

Testing Components versus Testing Mailing Packages

In the endless search for breakthroughs, the question continually arises: In direct mail, should we test components or mailing packages? There are two schools of thought on this. The prevailing one is that the big breakthroughs come about through the testing of completely different mailing packages as opposed to

Exhibit 20-1. Test Sample Sizes Required for 95 Percent Confidence Level for Mailing Response Levels from 0.1 Percent to 4.0 Percent

R (Response)	Limits of Error (Expressed as Percentage Points)														
	.02	.04	.06	.08	.10	.12	.14	.16	.18	.20	.30	.40	.50	.60	.70
.1	95,929	23,982	10,659	5,995	3,837	2,665	1,957	1,499	1,184	959	426	240	153	106	78
.2	191,666	47,916	21,296	11,979	7,667	5,324	3,911	2,994	2,366	1,917	852	479	307	213	156
.3	287,211	71,803	31,912	17,951	11,488	7,978	5,861	4,487	3,546	2,872	1,276	718	459	319	234
.4	382,564	95,641	42,507	23,910	15,303	10,627	7,807	5,977	4,723	3,826	1,700	956	612	425	312
.5	477,724	119,431	53,080	29,858	19,109	13,270	9,749	7,464	5,987	4,777	2,123	1,194	764	530	390
.6	572,693	143,173	63,632	35,793	22,908	15,908	11,687	8,948	7,070	5,727	2,545	1,432	916	636	467
.7	667,470	166,867	74,163	41,717	26,699	18,541	13,622	10,429	8,240	6,675	2,966	1,669	1,068	741	545
.8	762,054	190,514	84,673	47,628	30,482	21,168	15,552	11,907	9,408	7,621	3,387	1,905	1,219	847	622
.9	856,447	214,112	95,160	53,528	34,258	23,790	17,478	13,382	10,573	8,564	3,806	2,141	1,370	951	699
1.0	950,648	237,662	105,628	59,415	38,026	26,407	19,401	14,854	11,736	9,506	4,225	2,376	1,521	1,056	776
1.1	1,044,656	261,164	116,072	65,291	41,786	29,018	21,319	16,322	12,897	10,446	4,643	2,611	1,671	1,160	853
1.2	1,138,472	284,618	126,496	71,155	45,539	31,624	23,234	17,788	14,055	11,385	5,060	2,846	1,821	1,265	929
1.3	1,232,097	308,024	136,899	77,006	49,284	34,225	25,145	19,251	15,211	12,321	5,476	3,080	1,971	1,369	1,006
1.4	1,325,529	331,382	147,280	82,845	53,021	36,820	27,051	20,711	16,364	13,255	5,891	3,314	2,121	1,473	1,082
1.5	1,418,769	354,692	157,640	88,673	56,751	39,410	28,954	22,168	17,515	14,188	6,305	3,547	2,270	1,576	1,158
1.6	1,511,818	377,954	167,980	94,489	60,473	41,995	30,853	23,622	18,664	15,118	6,719	3,780	2,419	1,680	1,234
1.7	1,604,674	401,168	178,297	100,292	64,187	44,574	32,748	25,073	19,811	16,047	7,132	4,012	2,567	1,783	1,310
1.8	1,697,338	424,334	188,592	106,083	67,894	47,148	34,639	26,521	20,955	16,973	7,543	4,243	2,716	1,886	1,385
1.9	1,789,810	447,452	198,868	111,863	71,592	49,717	36,526	27,966	22,096	17,898	7,955	4,474	2,863	1,988	1,461
2.0	1,882,090	470,523	209,121	117,631	75,284	52,280	38,410	29,407	23,235	18,821	8,365	4,705	3,011	2,091	1,536

Exhibit 20–1 (Continued).

R (Response)	Limits of Error (Expressed as Percentage Points)														
	.02	.04	.06	.08	.10	.12	.14	.16	.18	.20	.30	.40	.50	.60	.70
2.1	1,974,178	493,544	219,352	123,386	78,967	54,838	40,289	30,846	24,372	19,742	8,774	4,935	3,158	2,193	1,611
2.2	2,066,074	516,518	229,564	129,129	82,643	57,391	42,165	32,282	25,507	20,661	9,182	5,165	3,306	2,295	1,686
2.3	2,157,778	539,444	239,753	134,861	86,311	59,938	44,036	33,715	26,638	21,578	9,590	5,394	3,452	2,397	1,761
2.4	2,249,290	562,322	249,920	140,581	89,972	62,480	45,903	35,145	27,769	22,493	9,997	5,623	3,599	2,499	1,836
2.5	2,340,609	585,152	260,068	146,288	93,624	65,017	47,767	36,572	28,896	23,406	10,403	5,851	3,745	2,600	1,911
2.6	2,431,737	607,934	270,192	151,983	97,269	67,547	49,627	37,996	30,021	24,317	10,807	6,079	3,891	2,702	1,985
2.7	2,522,673	630,668	280,296	157,667	100,907	70,074	51,483	39,416	31,144	25,227	11,211	6,307	4,036	2,803	2,059
2.8	2,613,416	653,354	290,380	163,339	104,537	72,595	53,335	40,834	32,264	26,134	11,615	6,534	4,181	2,904	2,133
2.9	2,703,968	675,992	300,440	168,998	108,159	75,110	55,183	42,249	33,382	27,039	12,017	6,760	4,326	3,004	2,207
3.0	2,794,328	698,582	310,480	174,645	111,773	77,620	57,026	43,661	34,497	27,943	12,419	6,986	4,471	3,105	2,281
3.1	2,884,495	721,124	320,499	180,281	115,380	80,125	58,867	45,070	35,611	28,845	12,820	7,211	4,615	3,205	2,355
3.2	2,974,470	743,618	330,496	185,904	118,979	82,623	60,702	46,476	36,721	29,745	13,220	7,436	4,759	3,305	2,428
3.3	3,064,254	766,063	340,471	191,516	122,570	85,118	62,535	47,878	37,830	30,642	13,619	7,660	4,903	3,404	2,501
3.4	3,153,845	788,461	350,427	197,115	126,154	87,607	64,364	49,278	38,936	31,538	14,017	7,884	5,046	3,504	2,574
3.5	3,243,244	810,811	360,360	202,703	129,730	90,089	66,188	50,675	40,040	32,432	14,414	8,108	5,189	3,603	2,647
3.6	3,332,452	833,113	370,271	208,278	133,298	92,568	68,009	52,069	41,141	33,325	14,811	8,331	5,332	3,702	2,720
3.7	3,421,467	855,367	380,163	213,842	136,859	95,041	69,825	53,460	42,240	34,214	15,207	8,554	5,474	3,801	2,793
3.8	3,510,290	877,572	390,031	219,393	140,412	97,507	71,638	54,848	43,336	35,103	15,601	8,776	5,616	3,900	2,865
3.9	3,598,921	899,730	399,878	224,932	143,957	99,969	73,446	56,233	44,430	35,989	15,995	8,997	5,758	3,998	2,938
4.0	3,687,360	921,840	409,706	230,460	147,494	102,426	75,252	57,615	45,522	36,874	16,388	9,218	5,900	4,097	3,010

testing individual components within a mailing package. Something can be learned from each procedure, of course. In my opinion however, the more logical procedure is to first find the big difference in mailing packages and then follow with tests of individual components in the losing packages, which can often make the winning packages even better.

In package testing, one starts with a complete concept and builds all components to fit the image of the concept. Consider the differences between these two package concepts:

	Package 1	**Package 2**
Envelope	9" x 12"	No. 10
letter	Eight-page, stapled	Four-sheet (two sides) computer written
Circular	None	Four-page, illustrated
Order form	8½" × 11", perforated stub	8½" × 3⅔"

The differences between these two package concepts are considerable. Chances are great that there will be a substantial difference in response. Once the winning package evolves, component tests make excellent sense. Let us say the 9" × 12" package is the winner. A logical subsequent test would be to fold the same inserts into a 6" × 9" envelope. A reply envelope could be considered as an additional test. Computerizing the first page of the eight-page letter could be still another test.

How to Test Print Advertising

For direct marketing practitioners who are multimedia users, testing print advertising is just as important as testing direct mail. And, as with direct mail, it is important that the tests be designed to produce valid results.

Gerald Schreck, media director of Doubleday Advertising Company, New York, gave the following pointers on A/B split tests in an *Advertising Age* feature article.

The split helps you determine the relative strengths of different ads. For example, you can run two ads, A and B, in a specific issue or edition of a publication so that two portions of the total run are equally divided and identical in circulation. The only difference is that Ad A will run in half of the issue and Ad B will run in the other half. For measuring the strength of the ads, a split includes an offer requiring your reader to act by writing or sending in a coupon. Then you simply compare the responses with the individual ads. If done properly, this method can be accurate to two decimal points. You also have the advantage of real-world testing to find out what people actually do, not just what they say they'll do. And because all factors are held equal, the difference in results can be attributed directly to your advertising. (See Exhibit 20–2.) Although the A/B split can't tell you why individuals respond to your

Exhibit 20–2.   Variations in the Uses of Splits

A/B Split	Clump Split	Flip-Flop Split
A	A	A
B	A	B
A	A	B
B	B	A
	B	
	B	

ad, the technique can tell you what they responded to. And a real bonus is that when you have completed your tests, you'll have a list of solid prospects.

A/B Splits.   In an ideal situation, an issue of a split-run publication will carry Ad A in every other copy and Ad B in the alternate copies.

Clump Splits.   Most often, however, publications cannot produce an exact A/B split. They will promise a clump. That is, every lift of 50 copies, for instance, will be evenly split, or even every lift of 25 or 10. The clump can be very accurate when the test is done in large circulations.

Flip-Flops.   For publications that offer no split at all, you can create your own. Take two comparable publications, X and Y. Run Ad A in X and Ad B in Y for the first phase. Then for the second phase, reverse the insertions: Ad B in X and Ad A in Y. Total the respective results for A and B and compare.

The Split That Is Not.   We recently asked one magazine publisher if he ran splits. The production manager told us, ''Oh, yes, we run a perfect split. Our circulation divides exactly—one-half east of the Mississippi and one-half west.'' Look out. That is not a valid split.

In the A/B split, how can you compare one run against another run of the same ad? Following are ideas for keying coupons or response copy:

1. **Dating.** On your coupons, try JA397NA for January 3, 1997, in *Newsweek* for Ad A and JA397NB for the same insertion of Ad B.

2. **Department numbers.** Use Dept. A for Ad A and Dept. B for Ad B in your company's address.

3. **Color of coupon.** One color for Ad A, another for Ad B.

4. **Color of ink**

5. **Names.** In Ad A ask readers to send correspondence to Mr. Anderson; for Ad B, have them write to Mr. Brown.

6. **Telephone numbers**

7. **Shape of coupon**

8. **The obvious.** Right on the coupon, use "For Readers of *Glamour*" in Ad A and "For *Glamour* Readers" in Ad B.

9. **Abbreviations.** In your address, New York for Ad A, N.Y. for Ad B.

10. **Typeface.** In Coupon A, all caps for NAME, and so forth, and in Coupon B, upper-and lowercase for Name, and so on.

The possibilities are virtually unlimited. All you need is a code that's in keeping with your ad and the publication, one you find easy to understand and use.

Telescopic Testing

Although it is certainly necessary to construct meaningful A/B split tests, they do have limitations. When marketers run an A/B split test, they don't know what would have happened if they had been able to run Ad C against Ads A and B and, additionally, Ads D, E, F, and G—simultaneously, all in the same edition, all under measurable conditions.

Today, testing to find the best ad among a multiplicity of ads all tested under the same conditions is quite feasible. The method is widely known as *telescopic testing*. Telescopic testing is simply the process of telescoping an entire season of test ads into one master test program. (Examples of telescopic testing were given in Chapter 18.) Regional editions of publications and other developments make telescopic testing possible. Indeed, with regional editions you can telescope a year's testing sequence into a single insertion, testing many ads simultaneously. *TV Guide* offers the best opportunity for telescopic testing. It publishes over 100 different editions.

Tom Collins, a pioneer in telescopic testing, has established a rule of thumb for estimating the minimum circulation you should buy for your ad tests to make results meaningful. First, start by assuming you need an average of 200 responses per appeal to be statistically valid. Then, multiply your allowable advertising cost per response by 200. Finally, multiply that figure by the number of key numbers in the test. This will give you the total minimum expenditure required to get meaningful results.

To clarify the technique further, let's say you want to test four new ads against a control ad, which we will call Ad A. Your tests for the four new ads against the control ad will be structured as follows: A versus B; A versus C; A versus D; A versus E. Thus we have a total of five ads requiring eight different keys. (Ad A, the control ad, is being tested against a different ad in four separate instances and therefore requires four different keys.)

To read the results in this kind of test, we simply convert Ad A to 100 percent, depending on the results achieved. In this way, Ad C can be compared with Ad E, for instance, even though they are not directly tested against one another. Now, let's say we want to test the four new ads in *TV Guide* against the control ad. Further, using the Collins formula, let's assume we need a circulation of 2 million to get 200 or more replies for each side of each two-way split. The type of schedule that would be placed in *TV Guide* to accomplish this objective appears in Exhibit 20–3. Note that a careful review of the markets selected for each split (region) shows that all markets are balanced geographically.

Exhibit 20–3.   Sample Schedule for *TV Guide*

Split 1—Ad A versus Ad B		Split 2—Ad A versus Ad C	
Edition	**Circulation**	**Edition**	**Circulation**
San Francisco–Metro	750,000	Northern Wisconsin	170,000
Pittsburgh	225,000	Philadelphia	230,000
Detroit	225,000	Cleveland	55,000
South Georgia	67,000	Kansas City	230,000
Iowa	210,000	Western New England	175,000
Phoenix	275,000	North Carolina	272,000
Western Illinois	87,000	Colorado	139,000
Northern Illinois	186,000	Illinois/Wisconsin	225,000
	2,025,000	Gulf Coast	125,000
		Minneapolis–St. Paul	126,000
		Central California	115,000
		Southeast Texas	64,000
		West Virginia	165,000
			2,091,000

Split 3—Ad A versus Ad D		Split 4—Ad A versus Ad E	
Edition	**Circulation**	**Edition**	**Circulation**
Central Ohio	210,000	Eastern New England	665,000
Michigan State	309,000	Chicago Metro	475,000
Western New York State	65,000	Orlando	140,000
Central Indiana	230,000	Oklahoma State	184,000
San Diego	255,000	St. Louis	235,000
New Hampshire	141,000	Eastern Illinois	100,000
Portland	195,000	Missouri	141,000
Eastern Virginia	160,000	Eugene	45,000
Kansas	92,000	Idaho	57,000
Tucson	70,000		2,042,000
North Dakota	65,000		
Eastern Washington St.	145,000		
Evansville–Paducah	104,000		
	2,041,000		

Telescopic testing is not limited to regional editions of publications. Newspaper inserts serve as an ideal vehicle for such testing. The test pieces are intermixed at the printing plant before being shipped to the newspaper. All test pieces, however, must be exactly the same size. Otherwise, newspapers cannot handle them on their automatic inserting equipment.

Using full-page card inserts in magazines is another way to test many ads simultaneously. Scores of magazines now accept such inserts. It is important to remember that in telescopic testing we are looking for breakthroughs, not small differences. As Collins puts it, "We are not merely testing ads, we are testing hypotheses. Then when a hypothesis appears to have been proved by the results, it is often possible to construct other, even more successful ads, on the same hypothesis."

Test hypotheses tend to fall into four main categories:

1. What is the best price and offer?

2. Who is the best prospect?

3. What is the most appealing product advantage?

4. What is the most important ultimate benefit? (e.g., pride, admiration, safety, wealth, peace of mind)

Idea development and testing are soul mates. The two things to keep uppermost in mind are: (1) strive for breakthrough ideas and (2) test the big things.

SELF-QUIZ

1. What strategy did Yamaha employ to solve the dormant piano market problem? _____

   _____

   _____

2. Name four traits of successful creative people.

   a. _____   c. _____

   b. _____   d. _____

3. What are the duties of the leader in brainstorming?

   a. _____

   b. _____

c. _____

d. _____

e. _____

4. What are the three phases of the brainstorming process?

a. _____

b. _____

c. _____

5. What are the six big things to test in direct marketing?

a. _____

b. _____

c. _____

d. _____

e. _____

f. _____

6. What is the safest rule to follow in testing mailing lists?

_____

_____

_____

7. In direct mail testing, which is preferable?

☐ Testing components   ☐ Testing complete mailing packages

8. Name six ways to key a print ad.

a. _____

b. _____

c. _____

d. _____

e. _____

f. _____

9. Define *telescopic testing*.

_____

_____

_____

10. Name the four categories into which test hypotheses seem to fall.

a. _____

b. _____

c. _____

d. _____

PILOT PROJECT

You are engaged in a fantasy game. Three wishes follow. Come up with at least three solutions for each of the wishes.

1. I wish that I could get all my customers to suggest friends who would likewise become customers.

2. I wish that I could get all my customers to pay their bills within 45 days.

3. I wish that I could reach all the people in this country who are over 6 feet tall.

CHAPTER TWENTY-ONE

Research for Direct Marketers

Since the inception of direct marketing, the primary method for assessing direct marketing programs has been the "in-market" or "in-mail" test.

What has made the direct marketing process particularly appealing to marketers is that the results produced by these tests have been measurable, quantifiable, and predictable. In other words, these results have provided a quantified measurement of overt response in terms of "making the sale," "producing a qualified sales lead," or "stimulating someone to request further information."

By overlaying this overt behavior with geodemographic data, it has been possible to build statistical models that can define high-propensity response groups, providing far more precise methods for marketing and prospecting.

Research and Testing the Big Things

The most important question concerning marketing research is: "When should I spend money on marketing research?" Yet direct marketers frequently treat research and testing as an either/or proposition, viewing the two activities as financial trade-offs and choosing to spend their money on either testing or marketing research. Such reasoning, however, overlooks the fact that testing is an integral part of the total marketing research process and that marketing research and testing are therefore not separate issues.

The question of when you should use marketing research was clearly answered in the last chapter. You should spend money on marketing research before testing "the big things."

Direct marketers who complain that research has not worked have frequently employed it to evaluate subtactical issues such as exposing to focus groups various offers or laundry lists of product attributes.

As shown in Exhibit 21–1, many direct marketers begin their testing considerations at this lower, subtactical level, which is where the test plan should be implemented, not researched. Thus overlay selections and specific offers are frequently considered before a new target audience is defined and selected, or headlines and product attributes are evaluated without first developing a strong, relevant product positioning for the new target segment. Many research dollars are wasted on researching such subtactical issues.

Marketing research dollars are most effectively spent on evaluating strategic issues—evaluating the big things to be sure they are worth spending the time and money for testing. The use of marketing research in testing the big things serves two functions. First, it provides the basis for the financial go/no-go testing decision. That is, the cost estimate of the research can be compared with the projected revenue and profits obtained if the test is successful. (For example, should we spend $20,000 on marketing research to evaluate our chances of making a million-dollar profit?)

Second, marketing research can serve as a valuable insurance policy against possible test failure if the strategic marketing variables to be tested turn out not to be "the big things." Thus the estimated cost of the research can be compared with the projected profit and time losses if the test is a failure. (For

Exhibit 21–1.   A Hierarchy of Test Variables

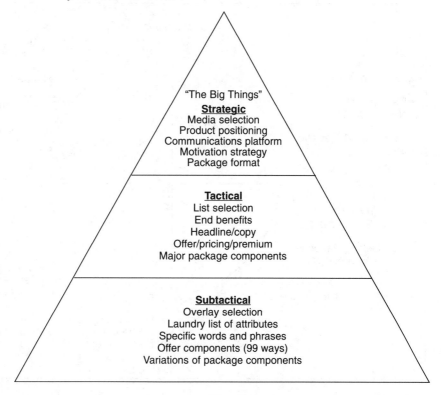

example, should we spend $30,000 on marketing research to help save a possible $20,000 loss as well as lose 6 months in developing a new test plan?)

The rest of this chapter demonstrates how marketing research has been and can be used to help in developing and testing the big things.

Testing and the Total Marketing Research Process

The testing process consists of four phases: (1) exploratory research, (2) pretesting, (3) testing, and (4) posttesting assessment. (See Exhibit 21–2.)

Phase 1: Exploratory Research

The exploratory phase of the testing process deals with defining and understanding your target audience as well as the marketplace in which you compete.

Exhibit 21–2. The Total Marketing and Research Process

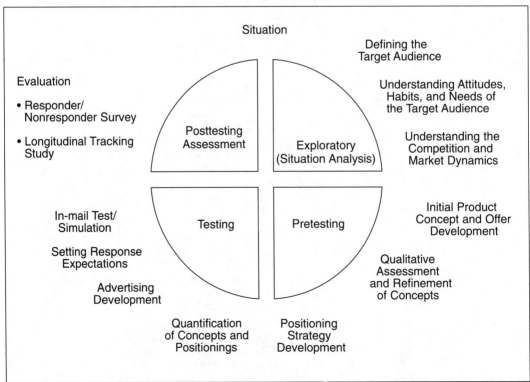

The focal point of the exploratory phase is situation analysis, which deals with understanding the geodemographic characteristics of your target audience as well as its attitudes, habits, and needs, particularly those characteristics that are most influential on heavy, regular usage of your product or service. The situation analysis should also cover the competition and market dynamics in terms of what attributes and benefits each competitive product or service brings to the market and why consumers are attracted to them. The end result of this situation analysis should be points of maximum leverage on which a direct marketing program can be developed. Such leverage points usually center on special ways of segmenting a target-audience, methods for reaching each specified target audience segment, and special ways of segmenting products or services.

Phase 2: Pretesting

The pretesting phase consists of developing, assessing, and refining the marketing and creative products before in-market testing. There are several issues that should be addressed in this phase:

- Determine that your product or service is offering an attribute or benefit that the consumer really wants—that is, something that is preemptive, setting it apart from the competition.

- Develop and refine the creative and the offer. In this area, qualitative research such as focus groups or in-depth individual interviews can help determine whether the creative approach is communicating information about the product or service and the offer in a manner that is clear, believable, and relevant to consumers in the target audience.

- Research usually referred to as *copy testing* can be used to assess alternative creative executions and offers. This research is usually quantitative in nature, that is, a survey, and is used to develop comparative profiles of the creative and the offer. Such research is useful in two ways. First, it helps to provide objective criteria for improving the creative or the offer, rather than giving them some subjective grade. Second and even of greater importance, however, is that this research can reduce the number of alternatives to be tested, thus greatly reducing test costs and increasing the accuracy of reading back-end results. Research done in the pretest phase can often help to uncover variables or clarify issues that should be addressed in the testing phase.

Phase 3: Testing

One question asked by businesses new to direct marketing is; ''When can we stop testing?'' And the answer, of course, is never. The testing process is dynamic and continuous (which is why the diagram in Exhibit 21–2 is a circle). The main objective in all testing is to learn, modify, and improve.

The testing phase brings together five key variables for assessment in the market:

- The product or service

- The medium or method of accessing the defined target audience

- The time or season

- The advertising/communication

- The offer or promotion

The test plan consists of the combinations in which these variables will be tested as well as the determination of response expectations and financial objectives.

Although all of the elements of the test plan are crucial, the most important single variable in direct marketing is the medium, or the access to the consumer, because this access provides the strongest point of leverage for all other test variables. In fact, if the medium cannot provide access to qualified consumers in sufficient quantities, the rest of the elements in the direct marketing mix become almost irrelevant by comparison. That is why testing is so critical to finding the lists that will access high-propensity prospects in sufficient quantities.

An alternative method of testing is simulation, which can be used in conjunction with five testing. Simulation systems such as STAR (Simulator Testing Advertising Response—a system developed by Direct Marketing Research Associates and Erard Moore Associates) predict response without running actual space advertising, package/statement inserts, or direct mail packages. Simulation can save time and costs by reducing the number of variables to be tested in-market and often by eliminating the need to address variables or issues that are of little importance to the direct marketing mix.

Simulation uses a close facsimile of an actual ad or direct mail package mailed to a sample of consumers with a questionnaire and letter. Separate packages are mailed to test and control cells. Data from the questionnaires are combined with actual responses to the simulated mailing to develop a prediction of relative response performance.

Phase 4: Posttesting Assessment

Posttesting assessment is potentially the area of greatest strength for direct marketing research. Assessment attempts both the analysis of test response and the development of diagnostic information in order to determine why the response rate was achieved and what can be done to achieve higher response rates.

The analysis of response rates is a measurement of overt behavior in terms of making a sale, a request for more information, or qualifying a sales lead. Marketing research can also provide diagnostic insights that can help to measure the quality of the response. For example, responder/nonresponder surveys can help pinpoint these issues:

- **Incremental sales:** The degree to which new consumers were attracted to the offer versus the sales' merely subsidizing current customers, particularly heavy or frequent buyers

- **Competitive conquest:** The degree to which competitive customers tried your product or service and were converted to regular customers

- **Attitudinal shifts:** The degree to which the brand image of your product or service was enhanced by direct advertising

In addition, questionnaires, which can help provide much added value to both the consumer and the marketer, can be included as an integral part of the mailing package.

- The response to relevant questions about the product or service helps to establish a vital two-way communication, or dialog, between the marketer and the consumer.

- The dialog can help establish a relationship with the consumer that can give the product or service a preemptive position in the mind of the consumer.

- The information provided by consumers can be used to qualify or segment them, giving the marketer valuable insights into subsequent positioning of products or services and more precisely targeting the appropriate message to the appropriate segment.

Marketing Research for Traditional and Nontraditional Direct Marketers

Let's begin by comparing the key direct marketing problems faced by traditional direct marketers versus those confronting nontraditional direct marketers. Once these issues are comprehended, it will be easier to understand the role that marketing research needs to play in each of the two areas.

It has been said that in the land of the blind, the one-eyed man is king. Traditional direct marketing today finds itself in exactly the opposite environment: How to compete when everyone has the eyesight of an eagle? Thus traditional direct marketers today find themselves in a maturing industry in which the major competitors are experienced and sophisticated, many of the market segments are glutted with similar products and services, and everyone's mailbox is cluttered with similar pieces.

Within such an environment, marketing research should address such issues as:

- Developing mailing pieces that cut through the mailbox clutter by being targeted more discretely and relevantly to specific consumer segments in terms of the offer and the visual and message elements. This could certainly help to dramatically increase response rates and enhance the marketer's image while making the sale.

- More effectively prospecting for new customers by developing an in-depth understanding of the types and numbers of "high-propensity prospects" available and translating these consumer segments into targetable groups that can be directly accessed. This could help reduce quantities mailed as well as mailing costs.

- Providing strategic direction of growing traditional direct marketing businesses in terms of identifying new product and service categories with high growth potential, assessing the most dynamic segments within each category, and screening for the most viable products and services within each segment.

Nontraditional direct marketers such as consumer goods manufacturers and retailers are just beginning to explore the many possible applications that direct marketers can offer their businesses. These applications include the following:

- Institutional direct marketing programs in which the use of major consumer brands can be extended from home consumption to include institutional consumption

- The use of direct marketing for a direct distribution system as an alternative or supplement to retail distribution (A direct marketing distribution system can be quite effective for name brands of clothing and gourmet food items that require an inordinate number of stockkeeping units and a great deal of copy and illustration to sell successfully.)

- The use of direct marketing as a vehicle for testing new positionings for a brand economically and discretely, without telling the media or competitors and without disturbing your current franchise

- Targeted promotions that can be used by retailers and manufacturers to provide specific measurable, projectable promotional programs to selected prospects and customers

- Customized communications that can be used by retailers and manufacturers to deliver discrete, measurable messages targeted to specific customer or prospect profiles

- The use of direct marketing as a media vehicle to provide direct access to selected customers and prospects for retailers and manufacturers

The role of marketing research as it relates to a number of nontraditional direct marketing approaches (see Exhibit 21–2) can include two broad areas: the front-end, or development of programs; and the back-end, which is concerned with the measurement and assessment of these programs.

Direct Marketing Research for Consumer Products

Let us now examine some specific examples in which marketing research can support direct marketing efforts for consumer products and services.

The first example will demonstrate the use of research in the initial phases, the exploratory and pretest phases, by defining target-audience segments, providing an understanding of these segments, and translating this understanding into product/service positionings, an offer, and a relevant, believable, understandable message.

In the past, direct marketers centered their research activities on analyzing consumers' geodemographic characteristics and purchase behaviors. Direct marketers used these approaches because these two variables are most readily linked with list and prospect selection. Attitudinal, psychographic, and lifestyle data have been much underutilized by direct marketers because these factors are not readily translated to list or prospect selection.

Four Research Levels

To realistically define, understand, reach, and communicate with target audiences, however, it is imperative that research deal with consumers on all four relevant levels:

- Geodemographics

- Psychographics and lifestyles

- Attitudes

- Purchase behavior

All four factors must be dealt with. They must all be integrated to form pictures of "real" consumers, who they are and where they live (geodemographics); what their basic attitudes and values toward life are and how these attitudes are translated into the way these persons live (psychographics and lifestyles); their perceptions, attitudes, and values with respect to various product and service categories (attitudes); and how these perceptions, attitudes, and values translate into selection making in the marketplace (purchase behavior).

Positive Attitude Group

The Stone & Adler Study of Consumer Behavior and Attitudes toward Direct Marketing was the first attempt to perform such an interdisciplinary synthesis. The study was designed, fielded, and analyzed with the help of Goldring & Company Inc. and the Home Testing Institute. Once the data were collected within each of the four levels, they were integrated through a software program called PAG (Positive Attribute Group).[1]

PAG is a comprehensive analytical technique for determining the combination of purchase activities, demographics, psychographics and lifestyles, and attitudes toward direct marketing at work in the direct marketing environment. PAG enabled us to segment the direct marketing environment and identify the four variables and their combinations that were active in each segment.

The PAG program subsequently produced six consumer clusters arrayed in an order (of importance) that breathed life into each of the clusters.

Cluster 1: Mailbox Gourmets.   Let us begin with the most important cluster for direct marketers. Mailbox Gourmets are the magical 26 percent of the population targeted by almost all direct marketers. In terms of psychographics and lifestyles, Mailbox Gourmets perceive themselves to be sophisticated. They want more of everything, especially travel. They are extremely active and involved and perceive themselves as not having enough leisure time.

Mailbox Gourmets are affluent. Their demographics show them to be above average in education and income and to be engaged in white-collar occupations. This cluster is also female-intensive. Although three-fourths are married, this percentage is slightly below marriage averages. The family structure is less traditional, with more two-paycheck families or single professionals, particularly women.

It is not surprising that their attitudes toward direct marketing are extremely positive. They enjoy it and are comfortable with it. Although most people perceive themselves to be novices when transacting by mail or phone, these people perceive themselves to be experts.

All of this information translates into direct marketing purchasing behavior that earns this cluster its name: they spend a lot (significantly more than any other cluster) and they buy often.

Cluster 2: Young Turks.   In terms of psychographics and lifestyles, the Young Turks are very trendy, as one would expect. They also consider themselves to be—whether they are, in fact, or not—sophisticated and worldly. Demographically, this group accounts for 10 percent of the households and form a perfect yuppie profile: They are single and male-intensive, well educated, and economically aspiring.

Although Young Turks are also very positive toward direct marketing, they tend to be cautious because they are emerging consumers. This makes them very "presentation sensitive." Because they are so active, they are more likely to order via an 800 number than any other cluster group. The Young Turks are the second highest group in terms of dollars spent and purchase frequency, but their expenditures are significantly less than those of the Mailbox Gourmets.

---

[1]Goldring & Company, © 1986.

Cluster 3: Life Begins at 50. The Life-Begins-at-50 cluster comprises 7 percent of households and is completely middle-of-the-road in terms of psychographics and lifestyle. Demographics indicate that these older consumers are "empty nesters": Their children are grown and away at college or married. As a group they are engaged in a mixture of blue- and white-collar occupations.

Like the Young Turks, the Life-Begins-at-50 cluster is also quite positive but cautious toward direct marketing. The cautiousness, in this case, is due to the fact that these people are the experienced "old pros" who have been shopping direct for 20–30 years. This experience has been transformed into a demanding attitude. They know what they want and the marketer had better give it to them.

These data translate into direct marketing dollar expenditures and purchase frequencies just below those of the Young Turks, but the products this cluster is likely to buy are vastly different. The Life-Begins-at-50 cluster is more likely to buy higher-ticket items such as home furnishings or housewares. They are also more likely to buy vitamins and minerals and to belong to a book club. Young Turks, on the other hand, are more likely to purchase products related to self-indulgence, such as electronic toys and sports equipment.

Cluster 4: Dear Occupant. Now we come to the great faceless, nameless masses that account for 14 percent of households—"Dear Occupant." Actually, they are the leftovers in the clustering process and therefore represent those who were:

- Neither too positive nor too negative in their attitudes

- Neither affluent nor destitute

- Neither the lightest nor the heaviest buyers

As such, they are truly the mundane, the moderate, the middle.

Cluster 5: Kitchen Patriots. When members of these households (23 percent of the total) are not out shopping at their favorite shopping mall or mass merchandiser, they are likely to be home reading the daily newspaper, a magazine, or their mail at the kitchen table à la Archie and Edith Bunker.

In terms of lifestyles and psychographics, this cluster is the backbone of traditional American morality and values:

- They are extremely patriotic.

- Home, family, and community are extremely important to them.

- They have sufficient leisure time, which is one reason they shop so much. In fact, many of them have more time than money.

Demographically, this group is blue-collar intensive, average in income and education, and indexes highest among those 55 years old and older.

Although the Kitchen Patriots' attitudes toward direct marketing are basically negative, they like to browse through their mail, including direct mail pieces and catalogs. But because of their negative attitudes toward direct marketing, coupled with their propensity toward retail shopping, Kitchen Patriots tend to be non-direct-marketing buyers or light, selective buyers at best.

Cluster 6: Above-It-Alls.   Finally, we have the most negative, the pro-retail cluster, the "Above-It-Alls" that account for 20 percent of all households. They are nearly a carbon copy of the Mailbox Gourmet, with a major difference: they are anti-mailbox. In terms of lifestyles and psychographics, this cluster is career-oriented, active, and involved in fads and causes. It perceives itself as taking a leadership position, and it is athletic.

Demographically, Above-It-Alls are somewhat more affluent than Mailbox Gourmets. They tend to be more traditional in household compositions. Wives are, more often than not, full-time homemakers—which, of course, gives them more time for retail shopping. This cluster also tends to be more strictly suburban than the Mailbox Gourmets, who are more split between suburbs and cities. The Above-It-Alls' attitude toward direct marketing is basically negative. In fact, not only do Above-It-Alls like mail, in general, much less than any other group, but they also don't like to browse. In particular, they don't see direct marketing as a convenience. Not surprisingly, this cluster rates as non-direct-marketing buyers or light, selective buyers at best. They want to see and touch the merchandise first, try it on, and obtain instant gratification both in purchasing and returning merchandise.

Putting Attitudinal Research to Work for Your Business

If information is to be useful to a business, it must be analyzed and interpreted for strategic implications that lead to specific actions. Let us now take a look at how attitudinal data can be directly applied to business in terms of the following:

1. Profiling target audiences and product categories

2. Segmenting customers for precise file selection and developing highly targeted products, services, and creative appeals

Profiling Target Audiences and Categories

There are two major reasons why a business might want to use target-audience and category profiling:

1. For new-business development

2. For expanding an established business

For new-business development, it is important to know who are the users within a category. Not only is it important to know who they are geodemographically for the purpose of list selection, but it is also important to know who they are attitudinally. Attitudinal understanding leads to meaningful positioning to the target audience. Thus the target audience can be communicated with in the most relevant, believable, and understandable manner.

For expanding an established business, profiling can provide an important perspective to the direct marketers by showing how high is up. Unfortunately, too many direct marketers are trapped by their house files; they don't have the necessary information to make the best strategic use of media when prospecting.

Profiling can provide these insights by allowing direct marketers to compare customers on their files against category users on a national basis. Thus direct marketers can judge whether they are obtaining their fair share of the target-audience pie. If they are not, they can fine-tune their demographics for media selection. Even more importantly, they can fine-tune their creative approach and offer so that they have a better chance of being seen and read by their target-audience prospect.

Let us briefly examine how such profiling and segmentation can be done. The first step is for the marketer to perform a buyer concentration analysis from its customer file, as shown in Exhibit 21–3. Such a buyer concentration study will segment the file into groups of heavy or frequent buyers, medium buyers, and light or infrequent buyers.

Exhibit 21–3.   Buyer Concentration Analysis

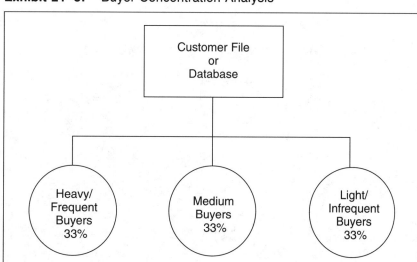

The second step consists of overlaying the buyer segments with attitudinal and lifestyle data, and then developing a second level of segmentation, as shown in Exhibit 21–4. This segmentation is accomplished by selecting a sample of names from the house file and administering a survey questionnaire containing attitudinal and lifestyle questions. By combining the answers to these questions with the geodemographic and purchase behavior data already on the file, PAG clusters can then be developed. At this stage, two analyses are critical: (1) the percentage of the customer file that comprises each of the six clusters and (2) the percentage of light, medium, and heavy buyers that comprised each of the six clusters.

The third step consists of developing a profile comparing your customer file and a nationally representative sample of consumers (i.e., a consumer database). This comparison allows you to determine whether you are getting your fair share of the following:

- Affluent/upscale consumers

- Younger or emerging consumers entering the marketplace

Exhibit 21–4.   Attitudinal and Lifestyle Overlay

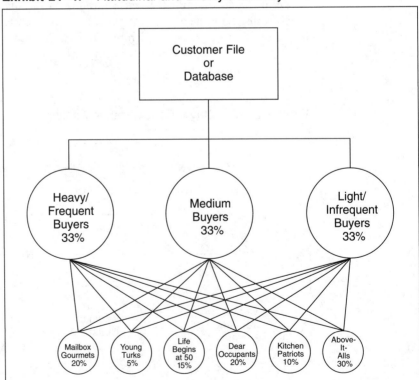

- Transitional consumers who are changing their lifestyles and their purchasing habits

For example, the comparative profile shown in Exhibit 21–5 points to a possible problem with the highest-propensity direct marketing consumers, who are significantly underrepresented in the customer file. There could be similar problems if the buyer concentration analysis shows that a disproportionate number of Mailbox Gourmets, Young Turks, and Life-Begins-at-50 consumers are merely medium and light buyers.

Applying Customer Segmentation

The use of national consumer databases can bring additional strategic marketing insights to your business when applied across a variety of product and service categories as well as segments within these categories. (See Chapter 2.) Let us review some examples of such applications in three diverse categories: insurance, credit cards, and clothing catalogs.

Insurance Profiles.   The *Stone & Adler Study of Behavior and Attitudes toward Direct Marketing* examined both the incidence of insurance inquiries and insurance purchases (by mail or phone) during a preceding 12-month period. The total incidence of inquiries was higher than expected at 25.9 percent. When the incidence of inquiries was analyzed by individual consumer clusters, it was observed that inquiries were relatively flat across all six clusters (see Exhibit 21–6).[2]

Thus inquiries were not skewed toward those clusters that were direct mail responsive. In other words, of the total inquiries, the extremely direct-marketing-

[2]Data for Exhibits 21–6 through 21–14 are from the Stone & Adler National Profile.

Exhibit 21–5.   Comparative Consumer Profile

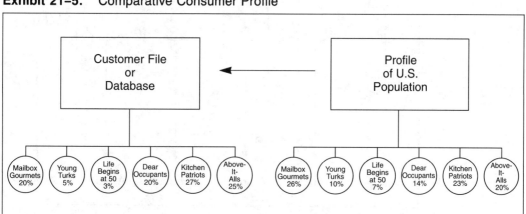

Exhibit 21–6.   Insurance Inquiries by Consumer Cluster

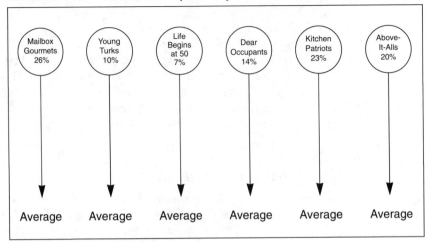

positive Mailbox Gourmets accounted for 26 percent of the inquiries, while the extremely direct-marketing-negative Above-It-Alls accounted for 20 percent of the inquiries, which is directly proportional to their representation in the general population. If the inquiries were indexed by cluster, therefore, each cluster would index at 100.

The incidence of insurance conversions by mail or phone totaled approximately 44 percent of the conversions, or 11 percent of the total sample (Exhibit 21–7). When the incidence of conversions was analyzed by individual consumer clusters, the same pattern emerged for conversions as for inquiries.

Exhibit 21–7.   Insurance Conversions by Consumer Cluster

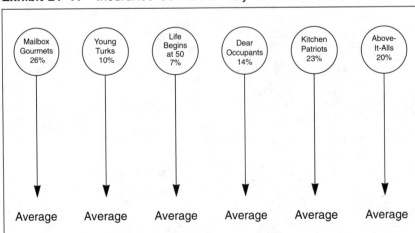

Conversions were also relatively flat across all six clusters. That is, conversions were not skewed toward those clusters that were the most direct mail responsive in other categories. Again, conversions were proportionate to each cluster's representation in the total U.S. population. All clusters would therefore index at or near 100.

The conclusion drawn was that insurance was one of the least direct marketing responsive of all the 26 product and service categories surveyed in the Stone & Adler study. However, the potential direct marketing audience for insurance is much larger than many other categories, because it has a less negative bias toward direct marketing.

But to take advantage of such an opportunity, direct marketers must strategically use research data of the type shown above to:

- Define the highest-propensity consumer segments for each type of insurance product

- Understand the needs for each type of insurance product from the perspective for each consumer segment

- Communicate the positioning, offer, and benefits of each insurance product in a manner that is understandable, relevant, and believable to the targeted consumer segments

Credit Card Acquisition Profiles.   Credit card acquisition in the Stone & Adler study included only new credit cards from new credit card sources that were obtained within the past 12 months. Acquisition did not include any credit cards that had expired and for which the company sent a new one. Acquisitions were based on either a solicitation received in the mail or a coupon sent in from a newspaper or magazine ad.

Acquisition profiles were developed for the four major categories of cards:

- Bank cards such as Visa and MasterCard

- Travel and entertainment cards such as American Express, Carte Blanche, and Diners Club

- Department store cards such as those from Sears, J.C. Penney, Wards, Neiman-Marcus, Saks Fifth Avenue, and local department stores

- Gasoline cards such as Amoco, Shell, and Texaco

The total incidence of bank card acquisition was 20 percent. As you can see in Exhibit 21–8, the incidence by cluster was heavily skewed toward the clusters that are the most positive toward direct marketing.

The total incidence of travel and entertainment card acquisition was 5 percent, which was the lowest of all four credit card market segments and a good

Exhibit 21–8. Bank Card Acquisition Patterns

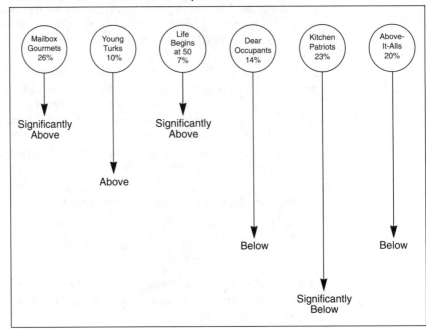

indication of the maturity that this segment is displaying. Again, acquisition of travel and entertainment cards, for the most part, is skewed toward the most direct-marketing-positive clusters. (See Exhibit 21–9.)

The total incidence of department store card acquisition was 23 percent. This percentage was the highest of all four credit card segments. The same skewed pattern that we observed in bank and travel and entertainment cards persists, except that it is even more accentuated. (See Exhibit 21–10.)

The gasoline credit card segment also showed a degree of maturity similar to that of travel and entertainment cards, with an incidence of acquisition at 12 percent. The skewing of acquisition toward positive direct marketing clusters is the least pronounced in this market segment. (See Exhibit 21–11.)

In summary, when above-average acquisition patterns are observed across all four credit card segments, clearly the most positive direct marketing clusters demonstrate the highest propensity to obtain credit cards. (See Exhibit 21–12.)

What are the implications of credit card acquisition being so heavily skewed toward positive direct marketing consumers? First, there is a general need for credit. Clearly, there is a new need for total credit in the form of multiple cards, not merely one card. But who are these high-propensity credit card acquirers? Supplementary work in this area shows that there are identifiable, targetable groups such as emerging and transitional consumers.

Emerging consumers can be found in the Young Turks cluster and among the younger Mailbox Gourmets. Demographically, these are recent college or technical school graduates, young aspiring professionals, newlyweds, and new

Exhibit 21–9. Travel and Entertainment Card Acquisition Patterns

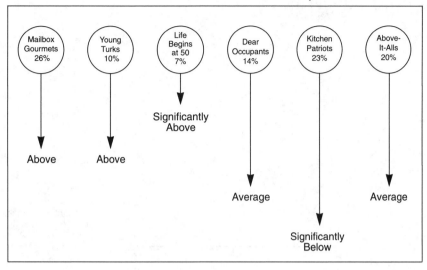

parents (Full Nest I). Transitional consumers can be most readily found in the Life-Begins-at-50 cluster and among the older Mailbox Gourmets. These people are undergoing major lifestyle changes such as divorce, remarriage, or a midlife career change, all of which affect credit needs.

Catalog Clothing Buyer Profiles.   Respondents to the Stone & Adler study were asked whether they had purchased any clothing within the past three months either at retail outlets or through mail order (where "you sent in a mail

Exhibit 21–10. Department Store Card Acquisition Patterns

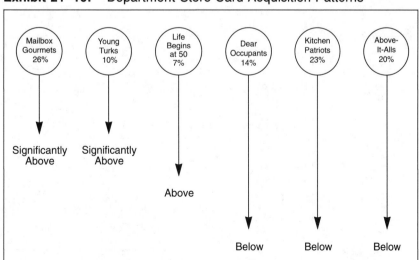

Exhibit 21–11. Gasoline Card Acquisition Patterns

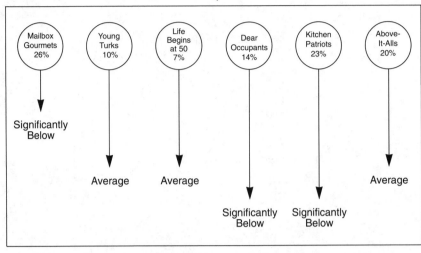

order form or phoned in your order, and the item was delivered to your home, office, or elsewhere''). At 74 percent, the total incidence of purchasing clothing from all sources, both retail and direct, was the highest of all 26 categories measured in the Stone & Adler study.

As can be seen in Exhibit 21–13, the Mailbox Gourmets and Young Turks, the two most positive direct marketing clusters, demonstrated the highest incidence; the Kitchen Patriots and Above-It-Alls, the most negative direct marketing groups, showed the lowest incidence.

Exhibit 21–12. Above-Average Acquisition Patterns

	Mailbox Gourmets 26%	Young Turks 10%	Life Begins at 50 7%	Dear Occupants 14%	Kitchen Patriots 23%	Above-It-Alls 20%
Bank cards	X	X	X			
T-and-E cards	X	X	X			
Department store cards	X	X	X			
Gasoline cards	X					

Exhibit 21–13. Clothing Buyer Profile—Retail and Direct

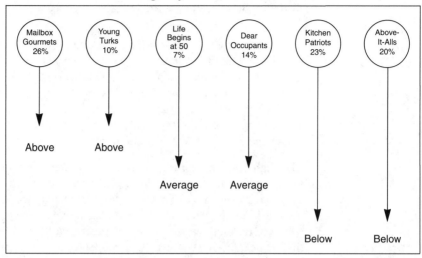

When we isolate catalog clothing purchases, a somewhat different pattern emerges (Exhibit 21–14). The incidence of purchase among Mailbox Gourmets registers significantly above average at 52 percent on an index of 200. Conversely, the incidence among Young Turks slips below average at 8 percent. And the incidence among Kitchen Patriots slips to under one-half of their representation in the sample of 11 percent, while purchase incidence of Above-It-Alls registers

Exhibit 21–14. Catalog Clothing Buyer Profiles

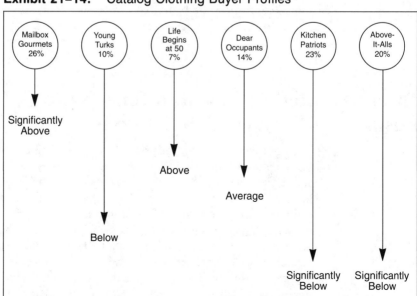

a mere 5 percent, or one-quarter of their representation in the sample. Several strategic implications can be drawn from these data:

- Mailbox Gourmets are conspicuous consumers in the clothing category. They buy more at both retail and catalog. Unfortunately, the growing mailbox clutter is also centering on this group because Mailbox Gourmets are on "everyone's" mailing list. Research should be used, therefore, to develop intrusive catalogs and mass media advertising to break through the clutter, and to develop unique types or lines of merchandise that will continue to attract the loyalty of Mailbox Gourmets.

- Although the Life-Begins-at-50 cluster exhibited the second highest propensity to buy clothing from catalogs, their purchases tend to be concentrated on a much narrower range of merchandise than the Mailbox Gourmets. Research should be used, therefore, to develop creative messages that motivate this cluster to try products they have not purchased by mail before, and to select the merchandise with the highest propensity to generate trial.

- The underperformance by the Young Turks represents a major lost opportunity to clothing catalog marketers, particularly in terms of an extremely high net present value. Research could help by directing catalog marketers on the best ways of communicating with and reassuring them about the key issues of styling and fit.

- Although the Kitchen Patriots and Above-It-Alls do not represent a major opportunity for direct mail clothing sales, they should not be summarily dismissed by direct marketers. Since direct mail, particularly catalogs, are used by both of these groups as reference materials for retail shopping, direct marketing can be used effectively among both groups as a targeted advertising vehicle to increase retail traffic.

Direct Marketing Research for Business-to-Business Applications

Many people ask whether the principles of marketing and research are the same for business-to-business products and services as they are for consumer products and services. After all, this line of reasoning goes, the people making purchases for businesses are the same consumers who buy television sets, automobiles, and toothpaste, aren't they? The answer is, "Not exactly."

When John Q. Consumer begins buying products for a business, the situation becomes much more complicated than it is for consumer products. In a business environment, he is part of a much larger, more complex institutional hierarchy. Thus responsibility for the purchase decision, as well as the ultimate consumption of the products or services, is a much more involved process.

For example, regardless of the organization of the business, the target audience within a business will normally have at least three hierarchical levels. (See Exhibit 21–15.) The purchaser is the person responsible for recommending and making the purchase, whether he or she is the purchasing agent, office manager, or director of human resources. The gatekeeper is a CEO or chief financial officer from whom the purchaser must often obtain approval. The end-user is often a department manager in the production, accounting, or marketing department whose department will actually be using the products or services purchased. In fact, either the gatekeeper or end-user can originate the purchasing process as well as influence it.

Finding Qualified Prospects

To make matters even more difficult, there are problems with finding qualified prospects on each of these three levels. First, we must understand that not everyone we contact is in the market for our products or services. At one extreme are those prospects who are simply not interested, either in our product or service category, or in the particular brand we are selling. Others might have recently purchased and made long-term commitments. Thus, although these prospects are in our category, they are not available to us for an extended time.

At the other extreme are those who are left, a group of prospects we call *active considerers*. And not even all of these prospects are available to us, because they must first be converted from prospects to serious shoppers.

Thus direct marketers often approach business-to-business marketing problems by merely testing and retesting rather than carefully defining and thor-

Exhibit 21–15.   Business-to-Business Purchasing Process

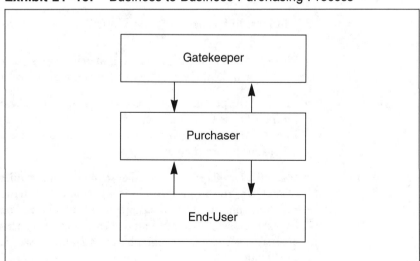

oughly understanding each level of prospect audience being targeted. You can readily see why the odds of success are so often slight. How can marketing research raise the odds of obtaining the highest-propensity prospects? Let's review a couple of examples.

Profiling

Business-to-business house files can be matched against a national database of businesses such as Dun & Bradstreet. This process will result in a more thorough knowledge of the current client base—a well-defined target market for future prospecting. With this knowledge comes a better understanding of the marketing and communications programs necessary to more effectively penetrate the desired segments.

The information and insights obtained through profiling can help the business-to-business marketer accomplish a number of objectives:

- **Marketing and creative:** To define and target business segments of the highest propensity; to provide creative and marketing guidance in communicating with high-propensity target audience segments on a clearer, more relevant, and believable basis

- **Promotional:** To provide creative and marketing guidance in developing specific reactivation and increased activity programs to the current customer file

- **Sales:** To help increase the efficiency of the sales force, by directing them to concentrate their efforts on the highest-propensity segments of the prospect universe

- **Media:** To attain greater efficiency in direct mail and other media

Business-to-business profiling is usually developed in three phases:

- **Phase I: Account identification and matching.** This phase consists of linking the national database operations files to the business-to-business house file.

- **Phase II: Appending data from the national database to the business-to-business house file.** This phase utilizes the existing compiled business establishment data (e.g., geographic, type of business, size of business, and type of location) from the national database.

- **Phase III: Development of market segmentation profiles.** This phase consists of analyzing the business-to-business customer file on the basis of the distribution and concentration of customers within specific market segments (e.g., the extent to which your current best customers are concentrated within certain areas such as SIC codes, geographic areas, company size, and revenue contribution groups).

Another way of analyzing the activities of current customers and assessing their potential is by drawing maps or creating matrixes of current purchasing activities, as shown in Exhibit 21–16. Based on the purchase activity quadrant in which the customer falls, we are in a position to segment our customer file and target specific messages and offers to best leverage the different opportunities:

- Quadrant 1 represents our best customers, those who spend the most dollars and purchase the most frequently. Clearly, the emphasis in this segment is on maintaining loyalty and providing rewards for continuity.

- Quadrant 2 represents customers who spend a lot of dollars but spend infrequently. Large average-order sizes combined with low levels of purchase frequency indicate that they might be using us for a few specialized purchases. Supplementary research, such as in-depth personal interviews among a sample of customers in this quadrant, can help uncover the reasons we are being used on an infrequent, specialized basis. These issues can then be addressed in both the creative and the offer to move them into Quadrant 1.

- Quadrant 3 represents customers who spend just a few dollars but make purchases relatively frequently. Small average-order sizes combined with high levels of purchase frequency indicate that these customers are "cherry picking" our inventory, concentrating on the lowest-cost sales items. Again, supplementary research, such as in-depth personal interviews among a sample of customers in this quadrant, can help us uncover problems that can be addressed with both creative and offers to stimulate purchases of a wider range of merchandise, particularly higher-ticket items.

Exhibit 21–16. Purchase Activity Matrix

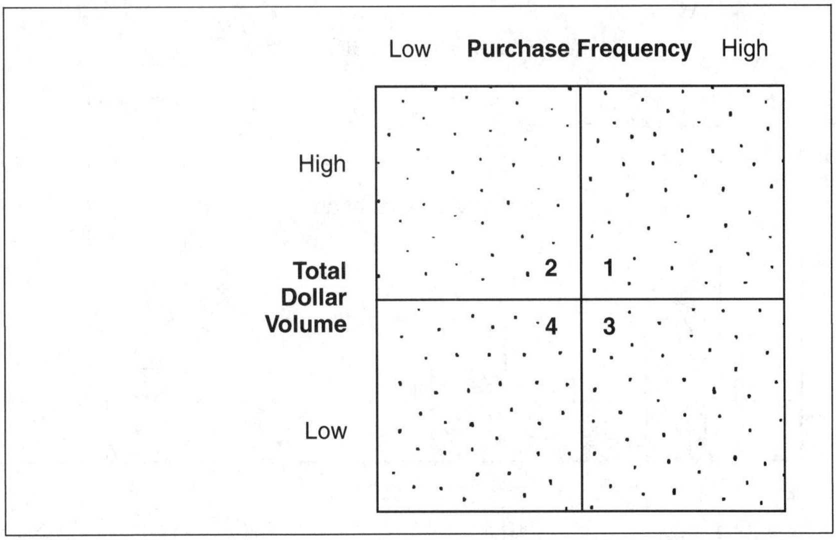

- Quadrant 4 represents the worst of all worlds: the customer who doesn't spend very much or very often. The potential payoff in identifying such customers is in saving money by targeting a higher proportion of spending toward customers in the first three quadrants.

We can further assess the potential of these customers by observing the degree to which companies with certain characteristics, such as SIC code, size, and geographic location, tend to be concentrated in certain quadrants. For example, if customers from four SIC codes are predominant within Quadrant 1 (highest sales volume, greatest purchase frequency), we should then analyze what our share of market or degree of penetration is in each of the four SIC codes. When this is done by comparing the customers in our house file against the total number of businesses within each SIC code on the national database, a profile of our market penetration can be drawn, as shown in Exhibit 21–17.

Primary Research for Marketing and Creative Development

Sometimes there is insufficient information available for profiling, particularly when a new market or segment is being entered. Such situations call for the marketer to obtain primary information directly from prospects in the form of qualitative information (focus groups or in-depth personal interviews) and/or quantitative data (surveys).

Exhibit 21–17.   Company Penetration in Selected Market Segments

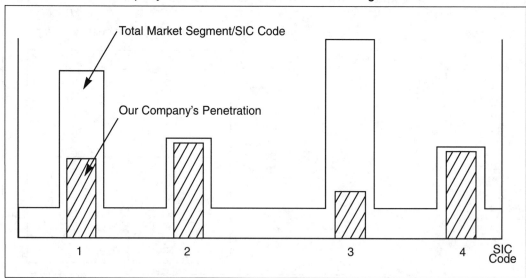

The need for research relating to a new marketing venture arose when the Harris Corporation called on Stone & Adler to develop qualified leads for marketing a state-of-the-art office automation system. This unique system performed both word-processing and data-processing functions from a single workstation and could function as a compatible component of the current user's data-processing network.

Because this was a new marketing venture for Harris, research was needed to provide a basic understanding of the attitudes toward, and the decision-making process involved in, selecting office automation systems:

- How is the need for office automation systems arrived at? How is the purchase process initiated?

- Who is involved in the decision-making process?

- What criteria are used in the decision-making process?

- What information sources are used in the decision-making process?

Research was also needed to understand what the effect of the low recognition level of Harris Corporation as an entrant in this market would have on key prospects.

Because the proposed target audience for this system were the *Fortune* 1,000 companies, the research process began with focus groups consisting of key decision makers for office automation systems selected from a sample of these companies. A wide variety of industry groups were included.

To begin with, the exercise of finding the real key decision makers in the sample corporations became a survey unto itself. Often, three to five contacts had to be made before the actual decision maker was reached. This knowledge had major implications for our ultimate targeting, because the actual titles of the decision makers varied widely. Some had traditional titles such as manager/ director of management information systems, manager/director of office automation systems, or manager/director of information services. But most decision makers had titles that appeared to be unique to each sample company and contained several functions under one hat, such as manager of office information systems and corporate planning and administration, manager of office automation systems and information center, or director of office automation systems and information technology.

Decision-Making Process

Regardless of the decision maker's title however, he or she (approximately 20 percent of the persons in our sample were female) formed one level within a three-level purchase process hierarchy. (See Exhibit 21–18.)

The purchase process centered around the manager/director of management information systems (MIS) or office automation systems (OAS) as the functional

Exhibit 21–18.   Purchase Process Hierarchy

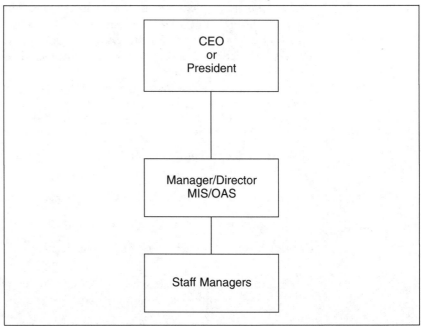

leader, the technical expert. The CEO or president's involvement in the decision-making process tended to revolve around the issue of financial considerations and the effect of the computer systems on the operating efficiencies of the departments obtaining the equipment. In some instances, however, the CEO or president was the originator of the purchasing process.

The perspective of the staff managers was specifically applications-oriented in terms of "What functions will the machine perform for my department?" "How easy is the equipment for my people to learn, because they aren't EDP experts?" "How compatible is the software with our current software?" "What happens if something breaks?" The purchase process frequently began from this perspective. Usually one of three scenarios occurs:

1. The department manager wishes to have an additional piece of equipment that is already in another department of the company.

2. The department manager wishes to have an additional piece of equipment from a "nonapproved" vendor.

3. The department manager requests a major new system, which requires a system study to be conducted.

Scenarios 2 and 3 will require major involvement on the part of the MIS/OAS director.

Current Marketing Environment

The Harris Corporation was facing a marketing environment in which much of the investment in major office automation equipment had already been made. Hence for most target prospects, the emphasis was on updating and refining the systems already in place. (Current systems were generally decentralized. Each division operated its own mainframe; a few were without mainframes.)

The procedures for purchasing this type of equipment appear to be ritualized and formal. Many corporations have ongoing equipment investigation committees. Purchases are often made based on an "approved vendor list" consisting of large, well-known companies such as IBM, Wang, and DEC. (Harris was not on approved vendor lists.) These decisions are of such high visibility that most MIS and OAS key decision makers tend to be relatively conservative in terms of not looking to be "the first" to try a product or system. In the eloquent words of one battle-scarred OAS director, "I have no desire to be on the bleeding edge."

Major Criteria for Office Automation System Selection.

A major requirement when purchasing new equipment appears to be system compatibility, for two basic reasons. First, a significant amount of money has been spent on the current equipment, and additions must therefore be able to interface with it. Second, most systems purchases involve software rather than hardware and are being purchased for ordinary managers and clerical workers rather than for data-processing people. Therefore, new equipment must require minimum training and run current software programs. The second major requirement is for equipment and systems that satisfy basic functional needs of the department.

Other key aspects of office automation equipment that decision makers looked for during their last purchase of equipment included the following:

- Ease of use

- Ability to share the system among other operators

- Support with installation, software, and maintenance

- Communication with other equipment

- Staying power of the vendor company

Sources of Information in Decision Making

When looking for information on new products, key decision makers tended to rely on the following:

- Word of mouth from peers in the field and other technical people at work, which was viewed as the most important source of information

- Marketing representatives and their companies' literature

- Seminars

- Trade publications

Other Information Developed

A variety of other information was developed from the study: reactions to concept statements describing the proposed office automation system on a blind (nonbrand) basis, research to determine which current competitors would most likely market such a system, and reactions to Harris Corporation's marketing such a system.

Conclusions and Implications

The conclusions and implications on which the subsequent advertising strategy was developed revolved around four issues:

- Credibility, or the ability to convince prospects that Harris Corporation's high level of experience and technical expertise in other markets was being transferred to the office automation equipment market

- Complexity of the decision-making process with multiple levels of target audiences, each having its own needs and points of view

- Conservatism on the part of key decision makers because of the high visibility of the decision and the concomitant need for risk reduction through vendor approval lists

- Compatibility with current systems in terms of both hardware and software

The Future of Research in Direct Marketing

The future of research will be dictated by the problems that it is asked to address. For example, as traditional marketing categories continue to mature and competitors face increasing clutter in the mailbox, in print, and on TV, the problem of identifying, understanding, and reaching the highest-propensity prospects looms larger and larger.

Hence the major problem common to both traditional and nontraditional direct marketers, given the current environment, is identifying and understanding key target audience segments. This is particularly true in terms of focusing on points of greatest strategic leverage and developing techniques to gain direct access to these segments. The problem is shared and must be jointly solved by research and media working in tandem. At first glance, this might seem to be a relatively simple, straightforward problem to solve, but it isn't.

Consumer Insights and Delivery Process

As long as the disciplines of research and media are treated as separate functions, they will not be able to participate in the consumer insights and delivery process that is needed to address the problems of both traditional and nontraditional direct marketers.

As you can see by the integrated process shown in Exhibit 21–19, the process begins with research defining who the target audience is and why it behaves the way it does.

The primary purpose of this chapter has been to show direct marketers and would-be direct marketers the true value of research and the types of research that can identify target markets and lead to well-executed direct response advertising. Conducting the actual research is best left to professional researchers. For the direct marketer, knowing what should be researched is imperative.

Exhibit 21–19. Consumer Insights and Delivery Process

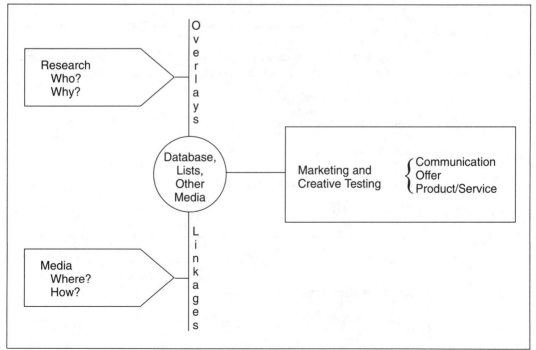

SELF-QUIZ

1. Name the last two of the four phases in the marketing research process.

   a. Exploratory research   c. _____

   b. Pretest   d. _____

2. The exploratory phase deals with defining and understanding the _____ audience.

3. The pretesting phase consists of developing, assessing, and refining the _____ and _____ products before in-market testing.

4. The testing phase consists of bringing together five key variables for assessment in the market:

   a. The product or service

   b. The media or method of accessing the defined target audience

   c. The time or season

   d. _____

   e. _____

5. Posttesting assesses reactions of both responders and nonresponders. Responder/nonresponder surveys can help pinpoint such issues as:

   a. Incremental sales

   b. Competitive conquest

   c. _____

6. Define *high-propensity prospects:*

   _____

   _____

   _____

7. Define these terms:

   Geodemographics _____

   _____

Psychographics and lifestyles _____

_____

8. PAG identifies six consumer clusters:

   a. Mailbox Gourmets   d. _____

   b. Young Turks   e. _____

   c. Life Begins at 50   f. _____

9. Why is it important to profile a target audience?

_____

_____

_____

10. Research principles are the same for business-to-business products and services as they are for consumer products and services.

   ☐ True   ☐ False

PILOT PROJECT

Suppose that your company acquired a product line in a category totally unfamiliar to you. No information exists about who uses such products or why. Consumer attitudes toward the line and competitive products are unknown.

Your assignment is to prepare a research plan that will provide the basic information necessary to market this product line. This plan should include a statement of research objectives for each project item and the specific type of technique best suited to meet the objectives.

Careers in Direct Marketing

Direct Marketing: An Excellent Career Choice

Forecasts from the 1995 DMA quantitative study "Economic Impact: U.S. Direct Marketing Today" have some dramatic implications for students and job seekers:[1]

- Direct marketing generated an estimated $594.4 billion in consumer sales and $498.1 billion in business-to-business sales. $1 out of every $15 in sales is related to a direct marketing sales activity.

- Growth in direct marketing sales in both consumer and business-to-business markets is fast outpacing the sales growth of the entire U.S. economy.

- One in every 13 jobs in the United States in 1995 is the result of direct marketing sales activity. About 4 million new jobs will be added between 1995 and 2000.

- More than half (57.1%) of U.S. advertising expenditures in 1995 is related to direct marketing.

With such statistics, a constant stream of talent will be required to fill positions in companies that are expanding their direct marketing efforts and in companies entering direct marketing for the first time—either exclusively or as an integrated function of their marketing and advertising mix. Those who have

Laurie Spar, Vice President, Direct Marketing Educational Foundation.
[1]Study conducted by the WEFA Group (formed in 1987 through a merger of Chase Econometrics and Wharton Economic Forecasting).

a basic understanding of the principles and practices of direct marketing will have a chance to start a very exciting career.

Advantages of a Direct Marketing Career

Direct marketing is growing daily and changing constantly. It's testable, measurable, and accountable and direct marketers know almost immediately what's working (and what's not). The constant emphasis on testing offers, new ideas, premiums, lists, etc., and the ability to measure the return on the investment, makes direct marketing accountable and therefore different from general marketing and advertising. There's a constant opportunity to learn, along with an opportunity for advancement. It's fun, and it's never dull!

Direct marketing is "smart" marketing/advertising, and the database is the key. Marketing databases help target the right message to the right prospect at the right time and establish relationships with customers. With businesses now more *customer*, rather than *market* driven, direct marketing helps establish and maintain vital relationships. Databases help to build brands, encourage repeat purchase, and enhance customer loyalty.

Who's Using Direct Marketing?

Virtually any kind of organization can use direct marketing to sell its products and services; raise funds; generate inquiries; call attention to issues; elect candidates; build store traffic; build brands, and generate leads for salespeople. These include consumer product manufacturers; financial service organizations (banks, savings and loan companies, personal credit and insurance companies); consumer mail order marketers; business and industrial mail order marketers; publishers (newspapers, magazines, book publishers); book-and-tape clubs; industrial manufacturers; business equipment manufacturers; retailers; public utilities; travel and transportation companies; package goods manufacturers and distributors; fund raisers; and service organizations (public relations, associations, management consultants, etc.). Many are *Fortune* 500 and 1,000 companies. Even companies that have traditionally used image-building general advertising are now integrating direct marketing into their marketing and advertising mix.

Global opportunities—companies using direct marketing within other countries, as well as U.S. firms doing business direct in foreign countries—represent yet another example of the growth of the field and a good reason for you to be in it.

Finally, interactive marketing (selling via TV and the Internet) represents the latest player in the direct marketing arena. Technological innovations and the fact that more and more individuals are using PCs and on-line services will make a knowledge of direct techniques more valuable and will open up an entire host of new career opportunities. Job titles and descriptions vary from company to company. Listed below are some general ideas.

Careers in Direct Response Advertising Agencies

A long time ago, David Ogilvy advised agency leaders not to hire anyone unless they had direct response experience. "Direct marketers know what works!" Indicative of the growth of direct marketing is the fact that every major advertising agency has formed or acquired a direct response division so they can offer clients "integrated" or complete direct marketing campaigns. Also, several independent agencies specialize in direct response.

Job titles and departments in direct response agencies are similar to those in general advertising agencies, but the opportunity for advancement can be more rapid in direct. Trends in integrated marketing and advertising, where direct is often used in tandem with sales promotion, public relations, and media advertising, make the individual with the knowledge of direct response advertising much more valuable.

Depending on background, interests and goals, an individual can choose a direct response agency career in traffic, account management/client services, media, creative, or production. With increased sophistication, many agencies now have research, database, or interactive departments. Many agencies are "full-service" agencies, with additional departments to service client needs in telephone marketing, list consulting, and lettershop services.

There are direct response agencies that deal solely with the consumer market or business-to-business market or fundraising, as well as agencies that deal solely with catalog marketing. Some agencies deal exclusively with interactive media, and many larger agencies have interactive services. Obviously, an understanding of these markets and of direct marketing techniques is critical to success in an agency career.

As an entry-level applicant, you should decide whether to begin on the agency side or the client side and whether to work for a large agency or a small agency. Obviously, there are pluses and minuses on both sides, but the applicant will have to compare his or her goals, aspirations, and personality with the information gleaned from research about individual companies.

Traffic. Traffic is an excellent entry-level opportunity, providing opportunities to advance into other areas. The traffic coordinator is responsible for coordinating the component parts of a total advertising project with each of the agency's departments.

Account Executives. Account executives are responsible for liaison with the client, involvement in marketing strategy, coordinating with various other departments involved in creating the advertising and its implementation. Although a background in marketing, business, advertising, or communications is not necessarily a prerequisite, it is extremely helpful for this position.

Copywriters.   Unlike general advertising, which seeks to create awareness (often through clever, creative ads), direct response advertising must sell. The copywriter, working closely with all departments of the agency, must have a thorough knowledge of the target audience: what it wants, why it buys, and how it reacts. Direct copywriters are really salespeople who must have a thorough knowledge of the product or service and be able to sell its benefits, rather than its features. They must tell what the product or service can do for the customer, rather than what it is. The copy, along with the proper offer and media, is what does the selling. Aspiring copywriters should write, create a personal portfolio, and collect samples of direct mail and direct response print advertising.

Assistant or junior copywriters can advance to copy supervisor/director and become vice presidents/creative directors who supervise both copywriters and graphic arts people.

Art and Layout.   Those with artistic talents can find jobs as artists, layout artists, or product photographers, working closely with the copywriters in developing the creative concept and "marrying" the copy to the graphics. Obviously, talent—as demonstrated by a portfolio and ultimately through experience—is positively required.

Media Buying and Production.   Some agencies handle all direct response media (mail, print, broadcast, and telephone), and others specialize. When hiring, these departments generally look for a background in direct response media, communications, and sometimes, liberal arts. Knowledge of direct response techniques, through actual experience or reading and course work, is helpful. Students who have worked in production or management of campus radio or TV stations will have had some valuable applicable experience. On-the-job-training will familiarize them with direct response details.

The advent of all the new electronic media, such as cable TV, home shopping networks, and interactive shopping via on-line services means that the individual interested in the future technology will have to keep up with the constantly changing times by reading trade press such as *Broadcasting, Cable Vision, Electronic Media, Television/Radio Age,* the *Media Industry Newsletter, Wired, Interactive Week,* and *Internet Monthly. PC Week, MacWeek,* and *AdWeek* have special sections on interactive distribution channels and the Information Superhighway. Some electronic media are still in the experimental stage, with a constant flux of newcomers and much room for success or failure.

Media personnel are responsible for the selection and purchase of lists, print space, or TV/radio time, as well as analysis of the results. Orders must be coordinated with agency personnel, brokers and publications and placed on a timely basis. Excellent negotiating skills, an analytical mind and the ability to effectively communicate recommendations are crucial for success.

The Newest Direct Medium: The Internet. World Wide Web sites can be used for marketing, sales, information, public relations, and relationship building. Marketing on the Internet requires very different skills. A prospect has to be guided to the Web site, be entertained, and given enough information (without requiring too much reading) to purchase the product or service, and later, be lured back to the site for repeat purchases.

Those interested in all the new media must be very smart about interactive channels, going beyond computer knowledge and language. They should "surf" the Net on a regular basis and see what others are doing.

Jobs in the interactive arena are generally divided into technical production/creative and marketing. Because the area is relatively new, there are no standard job descriptions and college background frequently doesn't matter. But programmers should have a strong understanding of the telecommunications and computer fields, with a background in HTML (Hyper Text Markup Language), and UNIX and a sense for computer graphics and design.

Agencies (or departments) that develop Web sites have employees who develop the content of the site. The content developer, who should have a marketing background, thinks about and develops ideas that will create excitement, encourage browsers to become buyers and to return to the site for repeat purchases. He or she is actually planning the content to help build the brand for the client.

With many companies developing Web sites and marketing via the Net, there is an increasing need for agencies to have the capability to help their clients. Many agencies now have interactive departments or individuals with this kind of expertise, and there are a small, but growing number of agencies or consulting groups that specialize in this area.

Production. Production staff must be detail-oriented, able to deal with change and work under the pressure of deadlines. Responsible for working with various suppliers such as printers and lettershops, they must see to it that the advertising message's component parts are complete, that colors are correct, that the copy is error-free (imagine what a misplaced decimal point could do to the client's bottom line!), and that postal regulations and size standards are adhered to.

Research. Because of the statistical nature of research, courses in research methodology, quantitative and behavioral statistics, psychology, sociology, and the like are obligatory. A research assistant can work up to senior management. Unlike some other areas of direct response marketing, an MBA might be required for advancement in the research department.

A Final Word. A career at a direct response agency is exciting and very challenging. The constant emphasis on testing means that there is always an opportunity to try new ways of getting an immediate response. Changing a word in the offer, using a different premium or list, changing the advertising medium, or any one of the many other variables can mean significant increases (or decreases!) in response rates. Feedback on what's working and what's not is almost immediate.

An agency career can be exciting, but it can also be extremely demanding. If you're a "nine-to-fiver," if you cannot work under the pressure of client demands and deadlines, if you are not a risk-taker and open to criticism, then an agency career is not for you.

Career Opportunities in Mailing Lists

The most creative mailing will be a failure if it is not sent to the right target audience or mailing list. An individual with a gift for numbers, for research, computers, analysis, or sales will find challenging and lucrative careers as a broker, manager, or compiler, as well as with computer service bureaus and database companies.

List Brokers.   The list broker serves the list owner and the mailer (user), helping the marketer select lists that will work best for the particular product or offer. The broker helps in planning the mailings, analyzing the response, forecasting future mailings, and often structuring the clients' marketing strategy. Brokers are measured by their client on the success of their recommendations.

List brokers must also be familiar with databases, knowing where they can be obtained and what they can do. Brokers frequently make recommendations to overlay demographic and lifestyle data on "house" (the mailer's own) or rented lists.

Entry-level jobs begin at the administrative assistant level or assistant account manager (or executive) and lead to senior account manager and vice president/ account supervisor. Client contact is part of the job. The assistant must be ambitious and eager to learn about new lists, pay attention to detail, and have good oral and written communications skills.

List Managers.   Lists are rented to brokers or directly to mailers by an internal or external manager. The manager, who should have a sales and marketing background with good computer skills, performs a sales function for the list owner and is also responsible for follow-up with the list owner (in the case of external list managers) and with the mailer. The manager must demonstrate potential benefits of the list by examining which companies have used it successfully in the past.

List Compilers.   Compilers "capture" data from a variety of commercial and public sources such as directories and voter and automobile registration lists. The very large compilers have databases with marketing-oriented information on millions of individuals and households. Compilers must have experience in developing sources for names and a methodology for producing lists with a high degree of accuracy. More technical in nature, this side of the business requires the services of data processors, computer programmers, program analysts, software engineers, and the like.

Service Bureaus.   The advent of ZIP codes, National Change of Address (NCOA), DMA's Mail Preference Service (MPS) and Telephone Preference Service (TPS), and customer information files has brought the list maintenance service bureau into prominence. Service bureaus perform sophisticated data processing and data conversion tasks such as merge/purge, personalized computer letters, postal presorting, model development and analysis, and list rental fulfillment, requiring the services of individuals with a computer and technical background. In addition, they require salespeople to sell their services to brokers and managers.

Printers

Printers are considered suppliers to the direct marketing field and must have an understanding of the techniques so they can sell the services of their company to mailers. The printer with a knowledge of ways to save the client money on increasing paper and postage costs is in great demand and can be very successful.

Generally, larger printing companies have formal training programs and hire entry-level candidates. New hires advance to become Customer Service Representatives, where they are in charge of the complete coordination of a client's account, from pricing to production to billing. The CSR is really the "relationship" manager, managing the entire process and matching the client needs with the capabilities of the printing company. CSRs can advance to management positions. Potential CSRs should be team players who are logical thinkers, able to coordinate the different steps of the particular job, possessing strong oral and written communication and math skills.

Technical positions are filled by people with printing backgrounds. Such people often cross over to sales and, because they know the services first-hand, can become an asset to the department. In most cases, the college major is not always crucial. What is important is the ability to efficiently and cost-effectively match the client's goals with the technology. A knowledge of the direct marketing process can be extremely helpful.

Lettershops

With the volume of direct mail, lettershops perform a critical function for the mailers, and hence represent good opportunities for sales positions, as well as mechanical or clerical jobs. Lettershops, which can be independently owned and operated or part of full-service direct response agencies, represent the last link in the direct mail process. Sales personnel give advice on how names and addresses should be delivered to the lettershop, specify requirements for insertion and labeling, and furnish written reports. Those who demonstrate the ability to save mailers money will be the most successful.

Catalogs

You have only to open your mailbox to realize the number of catalogs, and hence the number of job opportunities. Careers in catalogs (whether mail order, retail, or business-to-business) include merchandising; marketing; list maintenance, management, media, database operations; production; and forecasting. These are on the front end of the business.

Jobs in catalog agencies are similar to those already discussed in direct response agencies. Some mail order companies create their own marketing strategies, develop and rent their own lists, do their own testing, and so forth. If they have only some of the agency capabilities, they then utilize the services of agencies that specialize in design and production for the rest. The individual seeking a job with a particular catalog company will have to do corporate research to determine whether to apply to the company or its agency.

The most beautiful catalog in the world will be a dismal failure if the inventory, delivery, and customer service departments are inadequate. The "fulfillment" function of the catalog/mail order business presents some excellent entry-level training opportunities for newcomers who want to learn the catalog business. Customer service reps and inventory people are often in a position to make recommendations for improvement, thereby getting their names known to managers who make promotion and hiring decisions. Because customer service is critical to the success of all businesses, job candidates with such experience will be a step ahead of their competition, and the experience will prove invaluable throughout any business career.

Telemarketing

Telemarketing agencies are structured like advertising agencies, but their medium is the telephone. A client will hire a telemarketing agency to make or receive calls. A marketing representative or the executive responsible for new business will develop leads, make the "sales" presentation to the client, and formalize the "pitch" with a written marketing plan or proposal. The marketing rep is then responsible for client communications. Previous experience in telemarketing is helpful, but sales experience is certainly required.

A telemarketing account executive organizes and manages the client's program within the agency. Good written and oral communication, organizational, and analytical skills are required. The account executive coordinates script writing, testing, list preparation, and client reports.

Scriptwriters are the creative people of the telemarketing agency. Different copy skills are required in telemarketing, because the script must be written to be heard, anticipating questions and preparing responses in advance to prospect questions. Journalism and creative writing are helpful backgrounds for this line of work.

Some direct marketing companies do their own telemarketing in-house; others utilize outside telemarketing centers. It is the telemarketing center manager's responsibility to supervise the making or receiving of calls based on the client's marketing strategy, lists, and script requirements. The center manager must recruit, train, schedule, and motivate the center's "communicators."

A center manager should have a background in business administration and human resources. Telemarketing operations experience is essential, along with people management skills, logistics, and scheduling. Due to the increased automation technology in telemarketing, a background in computer science and telecommunications is advantageous.

Telemarketing trainers instruct the communicators about the products or services. In addition, they teach listening skills and sales techniques. They might monitor the communicators during the sales call, making sure all goes according to the script and marketing plan, and making any necessary adjustments.

Communicators often work part time and come from all walks of life: students, homemakers, actors, etc. For this reason, a communicator is a good entry-level job and provides excellent training and advancement opportunities. An individual interested in a sales career will get terrific training as a telephone communicator. Good communications skills are essential, but a business or marketing background is not required.

Where Do I Go From Here?

With the increasing employment projections in direct marketing, there is a need for trained professionals to fill the growing number of jobs. Individuals with academic and professional training in the form of internships will be a step ahead of the competition and have a head start on a challenging and rewarding career.

If you're interested in pursuing jobs in this field, you should read books on the various aspects of direct response. Be familiar with its jargon and be acquainted with its techniques. Read the trade press, do research on the Internet, keep up with who's doing what, with mergers and acquisitions, with promotions and career changes. Make lists of people and companies. Do research on individual companies by contacting them for copies of their promotional materials and annual reports.

The Direct Marketing Market Place, (National Register Publications), lists hundreds of companies in the direct marketing field by business category. Included are key contacts, addresses, and phone numbers and brief corporate descriptions.

The Direct Marketing Association's extensive reference library and resource center is available *by appointment* (212-768-7277; extension 1930). It's free of charge to full-time students with ID. (For others, there's a fee for one-time use.) The library contains a wealth of direct marketing information, including all books dealing with the subject, trade press, business category files containing reprints of articles, company files, portfolios of DMA's award-winning ECHO campaigns, and much, much more.

Join a local direct marketing organization. There are more than 40 of these scattered throughout the country and the world. Most of these groups have local Direct Marketing Days, which often include trade shows. These events offer wonderful networking and educational opportunities.

Internships help you gain actual work experience in direct marketing—a chance to turn theory into practice. The Direct Marketing Educational Foundation and some of the local clubs sponsor internship programs.

Full-time students interested in gaining hands-on experience might want to enter the Leonard J. Raymond Collegiate ECHO Awards Competition. This is a direct response advertising competition in which student teams act as a direct response agency, plan the marketing and creative strategies, the campaign, construct the budget, and project the results for a major corporate sponsor. Valuable prizes aimed at furthering direct response education (including attendance at a DMA Annual Conference or a local Direct Marketing Day or reference books) are available for winning teams and faculty advisors. Honorable mention certificates are awarded for creativity, marketing, budgeting, and most innovative campaign concept. Full-time seniors can apply for the Foundation's Collegiate Institute. This four-day seminar includes the basics of direct marketing and direct response advertising and is taught by leading practitioners using real-world examples.

The Direct Marketing Educational Foundation conducts other programs for students and professors. It also can provide general career information, course listings, sample course outlines, a bibliography of direct marketing texts, and a list of local direct marketing clubs. For more information about the programs of the Direct Marketing Educational Foundation, contact DMEF at 1120 Avenue of the Americas, New York, NY 10036-6700; 212-768-7277; ext. 1329.

Another way to learn more about direct techniques is to examine various forms of direct response ads that come in your mail, that you see on TV or on your computer, and in magazines. Pay attention to format, copy, order forms, positioning, and so forth. These real-world examples are excellent educational tools. Of course, your own portfolio should be maintained in a highly professional manner.

Where Are the Jobs?

Although New York, Chicago, and Los Angeles are referred to as direct marketing centers, jobs can be found in increasing numbers throughout the United States and abroad. Consult local classifieds and/or trade press advertisements and listings in club/association newsletters. Several executive recruiters deal with direct response positions, but rarely at the entry level.

A Word About Salaries

Dozens of variables for each job function make it practically impossible to quote typical salaries. Salaries depend on the location of the company, its size, the job responsibilities, benefits, and so forth. Job seekers would be advised to consult local classifieds to determine the going rate or range for a particular job title.

Entry-level salaries in direct marketing are competitive with salaries in other areas of marketing and advertising, but, due to direct marketing's testability, measurability, and accountability, opportunities for advancement are much greater. Although salary is an important consideration, it should never be the sole deciding factor. Responsibilities, educational opportunities, and promise for future advancement are equal, if not more important, considerations.

Marketing Yourself

The various techniques you have learned throughout this book will help you with the most important job—that of marketing yourself. Just as you would do research before marketing a product, you must do research about your own goals, likes and dislikes, and strengths and weaknesses and research prospective employers. The information you glean from directories, annual reports, trade publications, and through personal contacts will serve to make up your own personal database of prospects. The research will help you target your resume to your best prospects rather than "mass marketing" yourself.

Similar to the way you want your prospect to act immediately and buy your product or service, you want a prospective employer to *act* by calling you for an interview and then by hiring you. Remember that your resume is your ad; your cover letter is your sales pitch; your interview is your sales call; and your thank-you letter is your follow-up. Don't do anything that you wouldn't do in marketing a product or service. Remember to keep your resume benefit-oriented, telling what you can do for the company and stressing accomplishments rather than responsibilities. List only relevant information that will help you get the job you are seeking.

Glossary

ABC Audit Bureau of Circulations.

ACORN A Classification Of Residential Neighborhoods; a marketing segmentation system that enables consumers to be classified according to the type of area in which they live.

Accordion fold Two or more parallel folds that open like an accordion.

Account qualification matrix Scientific method of measuring each case as it is completed for potential future purchases.

Action devices Items and techniques used in direct mail to encourage positive response (e.g., tokens, scent strips).

Active buyer Customer whose latest purchase was made within the last 12 months. *See also* **Buyer** and **Actives**.

Active member Customer who is fulfilling the original commitment or who has fulfilled that commitment and has made one or more purchases in the last 12 months.

Active subscriber Customer who has committed for regular delivery of magazines, books, or goods or services for a period of time still in effect.

Actives Customers who have made purchases within a prescribed time, usually one year; subscribers whose subscriptions have not expired.

Additions New names, either of individuals or companies, added to a mailing list.

Add-on service Service of the Direct Marketing Association that gives consumers an opportunity to request that their names be added to mailing lists.

Address Coding Guide (ACG) List of beginning and ending house numbers, ZIP codes, and other geographic codes for all city delivery service and streets served by 31,540 post offices located within 6,601 ZIP codes.

Address Correction Requested Endorsement printed in the upper left-hand corner of the address portion of the mailing piece (below the return address), which authorizes the U.S. Postal Service, for a fee, to provide the known new address of a person no longer at the address on the mailing piece.

Advertisement rate card Printed card issued by the publishers of journals and newspapers detailing advertising cost, advertisement sizes, and the mechanical details of production.

Advertising schedule List of advertisements booked by media showing details of sizes, timing, and costs.

Against the grain Folding paper at right angles to the grain of the paper; a sheet of paper will fold easily along the grain but will possibly crack when folded against the grain.

AIDA Most popular formula for the preparation of direct mail copy. The letters stand for (get) Attention, (arouse) Interest, (stimulate) Desire, (ask for) Action.

Airbrush   Small pressure gun shaped like a pencil that sprays paint by means of compressed air. Used to obtain tone or graduated tonal effects in artwork.

Airtime   Jargon term denoting the amount of actual transmission time available for an advertisement on television and radio.

Alterations   Changes made in the copy after it has been set in type.

American Standard Code of Information Interchange (ASCII)   Widely used code adopted by the American Standards Association for transmission of information.

Antique paper   Rough-surfaced paper that is only slightly calendered.

Art paper   Paper coated with a mineral substance to produce a glossy surface.

Artwork   Finished layout consisting of drawings, photographs, lettering, and copy.

Assigned mailing dates   Dates by which the list user has to mail a specific list; no other date is acceptable without approval of the list owner.

Assumptive close   Closing technique in which the salesperson offers the product or service with the assumption that the target has made the decision to buy.

Asterisk bills   State laws that require telephone companies to advise subscribers that they can have an asterisk placed in front of their names if they do not want to receive telemarketing calls.

Audience   Total number of individuals reached by a promotion or advertisement.

Audit   Printed report of the counts involved in a particular list or file.

Automatic call distributor (ACD)   Equipment that automatically manages and controls incoming calls, sends calls to the telephone representative who has been idle the longest, answers and queues calls during busy periods, and plays recorded messages for waiting callers. It automatically sends overflow calls to a second group and provides management reports on the call activity. It can stand alone or be integrated with a PBX.

Automatic dialing recorded message player (ADRMP)   Machine that dials preprogrammed telephone numbers, automatically plays a prerecorded message (normally a sales pitch), then records responses.

Automatic interaction detection (AID)   Program for segmenting a list from a heterogeneous to a homogeneous market.

Automatic redial   Telephone feature that permits the last number dialed, to be automatically dialed again at the push of one button.

Automatic route selection (ARS)   Switching system that chooses the least costly path from available owned or leased circuits.

Backbone   Back of a bound book connecting the two covers; also known as the *spine*.

Back-end   Activities necessary to complete a mail order transaction once an order has been received; measurements of buyers' performance after they have ordered the first item in a series offering.

Bangtail   Promotional envelope with a second flap that is perforated and designed for use as an order blank.

Banker envelope   Envelope with the flap on the long edge.

Batch   Grouping of orders.

Batch processing   Technique of executing a set of orders/selections in batches as opposed to executing each order/selection as it is received; batches can be created by computer programming or manually by date.

Benefits   Features of a product or service. Benefits are what sells the product or services.

Bill enclosure   Promotional piece or notice enclosed with a bill, invoice, or statement.

Bindery   Place where final trimming, stitching/stapling, order-form insertion, and any necessary off-press folding is done.

Binding   Finishing process that glues, staples, or stitches the pages of a catalog to the cover.

Bingo cards   Reply card inserted in a publication and used by readers to request literature and samples from companies whose products and services are either advertised in the publication or mentioned in its editorial columns and feature articles.

Bleed Extension of the printed image to the trim edge of a sheet or page.

Block Metal, rubber, or plastic plate engraved, cast, or molded for printing.

Blocked calls Calls that receive busy signals.

Blocking out Operation of eliminating undesirable backgrounds and portions of a photographic negative by opaquing the image.

Blueprint Sometimes called *blues* or *bluelines*, a prior-to-printing proof made from a photographic negative or positive, used for checking type/photo position.

Body type Types used for the main body of the text as distinct from its headings.

Boiler room/bucket shop Term to describe outbound phone rooms where facilities are less than ideal for the telephone sales representative and sometimes for the activity itself. High turnover of representatives and low overhead for the owners are trademarks of this kind of operation.

Boldface type Type that is heavier than standard text type, often used for headlines and paragraph lead-ins, and to emphasize letters, words, or sentences.

Bond paper Grade of writing or printing paper used when strength, durability, and permanence are essential.

Book Catalog.

Booklet Usually, a small flyer-type promotional piece.

Boom In broadcasting, a semirigid tubelike apparatus that extends from the headset and positions the microphone close to the user's mouth.

Bounce-back Offer enclosed with a mailing sent to a customer in fulfillment of an order.

Bringing up the color Color correcting; intensifying color on press or in separations.

Broadcast media Direct response source that includes radio, television, and cable television.

Broadside Single sheet of paper, printed on one or two sides, folded for mailing or direct

distribution, and opening into a single, large advertisement.

Brochure Strictly defined, a high-quality pamphlet, with specially planned layout, typography, and illustrations; also used loosely to describe any promotional pamphlet or booklet.

Broker Agent authorized to buy or sell for an organization or another individual.

Bromide Photographic print made from a negative, or a positive used as a proof.

Bulk Thickness of paper.

Bulk mail Category of third-class mail involving a large quantity of identical pieces addressed to different names and specially processed for mailing before delivery to the post office.

Bulk rebate Category of postage that allows rebate for second-class presorted mailing; delivery will normally be made within seven working days. Amount of rebate depends on the volume of mail.

Burnout Exhaustion and lack of motivation often experienced by telephone sales representatives working long shifts without proper training or compensation.

Burst To separate continuous-form paper into discrete sheets.

Business list Any compilation of individuals or companies based on a business-associated interest, inquiry, membership, subscription, or purchase.

Business reply service Reply-paid service in which postage for the respondent's reply is paid for by the advertiser.

Business-to-business telemarketing Telemarketing to industry.

Buyer One who orders merchandise, books, records, information, or services.

C/A Change of address.

Call In telemarketing, this term encompasses uncompleted and completed connections, busys, temporarily disconnected, disconnected–no referral, disconnected but referred, and no-answers; does not include status of results such as sale/no-sale/follow-up.

Call-back Any contact required to follow up an activity.

Call card Record of details on prospects or customers; often arranged chronologically.

Call forcing Call distribution feature that automatically directs a waiting call to an available agent. The agent receives an audible tone burst that signals the call coming through. A button need not be pressed to receive this call.

Call guide Informal roster of points to be covered during a telephone sales presentation that allows for personalization.

Call management Process of selecting and managing the optimum mix of equipment, network services, and labor to achieve maximum productivity from a telemarketing center.

Call management system Equipment that gives detailed information on telephone activity and cost.

Call objective Clear reason for the call; the best calls are those that tend to have only one objective.

Call objective guideline Worksheet that allows preparation for the specific objective; often used in training and for new-product introductions.

Call queuing Placing incoming calls in a waiting line for access to an operator station.

Call restriction Procedure designed to limit the range of calling power given to employees, as when only selected personnel are able to make long-distance calls.

Carriers Transportation facilities suppliers.

Case Complete and measurable telephone sales cycle from beginning to end (e.g., 100 names on a list equals 100 cases).

Cash buyer Buyer who encloses payment with order.

Cash on delivery (COD) Expression meaning that a customer pays for an order when it is received.

Cash rider Also called *cash up* or *cash option*, an addition to an order form offering the option of full cash payment with the order,

at some saving over the installment-payment price as an incentive.

Cash with order Requirement made by some list owners for full payment at the time an order is placed for the list.

Catalog Book or booklet displaying photos of merchandise, with descriptive details and prices.

Catalog buyer Person who has bought products or services from a catalog.

Catalog request Order for the catalog itself. The catalog might be free; there could be a nominal charge for postage and handling, or there could be a more substantial charge that is often refunded or credited on the first order.

Cell size Smallest unit or segment quantity of an individual variant within a test program.

Census tract Area within a ZIP code group denoting households with uniform social and economic characteristics.

CHAD Change of address; also called *C/A*.

Charge buyer Person who has charged merchandise ordered by mail; or a person who has paid for merchandise only after it has been delivered.

Cheshire label Specially prepared paper (rolls, fanfold, or accordion fold) used to reproduce names and addresses to be mechanically affixed to mailing pieces.

Chromalins One method of proofing a color separation. Four separate, extremely thin plastic sheets (one for each color) are overlaid, producing a color reproduction of the separations.

Chromes Often misused term actually referring to color transparencies; also used as nickname for chromalins.

Circulars General term for printed advertising in any form, including printed matter sent out by direct mail.

Closed case Any case that has completed the sales cycle and has ended in a sale, no sale, or no potential.

Clustering Grouping names on a telemarketing list according to geographic, demographic, or psychographic characteristics.

Cluster selection Selection routine based on taking a group of names in a series (e.g., a cluster selection on an *n*th name basis might be the first 10 out of every 100 or the first 125 out of 175; a cluster selection using limited ZIP codes might be the first 200 names in each of the specified ZIP codes).

COAM Customer owned and maintained equipment.

Coding (1) System for ascertaining from replies the mailing list or other source from which an address was obtained; (2) structure of letters and numbers used to classify characteristics of an address on a list.

Cold calls Sales calls to an audience unfamiliar to the caller.

Cold lists Lists that have no actual or arranged affinity with the advertiser (i.e., they have not bought from, belonged to, or inquired of the advertiser itself or of any particular affinity group).

Collate (1) To assemble individual elements of a mailing in sequence for inserting into a mailing envelope; (2) program that combines two or more ordered files to produce a single ordered file; also the act of combining such files. *See also* **Merge/purge**.

Collation Orderly assembly of sheets or signatures during the bindery process.

Color print Printed reproduction of a transparency or negative, inexpensive but not of top quality; also called a *"C" print*.

Commercial envelope Oblong envelope with a top flap.

Communicator call report (CCR) List identifying for each telephone sales representative what calls were handled during a shift, the date, the contact name, and all information pertaining to the details of each call made.

Compiled list Names and addresses derived from directories, newspapers, public records, retail sales slips, trade show registrations, and the like, to identify groups of people with something in common.

Compiler Organization that develops lists of names and addresses from directories, newspapers, public records, registrations, and other sources, identifying groups of people, companies, or institutions with something in common.

Completed cancel Person who has completed a specific commitment to buy products or services before canceling.

Completed contact Any contact that finalizes a preplanned portion of a sales cycle.

Comprehensive Complete and detailed layout for a printed piece; also called *comp* or *compare*.

Computer letter Computer-printed message providing personalized, fill-in information from a source file in predesignated positions; full-printed letter with personalized insertions.

Computer personalization Printing of letters or other promotional pieces by a computer using names, addresses, special phrases, or other information based on data appearing in one or more computer records; the objective is to use the information in the computer record to tailor the promotional message to a specific individual.

Computer record All of the information about an individual, a company, or a transaction stored on a specific magnetic tape or disk.

Computer service bureau Facility providing general or specific data-processing.

Consultative selling Personalized method of sales that identifies a customer's needs and then sells a product or service to meet those needs.

Consumer list List of names (usually with home address) compiled or resulting from a common inquiry or buying activity indicating a general buying interest.

Consumer location system Market identification system containing information derived from Target Group Index and ACORN.

Contact Any conversation with a decision

maker or any communication that advances a case toward completion.

Contact-to-closed-case ratio   Number of completed contacts required to complete a case (e.g., contact mail contact would be a two-contact-to-closed-case ratio).

Continuity program   Products or services bought as a series of small purchases, rather than all at one time, generally based on a common theme and shipped at regular or specific time intervals.

Contributor list   Names and addresses of persons who have given to a specific funding effort. *See also* **Donor list.**

Control   Last successful mailing package without any changes that allows a true measurement of the performance of each of the variants on test; generally used to test against new variants.

Controlled circulation   Distribution at no charge of a publication to individuals or companies on the basis of their titles or occupations; typically, recipients are asked from time to time to verify the information that qualifies them to receive the publication.

Controlled duplication   Method by which names and addresses from two or more lists are matched (usually by computer) in order to eliminate or limit extra mailings to the same name and address.

Conversion   (1) Process of reformatting, or changing from one data-processing system to another; (2) securing specific action such as a purchase or contribution from a name on a mailing list or as a result of an inquiry.

Conversion rate   Percentage of potential customers who, through a direct mail solicitation, become buyers.

Co-op mailing   Mailing of two or more offers included in the same envelope or other carrier, with each participating mailer sharing the mailing cost based on some predetermined formula.

Copy   Written material intended for inclusion in the various components of a mailing package or advertisement.

Copy date   Date by which advertising material ready for printing must reach a publishing house for inclusion in a particular issue.

Cost per inquiry (CPI)   Simple arithmetical formula derived by dividing the total cost of a mailing or an advertisement by the number of inquiries received.

Cost per order (CPO)   Similar to cost per inquiry but based on actual orders rather than inquiries.

Cost per thousand (CPM)   Common rate for list rentals when fee is based on every 1,000 names rented to telemarketers.

Coupon   Part of an advertising promotion piece intended to be filled in by the inquirer or customer and returned to the advertiser; it often entities the bearer to a discount on an item at time of purchase.

Coupon clipper   Person who has given evidence of responding to free or nominal-cost offers out of curiosity, with little or no serious interest or buying intent.

Creative   Preprinting aspects of catalog preparation: design, layout, copy writing, and photography; used as a noun in the catalog business.

Crop   To trim part of a photo or copy.

CTO   Contribution to overhead (profit).

Cyberspace   This is a coined word from the novel *Neuromancer* by William Gibson. The word referred to a computer network that people plugged their brains into. Today the word is used to refer to the Internet or BBS services such as CompuServe.

Databank   Information resources of an organization or business.

Database   Collection of data to support the requirements and requests for information of a specific group of users.

Database definition   The clear understanding between telemarketing, management and database management about what will be captured and displayed from the database.

Data capture/entry   Any method of collecting and recording information.

Data processing   Organization of data for the

purpose of producing desired information; involves recording, classifying, sorting, summarizing, calculating, disseminating, and storing data.

Data sheet   Leaflet containing factual information about a product or service.

Deadbeat   Person who has ordered a product or service and, without just cause, hasn't paid for it.

Decoy   Unique name especially inserted in a mailing list for verifying list usage.

De-dupe   *See* **Duplication elimination**.

Delinquent   Person who has fallen behind or has stopped scheduled payment for a product or service.

Delivery   Method of oral presentation used (e.g., businesslike, informal, formal).

Delivery date   Date a list user or designated representative of the list user receives a specific list order from the list owner.

Demographics   Description of the vital statistics of an audience or population; includes personal characteristics, name, title, occupation, address, phone number, etc.

Direct mail   Printed matter usually carrying a sales message or announcement designed to elicit a response from a carefully selected consumer or business market.

Direct mail advertising   Any promotional effort using the Postal Service, or other direct delivery service, for distribution of the advertising message.

Direct Mail Order Action Line   Service provided by the Direct Marketing Association that attempts to help consumers resolve problems encountered when shopping by mail.

Direct Marketing Association (DMA)   Organization representing special interests of those in the business of direct marketing.

Direct response   Advertising through any medium inviting direct response by any measurable means (mail, telephone, walk-in, etc.).

DMA Mail Preference Service   Service provided by the Direct Marketing Association that allows consumers to request that their names be added to or deleted from mailing lists.

Donor list   List of persons who have given money to one or more charitable organizations. *See also* **Contributor list**.

Doubling day   Point in time established by previous experience by which 50 percent of all returns to a mailing will normally have been received.

Drop closing   Process of completing a sale by initially offering top-of-the-line items or services and then adjusting the offer to a lower range of prices.

Drop date   *See* **Final date**.

Drop out   Deletion of type from all four colors, resulting in "white" type.

Drop ship   Fulfillment function whereby the manufacturer of the product does the actual shipping of the item to the customer.

Dummy   (1) Mock-up giving a preview of a printed piece, showing placement of the material to be printed; (2) fictitious name with a mailable address inserted into a mailing list to verify usage of that list.

Dummy name   Fictitious name and address inserted into a mailing list to verify usage of that list; also known as a *sleeper*.

Duplicate   Two or more identical name-and-address records.

Duplication elimination   Specific kind of controlled duplication providing that no matter how many times a name and address is on a list or how many lists contain that name and address, it will be accepted for mailing only once by that mailer; also known as *dupe elimination*.

Dye transfer   High-quality, four-color print made from a transparency; most often used when retouching is needed.

800 service   Inbound long-distance service that is free to the caller and paid for by the recipient.

Enamel   Coated paper that has a glossy finish.

Envelope stuffer   Any advertising or promotional material enclosed with business letters, statements, or invoices.

Ergonomics   Study of the problems of people adjusting to their environment, especially seeking to adapt work or working conditions to suit the workers.

Exchange   Arrangement whereby two mailers exchange equal numbers of mailing list names.

Exhibition list   List of people who have registered as attendees at trade or consumer exhibitions.

Expiration   Subscription that is not renewed.

Expiration date   Date on which a subscription expires.

Expire   Former customer who is no longer an active buyer.

File maintenance   Activity of keeping a file up to date by adding, changing, or deleting data. *See also* **List maintenance** and **Update**.

Fill-in   Name, address, or words added to a preprinted letter.

Film positive   Photographic print on transparent film taken from artwork for use by the printer.

Final date   Targeted date for mail to be in the hands of those to whom it is addressed.

Finished size   Overall dimensions of a piece of printed matter after folding and other procedures have been completed.

First-class letter contract   Post office service for mailers that consist of at least 5,000 identical items, can sort into towns, and require first-class service; offers discounts of up to 12 percent.

First-time buyer   Person who buys a product or service from a specific company for the first time.

Fixed field   Way of laying out, or formatting, list information in a computer file that puts every piece of data in a specific position relative to every other piece of data. If a piece of data is missing from an individual record, or if its assigned space is not completely used, that space is not filled. Any piece of data exceeding its assigned space limitation must be abbreviated or contracted.

Fixed lists   Cost per sale including all other costs except promotions.

Flag   Computerized means of identifying data added to a file; usage of a list segment by a given mailer.

Flat   Paper industry's term for unprinted paper adopted by the direct mail industry to refer either to unprinted paper or, more particularly, to printed paper prior to folding.

Flat charge   Fixed cost for the sum total of a rental list; usually applies to smaller lists.

Flight   A given mailing, particularly when multiple drops are to be made on different days to reduce the number arriving at one company at one time.

Folio   Page number as it appears on a printed page.

Follow-up contact   Any contact required to finalize a previous commitment or to close a transaction.

Follow-up system   Part of an automated telemarketing system that keeps track of calls that should be recycled into the outgoing program and rescheduled at a later time; its purpose is to trap information and release it to communicators at the appropriate time.

Foreign mail   Lists of householders and businesses outside the United States.

Format   Size, style, type page, margins, printing requirements, and the like that are characteristic of a publication.

Former buyer   Person who has bought one or more times from a company but has made no purchase in the last 12 months.

***Fortune* 1,000**   Thousand largest industrial companies in the United States, as published by *Fortune* magazine; almost all have sales volumes per year of over $1 billion.

***Fortune* 300**   *Fortune* magazine's selection of the 50 largest companies in 6 classifications: banking, retailing, wholesaling, insurance, construction, and utilities.

Four-line address   Typical individual-name list with at-business addresses requires a minimum of four lines: name of individual, name of company, local address, city, state, and ZIP code.

Four-up, three-up, two-up   Number of similar items printed on one sheet of paper (e.g., four-up indicates the sheet will be guillotined to print four finished articles). Also called *four-to-view*, *three-to-view*, etc.

Fourth-class mail   Parcel post, the U.S. Postal Service delivery of mail parcels weighing over 16 ounces.

Free lancer   Independent artist, writer, or photographer who is not on staff but works on a per-project or hourly rate as the need arises.

Free-ride   *See* **Envelope stuffer** and **Piggyback**.

Freesheet   Paper without mechanical wood pulp.

Free-standing insert   Promotional piece loosely inserted or nested in a newspaper or magazine.

Frequency   Number of times an individual has ordered within a specific period of time. *See also* **Monetary value** and **Recency**.

Friend of a friend   Name of someone thought to be interested in a specific advertiser's product or service; submitted by a third party.

Front-end   Activities necessary, or the measurement of direct marketing activities, to obtain an order.

Fulfillment   Process of supplying goods after an order has been received.

Fund-raising list   List of individuals or companies based on a known contribution to one or more fund-raising appeals.

Galley listing or sheet list   Printout of list data on sheets, usually in ZIP or alphabetic order.

Galleys   Proofs of typesetting in column width taken before page make-up.

Gathering   Assembly of folded signatures into correct sequence.

Genderization   Program run to add gender to mailing lists (based on first names where available).

Geographics   Any method of subdividing a list based on geographic or political subdivisions (ZIP codes, sectional centers, cities, counties, states, regions).

Gift buyer   One who buys a product or service for another.

Giftees   List of individuals sent gifts or magazines by mail, by friends, donors, or business firms. Giftees are not truly mail order buyers; rather they are mail order recipients and beneficiaries.

Gimmick   Attention-getting device, usually dimensional, attached to a direct mail printed piece.

Gone-aways   *See* **Nixie**.

Governments   Often-overlooked source of lists (e.g., lists of cars, homes, dogs, bankers, hairdressers, plumbers, veterinarians, buyers, subscribers, inquirers, TV stations, ham operators, and CBs).

Grid test   Means of testing more than one variable at the same time; a useful method for testing different offers by different packages over a group of prospect lists.

Groundwood pulp   Paper that contains wood pulp.

Groups   Number of individuals having a unifying relationship, (e.g., club, association, membership, church, fraternal order, political group, sporting group, collector group, travel group, singing group).

Guarantee   Pledge of satisfaction made by the seller to the buyer and specifying the terms by which the seller will make good his pledge.

Gummed label   *See* **Label, gummed**.

Half-life   Formula for estimating the total response to be expected from a direct response effort shortly after the first responses are received; makes valid continuation decisions possible based on statistically valid partial data.

Halftone   Photograph or other tonal illustration reproduced by lines of small dots.

Handling charge   Fixed charge added per segment for special list requests; also shows up as part of shipping and handling charges for transportation of labels, cards, sheets, or tape.

Hard copy   Printout on a sheet list or galley of all data available on a magnetic source such as a tape, hard disk, or floppy disk.

Head of family   From telephone or car data, the name and sex of the individual on the registration file.

Headline   Primary wording utilized to induce a direct marketing recipient to read and react.

Heat transfer   Form of label that transfers reverse carbon images on the back of a sheet of mailing pieces by means of heat and pressure.

High-Potential/Immediate-Need   Any case that requires immediate contact by the outside sales force.

High school student list   Several compilers provide lists of high school juniors and seniors with their home addresses; original data, usually printed phone rosters, are not available for all schools or localities.

High-ticket buyer   Buyer who has purchased expensive items by mail.

Hit   Name appearing on two or more mailing lists.

Home office   For major businesses, the executive or home office location as differentiated from the location of branch offices or plants.

Homogenization   Unfortunate and misleading combination of responses from various sources; often the use of a single "average" response for a mailing made to customers and prospects alike.

Hot line   Most recent buyers on a list that undergoes periodic updating. (Those who have just purchased by mail are the most likely buyers of other products and services by mail.)

Hot-line list   The most recent names available on a specific list, but no older than three months; use of the term *hot line* should be modified by *weekly*, *monthly*, etc.

Households   Homes selectable on a demographic basis; householders (consumers) can be selectable on a psychographic basis.

House list   Any list of names owned by a company as a result of compilation, inquiry or buyer action, or acquisition, that is used to promote that company's products or services.

House list duplicate   Duplication of name-and-address records between the list user's own lists and any list being mailed by the list user on a one-time use arrangement.

ICSMA   International Customer Service Manager's Association.

Imposition   Way in which pages are positioned in order to print and fold correctly on a press.

In-house   Related to services or products that can be furnished by the advertiser himself (e.g., in-house lists, in-house print).

In-house telemarketing   Telemarketing done within a company as a primary or supplementary method of marketing and selling that company's own products.

Inactive buyer   Buyer who has not placed an order or responded during a specified period.

Inbound calls   Calls that come into a telemarketing center.

Inbound telesales   A department within a telemarketing operation devoted to the handling of incoming calls.

Income   Perhaps the most important demographic selection factor on consumer files. Major compiled files provide surprisingly accurate individual family incomes up to about $40,000. Incomes can be selected in $1,000 increments; counts are available by income ranges for every ZIP code.

Incoming specialist   Trained professional telephone specialist skilled at handling incoming order requests and cross-selling or up-selling to close a sale.

Indexing   Creation of a standard, say, 100 percent of recovery of promotion cost, to allow comparison between mailings of different sizes.

Indicia   The required indication in the area usually reserved for the postage stamp designating the type of mailing.

Individual   Most mailings are made to individuals, although all occupant or resident mail is, in effect, to an address only. A portion of business mail is addressed to the establishment (by name and address) only, or to a title and not to an individual.

Influentials In business mail order, those executives who have decision-making power on what and when to buy; those who exercise clout in their business classification or community; in consumer mail, those individuals (executive, professionals, educators, clergy, etc.) who make a difference in their localities or workplaces.

Initial source code Code for the source that brought the name to the customer file for the first time.

Ink-jet Computer-generated ink droplets that apply ink through a small orifice to form characters; often used for purposes of personalization.

Input data Original data, usually in hard copy form, to be converted and added to a given file. Also, taped lists made ready for a merge/purge, or for a databank.

Inquiry (1) Request for literature or other information about a product or service; (2) response in the form of an inquiry for more information or for a copy of a catalog.

Inset Leaflet or other printed material bound in with the pages of a publication rather than inserted loose.

Insert Leaflet or other printed material inserted loose in a publication or mailing package.

Installment buyer Person who orders goods or services and pays for them in two or more periodic payments after their delivery.

Insurance lists Lists of people who have inquired about or purchased various forms of insurance; lists of insurance agents, brokers, adjustors, executives.

Intelpost Royal Mail electronic transmission service for copy, artwork, and other urgent documents.

International 800 service Telephone service allowing toll-free calls to another country.

Internet A large network of networks and computers, all of which use the Internet protocol. The Internet was first developed by the U.S.

Department of Defense in the 1960s and 1970s.

Intralist duplication Duplication of name and address records within a given list.

Italic Sloping version of a typeface, usually used for emphasis.

Item In the selection process for a mail order list, term denoting the type of goods or service purchased; in input terms, it is a part of a record to be converted.

Julian dating Three-digit numerical system for date-stamping a transaction by day: January 1 is 001, December 31 is 365.

Key code Means of identifying a given promotional effort so that responses can be identified and tracked.

Key code (generic) Form of hierarchical coding by which promotional vehicles can be analyzed within type of media—newspapers, magazines, Sunday supplements, freestanding stuffers, mailing-lists, radio promotion, TV promotion, takeovers, and so on.

Key code (key) Group of letters and/or numbers, colors, or other markings, used to measure the specific effectiveness of media, lists, advertisements, offers, etc., or any parts thereof.

Keyline Any of many partial or complete descriptions of past buying history codes to include name-and-address information and current status.

Keystroke Means of converting hard copy to machine-readable form through a keyboard or similar means.

Key verifying For 100 percent accuracy, having two operators at the data-entry stage enter the same data.

Kill To delete a record from a file.

Label Slip of paper containing the name and address of the recipient that is applied to a mailing for delivery.

Label, gummed Perforated label form on paper stock that must be individually separated and moistened before being applied with hand pressure to the mailing piece.

Label, one-up Conventional pressure-sensitive labels for computer addressing are four-across horizontal; one-up labels are in a vertical strip with center holes for machine affixing.

Label, peel off (pressure-sensitive) Self-adhesive label form that can be peeled off its backing form and pressed onto a mailing piece.

Laid paper Paper having parallel lines watermarked at equal distances, giving a ribbed effect.

Laser letters Letters printed by a high-speed computerized imaging method. Lasers can print two letters side by side, each of 35 or 40 lines, in one second.

Late charge Charge imposed by some list owners for list rental fees not paid within a specific period.

Layout (1) Artist's sketch showing relative positioning of illustrations, headlines, and copy; (2) positioning of subject matter on a press sheet for most efficient production.

Lead generation Mailing used to invite inquiries for sales follow-up.

Lead qualification Determination, by telemarketing, of customer's level of interest in and willingness and ability to buy a product or service.

Length of line The computer, which has the capacity to print 132 characters across a 14½" sheet, has forced discipline in the choice of line length. In four-across cheshiring, the longest line cannot be more than 30 characters; for five-across this limit is 23 characters. Capable data processors, utilizing all 8 lines available on a 1"-deep label, can provide two full lines, if need be, for the title line.

Length of residence Major compilers who utilize telephone or car registration data maintain the number of years (up to 16) a given family has been at the same address, thereby providing another selection factor available from these stratified lists.

Letterhead Printing on a letter that identifies the sender.

Lettershop Business organization that handles the mechanical details of mailings such as addressing, imprinting, and collating; most offer some printing facilities, and many offer some degree of creative direct mail services.

Lifestyle selectivity Selectivity based on the lifestyle habits of segments of the population as revealed through lists indicating what people need, what they buy, what they own, what they join, and what they support; major lists based on consumer surveys provide data on hobbies, ownership, and interests.

Lifetime value (LTV) In direct mail and marketing, the total profit or loss estimated or realized from a customer over the active life of that customer's record.

Lift letter Separate piece added to conventional solo mailings asking the reader to consider the offer just once more.

List acquisition (1) Lease or purchase of lists from external services; (2) use of internal corporate lists.

List affinity Correlation of a mailing offer to selected mailing list availabilities.

List bank Names held in inventory for future use.

List broker Specialist who makes all necessary arrangements for one company to use the list(s) of another company. A broker's services include research, selection, recommendation, and subsequent evaluation.

List building Process of collecting and utilizing list data and transaction data for list purposes.

List bulletin Announcement of a new list or of a change in a list previously announced.

List buyer Technically, one who actually buys mailing lists, in practice, one who orders mailing lists for one-time use. *See* **List user** and **Mailer**.

List card Conventional 5" × 8" card used to provide essential data about a given list.

List catalog Directory of lists with counts prepared and distributed, usually free, by list managers and list compilers.

List cleaning List updating or the process of correcting a mailing list.

List compilation Business of creating lists from printed records.

List compiler One who develops lists of names and addresses from directories, newspapers, public records, sales slips, trade show registrations, and other sources for identifying groups of people or companies having something in common.

List count Number of names and addresses on a given segment of a mailing list; a count provided before printing tapes or labels; the universe of names available by segment or classification.

List criteria Factors on a mailing list that differentiate one segment from another; can be demographic, psychographic, or physical in nature.

List, customer-compiled In prior years, list typed and prepared to customer order. Today, virtually all lists are precompiled on tape for any selection the user orders.

List, mailing Names and addresses of individuals and/or companies having in common a specific interest, characteristic, or activity.

List databank *See* **Databank**.

List enhancement Addition of data pertaining to each individual record that increases the value of a list.

List exchange Barter arrangement between two companies for the use of a mailing list; may be list for list, list for space, or list for comparable value other than money.

List franchise Provision by major compilers, on a franchise basis and usually for only a few years, of copies of all or parts of their files to list wholesalers and mailing shops.

List key *See* **Key code**.

List maintenance Any manual, mechanical, or electronic system for keeping name-and-address records (with or without other data) up to date at any specific point(s)in time.

List management system Database system that manages customer and prospect lists, used to merge and purge duplicates between in-house lists and those obtained from outside sources and to select names for direct mail promotions and outgoing telemarketing programs.

List manager Person who, as an employee of a list owner or as an outside agent, is responsible for the use, by others, of a specific mailing list(s), and who oversees list maintenance, list promotion and marketing, list clearance and record keeping, and collecting for use of the list by others.

List manager, in-house Independent manager serving multiple lists. Some large list owners opt to manage the list rental activity through full-time in-house employees.

List monitoring *See* **Monitoring**.

List owner Person who, by promotional activity or compilation, has developed a list of names having something in common; or one who has purchased (as opposed to rented, reproduced, or used on a one-time basis) such a list from the list developer.

List performance Response logged to a mailed list or list segment.

List protection Safeguarding of a list through review of mailing and mailer, insertion of list seeds, and obtaining of a guarantee of one-time use only.

List ranking Arranging list items in descending order on the basis of logged response and/or logged dollars of sales.

List rental Arrangement whereby a list owner furnishes names to a mailer and receives a royalty from the mailer.

List rental history Report showing tests and continuations by users of a given list.

List royalty Payment to a list owner for use of a list on a one-time basis.

List sample Group of names selected from a list in order to evaluate the responsiveness of that list.

List selection Process of segregating smaller groups within a list, i.e., creating a list within a list. Also called *list segmentation*.

List sequence Order in which names and addresses appear in a list: by ZIP code, alphabetically, chronologically, etc.

List sort   Process of putting a list in a specific sequence.

List source   Original source used to generate names on a mailing list.

List test   Part of a list selected to try to determine the effectiveness of the entire list. *See* **List sample**.

List user.   Company that uses names and addresses on someone else's lists as prospects for its product or service.

Load up   Process of offering a buyer the opportunity of buying an entire series at one time after the customer has purchased the first item in that series.

Logotype (logo)   Symbol or statement used consistently to identify a company or product.

Look-up service   Service organization that adds telephone numbers to lists.

Machine-coated paper   Paper coated on one or both sides during manufacture.

Machine-readable data   Imprinted alphanumeric data, including name and address, that can be read and convened to magnetic form by an optical character reader.

Magalog   Mail-order catalog that includes paid advertisements and, in some cases, brief editorials, making it similar to a magazine in format.

Magnetic tape   Film for storing electronically recorded data, often in list format to allow computerized matching with other lists for purposes of appending phone numbers or eliminating duplications.

Magnetic tape charge   Charge made for the tape reel on which a list is furnished and which usually is not returnable for credit.

Mail Advertising Service Association (MASA)   Major trade association of mailing houses responsible for fulfillment in the United States; has some 500 members and over 6,000 lettershops and mailing houses.

Mail count   Amount of mail deposited with the Postal Service on a given date as reported on the certification form.

Mail date   Drop date planned for a mailing, usually as agreed upon by the mailing list owner and the list user.

Mailer   (1) Direct mail advertiser who promotes a product or service using outside lists or house lists or both; (2) printed direct mail advertising piece; (3) folding carton, wrapper, or tube used to protect materials in the mails.

Mailer's Technical Advisory Committee   A group of representatives from virtually all associations involved in any form of mailing and related services that meets periodically with Postal Service officials to provide advice, technical information, and recommendations on postal policies.

Mailgram   Combination telegram-letter, with the telegram transmitted to a postal facility close to the addressee and then delivered as first-class mail.

Mailing house   Direct mail service establishment that affixes labels, sorts, bags, and ties the mail, and delivers it in qualified ZIP code strings to the Postal Service for certification.

Mailing List/Users and Suppliers Association   Association founded in 1983, specifically targeted to mailing list uses and abuses.

Mailing machine   Machine that attaches labels to mailing pieces and otherwise prepares such pieces for deposit in the postal system.

Mailing package   The complete direct mail unit as it arrives in the consumer's mailbox.

Mail monitoring   Means of determining length of time required for individual pieces of mail to reach their destinations; also utilized to verify content and ascertain any unauthorized use.

Mail order   Method of conducting business wherein merchandise or services are promoted directly to the user, orders are received by mail or telephone, and merchandise is mailed to the purchaser.

Mail Order Action Line (MOAL)   Service of the Direct Marketing Association that assists consumers in resolving problems with mail order purchases.

Mail order buyer Person who orders and pays for a product or service through the mail.

Mail Preference Service (MPS) Service of the Direct Marketing Association for consumers who wish to have their names removed from national commercial mailing lists.

Make-up Positioning of type and illustrations to conform to a layout; in lithography usually called a *paste-up*.

Makeready In letterpress, the building up of the press form so that heavy and light areas print with the correct impression.

Management information system (MIS) System, automated or manual, that provides sales support information for both the sales representative to enhance sales activity and management to evaluate sales performance.

Manual telephone sales center Completely paper-driven telephone sales center.

Marginal list test Test that almost, but not quite, qualifies for a continuation.

Market Total of all individuals or organizations that represent potential buyers.

Market identification Establishment of criteria to predetermine specific markets that will be primary targets of a telemarketing project.

Market penetration Proportion of buyers on a list to the total list or to the total area. For business lists, penetration is usually analyzed by two-digit or four-digit Standard Industrial Classification codes.

Marketing mix Various marketing elements and strategies that must be used together to achieve maximum effectiveness.

Markup Details of the size and style of type to be used; also known as *type specification*.

Marriage mail Form of co-op in which the offers of two or more disparate mailers are combined in one folder or envelope for delivery to the same address.

Master file File that is of a permanent nature, or regarded in a particular job as authoritative, or one that contains all sub files.

Match To cause the typing of addresses, salutations, or inserts into letters to agree with other copy that is already imprinted.

Match code Code determined by either the creator or the user of a file for matching records contained in another file.

Matched city pairs For testing purposes when individual markets must be utilized, a means to do A in City Y but not B, doing both A and B in City X with the premise that the two cities are reasonably matched as to size, income spread, and lifestyles.

Matte finish Dull paper finish that has no gloss.

Maximum cost per order Lifetime value of each major cell of customers on a customer file; helps set a limit on the price to pay for a new customer.

Mechanical Finished artwork ready for printing production; generally includes matter pasted in position.

Mechanical addressing systems System in which small lists are filed on cards or plates and addressing is done by mechanical means.

Media Plural of *medium*, the means of transmitting information or an advertising message (direct mail package, inserts, magazines, posters, television, etc).

Media data form Established format for presenting comparative data on publications.

Media insert Insert, either loose or bound, generally in business and consumer publications.

Median demographic data Data based on medians rather than on individuals (e.g., a census age is the median for a group of householders).

Medium Channel or system of communication (e.g, specific magazine, newspaper, TV station, or mailing list).

Member get member A promotion where existing members are offered a gift for enrolling new members.

Merge To combine two or more lists into a single list using the same sequential order, and then to sort them together, usually by ZIP code.

Merge/purge To combine two or more lists for list enhancement, suppression, or duplication elimination by a computerized matching process.

Military lists Lists of persons in military service.

Minicatalog New prospecting device consisting of a fanfolded set of minipages 3" × 5" used as cardvertisers, billing stuffers, and package inserts; also utilized by some mailers as a bounce-back.

Minimum (1) Minimum billing applied to list rentals involving a small number of names; (2) minimum billing for given mailing and/or computerized sources.

Minimum order requirement Stipulation, irrespective of the quantity ordered, that payment of a given number of dollars will be expected.

MOAL *See* **Mail Order Action Line**.

Mobility rate Annual rate at which families move or businesses fail, change names, or are absorbed each year.

Modeling Process involving the use of spreadsheets via a computer that provides reasonable answers to "what-if" scenarios.

Modem The hardware that translates between digital and analog enabling a digital computer to talk through an analog phone line.

Monetary value Total expenditures by a customer during a specific time, generally 12 months.

Monitoring Listening in on telephone conversation from extensions, usually for training of telephone sales representatives; also known as *service observing*.

Mono In printing, printed in a single color.

MPS *See* **Mail Preference Service**.

Multibuyers Identification through a merge/purge of all records found on two or more lists.

Multifamily *See* **Multiple dwelling**.

Multiple buyer Person who has bought two or more times (not one who has bought two or more items at one time only); also known as *multibuyer* or *repeat buyer*.

Multiple contact case Situation in which more than one contact with a prospect or customer is needed to complete or close a sale.

Multiple dwelling Housing unit for three or more families at the same address.

Multiple regression Statistical technique that measures the relationship between responses to a mailing with census demographics and list characteristics of one or more selected mailing lists; used to determine the best types of people/areas to mail to, and to analyze customers or subscribers.

Multiple regression analysis Statistical procedure that studies multiple independent variables simultaneously to identify a pattern or patterns that can lead to an increase in response.

Multiple SICs On major files of large businesses, the augmentation of the primary Standard Industrial Classification with up to three more four-digit SICs. Business merge/purges often disclose multiple SIC alignments unavailable on any single list source.

Name Single entry on a mailing list.

Name acquisition Technique of soliciting a response to obtain names and addresses for a mailing list.

Name drain Loss, mainly by large businesses, of the names and addresses of prospective customers who write to them or visit their stores.

National change of address Service of the U.S. Postal Service that provides national data on changes of address.

Negative Photographic image on film in which black values in the original subject are transparent, white values are opaque, light greys are dark, and dark greys are light.

Negative option Buying plan in which a customer or club member agrees to accept and pay for products or services announced in advance at regular intervals unless the individual notifies the company, within a reasonable time after announcement, not to ship the merchandise.

Nesting Placing one enclosure within another before insertion into a mailing envelope.

Net name arrangement Agreement, at the time of ordering or before, whereby a list owner agrees to accept adjusted payment for less than the total names shipped to the list user. Such arrangements can be for a percentage of names shipped or names actually mailed or for only those names actually mailed.

Net names Actual number of names on a given list mailed after a merge/purge; the concept of paying only for such names.

Net-net names Agreement made by a renter with a list owner to pay only for names that survive such screens as income, credit, house list duplicates, prior-list suppress names, and ZIP suppress programs; the surviving portion can be quite small.

Net unique name file Resultant one-per-record unique unduplicated list, one of the chief outputs of a merge/purge operation.

New case Telephone contact yet to be made.

New connects New names added to the connected lines of telephone, gas, and electric utilities.

New households New connects by local phone companies; data on new names from one telephone book to another are over one year old.

Newspaper lists List data on engagements, births, deaths, and newsmaking items and changes published in newspapers.

Nine-digit ZIP code Postal Service system designed to provide an automated means of utilizing an extended ZIP code to sort mail down to small contiguous areas within a carrier route.

Nixie Mailing piece returned to a mailer (under proper authorization) by the Postal Service because of an incorrect, or undeliverable, name and address.

Nonprofit rate Preferential Postal Service rate extended to organizations that are not maintained for profit.

No-pay Person who has not paid for goods or services ordered. Also known as an *uncollectable*, a *deadbeat*, or a *delinquent*.

North/south labels Mailing labels that read from top to bottom and that can be affixed with Cheshire equipment.

Novelty format Attention-getting direct mail format.

***n*th name or interval** Statistical means of a given number of names equally selected over the full universe of the list segment being sampled. The *n*th number interval is derived by dividing the total names in the list by the sample number desired.

***n*th name selection** Method of selecting a portion of a mailing list for test mailings (e.g., every fifth, tenth, twentieth name).

Objective case Each telemarketing project has a specific objective for each case (e.g., make a sale, reactivate an account, arrange for an appointment).

Occupant list Mailing list that contain only addresses (no names of individuals and/or companies).

OCR *See* **Optical Character Reader**.

Offer The terms promoting a specific product or service.

Offices Compilations of businesses with telephones providing offices of professionals and of multiple professionals per office, where desired, brought together by their common telephone number.

Offset litho Method of transferring the printing image from flat plate to paper via a covered cylinder.

One-off *See* **One-time use of a list**.

One-shot mailing Offer designed to make the sale in a single transaction.

One-stage mailing Mailing designed to take orders directly without any follow-up process.

One-time buyer Buyer who has not ordered a second time from a given company.

One-time use of a list Intrinsic part of the normal list usage, list reproduction, or list exchange agreement in which it is understood that the mailer will not use the names on the list more than once without specific prior approval of the list owner.

One-year contract Form of lease in which the renter is granted unlimited use for one year of a given set of compiled records; usually treated as a "sale for one year."

On-line availability Linkup system in which an operator at a remote terminal can obtain list information from a data bank or database at another location.

Opacity Property of a sheet of paper that minimizes the show-through of printing from the reverse side or from the next sheet.

Open account Customer record that at a specific time reflects an unpaid balance for goods and services ordered without delinquency.

Operations review Annual or semiannual review of the entire telephone sales center and strategic plan of a company.

Opportunity seeker Class of mail-order buyer or prospect that seeks a new and different way to make an income; ranges from people who look for ways to work at home to expensive franchises.

Optical character reader (OCR) Electronic scanning device that can read characters, either typed with a special OCR font or computer created, and convert these characters to magnetic form.

Optical scanner Input device that optically reads a line of printed characters and converts each character to its electronic equivalent for processing.

"Or Current Resident" Line added by computer to a three-line consumer list in an attempt to obtain greater deliverability and readership in case of a change in residential occupants.

Order blank envelope Order form printed on one side of a sheet, with a mailing address on the reverse; the recipient simply fills in the order and folds and seals the form like an envelope.

Order card Reply card used to initiate an order by mail.

Order entry procedure Process of capturing the name, address, item, dollars, and key for a transaction, and connecting it to electronic data, which then trigger creation of a picking document, a billing document, and usually the effect of that transaction upon inventory and inventory control.

Order form Printed form on which a customer can provide information to initiate an order by mail.

Order margin Sum represented by the difference between all costs (except promotion) and the selling price (after returns).

Origination All the work needed to prepare a promotional package (e.g., copy, design, photography, typesetting, color separation).

Outbound calls Calls that are placed by the telemarketing center. *See also* **inbound calls.**

Outbound telesales Proactive approach to a given market by a planned program to develop leads and/or sales.

Outside list manager *See* **List manager.**

Overlay In artwork, a transparent or translucent covering over the copy where color breaks, instructions, or corrections are marked.

Overprinting Double printing; printing over an area that already has been printed.

Owners Owners of mail order response lists and operators of mail response companies who "own" the customer and inquiry lists that they offer on the list rental market. All such proprietary lists must be "cleared" by such owners or their agents to be rented for one-time mailing by others.

Package insert Any promotional piece included in merchandise packages that advertises goods or services available from the same or different sellers.

Package test Test of part or all of the elements of one mailing piece against another.

Page proofs Proofs taken after make-up into pages, prior to printing.

Paid cancel Person who completes a basic buying commitment before canceling that commitment. *See also* **Completed cancel.**

Paid circulation Distribution of a publication

to individuals or organizations that have paid for a subscription.

Paid during service Method of paying for magazine subscriptions in installments, usually weekly or monthly, and usually collected personally by the original salesperson or a representative of the publisher.

Pandering list List of individuals who have reported receipt of sexually offensive literature to the Postal Service to ensure that the same mailer cannot, except by facing criminal charges, mail to them again.

Panel Group of people having similar interests that is used for research purposes.

Para sales force Sales team that works as a supplement to another sales team either on the telephone or in the field.

Pass (1) One run of the paper through the printing press; (2) to clear a page for a subscription.

Pass-along effect Additional readership acquired as executives forward particularly interesting mail to their associates. Business catalog makers seek to harness this effect by printing a group of germane titles on the cover as a suggested routing for such pass-along readership.

Passing a file Process of reading a file sequentially by computer to select and/or copy specific data.

Past buyer *See* **Former buyer.**

Paste-up Process by which an artist puts together type copy and photographs into final artwork ready for photographic reproduction.

Payment, method of Record or tag showing how a customer paid for a purchase (by check or credit card or money order); available as a selection factor on a number of response lists.

Payment rate Percentage of respondents who buy on credit or take a trial on credit and who then pay.

Peel-off label Self-adhesive label attached to a backing sheet that is attached to a mailing piece. The label is intended to be removed from the mailing piece and attached to an order blank or card.

Peg count Tally of the number of calls made or received over a set period.

Pending case Case in which an initial contact has been made and the communicator is waiting for a response or additional information.

Penetration Relationship of the number of individuals or families on a particular list (by state, ZIP code, SIC code, etc.) compared to the total number possible.

Penetration analysis Study made of the "share of market" held by a given mailer within various universes by classification or other demographic characteristics; for business mailers, the chief means to ascertain which markets by SIC and number of employees are most successfully penetrated in order to prospect more efficiently.

Performance evaluation Weekly or monthly review of a salesperson's performance by first-line supervision.

Periodical Publication issued at specific intervals.

Peripheral listing Creation of a variant kind of audience from that specified (e.g., addressing to the parents of College Student or High School Student X, titling to Mrs. X from a list of doctors by name and address at home, addressing a child by name to attract the eye of the parent, or inviting the new neighbors to view a new car at a given address).

Personalization Adding the name of the recipient to a mailing piece, or the use of a computer to input data about the psychographics of the customer being addressed.

Phone list Mailing list compiled from names listed in telephone directories.

Photosetting Production of type matter in positive form on bromide or film by the use of electromechanical equipment that is usually computer-assisted.

Pick-up and delivery charges Charges relating to collection or delivery of outside lists or components involved in the mailing process.

Piece rate   Third-class mail breaks into two main rate categories—third-class bulk rate (for discounts) and third-class piece rate. For the price of a first-class stamp, a piece weighing up to 3-½ ounces may be placed in the mail stream without any prior sortation, a charge that is currently over 40 percent greater than the unit charge for third-class bulk mail.

Piggy-back   Offer that hitches a free ride with another offer.

Pigment   Powdered substance used to give color, body, or opacity to printing inks.

Pilot   Trial program designed to test the feasibility of a possible telemarketing program.

Platemaking   Process by which artwork is converted into letterpress or off-set plates for printing.

Pocket envelope   Envelope with the flap on its short side.

Point   Measure used to describe type sizes.

Political lists   Mailing lists that break into two main categories: voter registration files mailed primarily during political campaigns and fund-raising files of donors to various political causes.

Poly bag   Transparent polyethylene bag used as envelopes for mailings.

Pop-up   Printed piece containing a paper construction pasted inside a fold that, when the fold is opened, ''pops up'' to form a three-dimensional illustration.

Positive   Photographic image on film that corresponds to the original copy; the reverse of a negative.

Positive option   Method of distributing products and services incorporating the same advance notice techniques as a negative option but requiring a specific order each time from the member or subscriber, generally more costly and less predictable than negative option.

Postage refund   Sum returned to a mailer by an owner or manager for nondeliverables exceeding a stipulated guarantee.

Postcard   Single sheet self-mailer on card stock.

Postcard mailers   Booklet containing business reply cards that are individually perforated for selective return to order products or obtain information.

Post codes   Codes added to the addresses on a mailing list that define sales and distribution areas; a fully post-coded address list earns an additional discount when bulk mailing under the first- and second-class discount schemes.

Post-paid impression (PPI)   *See* **Printed postage impression**.

Precall planning   Preparation before a sales call to promote maximum effectiveness.

Preclearance   Act of getting clearance on a rental before sending in the order.

Premium   Item offered to a potential buyer, free or at a nominal price, as an inducement to purchase or obtain for trial a product or service offered via mail order.

Premium buyer   Person who buys a product or service in order to get another product or service (usually free or at a special price), or person who responds to an offer of a special premium on the package or label (or sometimes in the advertising) of another product.

Preprint   Advertising insert printed in advance for a newspaper or magazine.

Prerecorded message   Taped message often recorded by a celebrity or authority figure that is played to inbound callers or included in an outbound call.

Presort   To prepare mail for direct delivery to post offices or to carriers at post offices. Over half of all for-profit third-class bulk mail is now mailed at carrier-route presort discount rates.

Press date   Date on which a publication goes to print.

Prestructured marketing   Marketing using computer software that provides a highly efficient system for annual fund-raising and capital drives, special events, and membership development by providing detailed information on specific target groups.

Price lining   Setting of prices by a seller in accordance with certain price points believed to be attractive to buyers.

Printed postage impression (PPI)   System enabling producers of bulk mailings to preprint "Postage Paid" on their envelopes; a wide range of designs is available allowing compatibility of style with other print detail on the envelope.

Printer's error   Error in printed copy that is the fault of the typesetter and corrected at the printer's expense.

Printout   Copy on a sheet of a list, or of some selected data on a list such as matched pairs indicating duplication from a merge/purge, or an array of largest buyers or donors.

Priority   For a continuation, method of arranging the tested lists and list segments in descending order on the basis of number of responses or number of dollars of sales per thousand pieces mailed; for political mail, a special next-day delivery service offered by the Postal Service.

Prior list suppress   Utilization of prior data to remove matching data from a new run and thus reduce the payment for the list data as used.

Private mail   Mail handled by special arrangement outside the Postal Service.

Proactive telemarketing   Seller-initiated or outbound calling.

Process colors   Black and three primary colors—magenta (red), cyan (blue), and yellow—into which full-color artwork is separated before printing.

Product information cards   Business reply cards bound in a booklet for selective return to order products or obtain information; also sometimes mailed loose in the form of a pack of cards.

Professional lists   Direct marketing lists that break down into some 30 categories, from architects to veterinarians. For example, a new list on the market based on a classified list of doctors (MDs) with phones has verified addresses and phone numbers of over 100,000 of some 190,000 physicians in private practice.

Projected roll-out response   Based on tests results, the response anticipated from a large continuation or program.

Prompt   Form of sales presentation by a professional telesalesperson that is comprised of predetermined but unscripted steps in the telephone call that will be presented in every closed case.

Proof   Impression taken from types, blocks, or plates for checking for errors and making amendments prior to printing.

Prospect   Name on a mailing list considered to be that of a potential buyer for a given product or service who has not previously made such a purchase.

Prospecting   Using mailings to get leads for further sales contacts rather than to make direct sales.

Protected mailing period   Period of time, usually one or two weeks prior to and one or two weeks after the mail date for a large quantity of names, in which the list owner guarantees no competitor will be given access to the list.

Pseudocarrier routes   The Postal Service Carrier Route (CRIS) tape lists millions of bits of data delineating 160,000 individual carrier routes. Major consumer compilers break up the areas not serviced by individual carriers into 240,000 extra pseudocarrier routes for marketing penetration selection or omission.

Pseudo SICs   Modifications of the U.S. Department of Commerce Standard Industrial Classification codes. By adding a fifth character to the SIC four-digit designations, major compilers now provide 4,600 SIC classifications with greater specificity. When the phone companies provide all of their classified listings, the number of different classifications for selection can total over 8,500. A six-digit SIC system is now under construction by Dun & Bradstreet and Data Base America.

Psychograhics   Characteristics or qualities used to denote the lifestyle or attitude of customers and prospective customers.

Publisher's letter   Letter enclosed in a mailing package to stress a specific selling point.

Pull   Proportion of response by mail or phone to a given promotional activity.

Purge   Process of eliminating duplicates and/ or unwanted names and addresses from one or more lists.

Pyramiding   Method of testing mailing lists that starts with small numbers and, based on positive indications, follows with increasingly large numbers of the balance of the list until the entire list is mailed.

Qualification sortation   Third-class bulk mail sorted to meet Postal Service qualifications for three different mail streams.

Qualified lead   Potential customers that have been determined to need, want, and be able to purchase a specific product or service.

Quantity pricing   Pricing, usually by compilers, offering price breaks for varying list quantities rented over a period of a year.

Queue   A function of an automatic call distributor that holds all (incoming) calls in the order in which they arrive until the next available agent takes the first in line, moving the next call up in sequence.

Questionnaire   Printed form presented to a specific audience to solicit answers to specific questions.

Quotation   Price presented to a prospective mailer before running a list order requiring special processing.

Random access   Access mode in which records are obtained from or placed into a mass storage file in a nonsequential manner so that any record can be rapidly accessed.

Rate of response   *See* **Response rate**.

Rating points   Method of measurement of TV or radio audience size.

Reactive telemarketing   Customer-initiated buying by telephone (inbound calling).

Readership   Number of people who read a publication as opposed to the number of people who receive it.

Rebate   *See* **Bulk rebate**.

Recency   Latest purchase or other activity recorded for an individual or company on a specific customer list. *See also* **Frequency** and **Monetary value**.

Record   Name-and-address entry on a file.

Record layout   Description covering the entire record length to denote where on a tape each part (or field) of the record appears, such as name, local address, city, state, ZIP code, and other relevant data.

Record length   Number of characters occupied by each record on a file.

Referral name   *See* **Friend of a friend**.

Reformatting   Changing a magnetic tape format from one arrangement to another, more usable format; also called *conversion*.

Refund   (1) For a list, return of part of payment due to shortage in count or excessive nondeliverables (over the guarantee); (2) for a product sold by mail, a return of the purchase price if an item is returned in good condition.

Registration list   List constructed from state or local political-division registration data.

Regression analysis   Statistical means to improve the predictability of response based on an analysis of multiple stratified relationships within a file.

Renewal   Subscription that has been renewed prior to or at expiration time or within six months thereafter.

Rental   *See* **List rental**.

Repeat buyer   *See* **Multiple buyer**.

Repeat mailing   Mailing of the same or very similar packages to the addresses on a list for the second time.

Reply card   Sender-addressed card included in a mailing on which the recipient can indicate a response to the offer.

Reply-O-Letter   One of a number of patented direct mail formats for facilitating replies from prospects, featuring a die-cut opening on the face of the letter and a pocket on the reverse; an addressed reply card is inserted in the pocket and the name and address shows through the die-cut opening.

Reprint   Special repeat printing of an individual article or advertisement from a publication.

Repro High-quality reproduction proof, usually intended to be used as artwork for printing.

Reproduction right Authorization by a list owner for a specific mailer to use that list on a one-time basis.

Request for proposal (RFP) Pro-forma device for outlining specific purchasing requirements that can be responded to in kind by vendors.

Response Incoming telephone contacts generated by media.

Response curve Anticipated incoming contact volume charting its peak and its decline, based on hours, days, weeks, or months.

Response rate Gross or net response received as a percentage of total promotions mailed or contacts made.

Return envelopes Addressed reply envelopes, either stamped or unstamped—as distinguished from business reply envelopes that carry a postage payment guarantee—included with a mailing.

Return postage guaranteed Legend imprinted on the address face of envelopes or other mailing pieces when the mailer wishes the Postal Service to return undeliverable third-class bulk mail. A charge equivalent to the single-piece, third-class rate is made for each piece returned. *See also* **List cleaning**.

Returns Responses to a direct mail program.

Reverse out To change printing areas so that the parts usually black or shaded are reversed and appear white or grey.

RFMR Acronym for recency-frequency-monetary value ratio, a formula used to evaluate the sales potential of names on a mailing list.

ROP *See* **Run of paper**.

Roll-out Main or largest mailing in a direct mail campaign sent to the remaining names on the list after tests to sample portions of the list have shown positive results.

Rough Rough sketch or preliminary outline of a leaflet or advertisement; also known as *a comp*.

Royalty Sum paid per unit mailed or sold for the use of a list, an imprimatur, a patent or the like.

Running charge Price a list owner charges for names run or passed but not used by a specific mailer.

Run of Paper (ROP) (1) Term applied to color printing on regular paper and presses, as distinct from separate sections printed on special color presses; also called *run of press*. (2) Term sometimes used to describe an advertisement positioned by publisher's choice—in other than a preferred position—for which a special charge is made.

Run-on price Price from a supplier for continuing to produce (generally print or envelopes) once an initial run is in process; includes only materials and ongoing charges, and not origination or machine makeready.

Saddle stitching Stapling a publication from the back to the center.

Sale Formal agreement to buy, make an appointment, or any other definition of a sale as determined by the objective of a specific case.

Sales conversion rate Number of sales in relation to number of calls initiated or received.

Sales message Description of the features and benefits of a product or service.

Sales presentation Structured anatomy of an offer describing how the product or service works.

Salting Deliberate placing of decoy or dummy names in a list for the purpose of tracing list usage and delivery. *See also* **Decoy** and **Dummy**.

Salting via seeds, dummies, or decoys Adding names with special characteristics to a list for protection and identification purposes.

Sample package (mailing piece) Example of the package to be mailed by the list user to a particular list. Such a mailing piece is submitted to the list owner for approval prior to commitment for one-time use of that list.

Scented ink Printing ink to which a fragrance has been added.

Score Impressing of an indent or a mark in the paper to make folding easier.

Scratch and sniff *See* **Scented ink.**

Screen (1) Use of an outside list (based on credit, income, deliverability, ZIP code selection) to suppress records on a list to be mailed; (2) halftone process in plate-making that reduces the density of color in an illustration.

Screen printing Method of printing from stencils placed on a fine mesh tightly stretched on a frame, through which ink or paint is forced.

Script Prepared text presentation used by sales personnel as a tool to convey a sales message in its entirety.

Seasonality Selection of time of year; the influence of seasonal timing on response rates.

Second class Second-class mail in the postal rate system; covers periodicals.

Sectional center (SCF or SCF center) Postal Service distribution unit comprising different post offices whose ZIP codes start with the same first three digits.

Sectional center facility (SCF) Geographic area designated by the first three digits of a ZIP code.

Seed Dummy or decoy name inserted into a mailing list.

Seeding Planting of dummy names in a mailing list to check usage, delivery, or unauthorized reuse.

Segment Portion of a list or file selected on the basis of a special set of characteristics.

Segmentation Process of separating characteristic groups within a list for target marketing.

Selection Process of segregating or selecting specific records from a list according to specific criteria.

Selection charge Fee above the basic cost of a list for a given selection.

Selection criteria Characteristics that identify segments or subgroups within a list.

Self-cover Cover printed on the same paper as the test pages.

Self-mailer Direct mail piece mailed without an envelope.

Self-standing stuffers Promotional printed pieces delivered as part of a daily or Sunday newspaper.

Senior citizen lists Lists of older individuals past a specific age, available for over age 50, 55, 60, or 65.

Separations Color separations either prepared by an artist using separate overlays for each color or achieved photographically by use of filters.

Sequence Arrangement of items according to a specified set of rules or instructions.

Series rate Special rate offered by publications and other media for a series of advertisements as opposed to a single insertion.

Set-up charge Flat charge assessed on some lists in addition to the cost per thousand.

Shared mailing Mailing that promotes the products of two or more companies, with the participants sharing the mailing list and all other costs.

Sheet fed Relating to a printing technique whereby paper is fed into the printing press in single sheets, as opposed to paper on a roll.

Shipping time Approximate number of days required for production of a list order.

SIC (Standard Industrial Classification) Classification of businesses, as defined by the U.S. Department of Commerce.

SIC count Count of the number of records available by two-, three-, four-, or five-digit Industrial Standard Classification.

Signature In book, magazine, and catalog production, name given to a large printed sheet after it has been folded to the required size; a number of signatures make up a publication.

Significant difference In mathematical terms, difference between tests of two or more variables, which is similar differentiation. The significant difference varies with the confidence level desired. Most direct mail penetration utilizes a 95 percent confidence level, wherein 95 times out of 100 the results found in the test will come close to duplicating on a retest or combination.

Single-family household   Private home, housing only one household, as distinct from multiple-family residences.

Singles   (1) One- or single-person household; (2) list of unmarried adults, usually for social linking.

Single-step   *See* **One-stage mailing**.

Sleeper   *See* **Dummy name**.

Solo mailing   Mailing promoting a single product or a limited group of related products, and usually consisting of a letter, brochure, and reply device enclosed in an envelope.

Sorting   (1) Computerized process of changing the given sequence of a list to a different sequence; (2) interfilling two or more lists.

Source count   Number of names and addresses, in any given list, for the media (or list sources) from which the names and addresses were derived.

Space ads   Mail order ads in newspapers, magazines, and self-standing stuffers; one of the major media utilized for prospecting for new customers.

Space buyer   Media buyer (usually in an advertising agency) who places print mail order advertising.

Space-sold record   Any record on a house file (customers, inquirers, catalog requests) that has been generated through advertising space placed in publications.

Spanish lists   Lists based on surname selects available to reach the Hispanic market.

Special position   Designated location in a publication ordered by the advertiser for his advertisement, usually at extra cost.

Specific list source   Original source material for a compiled file.

Specific order decoy   Seed or dummy inserted in the output of a list order for that order only. The specific seed, which identifies the order, is usually in addition to list protection decoys in the same list.

Specifier   Individual who can specify or purchase a product or service, particularly at larger businesses; in many cases, this is not the individual who enters the order.

Spine   *See* **Backbone**.

Split run   Printing of two or more variants of a promotional ad run on an *n*th or A/B split through the entire printing: use of geographic segments of a publication for testing of variants.

Split test   Two or more samples from the same list, each considered to be representative of the entire list and used for package tests or to test the homogeneity of the list.

Spot color   Use of one additional color in printing.

SRDS   Standard Rate & Data Service, which prints a rates and data book covering basic information on over 20,000 mailing lists.

Standard Industrial Classification (SIC)   Classification of businesses as defined by the U.S. Department of Commerce, used to segment telephone calling lists and direct marketing mailing lists.

Standard Metropolitan Statistical Area (SMSA)   U.S. Bureau of the Census term for an area consisting of one or more counties around a central urban area.

State count   Number of names and addresses, in a given list, for each state.

Statement stuffer   Small printed piece designed to be inserted in an envelope carrying a customer's statement of account.

Step up   Use of special premiums to get mail order buyers to increase their unit of purchase.

Stock art   Art sold for use by a number of advertisers.

Stock cut   Printing engravings kept in stock by the printer or publisher.

Stock format   Direct mail format with preprinted illustrations and/or headings to which an advertiser adds its own copy.

Stopper   Advertising slang for a striking headline or illustration intended to attract immediate attention.

Storage Data-processing term indicating the volume of name-and-address and attached data that can be stored for future use on a given computer system.

Stratification Capacity to offer demographic segmentation on a list; the addition of such demographics to a customer file.

Student lists Lists of college or high school students. For college students, both home and school addresses are available; for high school students, home addresses for junior and seniors are available.

Stuffers Printed advertising enclosures placed in other media (e.g., newspapers, merchandise packages, and mailings for other products).

Subblock Along with enumeration districts, the smallest geographic segment of the country for which the U.S. Census Bureau provides demographic data.

Subscriber Individual who has paid to receive a periodical.

Success model Set of logical steps followed by successful salespeople to sell a product or service and used as a training example for new salespeople.

Suppression Utilization of data on one or more files to remove any duplication of specific names before a mailing.

Suppression of previous usage Utilization of the previous usage or match codes of the records used as a suppress file. Unduplication can also be assured through fifth-digit pulls, first-digit-of-name pulls, or actual tagging of each prior record used.

Suppression of subscribers Utilization of the subscriber file to suppress a publication's current readers from rental lists prior to mailing.

Surname selection Ethnic selection based on surnames; a method for selection of such easily identifiable groups as Irish, Italian (and hence Catholic), Jewish, and Spanish. Specialists have extended this type of coding to groups such as German, English, Scots, and Scandinavian.

Suspect (1) Prospect somewhat more likely to order than a cold prospect; (2) in some two-step operations, a name given the initial inquirer when only one in X can be expected to convert.

Swatching Attaching samples of material to a printed piece.

Sweepstakes list (sweeps) List of responders, most of them nonbuyers, to a sweepstakes offer.

Syndicated mailing Mailing prepared for distribution by firms other than the manufacturer or syndicator.

Syndication (1) Selling or distributing mailing lists; (2) offering for sale the findings of a research company.

Syndicator Operation that makes available prepared direct mail promotions for specific products or services to a list owner for mailing to its own list; most syndicators also offer product fulfillment services.

Tabloid Preprinted advertising insert of four or more pages, usually about half the size of a regular newspaper page, designed for insertion into a newspaper.

Tagging (1) Process of adding information to a list; (2) transfer of data or control information for usage and unduplication.

Take-one Leaflet displayed at point of sale or in areas where potential consumers congregate (e.g., credit card recruitment leaflets, display and dispenser units at hotels and restaurants).

Tape Magnetic tape, the principal means of recording, storing, and retrieving data for computerized mailing list operations.

Tape conversion Conversion of hard-copy data to magnetic tape.

Tape format (layout) Location of each field, character by character, of each record on a list on tape.

Tape record All the information about an individual or company contained on a specific magnetic tape.

Tape reel Medium on which data for computer addressing or merge/purge are handled.

Target Person to whom a sales call is directed.

Target group index (TGI) Analysis of purchasing habits among consumers covering 4,500 brands/services in over 500 product fields.

Target market Most likely group determined to have the highest potential for buying a product or service.

Tear sheet Printed page cut from a publication; sometimes used in place of a complete voucher copy as evidence of publication. *See also* **Voucher copy**.

Teaser Advertisement or promotion planned to excite curiosity about a later advertisement or promotion.

Telco Telephone-operating company.

Telecommunication Any electrical transmission of voice or data from sender to receiver(s), including telegraphy, telephony, data transmission, and video-telephony.

Telecommuting Practice of employees working in their homes while linked to their office by telephone and, in most cases, a computer, sometimes referred to as *telework*.

Telecomputer Nontechnical term for an Automatic Dialing Recorded Message Player (ADRMP), a machine that automatically dials, plays a prerecorded message, and records responses.

Telemarketing Use of the telephone as an interactive medium for promotion or promotion response; also known as *teleselling*.

Telemarketing-insensitive medium Any medium used to advertise a product or service that does not properly highlight a telephone number.

Telemarketing service vendor One who sells the service of conducting telemarketing calls; also called *telemarketing agency* or *telemarketing service bureau*.

Telephone household Household with a listed phone number. (Random access calling can ring unlisted and nonpublished numbers.)

Telephone list List of consumers or establishments compiled with phone numbers from published phone directories.

Telephone list appending Adding of telephone numbers to mailing lists.

Telephone marketing Any activity in direct marketing involving the telephone (e.g., list, building or telephone follow-up to a lead-generation program).

Telephone Preference Service (TPS) Program of the Direct Marketing Association that allows consumers who do not want telemarketing calls to have their names removed from most telemarketers' lists with only one request.

Telephone sales Implementation of the telemarketing plan.

Telephone sales representative (TSR) Person who markets and sells by telephone; also known as a *telemarketer* or *agent*.

Telephone sales supervisor (TSS) Person who oversees the performance of TSRs.

Telephone sales techniques Formalized methods that structure the entire sales process.

Telephone service center *See* **TSC**.

Teleprospecting Cold canvassing of telephone households or telephone nonhouseholds by personal phone calls (not to be confused with telemarketing, which pertains to calls made to customers or inquirers).

Teleprospecting list List of prospects with phones used for telephonic (cold calling) prospecting.

Telesales Function dedicated to receiving or making outgoing contact by telephone.

Test Period of time in which a minimum of 100 cases are completed for analysis and management decisions about whether a particular project or program is viable.

Test campaign Mailings of test pieces to a number of outside lists to establish a bank for continuation mailings; must not be to only one list, which is a "continuous series of one experiment."

Testing Preliminary mailing or distribution intended as a preview or pilot before a major campaign. Test mailings are used to determine probable acceptance of a product or service and are usually made to specially selected lists.

Test market Trial market for a new product or service offer.

Test panel List of the parts or samples in a split test.

Test quantity Test mailing to a sufficiently large number of names from a list to enable the mailer to evaluate the responsiveness of the list.

Test tape Selection of representative records within a mailing list that enables a list user or service bureau to prepare for reformatting or converting the list to a more efficient form for the user.

Text Body matter of a page or book as distinguished from the headings.

TGI *See* **Target group index.**

Third-class mail Bulk mail. The U.S. Postal Service delivery of direct-mail promotions weighing less than one pound.

Third-party endorsement In a mailing made for the joint benefit of an outside mailer and a company over the company's customer file, the imprimatur of the company (e.g., Britannica mailing the *Farm Journal* list with an offer ostensibly from the publication to its subscribers).

Third-party unit Service bureau that makes calls for hire; also known as a *contract unit.*

Three-digit ZIP First three digits of a five-digit ZIP code denoting a given sectional center facility of the Postal Service.

Three-line address For consumer mail, a conventional home or household address of an individual; for business mail, the name and address of an establishment without the name of an individual.

Three-up *See* **Four-up.**

Throwaway Advertisement or promotional piece intended for widespread free distribution. Generally printed on inexpensive paper stock, it is most often distributed by hand to passersby or house to house.

Tie-in Cooperative mailing effort involving two or more advertisers.

Till forbid Order for service that is to continue until specifically canceled by the buyer; also known as *TF.*

Time Media buyer (usually at a specialized agency for direct response electronic) who "buys" time periods and spots for direct response radio or TV promotion.

Time zone sequencing Preparation of national telemarketing lists according to time zones so calls can be made at the most productive times.

Tint Light color, usually used for backgrounds.

Tip-on Item glued to a printed piece.

Title Designation before (prefix) or after (suffix) a name to accurately identify an individual (prefixes: Mr., Mrs., Dr., Sister, etc.; suffixes: M.D., Jr., President, Sales, etc.).

Title addressing Utilizing the title or function at a business; adding a title to a business address rather than addressing to a specific person by name.

Token Involvement device, often consisting of a perforated portion of an order card designed to be removed from its original position and placed in another designated area on the order card, to signify a desire to purchase the product or service offered.

Town marker Symbol used to identify the end of a mailing list's geographic unit; originated for towns but now used for ZIP codes and sectional centers.

Track record Accounting of what a given list or list segment has done for given mailers in the past.

Trade show registrants (1) Persons who stopped at a given trade show booth and signed up to receive additional information or a sales call; (2) persons assigned by their companies to operate a trade show booth or booths.

Traffic Number of calls made or received per hour, day, or month on a single line or trunk of a telephone system.

Traffic builder Direct mail piece intended primarily to attract recipients to the mailer's place of business.

Transparency   Positive color film such as a slide.

Trial buyer   Person who buys a short-term supply of a product, or who buys the product with the understanding that it may be examined, used, or tested for a specified time before they need to decide whether to pay for it or return it.

Trials   Individuals who ordered a short-term subscription to a magazine, newsletter, or continuity program. In list rental, trials are not equal to those who convert to customer status.

Trial subscriber   Person who orders a service or publication on a conditional basis, which may relate to delaying payment, the right to cancel, a shorter than normal term, or a special introductory price.

Truncation   Dropping the end of words or names to fit an address line into 30 characters for four-across Cheshire addressing.

TSC   Telephone sales center, the department that is responsible for making and receiving telemarketing sales contacts.

Turnover rate   Number of times within a year that a list is or can be rented.

Two-stage sell   Process that involves two mailings or approaches—the first inviting an inquiry and the second converting the inquiry to a sale.

Typeface   All printing type of a specific design.

Typesetting   Assembly of reading matter by the use of handpicked metal type, by keyboarding, and/or by casting or phototypesetting.

Type specification   *See* **Markup**.

Uncollectible   One who hasn't paid for goods and services at the end of a normal series of collection efforts.

Undeliverable   Mailing piece returned as not being deliverable; also known as a *nixie*.

Unique ZIP code   Five-digit ZIP code assigned by the Postal Service to a company or organization to expedite delivery of its large volume of incoming letter mail. With the advent of ZIP + 4, a large number of businesses and institutions now have their own unique ZIP code.

Unit of sale   Average dollar amount spent by customers on a mailing list.

Universe   Total numbers of individuals that might be included on a mailing list; all of those fitting a single set of specifications.

Update   Addition of recent transactions and current information to the master (main) list to reflect the current status of each record on the list.

Up front   Securing payment for a product offered by mail order before the product is sent.

UPS   United Parcel Service, a major supplier of small-package delivery.

Up-scale list   Generic description of a list of affluents; can be mail-responsive or compiled.

Up-selling   Promotion of more expensive products or services over the product originally discussed.

Usage history   Record of the utilization of a given list by mailers, managers, or brokers.

U.S. Business Universe   Database containing the names and addresses of virtually every business, institution, and office of a professional in the United States.

User   Firm that uses telemarketing in its overall marketing program, whether it is executed in-house or by a telemarketing service vendor.

Utilities   One of the major groupings of business lists, public service industries (such as water, power, light), often included with mining, contracting, manufacturing, and transportation as part of the industrial complex.

Validation mailing   Second modest mailing to confirm initial test results prior to making a large continuation or rollout.

Variable field   Way of laying out list information for formatting that assigns a specific sequence to the data, but not specific positions.

Variable-length record   Means of packing characters on a name and address record so as to eliminate blank spaces. For most rental work such lists must then be reformatted to fixed fields in which each field, whether filled or unfilled, occupies the same numerical positions on a tape.

Variables (criteria) Identifiable and selectable characteristics that can be tested for mailing purposes.

Vendor Supplier of any facet of direct response advertising: lists, creative, printing, marketing, computerization, merge/purge, fulfillment.

Verification Process of determining the validity of an order by sending a questionnaire to the customer.

Volume discount Scheduled discount for volume buyers of a given compiled list.

Voters registration list List utilized to add multiple family members as well as age data to compiled consumer files.

Voucher copy Free copy of a publication sent to an advertiser or organization as evidence that an advertisement has been published.

Wallet flap envelope Special business reply envelope that utilizes the inside of a large flap to serve as the order form.

Warranty list List of buyers who mail in warranty cards identifying the particular product and its type, with or without additional demographic data.

Web browsers Graphical interface to content on the World Wide Web (e.g., Netscape, Mosaic).

Weighting (1) For evaluation of customer lists, a means of applying values to the RF$UISM data for each cell. (For larger lists this is better done by a computer regression analysis); (2) for merge/purge, a means of applying a form of mathematical analysis to each component for unduplicating.

White mail Incoming mail that is not on a form sent out by the advertiser; all mail other than orders and payments.

Wholesaler (reseller) Merchandiser of lists compiled or owned by others, usually working with compiled lists mainly covering a local area; differentiated from a broker by type of list and coverage.

Window envelope Envelope with a die-cut portion on the front that permits viewing the address printed on an enclosure; the die-cut window may or may not be covered with a transparent material.

Wing mailer Label-affixing device that uses strips of paper on which addresses have been printed.

With the grain When folding paper, parallel to the grain.

Word processor Computer software utilized to produce individualized letters; also useful in updating and expanding smaller mailing lists.

Working women In direct mail, a relatively new selection factor. Lists may be either compiled (e.g., women executives of S&P major companies) or mail order responsive (e.g., paid subscribers to *Working Woman* magazine).

Workstation Area where telephone reps perform their jobs; (2) integrated voice/data terminal.

Yield (1) Count anticipated from a computer inquiry; (2) responses received from a promotional effort; (3) mailable totals from a merge/purge.

Yuppies Young, upwardly mobile professional people.

ZIP Code Registered trademark of the Postal Service; a five- or nine-digit code identifying regions in the United States.

ZIP code count In a list, the number of names and addresses within each ZIP Code.

Zip code omission Loss of a ZIP code on a given mailing list.

ZIP + 4 code Designation by the Postal Service for the nine-digit ZIP-coding structure.

ZIP code sequence Arrangement of names and addresses on a list according to the numeric progression of the ZIP code in each record. This form of list formatting is mandatory for mailing at bulk third-class mail rates, based on the Postal Service sorting requirement.

Zip code string Merging of multiple selections into one ZIP code string to avoid minimums.

Index

DATE DUE

JA 12

Demco, Inc. 38-293